The FBI in Latin America

RADICAL PERSPECTIVES:

A RADICAL HISTORY REVIEW BOOK SERIES

Series editors: Daniel J. Walkowitz, New York University

Barbara Weinstein, New York University

The FBI in Latin America

THE ECUADOR FILES

MARC BECKER

DUKE UNIVERSITY PRESS *Durham and London* 2017

Library of Congress Cataloging-in-Publication Data
Names: Becker, Marc (Professor of history), author.
Title: The FBI in Latin America : the Ecuador files / Marc Becker.
Description: Durham : Duke University Press, 2017. | Series: Radical perspectives :
a radical history review book series | Includes bibliographical references and index. |
Description based on print version record and CIP data provided by publisher;
resource not viewed.
Identifiers: LCCN 2017007585 (print) | LCCN 2017011972 (ebook)
ISBN 9780822372783 (e-book)
ISBN 9780822369592 (hardcover : alk. paper)
ISBN 9780822369080 (pbk. : alk. paper)
Subjects: LCSH: Ecuador—Politics and government—1944–1984. | United States.
Federal Bureau of Investigation—History—20th century. | Espionage, American—
Ecuador—History—20th century. | Espionage, American—Latin America—
History—20th century. | United States—Foreign relations—Latin America. | Latin
America—Foreign relations—United States.
Classification: LCC F3738 (ebook) | LCC F3738 .B43 2017 (print) |
DDC 327.7308/0904—dc23
LC record available at https://lccn.loc.gov/2017007585

Cover art: Kathryn Sutton/Fine Arts Design at Truman State University

CONTENTS

This project began rather serendipitously with an invitation in November 2013 from the Universidad Andina Simón Bolívar (UASB) in Quito, Ecuador to present at a colloquium on the seventieth anniversary of the May 28, 1944, revolution. In research for my previous book, *Indians and Leftists in the Making of Ecuador's Modern Indigenous Movements*, I had searched without success at the National Archives and Records Administration (NARA) in College Park, Maryland, for information on rural participation in this mass uprising. Along with many other Latin American historians, I had discovered that the U.S. State Department cables in Record Group 59 Central Decimal Files provide an excellent source of information on the domestic affairs of other American republics. Every time I was in Washington, DC, for an academic conference, I always made a short side trip to NARA to see what new and interesting tidbits of information I might discover that would assist in my study of Latin America's social movements.

Two months after the UASB's invitation, the American Historical Association (AHA) held its annual meeting in Washington, DC. I decided once again to see what information the national archives might hold on peasant organizations. Maybe I had missed something in my previous, admittedly hasty, visits. While I did not find the information I sought on rural mobilizations, I was stunned to encounter extensive documentation of the Federal Bureau of Investigation (FBI) surveillance of urban labor leaders and leftist militants. Like most, I had assumed that government regulations limited the FBI to domestic surveillance within the United States and charged the Central Intelligence Agency (CIA) with spying operations outside the country. Yet here were FBI agents in Latin America. . . .

I quickly found myself falling down a rabbit hole as I was drawn into this previously unknown (at least to me) story of FBI counterintelligence activities in Latin America. I had hit one of those mother lodes of primary source documents that so excite historians. I began skipping sessions at the AHA to spend more time reading archival reports. I placed my camera on a copy stand

and shot thousands of images of documents as quickly as I could. (The most important of these are available in an electronic appendix for this book at http://www.yachana.org/fbi.) When a blizzard delayed my departure from Reagan National Airport, I was delighted to have gained even more time to collect information on the FBI's program.

It did not surprise me that the U.S. government would intervene in the internal affairs of another country. In the 1980s, I worked with the organization Witness for Peace to document U.S.-funded contra attacks against the civilian population in Jinotega, Nicaragua, where such interference was all too obvious. When I began graduate school, I wanted to study the region from a Latin American perspective rather than focusing on U.S. imperial interventions, an objective that my training as a social historian under Elizabeth Kuznesof's expert guidance facilitated. My research on the Peruvian Marxist José Carlos Mariátegui and popular movements in neighboring Ecuador advanced that goal of decentering empire. Rather than only critiquing problems that were often all too obvious, I wanted to learn from solutions that our counterparts in Latin America had proposed.

Discovering the FBI surveillance excited me not because of what it might tell us about U.S. imperial adventures in Latin America, about which much has been written, but because of the insights that spying might provide on popular movements' struggles to create a more just and equal society. The FBI documentation offers a unique opportunity to gain a richer and fuller understanding of the Latin American left. This study focuses largely on the communists, both because that is where the FBI dedicated its efforts and because the communists were often the ones who were most dedicated to imagining another world that would include the most marginalized peoples and create a society without racial discrimination, sexual violence, and economic exploitation. Studying the triumphs, shortcomings, and insights of previous generations can better equip us to achieve those goals today.

A brief note on capitalization: The *Chicago Manual of Style*, 16th ed., 8.37, calls for the names of ethnic and national groups to be capitalized, including adjectives associated with those names. Because "Indigenous" refers to such a group, the term is capitalized in this book. That convention is based on, and followed in respect for, the preference that the board of directors of the South and Meso American Indian Rights Center (SAIIC) specified as an affirmation of their ethnic identities.

ACKNOWLEDGMENTS

I thank Guillermo Bustos, Santiago Cabrera, Pablo Ospina, Katerinne Orquera, and my other colleagues at the UASB for the invitation to present at the colloquium on May 28–29, 2014, that provided the impetus for this book.[1] Other colleagues at the colloquium, including Valeria Coronel and Hernán Ibarra, offered key insights that improved this work. Su Flickinger and Doris Bartel graciously extend hospitality to me during my all too brief research trips to NARA. A fortuitous discussion with Anton Daughters led me to his grandfather Donald Daughters, the first person I was able to identify by name who had served as an FBI agent in Latin America. Anton courteously granted me access to an unpublished interview he had conducted with his grandfather before his death, and that interview furnished me with a much needed ethnographic feel for the FBI agents. Sally West kindly allowed me to present my initial ideas from this project at a Faculty Forum at Truman State University. Dan Mandell and Jason McDonald proffered penetrating feedback on an early draft of a prospectus, even though much of their advice and many of their suggestions will have to wait for my next book. The Provost Office at Truman State University funded a well-timed sabbatical leave that allowed for rapid completion of this book, and I thank that office for not complaining when I switched topics from what I had initially proposed.

Miguel Tinker Salas generously guided me to documents that significantly expanded and strengthened this work. Barry Carr responded to my questions and offered important guidance on the history of the left at key junctures in my research and writing. Steve Ellner's keen insights and probing questions on inter-American affairs bolstered my analysis. I am grateful for Margaret Power's support for a broader collaborative project on the FBI in Latin America. All are models of collegiality and politically engaged scholars, and I am fortunate to run in their circles. In the final stages of writing, Kelsey Smugala conducted a close and careful edit of the manuscript that immeasurably strengthened the final product. I truly appreciate Gisela Fosado's support and encouragement for publication with Duke University Press. It has been a pleasure to work with the entire Duke team, including editorial associate Lydia Rose Rappoport-Hankins, on this project. Once again, Bob Schwarz of Shearwater Indexing compiled the index in an excellent and efficient manner. To all of these colleagues and others, I extend my deepest gratitude.

ABBREVIATIONS

ADE	Alianza Democrática Ecuatoriana (Ecuadorian Democratic Alliance)
AFE	Alianza Femenina Ecuatoriana (Ecuadorian Feminist Alliance)
AFL	American Federation of Labor
ARNE	Acción Revolucionaria Nacionalista Ecuatoriana (Ecuadorian Nationalist Revolutionary Action)
CEDOC	Confederación Ecuatoriana de Obreros Católicos (Ecuadorian Confederation of Catholic Workers)
CIA	Central Intelligence Agency
CIG	Central Intelligence Group
CIO	Congress of Industrial Organizations
COI	Coordinator of Information
CTAL	Confederación de Trabajadores de América Latina (Confederation of Latin American Workers)
CTE	Confederación de Trabajadores del Ecuador (Confederation of Ecuadorian Workers)
FAC	Foreign Activity Correlation
FBI	Federal Bureau of Investigation
FDN	Frente Democrático Nacional (Democratic National Front)
FEI	Federación Ecuatoriana de Indios (Ecuadorian Federation of Indians)
FEUE	Federación de Estudiantes Universitarios del Ecuador (Federation of Ecuadorian University Students)
FEV	Frente Electoral Velasquista (Velasquist Electoral Front)
FPTG	Federación Provincial de Trabajadores del Guayas (Provincial Federation of Workers of Guayas)
FTP	Federación de Trabajadores de Pichincha (Pichincha Workers Federation)
MAE	Movimiento Antifasista del Ecuador (Ecuadorian Antifascist Movement)
MCDN	Movimiento Cívico Democrático Nacional (National Democratic Civic Movement)

MID	Military Intelligence Division
MPA	Movimiento Popular Antitotalitario (Popular Anti-totalitarian Movement)
OIAA	Office of Inter-American Affairs
OIR	Office of Intelligence Research
ONI	Office of Naval Intelligence
OSS	Office of Strategic Services
PCE	Partido Comunista del Ecuador (Communist Party of Ecuador)
PSE	Partido Socialista Ecuatoriano (Ecuadorian Socialist Party)
SADC	South American Development Company
SAIP	Sociedad Artística y Industrial de Pichincha (Artistic and Industrial Society of Pichincha)
SEDTA	Sociedad Ecuatoriana de Transportes Aéreos (Ecuadorian Aerial Transport Society)
SIS	Special Intelligence Service
UDE	Unión Democrática Universitaria (University Democratic Union)
VRSE	Vanguardia Revolucionaria del Socialismo Ecuatoriano (Ecuadorian Revolutionary Socialist Vanguard)
WFTU	World Federation of Trade Unions

FBI

PEDRO SAAD

DIPUTADO POR LOS TRABAJADORES

PEDRO SAAD received more attention from FBI agents than anyone else in Ecuador. Saad was born to Lebanese immigrant parents in Guayaquil. He studied law at the University of Guayaquil, but instead of practicing law he worked as an accountant with the family textile business. Saad was a leading labor activist and was the first of six deputies representing labor interests in the 1944–45 Constituent Assembly. In 1952, he was elected secretary-general of the Communist Party, a position he held for the next several decades. Source: León Borja, *Hombres de Mayo*.

Pedro Saad was concerned about government surveillance of his political activities. He had good reason to be apprehensive. The police had detained him several months earlier after cracking down on his attempt to organize a labor federation. Now he was free, and his friends wanted to throw him a party. Please don't, he told them. If we celebrate my release, it will only call more attention to other political activists. Government monitoring had already made life difficult for leftists, and Saad did not want to facilitate their investigations.

We know this story because an anonymous source informed an agent with the Federal Bureau of Investigation (FBI) of a private meeting that Saad held at the home of his fellow Communist Party member Hermel Quevedo. Enrique Barrezueta, another party member, was the only other person present.[1] It should be no surprise that the FBI would spy on communists; that was one of the bureau's main activities since its founding earlier in the twentieth century. What makes this story noteworthy is that it took place not in the United States but in 1943 in the South American country of Ecuador. The FBI report on Saad's private conversation raises important questions. Why was the FBI in South America? How did the agent acquire information on a small, secret, closed meeting of known Communist Party militants? And what did the bureau plan to do with the information it gathered?

This book explores a little-known chapter of U.S. intervention in Latin America. During World War II, U.S. President Franklin Delano Roosevelt (FDR) placed the FBI in charge of political surveillance in Latin America. The FBI is commonly thought of as a domestic police force, whereas the Central Intelligence Agency (CIA) is responsible for intelligence-gathering operations outside the United States, even though neither agency completely respects this division of responsibilities. The FBI presence in Latin America, however, came before the creation of the CIA in 1947 and in the midst of Director J. Edgar Hoover's attempt to build the bureau into a global investigatory agency.

Through a program called the Special Intelligence Service (SIS), the FBI placed about seven hundred agents in Latin America during the 1940s. The original justification for this program was "to gather secret intelligence in connection with subversive activities throughout the Western Hemisphere," which was understood to mean combating the influence of German Nazis in Mexico, Brazil, Chile, and Argentina.[2] The program quickly spread to other countries. The United States treated Central America and the Caribbean as within its geopolitical sphere of influence and as such considered surveillance of those areas to be key to national security concerns. In northern South America, Venezuela and Colombia had significant strategic importance because of their petroleum reserves. Peru on the west coast of South America had extensive mineral exports that the United States sought for the war effort. In addition, that country was home to more than seventy thousand people of Japanese descent. After the attack on Pearl Harbor in December 1941, the United States questioned the loyalty, often without a firm basis in reality, of those immigrants.

The FBI's mission did not stop in countries with large German or Japanese populations or those of geopolitical or strategic significance to the United States. As indication of the FBI's reach, the agency stationed forty-five agents, many of them clandestinely, in Ecuador, a country that never was the target of German espionage networks and lacked geopolitical or strategic significance. With the decline of the Nazi threat by 1943, Hoover shifted his entire international intelligence apparatus to focus on his primary obsession with communism. During the war years, many State Department officials supported political liberalization and democratization and were willing to work with leftist labor movements and political parties. The Allied fight against dictatorships in Europe led to a discrediting of authoritarian conservatives who traditionally had held power in Latin America, and at the same time the communist left gained prestige for having joined the battle against fascism.[3] The FBI under the notoriously xenophobic and anticommunist Hoover, however, had other priorities. Even as diplomatic officials welcomed openings to the left, FBI agents accelerated their surveillance of communist activists. Not only did a disconnect emerge between the justification for the FBI presence in Latin America (fascism) and the focus of their investigations (communism), but an additional disparity existed between the perceived threat of communism and the lack of danger that Latin American Communist Parties actually presented to U.S. security concerns.

The imperial gaze of the United States toward Latin America is immediately apparent in the FBI surveillance activities. That much should not come as a surprise, given what we know and what is already well documented about the nature of twentieth-century inter-American affairs.[4] The FBI presence in Latin America corresponded with a brief period in the 1940s of democratization and political openings that U.S. officials generally supported. These policy makers were often less concerned with ideological or political threats than with the economic competition that German goods posed to U.S. corporate financial interests, a danger that was repeated in the pages of the *New York Times*.[5] The United States attempted to maintain control over Latin America as a cheap source of raw materials and a lucrative market for finished industrial products, with the associated economic profits accruing to corporations based in the United States. Latin American leftists have long critiqued the region's economic dependence on industrialized countries and fought to break free from those restraints. They organized political parties and labor movements to fight against exploitation and oppression and for a more equitable distribution of resources. Socialists and communists opposed the attempts of U.S. monopolies to gain economic control over the rest of the hemisphere. They condemned loans from the United States that were designed to build an infrastructure to extract raw resources from Latin America. They denounced attempts "to make Ecuador an exclusively agricultural country, merely a source of raw materials for U.S. industry and a market for North American manufactured products." Instead, leftists argued, Latin America needed planned industrialization to raise living standards.[6] This political advocacy challenged the U.S. economic dominance over the hemisphere, which gained them the attention of its intelligence-gathering networks.

More interesting, and more useful for that matter, than attempting to understand or explain U.S. policy objectives is to examine what light counterintelligence documents shed on leftist organizing efforts in Latin America. This book interrogates the FBI documents not for what they reveal about the nature of U.S. political intervention in Latin America but, rather, for what they divulge about leftist struggles for a more equitable and just world. Ecuador is the focus of this study because it has a rich history of strong popular movements that pressed for social changes to end long-entrenched patterns of political exclusion and economic exploitation. In 1895, Eloy Alfaro led a liberal revolution that promised profound reforms that ultimately fell far short of expectations. In 1925, modernizing military leaders instigated a coup known as the Revolución Juliana (July Revolution) that attempted to introduce progressive social and labor reforms. The collapse of the cocoa export economy and the global economic depression led to a period of economic crisis and political instability during the 1930s that halted the promised improvements to society. A 1944 uprising commonly known as La Gloriosa, or the Glorious May Revolution, once again attempted but failed to open up political space for previously disenfranchised sectors of society. Each of these "revolutions" promised a fundamental transformation of society, but in each case the ruling class reasserted its control over economic and social structures, and life continued much as before. The Ecuadorian left faced a conundrum of being able to overthrow governments but of being too weak and internally fractured to implement positive policy alternatives.

The height of the FBI presence in Latin America corresponded with a particularly intense period of popular organizing in Ecuador. Working-class activists first failed and then succeeded in establishing a unified leftist labor federation. The Partido Comunista del Ecuador (Communist Party of Ecuador; PCE) in alliance with socialists and other progressives—and sometimes in competition with them—became a significant political force. These leftists drafted a new and progressive constitution that significantly expanded labor and social rights. Yet after initial successes, a coup, a conservative constitution, and a series of pro-U.S. governments reversed those gains. The FBI's fixation on a communist menace that allegedly emanated out of Moscow generated extensive documentation that provides an excellent avenue for gaining a deeper and better appreciation of those local struggles. A study of the successes and shortcomings of transformative movements provides important lessons for how to build a more just and inclusive society.

Police Sources

Political surveillance affords an important avenue to reconstruct the history of popular movements that contributed to transformational changes in society. Activists rarely had the time to maintain records to document their actions, or the interest in doing so. They commonly failed to preserve copies of periodicals they published—nor did libraries collect such ephemeral material. Militants often discarded their publications when their immediate political purpose passed, and they destroyed papers rather than risk facing persecution from military regimes. At times, the police confiscated the records of labor unions and leftist political parties. The CIA reported that during a coup in Ecuador in 1963, a military "raid on PCE headquarters netted several rank-and-file Communists, the PCE files and financial records, and two truckloads of propaganda."[7] The party's archive may still exist deep in the bowels of the military barracks, but if so, it has not emerged for public scrutiny. It does, however, provide a hint of the rich documentation that police archives potentially contain.

In the meantime, scholars are forced to turn elsewhere to reconstruct a history of the Ecuadorian left.

Scholars have written several good preliminary studies of the Ecuadorian left, although a lack of documentation has hampered a full treatment of this topic.[8] Many movement publications, including the periodicals *Bloque*, *Combate*, and *Ñucanchic Allpa*, are not readily available inside or outside the country. Only much later do historians become aware of the usefulness of these documents to chronicle a movement's history. Occasionally, copies made their way into police files where researchers subsequently discovered them.[9] Otherwise, we are left with fragments of these publications, including references to them in FBI reports. Surveillance reports may also provide the sole surviving documentation of internal PCE and labor union discussions. It is a truism that the police maintain the archives for leftist organizations and popular movements. The FBI's intelligence gathering offers scholars an unusually rich and much needed source of documentation and ethnographic evidence that creates a unique opportunity to gain a deeper appreciation for the Latin American left. Understandings that previously appeared only faintly now emerge more clearly, thanks to the contributions of foreign intelligence surveillance agencies.[10]

Very little has been written about the FBI in Latin America in the 1940s, and this episode in the agency's history remains largely unknown both in academic circles and among the general public. Surprisingly, none of the hundreds of FBI agents who worked in this program have published memoirs of their experiences, although some excellent oral histories are available.[11] The sole book-length treatment on the FBI in Latin America during this decade is the institutional history that the agency published in 1947 to justify its program.[12] Naturally, a very large literature exists on the FBI that provides a solid basis for further study.[13] Most popular histories of the FBI, such as Ronald Kessler's *The Bureau*, focus almost exclusively on the United States and contain only passing references to Latin America.[14] Rarely do these sources make mention of the secretive SIS program, and when they do they primarily examine administrative affairs in the United States rather than the agents' clandestine activities in Latin America. The former FBI agent Raymond Batvinis, for example, offers an insider view of the agency in *The Origins of FBI Counterintelligence*. Although he writes about the 1940s, he is mainly concerned with developments in Washington, DC, and provides little information on political processes in Latin America.

Authors who do examine FBI counterintelligence in Latin America limit their attention to the perceived German Nazi menace that originally justified the agency's presence or U.S. responses to that alleged threat.[15] Their writings contain very little analysis of the FBI's campaigns against the political left. Scholars who mention that surveillance understate its significance and do not appear to recognize its value for a study of the left.[16] This shortcoming exists despite the fact that in unpublished oral history interviews many former agents readily acknowledge that their efforts focused on domestic communists and not on the Germans. Very good books have been written about U.S. investigations of leftists in Latin America, but all of them focus on the Cold War rather than World War II.[17] These works, however, do provide a broader context and model on which the current study builds.

This book on the FBI in Latin America extends an analysis of political surveillance to an earlier period and complements other books that examine only the Nazi threat or read these events through the lens of U.S. policy concerns. This work contributes new insights into the purpose and nature of international surveillance, with a particular focus on what that intelligence gathering can tell us about social movements in Latin America. Other sources, including State Department correspondence, Latin American government reports, newspaper articles, and social-movement proclamations, facilitate and complement interpretations included in the FBI reports. Together, these sources provide a multifaceted perspective on grassroots efforts to build a strong movement for social justice and against oppression and exploitation in Latin America.

Good Neighbors

Beginning with his inauguration as U.S. president in 1933, Roosevelt marketed the principle of nonintervention in the internal affairs of other American republics as the cornerstone of his Good Neighbor policy. Secretary of State Cordell Hull publicly reiterated this policy at the Seventh International Conference of American States in Montevideo, Uruguay, in December 1933 when he agreed to abandon direct intervention in the Americas. The most overtly visible aspect of the policy was the withdrawal of the marines from the Central American and Caribbean countries of Nicaragua and Haiti that they had occupied on and off since the beginning of the century. It was not until twenty years later, with the overthrow of the progressive government of Jacobo Arbenz in Guatemala, that the United States once again actively conspired to intervene militarily in Latin America. Many scholars nostalgically reflect back on FDR's Good Neighbor policy as a positive model of the type of approach that the U.S. government should pursue toward the rest of the Americas.[18]

Despite these generally optimistic attitudes toward Roosevelt's foreign policies, the United States did not ignore political developments in Latin America during these two decades. Only a few years after proclaiming the Good Neighbor policy, Roosevelt ordered the FBI to act as a political intelligence agency to investigate first fascist and then communist groups, both domestically in the United States and internationally in Latin America and beyond. The FBI sent its secret intelligence agents into Latin American countries without the knowledge of the host government, and sometimes even without the awareness of U.S. diplomatic officials. This clandestine activity made a mockery of the noninterventionist tenets so central to the Good Neighbor policy. FDR's policies highlight the reality that even with the best of intentions the United States never relaxed its imperial grasp on Latin America.

The roots of the FBI lie in the creation of the Bureau of Investigation (BOI) in 1908. Almost from the beginning the BOI operated internationally. In 1917, the bureau joined the State Department, Secret Service, Army, and Navy in gathering intelligence in Mexico during its revolution. Duplication of efforts and conflicts among these different agencies was a persistent problem.[19] In 1935, FDR reorganized the bureau under the name Federal Bureau of Investigation as an independent agency within the Department of Justice. The president charged the bureau with criminal investigation and counterintelligence work. The FBI gained a positive reputation for capturing the famous criminals John Dillinger and Al Capone, but a chasm divided those agents engaged in criminal investigations and others working on political cases.[20] The bureau's work as a political police force remained largely hidden from public view and was controversial when it came to light. The surveillance often targeted peaceful protest rather than legitimate security threats, a misuse of government resources that remains a concern. From 2000 to 2009, for example, undercover agents infiltrated the School of the Americas Watch (SOAW), a group of nonviolent activists who work to close the U.S. Army School of the Americas. The FBI repeatedly acknowledged the protestors' peaceful intentions, which led the SOAW to highlight "the true role of the FBI." The SOAW depicted the bureau "as a political surveillance and intelligence operation that uses domestic terrorism authority against peaceful protesters and organizations."[21] Attempts to intimidate legitimate protest movements and political action have long characterized FBI surveillance activities.

Although the justification for the FBI surveillance was originally rooted in the rise of Nazi power in Germany, during his entire tenure in office Hoover was primarily obsessed with an alleged communist threat to U.S. national interests. On September 5, 1936, Hoover instructed his agents "to obtain from all possible sources information concerning subversive activities being conducted in the United States by Communists, Fascists and representatives or advocates of other organizations or groups advocating the overthrow or replacement of the Government of the United States by illegal methods."[22] The ambitious FBI director did not restrict his activities to the United States and soon sought to extend his reach to Latin America.[23] In 1936, FDR directed Hoover to coordinate the collection of intelligence information with the State Department, the Office of Naval Intelligence (ONI), and the War Department's Military Intelligence Division (MID, sometimes called G-2 in reference to the intelligence staff of a unit in the U.S. Army). The other agencies predated the FBI's arrival in Latin America. The Navy created the ONI in 1882, and in 1885 the Army formed the MID, originally called the Military Information (rather than Intelligence) Division.[24] Under Hoover, who served as director of the bureau for forty-eight years, from 1924 until his death in 1972, the FBI surpassed these other agencies as an international political police force.

Interagency squabbles led the other organizations to challenge FDR's preference for the FBI to investigate global "subversive" activities. In 1940, Adolf A. Berle Jr., the assistant secretary of state responsible for intelligence affairs, negotiated an agreement that was to limit the FBI to the Western Hemisphere; the Navy would hold responsibility for intelligence gathering in the Pacific while the Army controlled operations in Europe, Africa, and the Panama Canal Zone.[25] Even though the agreement placed the FBI in charge of the Americas, Army and Navy attachés as well as State Department diplomats continued to collect intelligence in the hemisphere. Informants sometimes served more than one agency, and the competition for informants caused continual conflicts.[26] The extensive duplication among the information-gathering agencies limited their overall productivity and effectiveness.

Hoover put a good face on these feuds and in his annual report for 1942 told of weekly conferences and close collaboration between the different intelligence agencies.[27] Jack Neal and Frederick B. Lyon headed a Division of Foreign Activity Correlation (FAC) in the State Department to process the sensitive political intelligence that the agencies collected. A history of the

State Department describes the FAC as "so secretive as to its activities that even the Secretary of State was not informed of some of its work."[28] Neither did the president inform Congress of the FBI's activities in Latin America. Instead, he funded the agency through a White House discretionary fund that required very little oversight.[29] Officials designed the entire intelligence-gathering operation to subvert administrative and congressional oversight.

Throughout much of the 1940s, Hoover forwarded FBI field reports from Latin America to the State Department in Washington. The communications followed a standard format, with a cover letter from Hoover first addressed to Assistant Secretary of State Berle and then later to Lyon or Neal at the FAC, with a copy to the chief of the Military Intelligence Division (Military Intelligence Service after March 1942) at the War Department and the director of naval intelligence at the Navy Department. Hoover commonly copied the local U.S. embassy on his correspondence, and if he did not do so, the State Department would forward the information to its diplomatic representatives. Hoover's letters to Berle were marked "personal and confidential by special messenger" and indicated the level of reliability and confidentiality of the source of the information. The levels varied from "reliable and confidential" or "confidential source believed to be reliable" to an indication that the reliability of the source could not be ascertained.[30]

John Speakes, an FBI field officer in Mexico, notes that Hoover was fond of the field reports because they provided him with information he otherwise would not receive. Speakes comments, "I believe he grew to like the idea of receiving his own reports of conditions in some foreign country written by his own personnel."[31] The historian John Bratzel notes that despite claims of reliability, overzealousness mixed with inexperience and personal ambition led to many highly inaccurate reports. Bratzel observes that while the FBI excelled at tracking down German radio transmitters through triangulation, its reports were plagued with the problem of "incredible overstatements and puffery."[32] Hoover forwarding the reports to other offices appears to be less an act of altruistic collegiality than an interdepartmental power play that reinforced his sense of self-importance.

Hoover commonly inflated the perceived importance of the information he provided. For example, in March 1942 he reported, "Information has been received from a highly confidential source that Coronel Ricardo Astudillo has been named Commander in Chief of the Armed Forces of Ecuador." A reader in the State Department circled the word "confidential" and noted, in rather snide fashion, "*New York Times*?" Indeed, several weeks earlier the *New York*

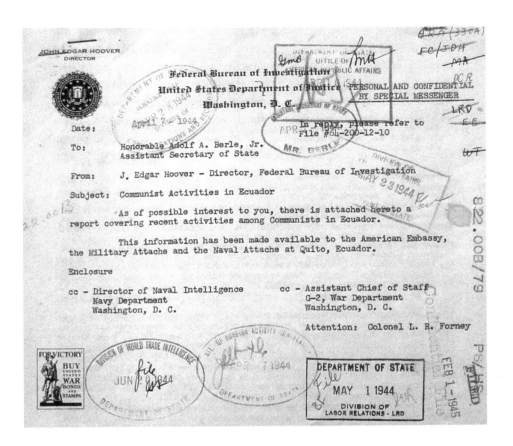

Times had reported on Astudillo's promotion.[33] The scholar María Emilia Paz Salinas observes, "The main success of the FBI in its counterintelligence battle was attributable to the unforgiveable mistakes committed by the Axis espionage agents rather than to the proficiency of the FBI people." She excoriates Hoover's reports for their "lack of depth and insight."[34] The author Chalmers Johnson, who was a consultant for the CIA from 1967 to 1973 and subsequently became a sharp critic of U.S. imperialism, noted, "The best reason to keep the national intelligence estimates secret . . . was their utter banality." He pondered whether classification simply hid the potential embarrassment "to have it known that such conventional journalism passed for strategic thought."[35] The security classification systems often appear to be quite random and provide an illusion rather than the reality of the sensitivity of the information contained within.

Initially, the State Department responded to Hoover's correspondence with a note of acknowledgment and appreciation for the information, although by 1942 interdepartmental tensions had reached the point at which such niceties were no longer observed. On occasion, the State Department would reciprocate with copies of its blandest, most innocuous correspondence that was classified "unrestricted" and contained publicly available information with an accompanying note that perhaps the information "will be of value" to bureau officials.[36] Despite a pattern of notoriously dysfunctional infighting among different government agencies, Hoover and Berle maintained a cordial relationship and on occasion Berle even defended the FBI from attacks from other agencies.[37] Berle pointed to the construction of an intelligence network in Latin America as the one area where the State Department had been able to collaborate effectively with the FBI during the war years.[38] In its annual reports and official history, the FBI insisted that it had very close and warm relations with embassies and, in particular, with Robert Scotten who served as ambassador in Quito from 1943 to 1947.[39] Hoover excelled at promoting his agency despite the institutional competition he faced.

The Office of Strategic Services (OSS), which FDR created in June 1942 to coordinate espionage and propaganda activities, also provided competition to the FBI. The OSS engaged in covert, anti-Nazi activities, whereas the FBI was to be restricted to intelligence gathering, a distinction that, as the historian Dirk Raat notes, "was easier to define than to put into practice."[40] The OSS was a forerunner to the CIA that U.S. President Harry Truman created with the National Security Act of 1947. Hoover thought that the OSS was encroaching on what should have been his territory, and, indeed, the OSS was sometimes more concerned with FBI snooping than the activities of Axis intelligence agencies. In fact, Hoover may have adopted the Special Intelligence Service (SIS) nomenclature for his Latin American program to usurp a similarly named Special or Secret Information Service (SI) of the OSS's precursor Office of the Coordinator of Information (COI).[41] As indication of the interagency rivalries, one former agent reported that when he resigned from the bureau to join the OSS, the FBI telegraphed his draft board so he would be inducted into the military instead.[42] The competing agencies hardly seemed to be collaborating in a fight against a common enemy.

In contrast to Hoover's hatred of leftists, General William Donovan, director of the OSS, quietly but actively recruited communists because of their facility with languages and ability to work effectively with communist-led antifascist movements. Donovan found that leftists were often his most useful field officers.[43] Communist activists reciprocated by recruiting party members as part of their contribution to the war against fascism.[44] Ultimately, Donovan was not able to marshal as many resources as Hoover. As a result, the OSS did not generate as voluminous a body of field reports as the FBI. Reports on Latin America by the OSS also were not necessarily any better than those by the FBI. Despite all evidence to the contrary, a COI report on insecurity in Ecuador from November 1941 claimed, "The activities of well-organized Axis agencies have been helped by the naturally pro-Fascist sentiment of a large proportion of the educated population." The same report, however, also astutely recognized that foreign companies exploited natural resources and took the profits out of the country.[45] Intelligence officers had extreme difficulty in distinguishing between a pro-Nazi and anti-U.S. position—nor did they understand the sentiments behind nationalist opposition to imperial exploitation. All anti-imperialist sentiments were painted with the same broad brush.

In addition to the State Department, MID, ONI, and OSS, the Office of Inter-American Affairs (OIAA), under the coordination of the wealthy U.S. capitalist and philanthropist Nelson Rockefeller, competed with the FBI to counter an alleged German political, economic, and cultural threat to Latin America and to maintain U.S. imperial control over the region. Despite opposition from the State Department, Roosevelt created the OIAA in August 1940 to combat Axis commercial and cultural influence and deepen U.S. economic control over Latin America. Its functions overlapped with those of other government agencies, which led to tension and conflicts. Career diplomats argued that the OIAA was a naïve and amateur operation that bungled complex international economic and political relations and ultimately did more harm than good to U.S. government interests during the war. In April 1941, the State Department claimed authority over foreign policy concerns and subjected the OIAA to its oversight. An executive order from April 1946 abolished the OIAA and brought most of its programs under the State Department's direct control. At the height of its operations, the OIAA had more than a thousand employees in the United States and three hundred technicians and field experts in Latin America. In addition, the OIAA employed almost seven hundred aides and assistants working with fifty-nine coordination committees in major Latin American cities. These coordination committees were composed primarily of prominent U.S. citizens engaged in business endeavors in Latin America that provided them with strong connections in local communities. The OIAA in particular spread propaganda to expand U.S. cultural influence in Latin America, including working with Walt Disney to make films that would advance its policy objectives.[46]

Although the agencies in Washington had their disagreements, agents on the ground in Latin America would sometimes collaborate with one another. For example, the FBI assigned Allan Gillies to an undercover position with an oil company in Maracaibo, Venezuela. As part of his position and with the consent of the FBI, he projected the OIAA's propaganda films.[47]

All of these overlapping and competing agencies with their interventionist agendas could become a little much for Latin American governments. In 1944, Harold Williamson, the consul general in Guayaquil, related, with a certain amount of surprise, private statements from Ecuadorian President Carlos Alberto Arroyo del Río that he was "fed up to the neck with the Gringos and that he is fed up to the top of his head with those Ecuadorans who like the Gringos." Another confidential source corroborated the president's "extreme resentment against American officials, notably those of the Embassy."[48] A week later, the consul reported with a good deal of relief that on further questioning the confidential source had revealed that the president's resentment was directed not against embassy officials but against "officers of independent Government agencies." The contact either believed that these officials were members of the embassy staff or had "permitted his imagination to enlarge upon the story."[49] Unfortunately, even in this "strictly confidential" correspondence, Williamson does not reveal who these unnamed officers were and whether they belonged to one of the competing intelligence agencies. Logically, though, the nature of his response indicates that they probably did. Regardless of the agency, leftists criticized these policies—as they also did with the subsequent Marshall Plan and Alliance for Progress—for subjugating other countries to U.S. economic control. Hemispheric security, from this perspective, was a justification rather than the purpose for the U.S. presence.

Surveillance as Documentation

This book illustrates that the FBI's original excuse of combating Nazism in Latin America does not explain the far-reaching surveillance of leftists' activities. Neither does Ecuador's small Communist Party justify the dedication of such extensive resources. Unsurprisingly, agents reported on the party's internal conflicts, although the available archival record does not reveal FBI attempts to infiltrate and disrupt the activities of leftist political parties, as occasionally was the intent of embassy personnel and, later and more explicitly, the modus operandi of the CIA.[50] Similar to what the historian Andrew Barnard observes for U.S. surveillance of Chilean leftists during the war years,

"So far as the available evidence shows, all these agencies were concerned with gathering information rather than with executive action."[51] The FBI infiltrated the Chilean Communist Party with an intent "to secure accurate advance reports on proposed changes in policy," and then share that intelligence with the embassy and State Department.[52]

In contrast, the OSS created a branch called Morale Operations (MO) that engaged in disinformation campaigns and psychological warfare designed to mislead or misdirect an opponent. The intent of this black propaganda was subversive, and agents disguised their sources so that the U.S. government could disown an operation and claim innocence if it backfired.[53] If the FBI engaged in similar tactics in Latin America during the war, that information has not come to light. Hoover apparently did treat the SIS as a genuine service agency that was tasked with conducting counterintelligence investigations for the benefit of others who could then analyze the information and decide what policies or other initiatives to pursue. He may have recognized that knowledge is power.

Although some of the targets of FBI investigation are understandable, in other cases the focus of the bureau's efforts is surprising, both for where it chose to dedicate resources and for the important leaders and activities that it missed. The agency was more concerned with labor leaders who might be positioned to challenge U.S. economic interests than ideological communists who forwarded radical critiques of society. The FBI also compiled information on members who seemingly had little importance or influence in the Communist Party, as if agents randomly and uncritically compiled information with little thought to its ultimate value. At the same time, agents remained largely oblivious to the activities of women, peasants, and Indigenous peoples who were not from the European-descended, male, upper-class society that the agents represented and from which they drew their confidential contacts. The race, class, and gender blind spots of those who collected information becomes one of the most significant limitations of using FBI investigations to re-create a history of the left. Nevertheless, the FBI's extensive surveillance provides a service that its original creators did not foresee: it documents domestic challenges to their imperial agenda. Thanks to those efforts, we are left with a better understanding of the thoughts and activities of leftist activists who sought to extend social rights to disenfranchised sectors of society.

CHAPTER 1

SIS

EXCELENTISIMO SEÑOR Dr.

JOSE MARIA VELASCO IBARRA
PRESIDENTE

The May 1944 revolution brought **JOSÉ MARÍA VELASCO IBARRA** back to power, and the 1944–45 Constituent Assembly confirmed him as president of the republic. This was his second of five times in office, but he managed to complete only one of those terms—the third, 1952–56. Military coups cut the other terms short, including the one from 1944 to 1946, when he could not live up to the promises that had led to initial popular support for his electoral campaigns. Source: León Borja, *Hombres de Mayo*.

The agents Thomas Finnegan Hannigan and Richard Crow received a teletype that they were to return immediately from their post in San Francisco to FBI headquarters in Washington, DC. Three days later, they were on a plane with all of their clothes and equipment, wondering what kind of trouble they were facing. In Washington, an FBI supervisor asked the two agents whether they were willing to serve in a foreign assignment. Both immediately responded that they would, not so much out of interest, but from a fear of being exiled to an undesirable assignment in Butte, Montana, if they refused. Hannigan and Crow formally resigned their positions in the FBI and were immediately sworn in as agents of the Special Intelligence Service (SIS). "They explained a little bit about what SIS was but not a lot," Crow later recalled. "They really didn't want us to know too much."[1]

After a crash course in Spanish, the FBI sent Hannigan and Crow, together with about twenty other agents, to Latin America, Hannigan to Chile and Crow to Bolivia. About half were assigned to Legal Attaché Offices in embassies, with the others traveling undercover as purported employees of a U.S. firm. The agents received very limited training in counterintelligence and counterespionage. Harold Judell, who arrived in Venezuela with the first group of twelve FBI agents, commented, "We were basically on our own."[2] James Kraus, who later followed as a stenographer, said he received no training, not even Spanish language instruction.[3] Agents were under the impression that they were "sent into a particular area just to nose around" and see what they could find.[4] The FBI transferred many to another country after only a few months, further limiting their ability to become experts on a specific situation.

Many of the agents arrived in Latin America with limited conversancy in Spanish and even more limited knowledge of the country to which they were assigned. In December 1944, Ronald Sundberg applied to the SIS. A week later, the agency asked whether he wanted to go to El Salvador, and he responded, "Fine—where is it?" As Sundberg noted, he "was green as grass." He knew little about the SIS and even less about what it was doing in El Salvador. "They stripped me of my credentials," he remembered, "told me not to tell anybody what I was doing in San Salvador. Well, that was easy, because I didn't really know what I was doing anyway." He concluded, "I went out there pretty much blind-folded."[5] The agents were outsiders to a reality they did not fully comprehend. That remained the modus operandi of the FBI in Latin America.

Few people, within the FBI or outside, knew of the intelligence-gathering operations in Latin America.[6] When the FBI told William Bradley that he was being considered for the SIS program, he "did not, at that time, know of its existence or what it was" or even for what the letters stood.[7] Similarly, Thomas Gaquin was confused when he was recruited into the SIS in June 1942 because he believed that the FBI worked only within the boundaries of the United States.[8] Decades later, the SIS program remained such a secret that even FBI historians had difficulty finding information about it or tracking down former agents. Crow observed, "You know it really is hard to believe it was such a well-kept secret during World War II. Even within the field offices." The former agent claimed he learned more about the SIS reading Leslie Rout and John Bratzel's book *The Shadow War*, but even that book did not have much detail.[9] Sundberg did not know that the SIS for which he worked was a precursor to the Central Intelligence Agency (CIA).[10] That lack of awareness of the nature of the FBI's operations in Latin America is also reflected in the scholarly literature. María Emilia Paz Salinas's masterful study of U.S. intelligence-gathering operations confuses the SIS with the ONI's Special Activities Branch or Special Intelligence Section.[11]

From humble beginning and with little public attention, the FBI's political surveillance in Latin America quickly grew to an impressive size in a short period of time. Broadly, the agents' activities fell into three categories: police trainers, undercover assignments with U.S. corporations, and legal attachés in embassies. Of the three, the police trainers had the most possibility to intervene directly in the internal affairs of another country, but it is also the realm for which the least amount of documentation remains. An assignment with a corporation inadvertently highlights the underlying economic motivation for the diplomatic presence, including blacklisting German firms that would allow them to be taken over by others friendly to U.S. economic interests. The legal attachés, and more generally the generation of extensive surveillance documentation, inadvertently creates a rich source on which scholars can draw. Seven hundred agents sent countless reports from across the hemisphere back to Washington that probed the depths of the local political landscape. While many agents arrived without much training or a clear sense of their duties, by just observing and reporting on what they saw they documented internal debates in Latin America that serve to reconstruct a history of the political left. An understanding of who the agents were and the roles they played facilitate an interpretation of the intelligence they produced, which contributes to a more complete and accurate analysis of the FBI's operatives in Latin America.

Arrivals

The FBI launched the Special Intelligence Service on July 1, 1940, to engage in foreign intelligence surveillance in the Western Hemisphere and "other specially designated areas."[12] The SIS was to be a service agency that provided the U.S. State Department, military, and FBI with information on financial, economic, and political activities that were detrimental to U.S. security concerns. Dallas Johnson later recalled that his fellow FBI agents did not call the agency the Special Intelligence *Services* but the Special Intelligence *Section*, possibly confusing it with the similarly named branch of the ONI. "I don't know where the services idea came," Johnson stated.[13] The term "services" may have formed part of FBI Director J. Edgar Hoover's branding effort to extend the reach of the bureau. Or perhaps the terminology the agency used to refer to the informal and clandestine operation was never entirely fixed. A collection of biographies of former FBI agents refers to the SIS as the Special *Investigative* Services, the *Secret* Intelligence Service (a name for the British foreign intelligence service MI6), or simply the SIS, as if readers would understand the reference.[14] In fact, Roy Britton, the longest-serving agent in Latin America, claimed that the FBI sent officials to London to study the British system and modeled the FBI program after it.[15] The agent Woodrow Lipscomb quipped, "There was always a constant discussion as to what SIS meant," and offered as alternatives "Security Intelligence Service," "Secret Intelligence Service," "and Security Investigative Service," none of which was its formal name. In Lipscomb's mind, the SIS was an undercover operation. If an agent worked openly with an embassy or consulate, that person returned to the status of FBI agent.[16]

Johnson recalled that Hoover sent the FBI agents Gus Jones and William Buys to Mexico and Cuba, respectively, even before President Franklin Roosevelt had formally approved the creation of the SIS. By 1939, Jones was sending reports from Mexico.[17] The following year, the agency dedicated significant resources to investigating Leon Trotsky's assassination, not to solve the crime, but to discover the extent of Soviet penetration in the hemisphere. Jones's activities formed part of the bureau's international intelligence gathering that had existed since the Mexican Revolution. As W. Dirk Raat notes, "The new organization was a dream come true for Hoover, who had been preoccupied with Mexico since the early 1920s."[18] Roosevelt's authorization allowed Hoover to expand his operations significantly. At the end of 1940, after six months of operation, the FBI had twelve undercover special agents in nine countries (Argentina, Brazil, Chile, Colombia, Cuba, Mexico, Nicaragua, Peru, and Venezuela), with one "special employee" traveling throughout South America. In 1941, this number grew rapidly. By July, the FBI had posted twenty-two undercover agents in twelve countries.[19] Within two years, the SIS had 137 agents stationed throughout Latin America, a number that later peaked at 360 agents.[20] Over the course of the entire program, the FBI placed about seven hundred agents in Latin America.

The initial dispatches from FBI agents were concerned primarily with threats from Nazi Germany, fascist Italy, and imperial Japan. The Germans established their major espionage networks in Mexico, Brazil, Chile, and Argentina, and at first the FBI focused its work mainly on Nazi encroachment into those countries. The bureau worked without the knowledge or agreement of host governments, especially those that were sympathetic to the Axis powers, and only joined the Allies once it was clear that they would emerge victorious in the war against Germany and Japan.[21] FBI agents paid for information on Nazis, which motivated informants to invent threats that greatly inflated U.S. perceptions of German activity. Despite the FBI's fears, the Nazis never came close to achieving their ambitions in the region, largely because of the Germans' lack of understanding of Latin America.[22]

Despite the original justification for the SIS program, many former agents deny that they were sent to Latin America to collect information on German or other Axis activities. Particularly after 1943, when the FBI had already rounded up and deported most Axis nationals and the SIS had reached its peak of activity, little surveillance activity in that realm remained for the agents. Mostly, what the agents did was collect information on the economic, financial, and political functioning of the country, which by its very nature involved a certain amount of duplication with State Department officials.[23] Because of his French-language skills, the FBI planned to send Fred Ayer to Haiti in 1943 but canceled the assignment because the State Department "did not feel that espionage, or even counter-espionage, was other than somewhat Un-American." Ayer reports that the FBI eventually sent another agent to Haiti, but in thirteen months "he had never seen a recognizable Nazi or a periscope." All the agent had to report was rumors of local intrigues. Eventually that agent resigned from the bureau and joined the military instead.[24]

The FBI sent agents to Latin America with minimal training. The most important consideration seemed to be that the agents were young and unmarried. In fact, agents were not allowed to take their families with them or have family visit them. Hoover assumed that older agents would face more difficulties in learning another language and adjusting to a different environment than those who had recently graduated from college, which to a certain extent may have been true. That decision also meant that the program suffered from a lack of administrative and technical knowledge that older agents would have brought.[25]

The FBI operated without previous experience in the region and thus had little advice or training it could offer to agents. As the program ramped up, the FBI provided first four, then six, then twelve weeks of intensive Spanish instruction (and later, training in Portuguese for Brazil), with the agents studying twelve hours a day from Monday through Saturday and half a day on Sunday. Before the FBI sent William Bradley to South America, the bureau provided him with Spanish lessons but then sent him to Brazil instead and he had to start over with Portuguese.[26] One agent claimed that the FBI put agents of Greek descent in the Portuguese class under the rationale that their heritage meant they "were smart and good linguists."[27] Often the FBI sent support staff with no language training at all. "They didn't even ask me whether I knew any foreign languages," Ronald Sundberg, who was stationed as a clerk in the Legal Attaché's Office in El Salvador, remembered, "and I didn't. I had absolutely no foreign languages." He arrived alone by plane and had to find his way to the U.S. Embassy. Once there, he took Berlitz lessons but in four months learned little. Later he was posted to Brazil for a year, during which time he learned more Portuguese.[28]

Initially, the bureau sent only men, but in 1944 the FBI began to assign female clerical support staff to Latin American posts. Hoover had arranged draft deferments for his agents, but the Selective Service put pressure on him to send men of draft age into the military and replace them with women. The FBI describes the contributions of female stenographers and clerical employees as enormously beneficial to the program. For safety, the FBI sent women to their posts in pairs.[29]

Nor did the FBI routinely debrief agents when they returned from the field.[30] The agent James Kraus did have an exit interview with Kit Carson, head of the SIS, but it focused on his feelings and whether he would be willing to return, not on the intelligence he had compiled.[31] The agents appeared to collect information without a clear understanding of its purpose or relation to a larger political environment. If the interviews and available documentation are to be believed, the agents did not engage in covert activity—nor would they have been particularly capable of doing so. Most merely functioned as the eyes and ears of a larger project that they probably never understood.

Edgar K. Thompson

On June 26, 1940, the FBI's special agent Edgar K. Thompson arrived by plane in Ecuador, several days before the formal launch of the SIS program. The FBI reported that although Thompson "was traveling on an official passport, his identity as an FBI Agent was not generally known in Quito."[32] A year before his arrival in Ecuador, the State Department, with Roosevelt's support, had sent Thompson to Rio de Janeiro, Brazil, to set up a "secret police system of a type similar to that considered necessary in the United States for dealing with espionage cases."[33] Martha Huggins surmises that in Ecuador he collaborated with the *carabineros*, a militarized police force modeled after their counterparts in Chile that the government employed as a bulwark against a potential military coup in the 1940 elections.[34] The U.S. government was eager to supplant the fascist Italian government's military mission that provided training of police forces throughout Latin America and turned to undercover FBI agents such as Thompson to achieve that goal.

Hoover selected Thompson for this first foray into South America because he was a young bachelor with previous experience in Puerto Rico, and he spoke Spanish. (The bureau apparently had no one who spoke Portuguese.) In this highly confidential assignment, Thompson assisted in the establishment of a Brazilian security service and provided the FBI with counterintelligence instruction. The undercover nature of Thompson's assignment created difficulties for making the appropriate financial arrangements, including confusion as to whether the Brazilian government or the State Department would cover his expenses, although in the end he was reimbursed quite lucratively out of Roosevelt's special appropriations fund. For five months, Thompson traveled extensively in Brazil as a visiting entrepreneur and succeeded in collecting extensive intelligence for the FBI.[35]

Following Brazil, the FBI assigned Thompson to Colombia, where the government had requested his expertise "in advising in the organization of an office similar to the Bureau" that would include "surveillance over the activities of aliens in Colombia." From his position, Thompson provided a steady stream of political intelligence back to Washington. Hoover subsequently pointed to Thompson's success in establishing important contacts with the police and gathering "a great deal of most interesting information" to justify an extension of this type of surveillance program to the rest of the Americas.[36] Hoover was eager to maintain tight control over his agents, as well as to build his own global intelligence-gathering empire. U.S. Ambassador Spruille Braden, however, complained that Thompson did little more than copy intelligence reports from embassy files and distribute them as his own to the State, War, and Navy departments.[37] FBI agents were aware that ambassadors did not like the idea of the bureau operating undercover in their country of assignment without their knowledge.[38] Interagency disputes over budgets and political control of intelligence operations led to constant conflicts, which contributed to Roosevelt's concern that the competing intelligence services "were often following the same matter at the same time and constantly crossing each other's tracks."[39] At one point, an embassy official in Colombia who resented the FBI's incursion into his territory had the local police department investigate an agent.[40]

Only a week before Thompson's arrival in Ecuador, Boaz Long, the U.S. envoy extraordinary and minister plenipotentiary, communicated a need to the secretary of state in Washington for someone to come immediately to Quito and remain until political conditions improved. The presidential election in January had been held under charges of electoral fraud and had left the country in a state of turmoil. The liberal candidate Carlos Arroyo del Río had won in a three-way race against the conservative archaeologist and historian Jacinto Jijón y Caamaño and the independent populist José María Velasco Ibarra. The sociologist Agustín Cueva characterized Arroyo del Río's win as a victory for "the most reactionary wing of the Liberal party" that had held power since Eloy Alfaro's liberal revolution in 1895.[41] Labor and leftist activists had long been antagonistic to the new president because of his role in suppressing a general strike in Guayaquil in November 1922 that led to a bloody massacre. U.S. officials feared that the unrest would persist until Arroyo del Río was inaugurated on August 10. In response, Long suggested that the FBI send Colonel Nicholas Campanole as a Secret Service agent. Campanole was familiar with the country and had the added advantage of being able to operate under the cover of working for an electric company. The FBI overruled

Long's suggestion, however, because it had "a representative who has already had considerable South American experience" that the bureau planned to send the following week. Depending on its representative's recommendations, the FBI might be open to sending more personnel.[42]

On July 1, 1940, Hoover forwarded Thompson's first report from Ecuador to Assistant Secretary of State Adolf A. Berle Jr. with a remark that the State Department might be interested in this intelligence and that he would follow up with more details. Hoover emphasized his agent's effectiveness in gathering information. "After consultation by the Special Agent with the United States Minister, the Provisional President of Ecuador and the Minister of Government," he commented, "the Special Agent's mission hereafter will be to investigate the belief that the Nazis through Víctor E. Estrada, a banker of Guayaquil, will finance a revolution against the President Elect about August 10, 1940." Hoover also noted, "The Government is reported as powerless as the army is under the control of the Italian Military Mission and the police are subverted by Estrada." Two days later, the State Department responded with a note acknowledging its appreciation for the FBI's communication. State Department officials consented that since "the FBI has its star agent in Quito, we leave it to him to have investigations made in U.S. by FBI."[43] With this green light from the State Department, Thompson proceeded to send a steady flow of political intelligence to the FBI.

Hoover soon followed up with a three-page memo to Berle that outlined the extent of German propagandizing in Ecuador. According to Thompson's intelligence, the Nazi Party, German merchants, and Estrada had contributed about $500,000 for propaganda. The German Legation paid about $1,000 a month for advertisements in newspapers in Quito and Guayaquil. The diplomatic mission also paid radio stations to broadcast anti-Semitic propaganda in the two cities. Both Germans and Ecuadorians wrote the propaganda that was directed against Jews, as well as against the United States. The advertisements outlined positive things Germany had done for Latin America and highlighted the nature of U.S. imperialism in Latin America. The Germans denounced a "dollar dictatorship" in which the prices of international trade were denominated in U.S. currency, with the U.S. government controlling monetary policy and financial value accruing to North American corporations. Thompson cautioned that "the so-called Communist, radical and socialist elements in Ecuador are being influenced by Nazi propaganda to believe that Germany is fighting against capitalism; that the United States is the symbol of capitalism, and that Dr. Arroyo del Rio, the incoming President who is pro-American, is the representative of the dollar."[44] Thompson's investigations highlighted just how much of the U.S. competition with Germany was commercial rather than political or ideological.

Subsequent memos from Thompson detailed the extent of Nazi propaganda in Ecuador's principal newspapers, including the conservative party's *El Debate*. The newspaper "has a very small circulation, confined almost entirely to members of the Conservative Party," and its editorial line was "violently anti-American and pro-Nazi," Thompson observed.[45] In a survey of Latin American newspapers, the State Department's Office of Intelligence Research likewise described *El Debate* as "ultra-conservative." The paper was anticommunist and "consistently attack[ed] liberal and socialist groups." *El Debate*'s "rightist and Falangist tendencies" and propensity to emphasize "religious aspects of every political question" limited its usefulness to advancing U.S. economic and political interests.[46] The British Legation also declared the newspaper "to be no friend of ours" and threatened to sanction its stalwartly conservative editor Mariano Suárez Veintimilla unless he changed his political line.[47]

Thompson wrote, "It seemed strange that this newspaper should be such a strong Nazi supporter since the Conservative Party is formed of the wealthiest landowners in Ecuador and it is common knowledge that the Nazi propaganda is actively working among leftist and labor organizations." The reason "for this apparent anomaly," he continued, "is that the Conservative Party of Ecuador was fanatically pro-Franco in the Spanish Civil War and its present attitude has naturally been influenced by Franco's leaning toward the axis powers."[48] Thompson described the actions of the Transocean news service that German representatives in Ecuador distributed free of charge to newspapers, as well as to government officials, military officers, and business leaders. Thompson charged that Quito's principal daily newspaper *El Comercio* had been paid to print Transocean news items.[49] In the early 1940s, some publications carried Transocean news largely because the Germans provided the wire service for free and the newspapers did not have the financial resources to subscribe to the United Press and Associated Press services out of the United States. While this did not necessarily reflect their political sympathies, it did represent a diminishment of U.S. influence in the hemisphere.

Thompson's concern about the growth of German propaganda was part of a broader U.S. fear of fascist appeal to the working class. In Mexico, for example, the Military Intelligence Division worried that President Lázaro Cárdenas's populist and corporatist style of governance reflected the influence of both Nazism and communism, which seemingly should be seen as opposing ideologies. Cárdenas, as with many others in Latin America, was motivated less by sympathy for Germany or fascist ideologies than by antipathy to the United States due to its long-standing imperial presence in the region. FBI agents in particular were not always attuned to the distinction between pro-German and anti–United States positions. Fear of fascists and communists plotting for control of Mexico as a base of operations to attack the United States increased after the Nazi-Soviet Non-Aggression Pact of 1939, although suspicions about a secret military treaty never were proved. The notorious Zimmerman telegram that proposed an alliance between Mexico and Germany in World War I remained a clear memory in Washington and influenced policy decisions in the lead-up to World War II. U.S. officials were determined to maintain their economic and political dominance over the hemisphere.[50]

Thompson also expressed concern that the presence of the Italian military mission meant that the Ecuadorian armed forces were under fascist influence.[51] This concern predated the war. In 1936, Federico Páez's conservative government announced the imminent arrival of an Italian mission to provide modern training for the Ecuadorian army. Government critics warned that the mission reflected warm relations with a fascist power.[52] The FBI later reported that Ecuadorian army officers were pleased with the work of the Italian mission and, as a result, were receptive to their fascist ideologies.[53] The Coordinator of Information (the precursor of the Office of Strategic Services [OSS]) echoed a similar concern that Italian influences contributed to the Ecuadorian military's sympathies for the Axis powers.[54]

On August 7, 1940, Thompson drafted a three-page memo outlining his activities in the little more than a month that he had spent in Ecuador. He had arrived "with the understanding that the purpose of [his] visit was to assist in the reorganization or training of a certain branch of the Ecuadorean police." Nevertheless, despite several meetings with Minister of Government Augusto Durango, Thompson's attempts to reorganize the detective section of the police had resulted in failure. At this point, that mission was a moot point, as the current government would soon be replaced with the incoming Arroyo del Río administration. Because of the Ecuadorian government's lack of interest in his original mission, Thompson decided to use his time "to secure information which might be of value to the United States Government as regards 5th Column and National Defense matters." During the recently concluded Spanish Civil War, the nationalist General Emilio Mola had referred to a "fifth column" of supporters inside Madrid who would support him as he approached with four columns of troops. According to Mola, those internal sympathizers would undermine the republican government from within. Their activities in support of an external attack might include sabotage, disinformation, and espionage. References to internal subversion as a "fifth column" became commonplace, and Thompson used this allusion to critique the suspicious activity of fifteen people of German and Italian descent in Ecuador. He also attempted to ascertain the source of funds that Estrada, the pro-Nazi banker from Guayaquil, had used for propaganda. Thompson also worked to decode the logs of clandestine radio stations. Finally, he compiled information on Nazi and fascist propaganda "and other topics of interest to our national defense of America and Latin America."[55] Thompson's reports reveal a preoccupation with fascism's potential influence, even though, as George Lauderbaugh notes, Nazi propaganda had made relatively minor inroads into Ecuador.[56]

While Thompson was in Ecuador, the journalist Russell Porter published a series of alarmist articles in the *New York Times* about a growing Nazi threat in Latin America, further fueling Washington's paranoia. Similar to Thompson, Porter pointed to a "fifth column" operating out of the German legations, with the German ministers directing large and efficient organizations of militant Nazi propagandists. Porter warned, "The Nazis are making a special drive among the lowest working classes most of whom, Indians or Cholas, are unable to read and write." Porter charged that the Nazis published a weekly paper, *Voz Obrera* (Workers' Voice), and paid "labor bosses, some previously regarded as communistic," to read it "to groups of illiterates." This concerted propaganda drive was allegedly designed to undermine U.S. economic and political influences in the region.[57]

The conservative Catholic *Voz Obrera* responded quite ferociously to the "insolence" of Porter's attack against it in "the press bought and paid for by international Jewry and a criminal and traitorous Masonry." The outrageous and imperialist statements of a reporter who had spent only three days in the country and possessed little understanding of its realities incensed *Voz Obrera*'s editor, Ciro Luis Tinajero. He denied that the newspaper was part of a fifth-column conspiracy and was particularly insulted by the implication that it was an organ for the lower class or that the paper sympathized with communism.[58] Tinajero's protestations notwithstanding, it had become quite common to characterize the publication as a Nazi propaganda tool. The renowned economist Robert Jackson Alexander, who interviewed leading political figures in Ecuador in the 1940s, also identified the periodical as a German Nazi propaganda organ because it carried wire reports from the Transocean news service.[59] In reality, *Voz Obrera* was more interested in attacking Freemasonry than in promoting fascism. Its sympathy for conservative European leaders, including Adolf Hitler in Germany and Benito Mussolini in Italy, as well as Portugal's Prime Minister António de Oliveira Salazar and Spanish General Francisco Franco, was due to their attacks on Masonry. Later, when the government blacklisted *Voz Obrera*, its editors proudly wore the status the paper had gained from the "Masonic-capitalist" English and Yankee governments.[60] The reactions to Porter's articles left the FBI scrambling to document that the journalist, who did not speak Spanish, had indeed reported from Quito and that his stories were not ghostwritten by people who sought to denigrate the Germans.[61] The FBI's collaboration with the *New York Times* was part of a campaign to advance U.S. interests in Latin America.

Porter acknowledged that while the Ecuadorian government was generally not pro-Nazi, it was too poor to invest resources in counterespionage. Porter was particularly concerned about Germany's commercial inroads into Latin America, including purchasing much of Ecuador's cacao and balsa exports and selling industrial products "with which the United States was unable to compete in price and credit terms." Porter warned, "Unless the United States takes definite action, Ecuador is likely to be one of the first South American nations to fall under Nazi domination."[62] As with Thompson, Porter's interest in counterespionage was not to protect Ecuador but to advance U.S. economic penetration into the region.

Porter cautioned against ignoring the "strategic importance" of the German airlines in the face of a looming war with the Axis powers. In particular, his concern was with Scadta (the Sociedad Colombo Alemana de Transporte Aéreo [Colombian-German Air Transport Society]) and Sedta (the Sociedad Ecuatoriana de Transportes Aéreos [Ecuadorian Aerial Transport Society]). "The fifth column here could foment a revolution and establish an Ecuadorean regime favorable to the Nazis," he wrote. The two airlines consistently lost money, Porter claimed, highlighting that their purpose was military rather than economic. He warned that they could be used to launch an attack on the Panama Canal.[63] Commentators and policy makers exploited Ecuador's assumed strategic location for defense of the canal as justification for U.S. intervention in the region. In July 1941, *El Comercio* in Quito reprinted an analogous article that the "eminent North American author" Edward Tomlinson published in the *New York Herald Tribune* identifying Ecuador, Colombia, and Venezuela as three key countries for the defense of the Americas because of their proximity to the Panama Canal. Like Porter, Tomlinson was particularly concerned with the German airlines Sedta and Scadta and the Italian military missions in Ecuador and Venezuela.[64] Journalists and policy makers repeatedly used the Panama Canal, itself an imperial outpost in the middle of the hemisphere, to justify U.S. economic policies.

Since April 1940, even before Porter and Tomlinson had raised these concerns in the press, the State Department had been quietly working behind the scenes to negotiate a plan for a U.S. airline to take over Sedta's routes. Ecuador's Defense Minister Galo Plaza resisted the plans and, in fact, informed the United States that the Ecuadorian military relied on Sedta's service and was looking to expand it. Plaza frankly told U.S. Minister Boaz Long that the Ecuadorian government would not accept less from a new contract than what it currently received from Sedta. Furthermore, Sedta had such a good reputation in Ecuador that "the public would probably rebel if they lost Sedta and got in exchange a less comprehensive or efficient service."[65] Both Sedta and Scadta were subsidiaries of the German airline Lufthansa and enjoyed a good reputation for their excellent service and affordable prices. The planes would carry anything, even pigs. The airlines held mail contracts and in exchange provided free rides to government officials and politicians, as well as cheap communication and transportation services to the military.[66]

Over the next several months, U.S. Secretary of State Cordell Hull and Minister Long engaged in a protracted and voluminous correspondence concerning how best to remove Sedta from Ecuador. Hull claimed that the primary concern of the United States was to safeguard the Panama Canal, even as he acknowledged a desire to protect "United States international aviation interests."[67] These diplomatic officials plotted to replace the German carriers with Pan American-Grace Airways, a joint venture of Pan American Airways and the Grace Line steamship company known as Panagra. One proposal was to have the Ecuadorian government buy out Sedta, even though it (and Panagra, for that matter) appeared to have little interest in doing so because of the financial cost of assuming the service.[68] Hoover inserted himself into the conversation by forwarding a pair of letters to the State Department, probably drawing on information from Thompson, complaining that Pan American Airways was doing little to remove Sedta from Ecuador.[69] The FBI, however, had little to offer to resolve the issue. More rational voices questioned how serious a threat Sedta, with its two old and slow planes, posed to the United States.

Rather, the German airlines were engaged in a "spirited competition" with Pan American Airways. Sedta kept cutting its rates, and Panagra was unwilling to match its prices or take over its routes without heavy government subsidies. Sedta also received a significant boost in public opinion in 1941 when it flew Ecuadorian military officers during a border dispute with Peru.[70] The FBI reported that the public retained positive attitudes toward the German airline, and Panagra faced difficulties in gaining the confidence of the people.[71] Panagra could not compete economically with Sedta, which deepened official fears of a German economic (rather than political) threat in the region.

Plaza demanded that if these plans moved forward and Panagra could not provide the military with the same level of service as Sedta, the U.S. government agree to supply planes and pilots. The negotiations led the British diplomatic mission in Ecuador to observe that Sedta's removal could open up new opportunities "for the development of a British service."[72] At the same time, Hull insisted that the diplomatic mission in Quito take a back seat in the negotiations between Panagra and the Ecuadorian government, even as the State Department was determined to guide and define the specific outcome of those negotiations.[73] Diplomatic interests never remained purely on the level of political policy but also commonly entered the realm of how to advance a country's economic interests, a point that subsequent scholars openly acknowledge.[74] The overt economic penetration led to concerted leftist opposition to U.S. imperialism.

By October 1940, the State Department thought it had finally negotiated an agreement to take over the airlines when additional wrinkles emerged. First, Sedta submitted a very attractive contract to the Ecuadorian government to offer mail service that Panagra had trouble countering.[75] Then the Ecuadorian government insisted on "moral guarantees" from the United States that Panagra's service would be permanent, something that the State Department could not provide for a private enterprise. Ecuador's foreign minister protested that if the new Panagra service were to be suspended for any reason after the elimination of Sedta, it would leave the government open to such criticism that it could result in its overthrow.[76] The U.S. government eventually forced Ecuador's hand by threatening to cut off oil and gasoline sales to the country unless the government canceled its contract with Sedta.[77] The Ecuadorian government responded by limiting the sale of aviation fuel to Sedta, but the airline simply switched to automobile fuel and continued operations.[78] That move raised safety concerns in many people's minds. Finally, on October 1, 1941, the Ecuadorian government suspended the contract, although it did so with a good deal of regret.[79]

In a surprisingly frank confession, British Minister Leslie Hughes-Hallett expressed alarm that the U.S. diplomatic mission's chief concern was to foster and support its country's commercial penetration of South America, while "matters more closely connected with the joint war effort receive very half-hearted attention."[80] His preoccupation, however, had to do with much more than military strategy. The United States was determined to replace Germany's economic position in South America, and the British were concerned that they were being squeezed out of economic opportunities in the process. The British mission also charged that the U.S. government was making improper use of censorship of the mail to intercept requests for British goods and redirect them to U.S. companies. The United States had "taken every advantage of the present situation to develop their own commercial interests," Hughes-Hallett complained, "and the exclusive domination which they have established over Ecuadorean economic life is a potential menace to any plans Great Britain may have for taking part in the development of this country after the war."[81] Economic penetration of Latin America was as much, if not more, of a concern for industrial powers as political ideologies, a fact that was not lost on leftists and labor activists dedicated to advancing working-class interests.

Edward Tomlinson was encouraged that Pan American Airways was taking over the German airlines and that the U.S. military was displacing the Italian missions, but he remained concerned with the continuing active German commercial presence in the region. In 1937, for example, Germany bought 60 percent of Ecuador's cacao exports, and German ships transported 43 percent of the country's exports. In the 1930s, Germany's imports into Latin America had dramatically risen, while the U.S. share had fallen.[82] By 1940, Germany surpassed Great Britain in imports to the region and was second only to the United States. Tomlinson advocated for the application of the Monroe Doctrine to reestablish U.S. control over the hemisphere.[83]

Similarly, at the end of his ten-week trip through South America in 1940, Porter concluded, "Germany wants South America and wants it badly," not for "its physical possession necessarily, but [for] its economic control, the real prize for which wars are fought." He urged U.S. policy makers to play their cards carefully so as not to "lose" Latin America to the Germans. Porter advocated for U.S. intervention in the face of potential Nazi success "in fomenting revolutions which appear to be purely internal movements," even if that meant a violation of the Good Neighbor policy.[84] Latin Americans reacted strongly against these ideas that they viewed as purely imperialistic. The Ecuadorian socialist leader Juan Isaac Lovato emphasized that a true Good Neighbor policy needed to respect independence and sovereignty and allow each country to find its own way forward.[85] The U.S. government did not share this perspective.

Police Trainers

Thompson's departure in September 1940 temporarily brought an end to regular FBI reports from Ecuador. After Thompson's brief stay in the country, Long wrote to Undersecretary of State Sumner Welles that "he has done well here. Above all, he has been discreet, and his report is modest enough." It was Long's desire that Thompson remain a while longer in Ecuador.[86] Half a year later, Long's wish for continued FBI presence in Ecuador was partially met with the assignment of a temporary agent, also to assist with police training. The success of that special mission led President Arroyo del Río, as well as the State Department, to agree in August 1941 after much urging from the FBI to request a permanent assignment for an agent to cooperate with the Ecuadorian government. The temporary agent convinced Arroyo del Río that "it would be possible to devote a great deal of time to intelligence work in addition to the police training."[87] Hoover was willing to use any excuse necessary to justify the expansion of his domain.

Whether under the guise of investigating Nazis or communists, the FBI continued to send police trainers to Latin America but always did so on its own terms. In November 1942, Colón Eloy Alfaro, Ecuador's ambassador to the United States, requested two police instructors and asked for an invitation for Héctor Salgado, the head of the carabineros, to visit the United States. The FBI responded that it was willing to send instructors if the embassy in Quito requested them, but the bureau was concerned that it did not have the proper facilities to handle a visit from the chief of police.[88] "The FBI has no intention of inviting any chief of police to the United States and does not wish to receive any," a State Department functionary stated in response to the request. The bureau "has always made it a rule never to discuss such matters with missions in Washington because they are not in a position to know the situation well enough to be of use," probably an implicit acknowledgment of the covert and possibly illegal nature of the trainers' activities. Rather, arrangements for such assignments should be made through the U.S. Embassy and the FBI agents attached to it.[89] Clarence Moore, an FBI agent in the embassy, advised that "no direct useful purpose would be served through a visit to the United States of the Jefe de Carabineros other than in the pursuance of our Good Neighbor policy."[90]

Eventually, the FBI capitulated and organized an eighty-two-day coast-to-coast trip for Salgado for "the purpose of acquiring training and an insight to methods employed by the Bureau in crime prevention, espionage, and sabotage investigations."[91] During the trip, newspapers in Quito carried stories of his experiences and impressions and his plans to return with the latest in police equipment.[92] Salgado declared that he was "a great admirer of the magnificent work of the FBI." After studying the FBI's methods, he was convinced that the Ecuadorian police could adopt many of them. He returned to Ecuador by way of Cuba and Chile, where apparently he consulted with his counterparts on the implementation of repressive police tactics.[93]

The embassy was open to receiving more police instructors. In February 1943, the FBI assigned Walter Gates as a police liaison officer to the embassy, with the FBI to pay his salary and expenses.[94] Gates provided training to officers in Quito, Guayaquil, and Cuenca. The police assigned graduates of this program to posts throughout the country, which notably increased and extended the ability of the FBI to conduct local surveillance. The program also allowed agents to draw up a list of "dangerous and undesirable aliens" from Axis countries, which the president subsequently had the carabineros arrest and deport.[95] When Alfaro requested even more instructors, the State Department again reiterated that such assignments would be made only on the recommendations of the FBI agents stationed in the embassy.[96] Rather than maintaining reciprocal relations with its counterparts in Latin America, such decisions were made with an eye to benefiting the United States. The FBI underscored its desire to act in a manner that would advance the bureau's agenda rather than strengthening antifascist struggles in Latin America.

As the FBI became institutionalized in Latin America, the bureau's work expanded from its original focus on police training to include counterintelligence. The FBI followed the permanent posting of an agent in Quito in August 1941 with a second one in Guayaquil a month later. They were two of thirty-six agents the FBI had stationed in sixteen countries by October 1941.[97] From that small beginning, the FBI presence began to grow rapidly. The FBI added another agent in Quito at the end of the year and an open representative to the embassy at the beginning of 1942. By July 1942, the FBI had two undercover agents in Guayaquil and three in Quito; two undercover special agents in Quito; two representatives at the U.S. Embassy in Quito; and a radio operator stationed in Quito, for a total of ten agents. One of the undercover agents had "the privilege of traveling to surrounding cities and towns keeping in touch and abreast of Axis activity."[98] With this large presence, in 1942 FBI communications on Ecuador's internal political affairs once again arrived regularly in Washington and continued until the withdrawal of agents from Latin America in 1947.

By 1943, with a realistic Nazi threat having largely evaporated, the FBI shifted its entire intelligence apparatus to focus on a perceived communist threat, both in the United States and in Latin America. In actuality, no significant fascist threat ever existed to justify such a major investment of resources. An FBI report from 1944 conceded as much: "There is absolutely no evidence of any kind that organized Axis subversive elements currently influence the manipulation of Ecuadoran political parties or the more prominent individuals thereof."[99] Almost as if to drive home the hypocrisy of U.S. policy on fascism, both the mainstream and socialist press in Ecuador carried stories, before and after the war, of Nazi propagandists operating openly in the United States even while FBI agents were monitoring what was largely an absence of such activity in Ecuador.[100] The duplicity—or, perhaps more accurately, the hidden objectives—of U.S. policies were readily apparent.

Undercover

FBI agents commonly entered Latin America under the cover of working for a U.S. corporation such as General Motors or Firestone. Although the corporations may have had underlying economic motivations, they presented their collaboration as a patriotic desire to help with the war effort, and one way to do so was by hosting an FBI agent. The FBI provided staffing, and the corporation furnished the cover, even if in reality the agents did little work for the business.[101] Pan American Airways was a favorite post because it gave agents the ability to monitor movement in the country in which they were stationed. Decades after the end of the program, the FBI still treats the names of these corporations as classified information and redacts them from interviews and released documents. "The work of the undercover agents," the FBI reported in 1943, "has been integrated into the general work of the office and it has been possible for them to obtain much information and perform considerable work which would have been embarrassing or impossible if done by the agents of the Embassy." Their undercover status permitted the agents to travel to otherwise remote parts of South America "to obtain information of pertinent developments in those areas."[102] Nevertheless, these secretive intelligence-gathering operatives exacerbated tensions both with U.S. diplomatic officials in the country and among different government agencies.

The FBI's tactics frequently encroached on the realm of illegality. One agent worked as a journalist, and having a government agent reporting on Latin American affairs in the U.S. press should have raised constitutional issues.[103] The FBI trained the undercover agents in picking locks and other skills for so-called black bag jobs that would require breaking and entering into premises to collect information. The agent Thomas Gaquin recounted that he received instruction in sabotage techniques and espionage.[104] "We understood basically that the reason we were undercover is that we were going to be doing things that would be an embarrassment to the United States Government if we were caught," acknowledged Richard Crow. "They told us frankly we don't want you to know too much of what's going on so that, you know, you couldn't say anything." In fact, undercover agents were told to stay away from the U.S. Embassy so the FBI could deny any responsibility or affiliation if its agents were caught in the middle of a burglary attempt.[105] This became a problem in Recife, Brazil, when a naval commander attempted to neutralize an agent, but the bureau was not willing to admit to its presence or the nature of its work.[106] The FBI sent Gaquin to Mexico with "no credentials, no badge, no identification system relating to the government, nothing, zero." He entered with a tourist card that allowed him to stay eleven months. Gaquin's cover was that he was a French teacher from Boston who wanted to learn Spanish. Rather than being given a specific mission, the FBI ordered him to collect "anything that could conceivably interest the United States Intelligence community." Despite the war, he did not specifically target Germans, Italians, or Japanese, inadvertently conceding that the true interests of the program lay elsewhere.[107]

The FBI sent Fred Woodcock to Peru with no knowledge of Spanish. The bureau told him that he would be on his own, with little chance of assistance if he ran into trouble. In such a situation, agents were expected "to go underground and get back as best they could."[108] The FBI assigned William Horan to Paraguay but told him "that all future contact with the Bureau would cease." Agents were to arrange their own travel to South America, but a limited number of seats on planes meant that Horan had to wait for weeks in Miami for a flight. Soon, it became common knowledge that he was working with the FBI, and his cover was blown even before he arrived in Paraguay.[109] After waiting two or three weeks for a flight, Charles Dickey gave up on his FBI assignment and joined the Marine Corps instead.[110]

With hundreds of agents on the continent, many covers were not located in areas of the economy that would facilitate useful intelligence gathering. The result was that some undercover agents had few surveillance activities to occupy their time and instead hung out with wealthy individuals at country clubs. One agent in Colombia admitted, "Most of my life there was social."[111] In Venezuela, Allan Gillies claimed to have played tennis with the son of the Italian ambassador, even though the United States was at war with the fascist power. Gillies was assigned to investigate Germans but concluded that they were engaged only in business endeavors, not in espionage activities.[112] Woodrow Lipscomb distributed film in Ecuador, and his primary memory entailed simply going to work every day. After eight months, the FBI removed him because the limited information he acquired duplicated what a military attaché had already provided.[113] A common perception, as one agent stated, was that these undercover agents "had it easy." Many agents did not conduct significant counterintelligence work because "there wasn't much they could do."[114] Ultimately, the bureau was quite ineffective at halting German influence in the hemisphere. Seemingly, one of its few noteworthy achievements, and one that the FBI and its agents repeatedly mention, was breaking up a smuggling ring that moved platinum from Colombia to Argentina, where it was shipped to Germany for use in airplane ignition systems.[115]

Exacerbating this futility was that sometimes the agents' cover stories were not very convincing. William Bradley's cover in Brazil was very fragile and raised suspicion among authorities, which forced the FBI to move him to a new assignment.[116] John Paul Larkin worked in such an inappropriate assignment in Costa Rica that "eventually people doubted the truth of my cover." He recalled, "They observed that I was young, an American, it was wartime, and it wasn't very long before people were telling me that I must work for the FBI." Larkin remained in Costa Rica for eighteen months, and the FBI eventually withdrew him when a bureau inspector concluded that his unsuitable cover meant that there was little productive work he could undertake in the country.[117] Others told similar stories. "What's an American doing down there?" Gaquin remembered people asking. "He's got no uniform on, he's not in the Army and the Navy, what the hell is he doing?" Often it quickly became obvious that they were undercover agents. As Gaquin said, "A cop could taste another cop two blocks away." The local authorities immediately knew that he was with the FBI and that he was engaged in illicit police activities in the country.[118] In its own evaluation of the SIS program, the FBI "noted for possible future reference that commercial covers generally in wartime are extremely weak and objectionable unless the employee to be assigned under same is somewhat elderly or otherwise obviously not good draft material."[119] One consequence of inexperience was not having thought through all of the implications for how a program was run.

Having one's cover blown could have a variety of consequences. Edward Sanders monitored Germans in Mendoza, Argentina, and many people suspected why he was there, but that did not seem to interfere with his assignment.[120] John Diesing worked with a U.S. insurance company in Buenos Aires. He monitored Italian radio transmissions regarding Allied ship movements, but once his cover was blown, he could not remain in the country.[121] Donald Roney had to leave Argentina because someone wrote an anonymous letter to the U.S. ambassador naming him as an undercover agent who was targeted by an Argentine government official.[122] In Venezuela, the police arrested an informant who identified Frank Fawcett as his contact with the FBI. As a result, the government gave the undercover agent twenty-four hours to leave the country.[123] The more sensitive the agent's work, the more necessary it was to maintain their confidential status.

Many agents in undercover assignments suffered from low morale because they were not permitted to have contact with other U.S. diplomats while they were in a country. If they did not make their own social connections with local residents, they could easily end up feeling lonely and isolated. Some agents were not acclimated to Latin American cultures and reinforced "ugly American" stereotypes. Perhaps worst of all, they had no sense of the larger picture or understanding of the policy objectives the U.S. government was pursuing. For such agents, being sent back with dysentery or other tropical diseases could be a relief.[124] Others resigned from the bureau and joined the military because they believed that they would be of more use participating directly in the war. Their defections highlighted the ineffectiveness of the bureau's activities.

Still, not all agents felt alienated in their assignments. The radio operator Richard Leahy concluded, "If I was going to be of any service to the Bureau, I had to get enmeshed with the Chilean people." As a result, he had very positive experiences during his time in the country. "I think the Bureau did a pretty good job down there," Leahy stated, even as he acknowledged that, for the most part, the efforts of undercover agents were not properly rewarded.[125] Donald Daughters provides an even clearer example of a positive experience with an FBI assignment. He arrived in Santiago, Chile, without knowing anything about the country. Initially he was lonely because he did not know anyone, but Daughters "found out very quickly that as soon as you knew someone it was so easy to establish relationships with Chileans, they're so friendly." He began dating Yvonne Fath, a Chilean secretary working at the Rockefeller Institution. Daughters returned to the United States when he came down with yellow jaundice. He worked for brief stints in the sis division in Washington, and then a bureau field office in Boston. Soon, however, he married Fath and several years later returned to Chile, where for the next thirty years he raised a family and worked with the United Shoe Machinery Company.[126] Some agents thrived in Latin America, and their assignments were transformative experiences.

Legal Attaché

In 1941, Minister Boaz Long cooperated with the FBI's plan to expand intelligence gathering by designating the FBI agent Clarence Moore a "legal attaché" in the embassy in Quito. Since Moore was a lawyer, the embassy thought that the title was proper.[127] As legal attaché, Moore worked closely with Government Minister Aurelio Aguilar Vázquez to provide technical training in the "Henry" method of police investigation.[128] Moore's collaboration with the Ecuadorian police represented an achievement for the FBI. After Thompson's departure, Long complained to the State Department that Arroyo del Río had not taken advantage of the agent to enact "certain reforms contemplated in Ecuador's secret service." However, Arroyo del Río rethought his position after Thompson left and welcomed Moore's contributions. Long warmly embraced Moore's work as a legal attaché and requested additional personnel from the FBI to expand the embassy's intelligence-gathering operations.[129]

The State Department also responded positively to Moore's title and assigned activities and subsequently instructed all of its South American embassies to provide an FBI representative with the same label.[130] One of the next legal attachés was William Bradley, who assumed that designation in Brazil in 1943, when his cover story became too fragile to maintain.[131] In August 1943, the FBI extended the practice to Europe with the appointment of Dennis Flinn, the first agent permanently posted to Europe, as a legal attaché in the U.S. Embassy in Lisbon, Portugal. Flinn's assignment was a special exception to an agreement to divide intelligence gathering between the FBI in the Western Hemisphere and the OSS in the Eastern Hemisphere.[132] After the war, the FBI continued to use the title "legal attaché," or "legat," as a euphemism for an agent in an embassy or a foreign liaison office, and the practice spread around the world.[133] In some countries, the agents were called "civil attachés" or vice-consuls to hide their FBI affiliation from the local government or if an ambassador sought to distance the embassy from the FBI.[134] Some embassy personnel were leery of having the FBI in their building out of fear that the agents were spying on their activities.[135] The FBI stationed legats in embassies in part so they would be in close proximity to the ambassador and thereby be able to smooth ruffled feathers over conflicting surveillance activities among different government agencies.[136] The number of legats or their equivalent at any one time varied depending on current needs but could grow to be quite large. At its height, the FBI had roughly fifteen of its agents positioned as vice-consuls in the Buenos Aires consulate.[137]

Fred Woodcock, an agent in charge of radio operations in Lima, Peru, recalled that agents formally left the bureau when they received an SIS assignment and ostensibly became State Department employees, including receiving State Department passports. He characterized the entire program as "highly confidential" and remarked that not many people knew of the FBI's involvement.[138] These agents enjoyed full diplomatic coverage, which provided them with a very safe environment.[139] Often the agents would deny that they worked for the FBI; instead, they claimed that they were embassy employees. Even so, none of the legal attachés were included on the State Department's Foreign Service lists that provided the rank and salary of all diplomatic officials. The embassy cover was so effective that subsequent scholars do not always recognize legal attachés as FBI agents.[140] In essence, the embassy provided diplomatic cover for a political police engaged in illegal spying in other countries.

Daughters, who operated as a legal attaché in the embassy in Chile, remarked that the label "was an innocuous name that they gave to the people who worked as special agents down there in order to avoid the frightening name of FBI." Nevertheless, word of their assignments would leak out. "It's always the Americans who are most interested in gossiping about anything that smells of secret intelligence," he observed. "It really gets people excited, gets the blood flowing, and they can't wait to talk about things that relate to secret intelligence." Daughters was one of four or five agents in the legat office. If someone asked what he did at the embassy, he would dismissively respond, "Oh, I'm a legal attaché." If someone inquired what a legal attaché did, he would "tell them that we were looking into problems that arise between Chile and the United States." The legal attachés would emphasize that they "were just fostering the best possible relations between the two countries. And then, we'd get off the subject pretty fast." The goal was to project themselves as "the most harmless people in the world."[141]

As part of their position in the embassy, the legal attachés had access to the diplomatic pouch to send dispatches to FBI headquarters in Washington. This privilege could be abused, however, as on occasion the transmissions contained nothing more than newspaper articles on Hoover's activities and awards that he received from local governments.[142] For example, in January 1944, Colón Eloy Alfaro, Ecuador's ambassador to the United States, conferred on Hoover the National Order of Merit with the rank of Commander First Class. Alfaro presented this honor in the name of the Ecuadorian government in recognition of Hoover's suppression of fifth-column activities and the training of Ecuadorian police officials in detective work. The ceremony took place at a dinner at the Mayflower Hotel in Washington in the presence of Vice President Henry Wallace, Attorney General Francis Biddle, Assistant Secretary of State Adolf Berle, high-ranking military officers, and members of the diplomatic corps. Legal attachés stationed in Colombia and Venezuela forwarded local newspaper clippings to the FBI of a United Press wire story on the award. Hoover or, more likely, one of his minions was sufficiently impressed with the designation that it was added to his official biography along with a note that he was recognized "for his accomplishments in effecting a closer law enforcement cooperation in the cause of the allied nations." Curiously, that notation was not included in the original press reports announcing the honor.[143]

In Ecuador, Arroyo del Río delegated extensive powers to the legal attaché, who essentially began to function as a member of the president's cabinet. The legal attaché provided the FBI with a wealth of information on internal political activities while allowing the U.S. government to dictate policies to other governments regarding the monitoring, arrest, punishment, and exile of supposed subversive elements. Legal attachés could become so entrenched with friendly governments that they would draft decrees and other formal documents for local officials to sign.[144] The FBI acknowledged that this "quasi-official" status gave the United States a free hand to target which Axis nationals to expel from Latin America. Clarence Moore drafted a list of undesirable Axis nationals, which led the Spanish minister in Ecuador to complain that in reality it was the United States and not the Ecuadorian government that was deporting people.[145] Arroyo del Río was unfamiliar with the names of Germans on the list, but several Italians had previously been clients in his law practice. Those names led Arroyo del Río to challenge the accuracy of Moore's work and to criticize the U.S. Legation for how it had responded to his generosity in meeting with their diplomats.[146] Maintaining these relationships required a certain amount of delicate negotiation.

With a growth in personnel, the FBI recounted in its annual report, the legal attaché "office changed from one agent with a borrowed typewriter to a well-equipped office similar to one of the Bureau's smaller Field Offices." This was an accurate description. The FBI operated the only Photostat machine in Ecuador out of the U.S. Embassy, as well as a continuous wave (CW) radio transmitter that broadcast without permission from the Ecuadorian government.[147] The radio station, as well as access to the embassy's diplomatic pouch, placed the FBI "in a position to forward by rapid means important and vital information which might come to the attention of SIS representatives."[148] In 1945, the FBI testified, "The Office of the Legal Attaché continues to maintain adequate coverage in the intelligence field." The bureau stated that due to the cultivation of confidential informants, it "has been possible to accurately follow political developments, economic activities and subversive movements" in Ecuador. The FBI reported that the relations between the legal attaché and Ambassador Robert Scotten were "very close" and that the embassy relied on this office "to secure reliable and confidential information" on internal political developments.[149] From the FBI's perspective, this intelligence gathering was proceeding very well.

An example of the close collaboration between the embassy staff and the FBI came in August 1943 as political opposition to President Arroyo del Río continued to grow. Many Ecuadorians saw his government as corrupt, and the president's credibility suffered after losing a border war with Peru in 1941. Arroyo del Río became exceedingly unpopular after signing the Rio de Janeiro Protocol in 1942, which ceded half of Ecuador's territory to its neighbor. Scotten claimed that he had been able to verify the accuracy of "a number of somewhat confused reports of unrest." Although he acknowledged that political predictions in Ecuador were hazardous, he believed that "an imminent danger of a revolution" before Congress resumed its session on August 10 did exist. He based this prediction on information that the legal attaché George Blue acquired from "a reliable official source." Blue indicated that the government found itself "in a precarious position due to the ever-increasing activities of the newly formed Alianza Democrática Ecuatoriana" (Ecuadorian Democratic Alliance; ADE) that was backing the candidacy of José María Velasco Ibarra. According to "a source high within the Ecuadoran Government," Arroyo del Río planned to arrest the opposition leaders in advance of the congressional assembly. Blue promised Scotten that he would "be kept fully advised of developments as we learn of them." Either Blue's intelligence proved to be faulty or the ADE's plans to launch an uprising fizzled because, as a note dated August 19 from the State Department's Division of the American Republics stated, "On August 10 nothing happened."[150] Nevertheless, the correspondence between State Department officials and the FBI does indicate close relations between the ambassador and the legal attaché and how reliant the embassy had become on that office for its intelligence gathering, however imperfect it might be.

In December 1943, Hoover notified the State Department that he was issuing instructions to a bureau representative in Quito to interview Army Major George Páez and the conservative leader Jacinto Jijón y Caamaño regarding charges that a sale of machine guns to the Ecuadorian government violated the mail fraud statute.[151] Several weeks later, the Legal Attaché's Office conducted the interviews, although it was Ambassador Scotten and not Hoover who forwarded the five-page report to the State Department. Further reflecting the growth in the size and importance of the Legal Attaché's Office and its intermeshing with embassy functions, the report listed three FBI agents as having conducted the interview: William Hulbert, assistant to the legal attaché; Walter Gates, assistant legal attaché; and Henry Johnson, assistant legal attaché.[152] This close collaboration between FBI agents and embassy personnel came despite the famously dysfunctional relationships among different government agencies.

Field Investigations

In October 1943, the FBI reached its height of operations in Latin America with a total of 583 employees. Twenty-one were assigned to Ecuador, with most concentrated in the capital city, Quito. The FBI assigned five agents to the Legal Attaché's Office in the embassy, in addition to four clerical officers; four worked as special undercover agents, two operated the radio, one served as a liaison officer with the local police department, and another functioned as a police security officer. Two agents were assigned to the consulate in Guayaquil, and a special agent operated undercover in both Guayaquil and the southern city Cuenca.[153] A declassified FBI report lists a total of forty-five agents in Ecuador from June 1940 through March 1947, all with their names and SIS numbers redacted. Nearly all were stationed in Quito or Guayaquil, with one each in Cuenca and Manta for short periods of time. In 1943, the FBI reassigned the agent in the coastal city Manta to Quito because of a lack of activity in that area. Since many "Axis nationals" had been relocated to Cuenca, the FBI briefly assigned an undercover agent to that area to monitor their activities more closely.[154]

Reports from the agent in Cuenca shed light on the modus operandi of the FBI operations in Latin America. The agent described the city as "very old-fashioned and conservative," isolated from the rest of Ecuador and the world and hence largely unaware of what was happening elsewhere. He found little evidence of fifth-column activity in the city but also acknowledged that local people would not recognize it even if it did exist. With seemingly little of political significance happening and no subversive activities to report, the agent resorted to describing the religious orders in a city that was almost entirely Catholic. The orders included the Salesian Brothers, with about one hundred mostly Italian members, and the Jesuit Fathers, with about twenty Spanish members. The Salesian Brothers ran a radio station with irregular broadcasts that the agent described as essentially a "ham" radio operation. Despite coming from countries under fascist rule, they represented no threat to either Ecuadorian or U.S. national interests. A list of Axis nationals revealed only German refugees and others who were well-established community members with no apparent subversive intent.[155]

An even more innocuous report described living and economic conditions in the central highland province of Tungurahua. The three-page report provided little information on security concerns that would have justified the FBI's presence in the country. The communiqué was largely limited instead to basic historical, geographic, and economic information that would have been of interest to a traveler through the region, including provision of housing and entertainment options. The only slightly political observation was that the local population was "somewhat anti-Allied in attitude" because German-trained members of the clergy had provided their education. The anonymous author of the report described the clergy as "a very ignorant group" who were "more swayed by emotion and superstition than by the light of intellect and reason." According to this author, "Considerable propaganda on the part of the Allies would be needed to change views which are almost apart [sic] of their inner nature." Rather than dwell on that topic, however, the author described the hot springs at Baños, complained about uncomfortable hotel beds, and made derogatory remarks about residents who lived "in their pristine state of squalor." Rather surprisingly, the FBI removed even such a tourist report with little counterintelligence value in its sweep of archival documents during its declassification review project.[156]

and its ramifications which was reported by the Ambassador had been
furnished by the Legal Attache's Office. It was sent by the Ambassador
to the State Department via Bureau radio facilities. (64-3301)

3. Personnel

The following Special Agents and Special Employees were
assigned to SIS work in Ecuador:

b7C
b2

NAME	SIS NO.	CITY	DATE	ASSIGNMENT
		Quito	5/42-11/42	Undercover
		Quito	7/45- 3/47	Police Liaison
		Quito	8/42-10/43	Official
		Quito	6/43-10/43	Official
		Guayaquil	8/44- 1/45	Official
		Quito	6/43-10/43	Undercover
		Cuenca	9/43- 2/44	Undercover
		Guayaquil	10/43- 3/44	Undercover
		Quito	1/46- 3/47	Legal Attache
		Quito	2/43- 2/45	Police Liaison
		Guayaquil	4/45- 8/46	Official
		Quito	2/43- 8/43	Legal Attache
		Quito	7/44- 2/45	Official
		Quito	5/42- 5/43	Legal Attache
		Quito	5/43-10/43	Undercover
		Quito	5/43- 1/44	Official
		Manto	2/43- 6/43	Official
		Quito	6/43- 1/44	Official
		Guayaquil	5/43- 6/44	Official
		Guayaquil	8/45-11/45	Undercover
		Quito	5/43- 1/44	Undercover
		Quito	1/42- 9/42	Undercover
		Guayaquil	5/43- 8/43	Undercover
		Quito	12/41-12/42	Legal Attache
		Guayaquil	5/46- 2/47	Police Liaison
		Guayaquil	10/43- 3/45	Official
		Quito	3/45-10/46	Legal Attache
		Guayaquil	2/42- 6/42	Undercover
		Quito	3/44- 6/45	Police Liaison
		Quito	5/43-11/43	Undercover
		Guayaquil	9/41- 9/43	Official
		Guayaquil	8/42- 1/43	Undercover
		Quito	3/43- 4/43	Plant Survey
		Quito	10/43-10/44	Legal Attache
		Quito	3/42- 2/43	Undercover
		Guayaquil	1/42- 7/42	Undercover
		Quito	11/43- 9/44	Undercover
		Quito	8/41- 6/42	Undercover
		Quito	7/45- 9/46	Official

The largest number of agents in Ecuador (seventeen) were listed as "under-cover" for their assignments, which often meant that the embassy and State Department may not have been aware of their presence in the country. The FBI identified sixteen agents as "official," including six as legal attachés and five as police liaisons. One agent conducted plant surveys in Quito during March and April 1943.[157] The plant surveys involved inspecting industrial plants re-lated to military production to look for weaknesses that might leave them open to sabotage and espionage, an undertaking that first took place in the United States before being extended to Latin America.[158] In January 1942, the War Department and Department of the Navy assumed responsibility for the plant surveys in the United States, but the FBI remained in charge of them in Latin America.[159]

The extensive surveillance led to a monograph in June 1942 on totalitar-ian activities in Ecuador, which formed part of a series of reports that the FBI assembled on different Latin American countries. "In evaluating the impor-tance of Ecuador to the war effort," the monograph states, "it must be borne in mind that Ecuador has been seriously neglected in the past, which can undoubtedly be attributed to her turbulent political history and her resultant lack of encouragement to foreign capital." Ecuador had become more attrac-tive to foreign capital, the FBI argued, and with the country's "almost wholly undeveloped natural resources, she is potentially one of the richest nations in South America." The FBI understood the economic nature of U.S. "national interests." Ecuador's geographic location gave it strategic importance for the defense of the Panama Canal, but its agricultural and potential mineral wealth was what made it significant to the United States. Of particular importance was the South American Development Company (SADC), which operated the only gold mine in the country. In addition, the United States had economic interests in the extraction of oil, coffee, and bananas. U.S. neglect had made the task of displacing German and Italian merchants particularly difficult, the monograph stated, but thanks to the Good Neighbor policy and FBI efforts, advances had been made on this front.[160]

After seven years of operations, FBI Director J. Edgar Hoover reported that the bureau had identified 888 Axis espionage agents in Latin America. Their investigations led to the arrest of 389 agents and resulted in 105 convictions under the laws of the local countries. The sentences totaled 1,340 years, plus one death sentence. In addition, the FBI identified 281 propaganda agents, 30 sabotage agents, and 222 smugglers of strategic war materials. Hoover also reported identifying 24 clandestine radio stations and the confiscation of 30 clandestine radio transmitters and 18 clandestine radio receiving sets. Hoover was determined to present FBI investigations as a resounding success.[161]

The FBI presence in Latin America grew so large that the State Department began to complain that the bureau was duplicating its work in economic, political, industrial, and financial realms. Because of those complaints and after the conclusion of the war that provided the justification for the surveillance, the FBI began to remove agents from the SIS program. By July 1946, the FBI reduced the number of agents in Ecuador to seven, and it began to shut down operations in the country. The last three agents were a police liaison in Guayaquil who left in February 1947 and a police liaison and legal attaché in Quito who left the following month. Missing from the list is the radio operator James Wilson, who later claimed, "In March, 1947, I decoded a message instructing the Legat to arrange to turn everything over to officials of the recently created Central Intelligence Agency. I then decoded the next message received at the same time as the other. This message instructed I was to leave the CW radio station as it was."[162] On March 12, 1947, the FBI closed its field office in Quito.[163]

From the FBI to the CIA

Many of the agents who volunteered for the SIS program did so out of patriotic sentiments to support the war effort. They assumed that they would be in Latin America only for the duration of the war and would return home once it was over.[164] The director of the FBI, however, had other plans.

Hoover was very resistant to give up control over his intelligence-gathering operations in Latin America. In fact, he pressed that the SIS be expanded into a worldwide intelligence system. In a memo to Attorney General Tom Clark dated August 1945, Hoover wrote, "It is a fact, as you well know, that the SIS program operated by the Bureau in the Western Hemisphere has been completely successful." Hoover bragged, "The program has produced results which were beyond our hope and expectations when we went into this field and these results were brought about without the slightest friction in the countries where we operated." With a certain amount of exaggeration, he claimed, "Not a single incident has arisen in which the Government of the United States was subject to any unfavorable or unfortunate publicity." He continued, "this is a rather remarkable achievement when you consider the fact that hundreds of agents operated both undercover and as open representatives of the Government of the United States throughout the Western Hemisphere, conducting thousands of investigations resulting in the acquisition, assimilation and distribution of great quantities of intelligence information."

Hoover championed his success as a call to expand his own empire. "It seems to me," he continued in the memo, "that taking for granted the recognition of the need for a world-wide intelligence service, it is most logical that the system which has worked so successfully in the Western Hemisphere should be extended to a world-wide coverage."[165] Indeed, the FBI was remarkably successful in avoiding negative publicity for its Latin American program, but this was largely due to Hoover's success in keeping the program hidden from public view. As Charles Ameringer observes, "Successful covert operations are rarely documented; only the failures receive publicity."[166] Hoover was a master at presenting his intelligence operations in a way that would build support for extending his domain.

President Harry Truman, however, feared Hoover's growing power, which led to his decision to remove foreign surveillance from FBI control. Truman was particularly concerned that having the FBI operate in Latin America was not consistent with the Good Neighbor policy. Truman worried that FBI surveillance would not give the United States a basis for complaint if Latin American countries engaged in similar endeavors in the United States. Furthermore, he opposed building a Gestapo-style operation with a secret political police that functioned free of federal oversight.[167] Truman's concerns reveal a surprisingly acute awareness of the liabilities of covert intelligence operations.

While the War Department and Navy Department opposed Hoover's plan to expand his domain, the State Department, despite some initial misgivings, generally supported it. In 1939, Spruille Braden, as the U.S. ambassador to Colombia, had been critical of FBI actions, but later, as assistant secretary of state for American republic affairs, he heavily advocated for keeping the agency in Latin America. Acting Secretary of State Dean Acheson emphasized, "Since the withdrawal movement started, messages of concern, apprehension or alarm have been received from *every American Ambassador* in Latin America, testifying to the excellent work accomplished since the establishment of the Legal Attaché service of the FBI in Latin America, and recommending with the utmost urgency that the change-over be gradual and orderly." Acheson reported, "the Ambassadors have in particular recommended that no FBI personnel be withdrawn until successors have arrived and have had sufficient time and opportunity to familiarize themselves with the work." Acheson noted that "the

Department of State shares in every respect the views expressed by our Ambassadors in the field" that it was a mistake to withdraw the FBI from Latin America.[168] State Department and FBI interests coalesced in the covert collection of intelligence.

Truman's removal of the FBI from the field of foreign intelligence met with a good deal of resistance from Hoover and his allies. They argued that the FBI had developed strong relationships in Latin America and that it was a mistake to terminate them. John Speakes, the legal attaché in Havana, later remembered, "Quality reporting about a country did not happen over-night. It required organization, trained personnel, and informants placed in many circles of Society." Speakes claimed, "Through the war years the Bureau's Latin American offices became more and more resourceful. By early 1947 when CIA came into existence and I was assigned to travel through Latin America closing down our wartime foreign offices, sending personnel home, and handing over the office keys to the just arrived Agency people, I was impressed with how excellently these offices had been functioning." He acknowledged that while State Department personnel initially viewed the FBI with suspicion, "The offices within a few years had become respected institutions within the Embassy hierarchy upon which our Ambassadors greatly relied."[169] Indeed, FBI field reports do bear out Speakes's assessment that their quality and usefulness improved over time.

Truman nevertheless stood firm in his decision to create a unified worldwide secret intelligence agency that was outside Hoover's control. A presidential directive issued in January 1946 formed the Central Intelligence Group (CIG) for that purpose. Acheson urged an orderly transfer from the FBI to the CIG and asked that the FBI agents remain until the new CIG personnel were firmly in place in Latin America. He implored Hoover to allow the FBI agents who wished to remain at their posts to transfer to the CIG, a provision that Hoover adamantly opposed.[170] Hoover claimed that if he was able to quickly mobilize the human resources necessary to establish an extensive surveillance network across the hemisphere during the war, his opponents in the CIG should likewise be required to do so during peacetime.[171] Hoyt Vandenberg, the director of central intelligence for the new CIG, finally consented to Hoover's demand but not without sniping, "I seriously doubt that the withdrawal from Latin America of all FBI representatives, many of whom would cheerfully elect to remain at their posts, is in the interest of the United States."[172] Once again, the legendary conflicts between the institutional interests of the different intelligence agencies were visible.

Hoover attempted to put a positive spin on this blow to his hegemonic control over hemispheric intelligence operations. Between July 1946 and April 1947, as the CIG replaced the SIS program in Latin America, Hoover reported, "On special request, FBI offices in Latin America were kept open until CIG representatives were available to handle the intelligence work in those areas."[173] When the FBI left in 1947, agents turned over their equipment and contacts to the CIG. According to Woodcock, despite the drawdown in the number of agents after the war, the final closing of the office in La Paz came quickly and as a surprise to him.[174] Hoover was determined to withdraw all of his agents, and he viewed those who left the FBI to work with the CIA as having "defected."[175] Many in the FBI felt a deep loyalty to Hoover, which served to reinforce his sense that he had been wronged in being removed from the Latin American field of operations.

Despite Hoover's opposition, some agents remained to work with the CIG and its successor organization, the CIA.[176] After Donald Daughters left the FBI in Chile, the newly formed CIA offered him what he considered a "plum assignment" in charge of the Mexico City station that was the center for gathering intelligence on the Soviets in the Western Hemisphere. He declined and instead returned to Chile to work in the private sector and raise a family. Daughters notes, however, that other FBI agents he knew from the SIS program stayed on to work with the CIA. One of those agents recruited Daughters to work as a cutout—someone who would surreptitiously receive information from Chilean informants and pass it on to the CIA to preserve the confidentiality of their arrangement. "I was back in the intelligence business without having ever planned it," Daughters remembered. He continued collaborating with the CIA during the remainder of his time in Chile.[177]

Francis Milovich, an agent in Venezuela, claimed that, upon departure, Hoover refused to reveal the names and locations of FBI personnel "because of his concern that providing the SIS agents' names and locations would put the SIS special agents at risk for exposure." According to Milovich, the undercover agents respected and appreciated Hoover's willingness to defend their interests.[178] Other agents related different stories of the transfer of materials and informants from one agency to another. John Walsh, for example, denied that the FBI in Argentina had failed to cooperate with the CIA. He claimed that the bureau in fact had facilitated the continuance of activities under the purveyance of its competitor.[179] In Bolivia, Woodcock physically turned over equipment and furniture to his successors, but the FBI agents burned all of their confidential records. That decision was made not locally but at FBI headquarters.[180] The destruction of records was part of the interagency conflicts, and it has an unfortunate side effect of depriving historians of what otherwise might have been a rich source of documentation on local popular organizing.

The FBI closed its last SIS office—in Port-au-Prince, Haiti—on April 28, 1947. Even as the FBI surrendered intelligence-gathering operations to the CIG, the FBI maintained police liaison offices in Brazil, Mexico, and Cuba in Latin America, as well as with the Royal Canadian Mounted Police, in Ottawa, and in London, Madrid, and Paris. This work was a continuation of the FBI's close cooperation with Latin American law enforcement agencies during the war, including providing them with training and information from the bureau's counterespionage programs in the United States.[181] In 1947, the FBI closed its Mexico operations and turned its files over to the CIA, yet only a few months later it resumed its operations in the embassy under the designation as the Legal Attaché's Office.[182] In the twenty-first century, the FBI maintained its global reach through Legal Attachés' Offices in U.S. embassies around the world.[183] Hoover effectively subverted Truman's executive decision to remove the FBI from the realm of international surveillance operations.

The FBI presence in Latin America in the 1940s formed the basis for long-term practices that survived the war years, particularly in the form of police assistance programs that targeted political leftists. The FBI's charter limits its foreign activities to investigation of international aspects of domestic cases and prohibits the bureau from collecting foreign intelligence. As a result, the FBI was to focus its efforts on political surveillance in the United States while the CIA would conduct such activities outside the country. Nevertheless, for example, Lyndon Johnson turned to the FBI rather than the CIA in 1965 to monitor the internal situation in the Dominican Republic after the U.S. military intervention to forestall what he claimed would become a "communist dictatorship."[184] Although the SIS program operated under the Good Neighbor policy, it laid the groundwork for subsequent U.S. interventions in Latin America.[185] In reality, during this entire period, the United States never relaxed its imperial grasp on Latin America.

Communism

RICARDO PAREDES

DIPUTADO POR LOS INDIGENAS

RICARDO PAREDES was the Communist Party's principal leader since its founding in the 1920s and served as its secretary-general on multiple occasions, although the FBI paid little attention to his activism. He was a medical doctor who worked closely with Indigenous communities. He was the last deputy to join the 1944–45 Constituent Assembly, with the Ecuadorian Federation of Indians selecting him as a representative of the Indigenous Race on August 10 just as the assembly started its deliberations. Source: León Borja, *Hombres de Mayo*.

The war years represented an expansion of the U.S. imperial presence in Latin America, and FBI Director J. Edgar Hoover repeatedly pointed to Axis activity to justify the bureau's presence in Latin America.[1] The greater the danger that Hoover could establish, the stronger the argument he could make to rationalize the FBI's intelligence-gathering operations. Hoover excelled at emphasizing these fears to pad his congressional budget requests, which put pressure on his agents to deliver sensationalistic reports. In reality, the Axis powers were never very active; nor did they present a serious challenge to U.S. hegemony over the American continents. While FBI headquarters in Washington played up the German Nazi, Italian fascist, and imperial Japanese threats in its annual reports, that focus did not carry over to agents' dispatches from Latin America.[2]

The agent Dallas Johnson readily admitted that the FBI was not only concerned with fascists but also with communists. Especially before the United States entered the war, the FBI was "probably more interested in Communist activities than German activities," he said. The undercover agent Stokes Davis, for example, arrived in Mexico with money to infiltrate a Communist Party cell, and other agents spent more time tracking left-wing refugees from Nazi Germany than fascist operatives.[3] Similarly, the FBI sent John Paul Larkin to Venezuela to investigate the German community, but instead he dedicated significant resources to collecting information on communists. Examining the communists rather than the Germans had the added benefit of helping Larkin develop close relations with the Venezuelan police, which further facilitated the FBI's surveillance of domestic political dissidents.[4]

Comparable stories could be told for almost every Latin American country. In the Legal Attaché's Office in El Salvador, Ronald Sundberg created index cards on communist organizations or others who leaned in that direction, even as the FBI acknowledged that, after a massacre in 1931, communists had little presence in the country.[5] Although FBI agents ostensibly were in Peru because of the country's mineral exports and large Japanese community, Legal Attaché Harold Judell highlighted that two of his best undercover agents focused their investigations on communists organizing among Indigenous workers who "were half starved to death working in the mines."[6] Even in Argentina where the U.S. government was deeply concerned with the antagonistic Juan Perón government's alleged connections with Nazi Germany, the FBI assigned John Walsh to investigate communist activities, including its main organizations and activities. "I always thought that the Russians were more of a danger to us than the Nazis were," he said.[7] A fear of communism became a common denominator in bureau activities across the hemisphere. In Chile, Wade Knapp and Richard Leahy spent as much time investigating communists as Germans, and similar stories also emerged from Brazil. "What the Bureau did especially well," Leahy remembered from his time in Chile, was that "we kept track of the activities of the Communist Party." One of his best informants worked at a bank and passed information on the Communist Party's account to the FBI.[8] Many FBI agents conducted their surveillance not on fascist agents or local government activities, but on politically engaged private citizens.

Before transferring to Chile, Knapp worked as an assistant to the consul in Guayaquil, where his first assignment was to write a report on the Communist Party of Ecuador. The newly arrived FBI had nothing on the topic, so he relied on the consulate files and a British intelligence officer for his information. His initial thirty-page report reflected a rather superficial understanding of Ecuador, as well as a good deal of disdain for communist partisans.[9] In 1947, at the close of the SIS program, the FBI readily admitted that these early intelligence reports had minimal value. Novice agents could do little more than report rumors without being able to verify their accuracy, and in retrospect the FBI did not seek to defend their contents.[10] After this slow beginning that offered little new data, the FBI director soon forwarded reports regularly to the State Department that drew on informed sources with intimate knowledge of the Communist Party's inner workings. Agents recruited locals to infiltrate leftist parties and labor unions and reported the intelligence they collected to FBI headquarters in Washington. Their function as effective data collectors was similar to that of Spanish inquisition officers of yore in that they recorded all sorts of "noise" for posterity while searching for their own brand of sins and crimes. We thank them even as we condemn their mission.[11] In practice, the SIS program did not function as a regular spy agency designed to infiltrate and report on the activities of another government. Instead, agents targeted political dissidents in those countries. The overarching purpose of extending one country's imperial control over the internal affairs of another, however, remained quite similar.

Although the initial justification of the FBI counterintelligence investigations was fascism, field reports quickly shifted to Hoover's primary obsession with leftists. That emphasis was only logical, given that the bureau strongly emphasized the communist menace in its training of agents. This focus carried over into assignments, in which Hoover instructed his agents that he was not as interested in the Nazis as in the communists.[12] A result of a lack of serious Axis infiltration into Latin America, combined with Hoover's anticommunist paranoia, contributes to a surprisingly useful documentary record of the Latin American left.

Communist Party of Ecuador

Long before the arrival of the FBI, U.S. diplomatic missions faithfully reported on leftist developments in Latin America. Together with other sources, their cables provide insights into the growth of the Marxist left in the region after the Bolshevik Revolution of 1917. In Ecuador, that left slowly coalesced and gained strength, and by the 1940s it had become a significant political force. Historians commonly point to the massacre of striking workers in the port of Guayaquil on November 15, 1922, as having given birth to Ecuador's labor movement through a baptism of blood. The modernizing military revolt known as the Revolución Juliana (July Revolution) of 1925 opened up space for political organizing that facilitated the founding of the Partido Socialista Ecuatoriano (Ecuadorian Socialist Party; PSE) a year later. U.S. diplomats expressed concern for the "many minor indications of Socialistic or even Bolshevistic tendencies now evident in Ecuador." Even though the U.S. Legation conceded it was too soon to know whether the country would become communist, and even characterized such concerns as exaggerated, it pledged to continue to watch the situation "very carefully" and inform the State Department of any developments.[13] Indeed, diplomatic officials did keep close tabs on subsequent developments.

Socialists divided over whether to affiliate with the Third, or Communist, International (Comintern), based in Moscow, which Lenin had created to lead a global revolution. Ricardo Paredes, the leader of the PSE, attended the Comintern's sixth congress in 1928, where he requested affiliation for the Socialist Party. When he returned to Ecuador, he assumed control of the party and attempted to bring it under strict communist control. In January 1929, he changed the name of the party to Partido Socialista Ecuatoriano, sección de la III Internacional Comunista (Ecuadorian Socialist Party, Section of the Third Communist International). In 1931, this group changed its name to the Partido Comunista del Ecuador (Communist Party of Ecuador; PCE).

In January 1933, dissidents who opposed the formation of a Communist Party rather than a Socialist Party reformed the PSE under the leadership of Luis F. Maldonado Estrada. The new PSE also faced divisions between a strong reformist tendency and a smaller, leftist revolutionary trend. The Socialist Party was larger than the Communist Party and remained the third most significant political force in the country, after the liberals and conservatives. The PSE played an important role in drafting social legislation, including minimum wage laws and a progressive labor code. The socialist base of support was largely rooted in the urban middle class, and most of its members were professionals. Communists, by contrast, maintained more of a presence among the laboring classes and Indigenous communities, even though many of the leaders were intellectuals. Although the communists were a smaller party than the socialists, they were better organized, with a more loyal following, and thus presented a more serious threat to U.S. imperial interests.

The intellectual Manuel Agustín Aguirre, who came from the left wing of the Socialist Party, drew a clear distinction between socialism and communism. The PSE, Aguirre emphasized, was an autonomous party that did not resort to nationalistic appeals—nor did it follow dogmatic formulas or foreign directives from Moscow. Nevertheless, the party did use Marxist tools of scientific socialist analysis to understand Ecuador's realities and to discover just and appropriate solutions to capitalist problems of poverty and exploitation.[14] Aguirre also emphasized that the PSE had never been a purely electoral organization with the limited goals of gaining seats in delegative bodies. From its beginning it had been a social movement with a political vision of making economic, technical, and cultural changes in society.[15] In contrast, the socialist leader Ángel F. Rojas acknowledged that little difference existed between communists and socialists. Communists, however, had gained a negative reputation, and strategically activists were better positioned if they assumed the label socialist because the government did not bother socialists.[16] The PSE and PCE had a shared goal of ushering in a socialist society, and often the differences between the two were strategic rather than ideological.

In addition to the PCE and PSE, the Vanguardia Revolucionaria del Socialismo Ecuatoriano (Ecuadorian Revolutionary Socialist Vanguard; VRSE) attracted progressive military personnel, industrialists, modernizing landowners, and urban professionals largely cut from a radical liberal ideological cloth. Its leadership included such colorful personalities as Juan Manuel Lasso Ascásubi, a wealthy landowner who in 1924 had led peons in a failed revolution and two years later participated in the founding of Ecuador's Socialist Party.[17] The VRSE explicitly identified itself as adhering to a Marxist interpretation of Ecuadorian reality, and committed itself "to the economic, moral, and spiritual liberation of the middle classes, workers, and peasants of Ecuador."[18] Rival leftist groups sometimes collaborated to form electoral popular fronts, and other times they fought with each other for the allegiance of the working class. In March 1934 in anticipation of the policy change in the upcoming seventh congress of the Comintern, the communists began to appeal for a united front with vanguardists, socialists, and liberals to keep the conservatives out of power. Subsequently, the political center and left would periodically coordinate activities. Competing political interests, however, frequently led to divisions on the left that opened up the way for conservative victories.

U.S. diplomatic officials carefully followed all of these developments and splinters on the left. In 1931, as part of a surveillance of leftist developments in Latin America, U.S. Minister William Dawson had his secretary, Charles Page, prepare a lengthy memo on communism in Ecuador. Page estimated the size of the party at ten thousand, with five thousand members in Guayaquil, two thousand in Quito, and the rest scattered throughout the country, with particularly strong pockets in Ambato and Riobamba. The party used the enticement of a two-year paid trip to the Soviet Union to study communism as an incentive for members to join, although only a handful of people took advantage of the offer. One of those who did was Luis Gerardo Gallegos who returned disillusioned with what he had seen. His criticisms contributed to a schism in the party over whether or not to ally with the Communist International.[19]

Page pointed to other problems that communists faced: a lack of capable leaders and sufficient funds, as well as "the generally unfavorable conditions in Ecuador for the acceptance of their doctrine." He described communism as "a loose federation of affiliated 'sindicatos'" with strong regional divisions between the coast and highlands rather than a unified national movement. These divisions made it difficult for the communists to stage a serious threat to the government. Despite government panic, these liabilities led Page to conclude that no immediate danger of a communist menace was present. Rather, Page argued that analysts had a historical tendency to exaggerate the communist threat in Ecuador. Dawson applauded Page for his discretion in conducting his investigation and his resourcefulness in drawing on extensive contacts to draft the memo. Even though Page had minimized the significance of a socialist threat, Dawson informed the secretary of state that the legation would continue to follow communist activities closely and promptly report any new occurrences.[20] Assistant Secretary of State Francis White responded to Page's memo with interest and was pleased to learn about plans to keep the State Department informed of future developments.[21] Two years later, the Ecuador mission reported, "The name of communism is unpopular in Ecuador, perhaps because it is invariably associated with terrorism." The legation described a situation in which communists were losing "unity, cohesion, and direction" while the competing Socialist Party was growing in size and strength.[22] Even though the party did not appear situated to challenge U.S. security concerns, the diplomatic mission continued to monitor its activities.

Dawson noted that Ecuadorian officials held quite divergent views as to the seriousness of the communist threat. The Liberal Party stalwart Miguel Ángel Albornoz confided to the diplomat that his principal reason for agreeing in 1930 to be minister of government in Isidro Ayora's administration was to combat communism. Albornoz used his position as head of the police to interdict communications among leftists and labor activists, and he planned to implement policies that would facilitate the arrest and exile of communists.[23] Albornoz asked Dawson for information and suggestions from the United States to combat communism. Albornoz was particularly interested in receiving agents to train their police in anti-communist tactics, a request that set off a diplomatic scramble in Washington.[24] Allan Dawson, chief of the State Department's Division of Latin-American Affairs, observed, "Previous despatches from the Legation at Quito have *reported* on radical activities in Ecuador; this one asks for material which, if given, might be interpreted as putting us in the position of *combatting* these activities." Dawson said he feared that diplomats "would be open to newspaper criticism on the ground of engaging in anti-communist propaganda abroad at the same time that we object to communistic propaganda in the United States." As he noted, "There is a real dynamite in this despatch if its substance should become known." Dawson pointed to diplomatic reports from Ecuador as evidence that all of the communist leaders were Ecuadorian. He considered communism "primarily a domestic problem of Ecuador," and if the United States moved beyond observation, it was "likely to have [its] fingers badly burned." Dawson's advice was to ignore Albornoz's request.[25]

Dawson was not alone in his recognition of a deep double standard in U.S. policies, with the government intervening in the internal affairs of other countries while objecting to foreign intervention in its own. When the head of state Alberto Enríquez Gallo threatened to nationalize the SADC gold mines in 1938, the U.S. State Department declared, "The Government of the United States neither asks nor expects especial or preferential treatment for United States citizens in business in Ecuador," a claim that, Albert Franklin observed, would appear "ironical to Ecuadorians."[26] Still, the principle of nonintervention remained the official policy. In 1945, Assistant Secretary of State Spruille Braden emphasized that the State Department was prepared to support all legitimate private economic enterprises in Latin America, but no U.S. corporation that involved itself in another country's internal affairs could expect to receive diplomatic protection. Not only would this interference complicate the State Department's conduct of foreign relations, but, from Braden's perspective, "It was also very poor business." Braden emphasized that all diplomatic missions in the Americas understood this policy of nonintervention and would carry it out vigorously.[27]

Similar to Braden, Harold Williamson, the U.S. consul in Guayaquil, accentuated that "regardless of good intentions, Americans have absolutely no right to interfere in the internal affairs of Ecuador."[28] James Gantenbein, chargé d'affaires in the U.S. Embassy in Quito, likewise declared that the U.S. government could not intervene in Ecuador's internal affairs. In a response to an Ecuadorian government request to halt leftist trends in the press, Gantenbein reiterated, "The Embassy will, of course, take no steps which might involve relations between the Ecuadoran Government and the press." He appeared to take the policy of nonintervention seriously.[29] Nevertheless, as the political scientist Cole Blasier aptly observes, principles "are one thing, and practice another."[30] The United States never hesitated to intervene in hemispheric affairs in defense of its perceived national security interests. As the U.S. ambassador to Argentina in 1945, Braden so famously and openly campaigned against Juan Perón's presidential bid that the candidate effectively leveraged the intervention to win election. Despite Braden's rhetorical support for nonintervention, on the eve of the Cold War it was not uncommon for him, unlike his predecessor Dawson, to express his long-standing desire "to guard against Communistic infiltration in the Americas."[31] In a variation of the truism that one person's freedom fighter is another person's terrorist, policy makers celebrate their international interventions as acts of solidarity while denouncing those of opponents as imperialist endeavors.

The State Department finally agreed to partial compliance with Albornoz's request for assistance in combating communism. Under no circumstances, the officers in Washington instructed, should trained agents be dispatched to Ecuador. Dawson was to inform Albornoz that "there is no Federal agency engaged in such tasks and that the Department is not currently informed as to what state, municipal or private agencies may be doing." Furthermore, the U.S. government "could not, of course, undertake to send agents to Ecuador, and you should so inform the Minister, if he again approaches you on the subject." The State Department would not provide information on anticommunist societies, and Assistant Secretary of State Francis White claimed not to be in possession of any such material. What he was willing to provide was a report of the 1930 Special Committee to Investigate Communistic Activities in the United States, commonly known as the Fish Committee, a precursor to the House Un-American Activities Committee.[32] A decade later, the FBI's response, and particularly Hoover's, to such requests was quite different.

Even while refusing to engage in the type of police training that the FBI would later provide, the State Department expressed concern in the 1930s of international financing of subversive movements. Officials constantly sought to confirm Soviet sources of funding for communist movements. Luis Mata, the Ecuadorian consul in Philadelphia, claimed that through the Comintern office in Argentina the PCE received $300 in gold from Moscow every month. Mata's assertion led White to request "reliable information with respect to the direction and control from Russia of communist activities outside of Russia." In particular, he sought "concrete evidence thereof in the form of documents, communications, statements, et cetera, secret or public."[33] Ecuador's Foreign Affairs Minister Gonzalo Zaldumbide likewise considered communism a serious menace, and he was convinced that its funding came from outside the country.[34] The U.S. Legation in Quito, however, reported that if the party had previously received funds from Moscow, that source had apparently stopped. The party held its meetings in a small, cheap room in an out-of-the-way part of town.[35] In Washington, Allan Dawson likewise conceded that the State Department had no proof of foreign financing.[36] Several years later, another report on communism in Ecuador admitted that "no definite evidence of the receipt of subsidies from Russia has been obtained."[37] In 1943, Wade Knapp searched for the party's international connections but concluded that they simply did not exist to any significant extent. The FBI similarly reported in 1945 that the PCE met in a place that "actually seems too small to satisfy the needs of the local Party."[38] Despite repeated attempts, the U.S. government never was able to document external roots of communist organizations in Latin America.[39] If the party did indeed receive "Moscow gold," no firm proof ever emerged—nor, for that matter, did other evidence of significant foreign intervention that should have caused the United States concern. Failure to recognize the domestic origins of leftist activism, and its goals to challenge long-standing patterns of economic exploitation and racial discrimination, hindered the ability of U.S. policy makers to understand those movements.

FBI Reports

In line with Hoover's paranoid fear of communism, initial FBI reports from Ecuador emphasized and sensationalized a communist threat, even as agents acknowledged the party's weaknesses. A monograph on totalitarian activities from 1942, for example, maintained that "Ecuador is an ideal nation for Communist propaganda" because "its population is poor; over ninety per cent of the people are either pure Indian or 'cholos' (mestizos); and the wealth of the nation is concentrated in the hands of a few large 'hacendados' and the Catholic Church." Nevertheless, FBI estimates of the party's strength in Ecuador varied from a "few dozen intellectuals" to several thousand militants.[40] Over the course of subsequent years, however, agents gained a more sophisticated understanding of the local landscape, and the FBI developed an infrastructure that allowed it to provide insightful intelligence reports on political developments. Although often partial and problematic, the FBI's counterintelligence activities highlight the commitment of communists to a fundamental social transformation of their local societies.

A report from a "confidential reliable source" dated July 1942 and titled "Communism and Trade Unions in Guayaquil" is a typical example of the type of information FBI agents initially provided to Hoover on a communist threat in Ecuador. The report revealed "evidence of Communistic influence" in labor unions in Guayaquil, "but no evidence of organizers from Communist Russia." The report continued, "The influence of Communism is manifested by the tendency of the Union members to call each other 'Comrade' and by the prominent display of the insignia of Communist Russia on buildings throughout the city." The author maintained that workers adopted communist slogans "without any understanding of [communism's] principles." With a certain amount of relief, the FBI agents conceded that their investigations had not uncovered "any evidence of representatives from Russia working among the natives." The exploitative conditions and poverty that the workers faced, together with the recent adoption of a labor code borrowed from the Mexican Constitution of 1917, however, threatened to lead to growth in the communists' power and influence. "The illiteracy, class distinction, low morals, and extremely low standards of living prevalent in this region," the report said, "contribute to the willingness of these workers to follow any leader who promises deliverance from the intolerable conditions under which they live." While currently communists did not present much of a threat, the FBI feared that the situation could change quickly.[41]

According to the FBI, communist militants in Guayaquil included the author Enrique Gil Gilbert, "an unscrupulous and degenerate cripple named Joaquín Gallegos L.," and "a strong-armed Lieutenant named Pedro Saad." These three men had "openly discussed the reprisals and executions they intend to carry out when Communism becomes the dominating force in Ecuador. They have openly boasted of executing all the bankers in Guayaquil." The FBI report expressed concern that unions in Guayaquil were "permeated with Communistic tendencies," and this made them "a force to be reckoned with as soon as the right leader appears." The FBI was concerned not only about the threat of communism but also that "dissatisfied workers offer[ed] a fertile field for Axis agents who wish[ed] to create disorder within Ecuador."[42] These claims highlight the FBI's partial and superficial understanding of Latin American realities. The PCE remained largely committed to a peaceful and institutional path to power, and targeted assassinations were not part of its modus operandi. Despite the field agents' attempts to link communism with fascism, little evidence existed of working-class support for fascist ideologies, and the bureau acknowledged as much. "There is no indication that the Communist Party is allied with the Axis," a memo dated May 1942 conceded, even as the bureau expressed concern that all of the communists' efforts were directed against the United States. The communists, for example, had "taken advantage of the recent arrivals of the U.S. armed forces in Ecuador and the Galapagos islands by spreading propaganda to the effect that once they are located they will never leave, and Ecuador will become a puppet of the United States."[43] The party's ardent anti-imperialist stance was an irritant for U.S. policy makers.

In June 1943, the FBI's legal attaché, presumably Wade Knapp, drafted a lengthy report on communist activities in Ecuador that reflects the agency's exaggerated fear of communism even as it recognized the PCE's weaknesses. The preamble to the report conceded, "Communism in Ecuador has not been up to the present a serious threat to the stability of the country." Knapp further acknowledged that "the party lacks organization and strength of numbers, appears to be hopelessly impoverished, has no press or radio facilities or other propaganda means, and is faced with the powerful opposition of the reactionary elements, supported by the all-dominant Catholic Church, which has organized and sponsored competitive workers' groups." Although "in theory there are great potentialities for Communist agitation in Ecuador because of its well defined proletariat (representing from 90 to 95 per cent of the population)," Knapp did not fear an immediate threat because "this group is so ignorant, illiterate, and utterly lacking in initiative, that it hardly lends itself to organization into a militant, well-disciplined and efficient entity." Even though the party was expanding in Guayaquil, its "leadership would seem to have remained the same small group of intellectuals, some of whom are periodically lodged in jail as political prisoners." The report stated, "The P.C.E. has never been a party of the masses," but it did not acknowledge that, as a vanguard party, this would not have been its priority. Instead, Knapp stated, "it has always been, and is today more than ever, a minority party, composed almost entirely of intellectuals." The party was most popular in Guayaquil, where it "directs some section of workers, especially the construction workers and the longshoremen, who at one time were prosperous enough, but who today live a miserable life unable to earn enough money for food and the necessities of life." Given long-standing patterns of oppression and exploitation, the FBI recognized, even as it feared, the party's immense potential.[44]

Among the range of sources Knapp cited in the report was the socialist novelist Jorge Icaza, who had been launched to fame through the publication of *Huasipungo* in 1934. The novel condemned the exploitation of Indigenous workers on large landed estates. Icaza deprecated the Communist Party's strength and organization, even though it was one of the main backers of Indigenous uprisings. He suspected that the dissolution of the Communist International would lead to the party's demise. Icaza told an FBI agent, based perhaps more on stereotypical assumptions than on documented evidence, that communists "have been living on what subsidy they could get out of the International and, now that this is being withdrawn from them, they will have to break up." He claimed that no more than twenty or thirty "real Communists" lived in Ecuador. A former party member contended that the PCE's leaders "were tired and disappointed because of the apparent lack of success and influence they were having," and that the best fighters had "retired after a long and bitter political struggle, disappointed by the indifference and lack of political consciousness of the masses." Among the retired or inactive leaders were Ricardo Paredes,

Hermel Quevedo, José Alvaro, and César Endara. José A. Moscoso had died, and Luis Gerardo Gallegos had defected to the Socialist Party. The party's political campaigns were failures. This combination of setbacks seriously eroded the prestige of the party. "All the Indian strikes ended with bloodshed and mass expulsions of the Indians," the report stated. Communist-led worker strikes similarly ended in defeat. Left unquestioned in the report was whether it was worth the dedication of the FBI's resources to investigate the party if it was bereft of a critical mass of militants to lead a significant political struggle.

Further evidence of the party's disunity was the fact that it lacked formal headquarters. Despite claims of being a national organization, it was largely confined to a presence in Quito, Guayaquil, Milagro, and Esmeraldas. The FBI recognized that the party had been stronger in the 1930s and flagged important people and markers in its struggle. Among the areas where the party previously held influence was Cayambe, which was "known as the Communist island" under the leadership of the schoolteacher Rubén Rodríguez and the Indigenous organizer Jesús Gualavisí. Agustín Vega had similarly led Indigenous struggles in Tigua, and the FBI identified Columbe as a place "where an Indian uprising of Communist nature took place in 1935." Ambato, Naranjito, Portoviejo, and Otavalo previously had been poles of communist activity but now had diminished in importance. The report indicated that Ricardo Paredes was "widely admired as a sincerely practicing Communist," but that he "gave up the fight some time ago and withdrew to private practice" in Esmeraldas. Leadership subsequently passed to "lesser personages," including the current Secretary-General Gustavo Becerra and the party militant Nela Martínez. All of these factors led to the demise of the party's importance.

Not only was the party too impoverished to publish a newspaper, but it also did not have the resources to distribute manifestos or other propaganda. Because it was an illegal underground party, it had not recently organized large public rallies or meetings. The FBI had not been able to uncover evidence that the PCE had succeeded in placing its members in any significant positions of power in the Ecuadorian government or that it had attempted to infiltrate the embassies or agencies of foreign governments. The party appeared to be isolated, and aside from some contact with Mexican labor groups and assumed connections with other Communist Party branches in South America, little evidence existed of extensive international relations.

The party's most distinguished and high-profile visitor was the Mexican labor leader Vicente Lombardo Toledano in October 1942, and Knapp questioned how explicitly a communist organizing effort that was. Lombardo Toledano had organized the Confederación de Trabajadores de América Latina (Confederation of Latin American Workers; CTAL) in 1938 as the regional bureau of the World Federation of Trade Unions (WFTU). The CTAL's goal was to unify Latin American labor movements in defense of national sovereignty and to advance anti-imperialist solidarity. The CTAL quickly emerged as the predominant inter-American labor organization and encouraged a leftward turn in Latin American politics. Lombardo Toledano had visited the Soviet Union in 1935 when the Comintern shifted its strategy at its seventh congress from a radical class-against-class line to a more moderate multi-class popular front strategy. This encounter influenced his political perspectives and, by extension, those of his labor collaborators in Ecuador. Lombardo Toledano was an ardent antifascist organizer and became an effective supporter of the Allies even as the FBI expressed concern that he was acting as "an agent of Moscow." The Mexican labor leader generally followed the Soviet political line, although he never joined the Communist Party. He denied that he received directives from Moscow, but he did receive financial support from the Soviets for his labor organizing. Lombardo Toledano subsequently played an outsize role in determining the direction of Communist Party policies and objectives.[45]

FBI surveillance of communist activities in Ecuador included the compilation of a list of bookstores in Quito where communist literature could be obtained. The party members César Endara and Gustavo Becerra both operated bookstores, and Primitivo Barreto frequented another one that the socialist novelist Jorge Icaza ran. Carlos Bravumalo sold a 430-page cloth-bound book on the history of the Communist Party of the Soviet Union for only ten *sucres* ($0.73) at his bookstore Fuente de Cultura when comparable books sold for up to three times that amount. A confidential source indicated, "The Communists of Ecuador as a Party are too impoverished to subsidise such sales and . . . in all likelihood the Soviet government is backing the distribution of the publication." The book carried a stamp from the Editorial Páginas, Ediciones Sociales in Havana, Cuba, denoting apparent distribution through that country.[46] The concern for the introduction of subsidized books indicates a long-standing fixation on searching for foreign influences on the party.

While the party languished in Quito, it enjoyed better fortunes in Guayaquil. A confidential source reported on a meeting with the communist sympathizer Manuel Rivas, who had returned to Quito in January 1944 after a month's stay in Guayaquil. Rivas stated that communists were gaining strength in Guayaquil, thanks in large part to Saad's organizing efforts that resulted in five new cells of 150 members each on the coast. In contrast, communist growth was slow in the highlands. Whereas Guayaquil had 150 new members, Quito did not have even fifty. "Practically speaking," the report stated, "Communism in the Sierra is paralyzed." Rivas blamed the lack of growth in the highlands on the influence of the Catholic church, as well as the ineffectiveness of the party's Secretary-General Gustavo Becerra.[47]

According to sources Knapp interviewed, as communists began to make significant inroads into organizing workers and peasants, conservatives also dedicated more resources to the organization of workers into Catholic unions. The most significant was the Confederación Ecuatoriana de Obreros Católicos (Ecuadorian Confederation of Catholic Workers; CEDOC), which conservatives used as a political tool to prevent the spread of communism. Knapp, however, did not find CEDOC an appealing alternative to the communists. Instead, he regarded the Catholic labor federation as "the best tool that the Catholic Church and the Conservative party have for their occasional anti-Democratic or anti-American campaigns." In addition, the government manipulated clientelist concessions and engaged in the strategic resolution of isolated social conflicts to attract workers, peasants, and Indigenous peoples to their side. These strategies served to weaken and marginalize the PCE.[48]

Intriguingly, rather than pointing only to external influences to explain the spread of communist influence, the FBI also acknowledged the role of poverty and income inequality in fostering political dissent. Knapp interviewed a Catholic priest with considerable knowledge of the political situation in Ecuador who believed that communist power was increasing. Rather than drawing its support from the Communist International and the Soviet government, as was the FBI director's mantra, the priest believed communism was gaining traction due to Ecuador's feudal economy, in which a few wealthy landholders exploited their workers. A rise in living costs also contributed to an erosion of workers' salaries. Communist demands for an equitable distribution of land and resources led to an increase in popular support for the communists. As was the pattern in the SIS program, Knapp communicated the priest's perspective to Washington without editorial comment or an apparent attempt to parse his statements.[49]

This report followed the general logic of FBI investigations of communism in the United States. As the historian Athan Theoharis observes, the FBI did not attempt to prove Soviet direction of the Communist Party but, rather, general communist influence over dissident political movements. Hints of inspiration or infiltration provided the rationale for surveillance.[50] Similarly, in Chile, although political confrontations subsequently came to be clothed in Cold War language, they were rooted in domestic conflicts and fought for domestic reasons.[51] Furthermore, the scale of reported communist activities was consistent with what the U.S. diplomatic mission had been reporting over the previous decade. Charles Page's lengthy memo of 1931 pointed to divisions within the left and described a Communist Party handicapped by a lack of leaders and funds. That report concluded that previous concerns of communism had been overstated.[52] An honest assessment would indicate that not enough had changed in ten years to justify the FBI's significant expenditures of resources on investigating an alleged international communist menace.

In July 1943, the naval attaché drafted a confidential intelligence report on Socialist Party and Communist Party activity in Ecuador that largely paralleled and duplicated what Knapp had included in his memo. The Navy report characterized the PCE as disorganized, with members who lacked the necessary enthusiasm and funds to carry out effective propaganda activities. The nucleus of their support was at Quito's Central University, with an additional presence in labor unions. In its current form, communism did not present a menace to the government of President Carlos Arroyo del Río or to the Liberal Party's dominant political position. The report depicted the PCE as being in very bad shape in Quito. The communists had a paucity of capital and organization, and older members were growing tired. Furthermore, the party lacked a clear political program. In comparison, and in line with Knapp's report, the PCE was gaining strength in Guayaquil, particularly with its work among labor organizations. Informants complained that the party masked its activities by presenting a public face as a labor union. In addition, the communists had developed a good nuclei of followers among farmers and "native Indians" in Cayambe and Milagro. The report implied that the PCE was not currently a danger to the country's stability, but, as if to justify the U.S. intelligence gathering operations, the naval attaché claimed that it might be so in the future. Despite continual searches for foreign sources of funding, the naval attaché concluded that the party was not under the direct control of the Soviet Union. It was torn by factional strife and had been for several years. Arrests of communist activists, however, indicated that the Ecuadorian government was aware of their activities and apparently feared them, which seemingly justified the U.S. investigation of the party.[53] Nevertheless, similar to the FBI, naval intelligence painted an image of a weak and disorganized party. That depiction remained largely consistent over the next several years.

Information from the FBI's confidential informants highlighted that communist strength lay in areas that otherwise would have escaped the attachés' attention. Saad estimated that there were about five hundred Communist Party members in Guayaquil, but he argued that the PCE's strength was not in its numbers but in its sympathizers. Saad said that about 80 percent of organized workers and a considerable number of professionals in the middle class were sympathetic to the party's goals and supported its program. Furthermore, the communists enjoyed the backing of agricultural workers and soldiers. Indicative of this rural orientation was the party's contemplation of holding its next annual congress in either Cayambe in the highlands or Milagro, "the most active communist center on the coast." The communist base of support in Milagro was in the agricultural cooperatives that the communist Neptalí Pacheco León led, and whose other primary leaders were either members of the PCE or sympathizers. The agricultural cooperatives also enjoyed the support of the urban communist activists Saad and Gil Gilbert. The main organizational goals of the agricultural cooperatives were to protest against the high rents and interest payments that the banks charged. They pressured the banks to buy land for the cooperatives to work rather than renting plots from private owners. Those successes were representative of the PCE's capacity to mobilize support well beyond its small numbers. The communists' ability to achieve significant policy initiatives fueled both the Ecuadorian government's and U.S. government's fear of a communist threat.[54]

An FBI report on communist activities in Guayaquil dated November 1943 apparently came from a well-connected source in the party. The informant reported on a secret congress of representatives of workers' unions that had met in Guayaquil on August 13–15, 1943, and elected Saad as general secretary of the "Federación de Obreros," or Workers' Federation. The informant then accompanied the well-known local communist leaders Víctor Hugo Briones and Enrique Gil Gilbert to a congress of rural cooperatives. The meeting was held on Neptalí Pacheco León's farm Ñauza, located about twelve kilometers from Milagro. The delegates elected Pacheco León director and Saad secretary of the meeting. Pacheco León and other speakers claimed that it was not a political meeting, but the informant emphasized that a common theme that ran through the congress was a workers' and peasants' demand to control the means of production. The unnamed author of the report characterized the speakers as providing "wild" denunciations of capitalist exploitation and imperialism. After the meeting, the anonymous informant accompanied Saad, Briones, the socialist

Ángel F. Rojas, and a representative of schoolteachers in the province of Guayas known as Cedeño to a political meeting at which the communists encouraged the local inhabitants to participate actively in the following year's presidential election.

The FBI's reports indicated multiple levels of spying on leftist and labor activities. In June 1943, the communists had decided not to admit any new members unless "an applicant is sufficiently well-known and his sincerity can be established" because too many of the recently admitted members had been sent by the secret police. Left unstated was the possibility that the FBI had trained the police in these infiltration tactics, and perhaps the report was intended as self-congratulatory on its success. While the FBI assigned a subversive intent to the PCE's activities, government repression forced the party into a semi-clandestine existence. That the apparent source of information in the FBI report was able to participate in private meetings indicates that the party may not have been paranoid enough with its internal security measures.[55]

Marginalized Voices

The FBI committed significant resources to careful monitoring of individuals whom Hoover believed presented a serious threat to U.S. commercial and political interests, and even of some who played seemingly minor roles in potentially subversive activities. Equally telling, however, is who the FBI did *not* investigate, or activists for whom it had difficulty verifying information. Surprisingly, agents spent little time shadowing the PCE's secretaries-general Ricardo Paredes and Gustavo Becerra.[56] Paredes, in particular, had provided key leadership to the party since its founding in the 1920s. Perhaps FBI agents saw him as less of a threat because he was a respected medical professional who did not resort to violent rhetoric. Or this focus may underscore that officials were less concerned with leftist ideologies than the direct economic challenges that labor leaders such as Saad provided to U.S. commercial interests in Latin America. Or the FBI's allocation of resources may simply have been an outgrowth of the information and leaders to which the bureau had convenient access. The FBI's lack of attention to the party's principal leaders reveals a degree of arbitrariness in the bureau's counterintelligence.

Almost all of the FBI's surveillance targeted men of European descent and, for the most part, ignored women, Indigenous peoples, and Afro-Ecuadorians, even when they made significant political contributions. In February 1944, the FBI estimated that out of a total population of three million people, only about one hundred thousand who were government employees or wealthy individuals took an active interest in politics. An additional half-million people from the lower middle class became politically engaged only when their economic livelihoods were endangered. "The remaining 70% of the population," the FBI report concluded, "are Indians who have never shown any interest in or exerted pressure in Ecuadoran politics."[57] Rather than reflecting reality, such statements highlighted the divided nature of Ecuadorian society and how isolated FBI informants were from rural mobilizations and, even more so, from women's activism. The bureau interpreted communism as a worldwide conspiracy emanating out of Moscow, and domestic concerns—particularly those focused on Indigenous peoples, Afro-Ecuadorians, and women—did not conveniently fit into that paradigm. The FBI was blinded by its own ideological assumptions.

Although largely unrecorded in FBI surveillance, four women—two white and urban and two rural and Indigenous—played key roles in the organization of Ecuador's Communist Party. Of the four—Nela Martínez, María Luisa Gómez de la Torre, Dolores Cacuango, and Tránsito Amaguaña—only one, Martínez, received any significant attention from the FBI, and even that was partial and problematic. Beginning in May 1945 and continuing for a little more than a year, FBI agents submitted a series of reports that focused on Martínez's activities. Informants occasionally mentioned Gómez de la Torre in passing as part of the surveillance of other activists, whereas FBI reports rarely mentioned the rural leaders Cacuango and Amaguaña, and when they did, only as part of longer lists of Indigenous activists.[58] The only woman other than Martínez whom the FBI deemed worthy of surveillance was Ana Moreno in Guayaquil. A single, four-page report focused on her personal life rather than her political life and noted that she became active in the Communist Party through her friendship with Isabel Herrería and Alba Calderón, the wives of Saad and Gil Gilbert, respectively.[59] Despite their long trajectories as political activists, Herrería and Calderón received even less attention than did the others. In fact, reflecting the FBI's gendered assumptions concerning who might represent a political threat, agents drafted a memo not on Herrería but on her brother Hugo Herrería. Not only was Hugo Herrería less active in the Communist Party than his sister, the FBI also identified him as Saad's brother-in-law rather than as Isabel Herrería's brother.[60] The FBI agents typically came from privileged backgrounds and did not readily understand those of other demographics, which hindered the effectiveness of their information gathering.

A lack of attention did not mean that these activists were not significant players in Ecuador's mid-twentieth century leftist politics. Gómez de la Torre, for example, was the secretary of an active women's cell known as La Pasionaría and a member of the Communist Party's Central Committee.[61] A monthly summary of communist activities for April 1946 highlighted a weekly mimeographed paper called *Combate* that the Communist Party had begun to publish. Paredes, Becerra, Martínez, Gómez de la Torre, and Secretary of Propaganda José María Roura contributed articles. A reader, presumably in the State Department, underlined with a red pencil one sentence that read, "The paper is mimeographed at the home of María Luisa Gómez de la Torre on a machine which was removed in pieces from an Ecuadoran Government office and reassembled by Party members." The reader added the snippy marginal note, "Talk about biting the hand that feeds you," thereby denigrating rather than applauding the serious dedication of party activists.[62] In November 1946, the FBI simply mentioned Gómez de la Torre as the second of two communists on a leftist slate for City Council elections in Quito, without acknowledging how rare it was for a woman to appear as a candidate. Gómez de la Torre did not win the election, although Primitivo Barreto, the other communist candidate, was one of three leftists who won seats on the eleven-person council.[63] Gómez de la Torre was an important activist who did not receive attention appropriate to her contributions, either in terms of FBI investigations or in subsequent studies of the Ecuadorian left.

In this context of a general disavowal of women's activism, Martínez stands out not so much for her unique contributions as for the attention she attracted from the FBI. Martínez was a writer and intellectual who was born in 1912 to a wealthy landholding family in Cañar, in southern Ecuador. Even though she was born into a life of privilege, she was an untiring fighter for social justice and the rights of women. According to an homage honoring her life, Martínez was committed to an internationalist ideology and dedicated to solidarity "with her people, with humble people, with the workers, Indians, and women."[64] She was actively involved in politics and deeply knowledgeable of current events. Martínez began her political life in 1934 as a member of the Communist Party and later served on the party's Executive and Central committees. She fought for the rights of women and denounced the sexual discrimination that they faced in the political, cultural, and social realms. During the revolution of May 1944 that removed Arroyo del Río from office, Martínez was the only woman in the presidential palace and briefly functioned as the minister of government before the all-male governing junta claimed power.

She later led the list of candidates for the popular front coalition for deputy for the province of Pichincha.

A FBI report dated September 1945 included Martínez's demographic information from the government registry, indicating the type and source of information agents collected on subjects of investigation. Martínez was five feet tall and of medium build; she had a light complexion, dark brown hair, dark brown eyes; and she had a secondary education, with some additional courses in domestic science. The report listed her birthdate as "11/1914 (Subject placed 'unknown' in space for day of month)," although in her autobiography Martínez lists her birthdate as November 24, 1912. It is not clear whether the government registry was in error, the FBI reported the information incorrectly, or Martínez did not know her birthdate when she registered, but this does highlight the partial nature of the FBI's information.[65] The FBI paid little attention to Martínez's first husband, Joaquín Gallegos Lara, a political activist in his own right, other than to note that "at the time of his marriage to the subject he was closely associated with Ecuadoran Communists." The FBI memo stated that Gallegos Lara was listed as Martínez's husband on her 1936 civil registration, but that "their marriage lasted a very short time." A registration from 1942 indicated that Martínez was divorced. An anonymous source told the FBI that Gallegos Lara was "a young writer who has been paralyzed from the waist down since birth." He exploited "his crippled condition" to draw attention to himself. Gallegos Lara employed "violent language in his articles" and posed "as a revolutionist."[66] Other passing mentions of Gallegos Lara included equally derogatory language and FBI agents never treated him as a serious political actor.

Martínez is primarily remembered for her feminist work. Together with Gómez de la Torre and other mostly upper-class, European-descent women in Quito, she formed the Alianza Femenina Ecuatoriana (Ecuadorian Feminist Alliance; AFE) in 1938.[67] Its objectives were to contribute to the cause of world peace, provide solidarity to victims of war, and promote the incorporation of women into political movements in opposition to the government. Although the AFE's leadership consisted largely of upper-class intellectuals, the alliance also had a presence in marginalized neighborhoods in Quito and in other cities throughout the sierra and on the coast.[68] While the AFE's social orientation would appear to betray condescending attitudes that reflected a paternalistic intervention in other people's struggles, Martínez emphasized that women's liberation had to come from women themselves, especially Indigenous women. These movements could not be isolated from broader struggles for social liberation.[69] In the aftermath of the May revolution, Martínez helped to reorganize the AFE and pressed for women to have a larger voice in the country's political affairs.[70] Martínez assumed a very public role in political activities, which presumably brought her to the FBI's attention.

Particularly important is how Martínez's feminism intersected with other social issues. Martínez helped organize a meeting of antifascist forces with Lombardo Toledano at the Teatro Sucre, Ecuador's premier performing arts theater, when he stopped in Quito on his South American tour. Martínez urged workers to unite to fight for their rights and aspirations as free citizens and lovers of democracy.[71] She became a key player in Ecuador's antifascist movements and often represented women in antifascist organizations. Similarly, Martínez played a key role in advancing the struggles of Indigenous peoples. She was one of the founding members together with Dolores Cacuango of the Federación Ecuatoriana de Indios (Ecuadorian Federation of Indians; FEI), which activists formed in the aftermath of the May revolution. She used her literary skills to edit the organization's newspaper, Ñucanchic Allpa.

One of the first foreign investigations into Martínez came not from the FBI but from the naval attaché. An intelligence report on leftist political parties from 1943 identifies her as a writer who was very active in "the feminine group in Quito." She attended a meeting at the Casa del Obrero (Workers' House, where workers commonly gathered) on July 4, 1943, that eulogized U.S. President Abraham Lincoln. "All orators attending complimented the United States," the attaché office noted, "but confusion reigned, most of them not knowing whether they were Communists, Socialists, or Liberals." In the context of the war, Martínez was part of a movement to build a broad popular front with the United States in defense of the Soviet Union. As part of those same antifascist organizing initiatives, Martínez reportedly received a note from President Arroyo del Río's administrative secretary saying, "If she did not desist attending 'Anti-Nazi Meetings' (many of which are sponsored by Communist-Socialist elements), she would be fired from the Fomento Corporation" where she worked in the quinine section.[72] That initial report and the intelligence on which it drew formed the basis for subsequent FBI reports on Martínez, which points to a level of information sharing on the ground, despite interagency conflicts in Washington. The FBI reports typically included only Martinez's name among lengthy lists of party members or collaborators, and often she was the only woman mentioned. One such list from 1943 that borrowed information from the naval attaché simply indicated that Martínez lived in Quito and was an "employee quinine secion [sic] of Fomento Corp.

Writer. Active in feminine section PCE." Apparently, FBI agents had not done any further study of her political activities.[73]

In a report on political and social conditions from April 1944, the FBI identified "Miss Nela Martínez" as the Communist Party representative to an ADE committee that consulted with José María Velasco Ibarra as he traveled from exile in Chile to Colombia in an attempt to return to power in Ecuador. The FBI in particular flagged Martínez for her desire to help Velasco Ibarra. An anonymous informant reported, "On February 22, 1944, at 8 P.M., the Colombian Ambassador Gustavo Santos, visited Nela Martínez in her house and the suspicion is expressed that Gustavo Santos has made arrangement to forward mail to Velasco (Ibarra) in Colombia via the Colombian diplomatic pouch." Santos also allegedly issued permits to Martínez and other members of the ADE committee to travel to Colombia, which led to strong protests from the Ecuadorian government.[74] Although largely operating outside the U.S. imperial gaze, Martínez still made significant contributions to political developments in Ecuador.

Beginning in May 1945 and at the height of FBI involvement in Latin America, agents drafted the first of a series of surveillance reports that focused exclusively on Martínez. In a cover letter to a two-and-a-half-page memo from "a reliable, confidential source," Hoover noted that she was "one of the principal feminine Communist leaders." The memo, as did subsequent ones, identified the subject as "Nela Martinez (Espinosa), with aliases Nella Martinez, Nela Martinez," even though it missed her birth name Mariana de Jesús Martínez Espinosa. The reports included partial and dated intelligence and largely repeated previously known or very basic information, saying, for example, that Martínez was a communist, resided in Quito (at Riofrio no. 148 and, later, at Flores no. 51), was an employee of the quinine section of the Corporación Ecuatoriana de Fomento, and earned a salary of $60.96 per month. She was politically active in labor unions, women's political movements, pro-Soviet activities, antifascist movements, and Velasco Ibarra's presidential campaign. The report cited newspaper articles rather than independent investigations to document her Communist Party activity, which reflected the lack of importance the agents assigned to her person.

A quote from Martínez at a Communist Party of Colombia meeting stands out in an otherwise bland and predictable report:

Although I belong to one of the best families of Ecuador, I am a member of the Communist Party of my country and I am striving to better the conditions of life of the Ecuadoran Indians. I am sure that when these Indians understand the Marxist principles they will accept them and defend them with their lives. After my return to Quito, I intend to go to Mexico City and from there I plan to travel to Russia in order to study Marxist tactics. Upon my return from Russia I will endeavor to put what I have learned into practice in Ecuador.

Martínez presented herself as a sincere and dedicated activist who struggled for human liberation. She called for the rest of Latin America to follow the example of Mexico, Cuba, and Chile and establish schools to train the youth "in Marxist theories because in the very near future there shall be but two trends in the world, Marxism and Capitalism." The report also stated that Martínez represented the FEI at the second CTAL congress in Cali, Colombia, in December 1944. What the memo does not say is that she attended as the personal secretary of the FEI's president, Dolores Cacuango, a role that Martínez would later emphasize when she recounted her life story.

If Martínez was indeed "very intelligent" and "one of the principal Communists in Ecuador," as the report proclaimed, the FBI seemingly did not give her due attention. Rather, the bureau's report resorted to repeating rumors, and even those it did not always get right. A "reliable source" told the FBI, "Although she is single, she has had two sons, the father of whom being Dr. Ricardo Paredes, presently Secretary General of the Ecuadorian Communist Party." This statement is repeated in a later memo.[75] In 1939, Martínez and Paredes did have a child together, Leonardo Paredes Martínez, and in the 1950s Martínez had three more children with her husband, Raymond Mériguet. Martínez and Paredes, however, did not have a second child. Despite recruiting infiltrators to report on Pedro Saad's party activities in Guayaquil and moles who collected Enrique Gil Gilbert's most mundane travel plans, the FBI failed to keep up to date on its *chismes quiteños* (local gossip) when it came to women activists.

In September 1945, FBI agents submitted a second short report on Martínez. She was actively involved in the work of the Communist Party's Central Committee, including assisting in the drafting of a letter to the minister of foreign relations demanding that the United States leave its military bases in Ecuador, an action that may have attracted the FBI's attention. In her job at the Corporación Ecuatoriana de Fomento, Martínez worked with a U.S. citizen named Ángel Sandoval who contemplated facilitating her visit to the United States. Sandoval returned to Washington in August, at which time Martínez was transferred to a new position in the counseling and credit office in the Ministry of Economy without having visited the United States. The Ministry of Economy sent her to Manabí, on the coast, to conduct a four-month course on domestic science, a topic on which she was a qualified instructor. According to the FBI, Martínez was scheduled to return to Quito at the end of the year, but the bureau had no information on any plans she might have to travel outside of Ecuador. The FBI memo concluded with a page of "undeveloped leads" that agents did not routinely include in the reports on surveillance of other leftists. The FBI office indicated that it would "follow and report pertinent activities of the subject" and "attempt to obtain a photograph and handwriting specimens of the subject," indicating that it maintained files with such items on other activists and now wanted to complete hers. Perhaps Martínez's level of political engagement led the FBI to realize that she might be a subject worthy of closer surveillance.[76] Unfortunately, FBI agents destroyed their files when they left Latin America in 1947, and the memos submitted to the FBI do not indicate whether agents were successful in completing her dossier.

Notably absent from the FBI surveillance was any mention of Martínez's extraordinary role as the first woman to participate in Congress. In July 1944, labor unions had named Martínez a *suplente*, or alternate, who could take a primary deputy's seat if that person was not able to attend the National Assembly. Originally, she was to be the second (after Saad) of six deputies to represent workers' interests, but other interests and a certain amount of intrigue denied her the position. Martínez points to her political disagreements with Saad, as well as a degree of sexism, as pushing her off of the original list.[77] In the end, labor unions named her a second alternate, after Segundo Ramos. On December 7, 1945, however, Martínez was part of a momentous event in Ecuador when she became the first woman to be seated as a deputy in Ecuador's National Assembly.[78] Martínez later noted that having women play a role in politics was so far removed from public consciousness that the congressional building had no restrooms for women, only urinals for men. "Never had they thought that a woman could go to the legislative palace," Martínez observed, "that she could be there discussing political issues with men."[79] Having a woman participate in Congress was a truly momentous occasion.

More significant than the bureau's failure to notice Martínez's achievement was a statement in a confidential memo that she did *not* participate in the assembly. This omission occurred despite an FBI report on communist negotiations regarding the United Nations charter and the Bretton Woods monetary agreements that deputies debated as Martínez was present in the assembly.[80]

The FBI observed that Martínez was an alternate deputy and on December 3 returned to Quito from Manabí to be on hand for the assembly's extraordinary session in case she was needed. "Martínez did not take part in the Assembly as the Deputy for whom she was a substitute was present throughout the session," the report notes. After the close of the session and a brief consultation with the Ministry of Economy, the FBI reported, Martínez returned to Manabí.[81] The FBI's neglect to acknowledge Martínez's participation in the assembly is stunning and reveals both the reach and limits of the bureau's political surveillance. Many of the political developments that the FBI reported as a result of its "investigations" were little more than what one could learn from reading the daily newspapers, seemingly a method of gathering information that foreign intelligence agents commonly employed.[82] While the FBI was not aware of Martínez's presence in the assembly, agents did know the dates that she traveled to Manabí, which were probably provided by a mole in the Panagra office, and that she visited the Ministry of Economy, probably provided by another mole in the government. It would appear that the FBI was more skilled at picking up mundane information and movements than politically significant activities. In cases such as Martínez's, as well as those of other women, Indigenous peoples, and Afro-Ecuadorians, this limits the usefulness of the FBI surveillance in reconstructing the history of the left.

Antifascist Movements

Even though investigating Nazi influences was the original justification for the FBI's presence in Latin America, the bureau dedicated significant resources to the surveillance of antifascist organizing. The most visible target of its investigations was the French activist Raymond Jean Mériguet Cousségal. Mériguet was born in Paris, where he met and married an Ecuadorian woman named Zoila Vázconez. In the midst of the global economic crisis in the 1930s, Mériguet joined a committee of unemployed workers through which he became involved in communist activities, including offering support to the Republicans in the Spanish Civil War. In 1936, he followed Vázconez to Ecuador. Later, in 1951, Mériguet divorced Vázconez and married his fellow communist Nela Martínez. He remained in Ecuador until his death in 1988.[83]

With Adolf Hitler gaining strength in Europe in the 1930s, Mériguet became deeply involved in antifascist organizing in Ecuador. By 1938, Ecuador's leftist parties had already issued a proclamation strongly denouncing fascism.[84] In October 1940, Mériguet formed an antitotalitarian committee in Quito and served as its secretary-general. After Germany's surprise invasion of the Soviet Union on June 22, 1941, which led to the collapse of the Nazi-Soviet Non-Aggression Pact of 1939 that denounced preparations for war and advocated for neutrality, communists became the earliest and most stringent opponents of fascism in Ecuador. The day after the attack, the PCE strongly denounced fascist aggression and defended the rights of oppressed people. Illustrating the rapid pivot away from the pact, the communists declared that the assault did not surprise them in the least, because "no one knows better than we do what National Socialism is capable of doing." The PCE claimed that the Soviet Union was the only country that had raised its voice in opposition to the growth of German armament. The party called on workers, peasants, intellectuals, and the middle class to support the Red Army in its battle against the Nazis, because the Soviet Union "constituted the assurance of the complete liberation of humanity."[85] Several weeks later, the Communist Party's Central Committee released another statement that denounced fifth-column elements. To halt such domestic and foreign efforts to advance a totalitarian agenda, it called for the immediate closure of the Italian, German, Japanese, and Spanish diplomatic missions, as well as of the German Transocean news service. The communists also proposed the formation of a committee to respond to pro-Nazi demonstrations.[86]

On November 21, 1941, the Movimiento Popular Antitotalitario (Popular Antitotalitarian Movement; MPA) convened an antifascist assembly at the Casa del Obrero in Quito. That assembly then organized an antifascist conference at Quito's Central University and reorganized itself as the Movimiento Antifasista del Ecuador (Ecuadorian Antifascist Movement; MAE). Mériguet remained the key organizer of the movement. He invited both "Ecuadorians and foreigners who sympathize with the struggle against fascism, for human freedom, and the liberation of people oppressed by Nazism" to join the struggle.[87] Mériguet emphasized that the committee was not opposed to Germany or Germans or to Italy or Italians; rather, its goal was to defend democratic ideals and engage in a peaceful campaign to repudiate the introduction of fascism into the Americas.[88] Leftists dominated the organization of the committee, with Juan Isaac Lovato, secretary-general of the Socialist Party, presiding over the opening session. Clotario E. Paz of the VRSE, the communists Nela Martínez and Gustavo Becerra, and other leftists took leading positions on the organizing committee. The MAE dedicated itself to publicizing Nazi atrocities and building a campaign in defense of democratic principles.[89]

As an indication of the organization's leftist orientation, Mériguet headed a celebration of the anniversary of the Bolshevik Revolution and called for solidarity with the Soviet Union in its heroic battle to contain the Nazi threat.[90]

Only four days after the Japanese attack on Pearl Harbor, the antitotalitarian committee published a manifesto in support of antifascist struggles. The manifesto said that Ecuador was particularly opposed to fascism because it was the first country in the Americas to suffer an invasion by totalitarian forces in the form of the 1941 war with Peru.[91] It condemned fascist attacks on the United States and Soviet Union and argued that the result of these tragedies was the unity of forces in favor of a heroic struggle for freedom. The attack at Pearl Harbor underscored that the Axis residents in the Americas formed a fifth column that threatened to prepare the way for a Japanese invasion. The statement said that all American countries—with the exception of Peru—were collaborating in a unified struggle for democracy and against the Axis powers.[92] Even for activists, Ecuadorian interests remained more nationalist than ideological in nature, with many seeing their neighbor as more of a concern than distant threats.

Despite Mériguet's antifascist activities that seemingly would serve Allied interests, the FBI monitored his movements because of his communist affiliations. The FBI included Mériguet in a lengthy list of Communist Party members and sympathizers. It identified him as a "Frenchman married to Ecuadoran" who was "said to have been Comintern representative." He "publishes the 'Antinazi' and is Secty Gen. of Movimiento Popular Anti-Fascista del Ecuador."[93] The FBI's legal attaché complained about a communist tendency to create antifascist organizations as front groups. While the PCE currently did not publish a newspaper, Mériguet's *Antinazi*, although it appeared only sporadically, served to advance the party's ideologies. The FBI repeated this characterization of *Antinazi* and charges of Mériguet's connections with the Comintern on multiple occasions, although he continued to deny the association. The French communist contended that only personal friendships tied him to the local party. The FBI acknowledged, "Competent observers are of the opinion that he studiously limits his connections to the leaders themselves," in particular Becerra and Martínez. According to the FBI informant, Mériguet never attended party meetings. Even so, the FBI feared his political activity.[94]

The FBI reported in its 1942 monograph on Nazi influence in Ecuador that "Mériguet has organized a workmen's anti-Totalitarian organization which has received some publicity." According to the FBI, Mériguet asked commu-

nists in Quito to inform the local inter-allied committee that Moscow had instructed the PCE "to cooperate with the democracies in their struggle against
Axis powers."[95] Similarly, in 1943 the naval attaché in Quito issued a confidential intelligence report on leftist political parties that flagged Mériguet's
work with MAE's periodical *Antinazi* as "[lending] itself amply to Communist propaganda."[96] The FBI reported on the contents of publication, including
summarizing "a pro–United States article on the Monroe Doctrine" that con-
trasted the Good Neighbor policy with Theodore Roosevelt's "fascist" policies.
It also highlighted a letter from Joseph Stalin that explained the justification
for the dissolution of the Communist International as a necessary step to defeat fascism. In general, the FBI depicted *Antinazi* as a publication supportive
of the Allied war effort.[97] In fact, the Office of Inter-American Affairs (OIAA)
had provided funding for its publication, although that support became complicated when Mériguet published a commemorative issue on the anniversary
of the Bolshevik Revolution.[98]

The FBI was not the only U.S. agency to monitor Mériguet's activities. The
Office of Strategic Services (OSS), for example, noted without comment or explanation that the pro–Charles de Gaulle Free French organization in Ecuador
refused membership to Mériguet.[99] Despite this extensive surveillance, State
Department officials did not appear to be overly concerned with Mériguet's activism. That lack of interest also becomes apparent during Vice President Henry
Wallace's visit to Ecuador in 1943. Wallace stayed at the house of the wealthy
landowner Carlos Mercado in Quito. As part of a security review of the area,
an embassy official checked the names of his neighbors against an index that it
maintained. Only one name appeared in the embassy files: Raymond Mériguet.
The embassy described him "as a leader in the local Free French movement, and
secretary of the Ecuadoran Popular Antitotalitarian Movement." The embassy,
however, concluded that Mériguet was "not . . . regarded as dangerous."[100] In response, Mériguet greeted Wallace's arrival with a front-page article in *Antinazi*
that characterized him as a fighter for true democracy. He encouraged Ecuadorians to give Wallace a warm welcome.[101] The FBI's concern appeared to be more
a reaction against Mériguet's communist affiliations than an accurate assessment of a true threat he presented to U.S. interests.

On July 14, 1943, Mériguet's antitotalitarian movement organized a Bastille
Day event at Quito's Central University. Labor unions, student groups, and
leftist political parties all participated. Students, workers, soldiers, and others
crowded into the venue and filled the hall to capacity before the event had
even started. The first speaker was Jorge Reyes y Reyes, editor of the liberal

newspaper *El Día*, who spoke on the history of the French Revolution. Various refugees addressed the current situation in Europe. The final presenter was the socialist Jorge Maldonado, who spoke on reconstruction in France and called on workers to support democratic countries in their fight against fascism.[102] The FBI reported that the sole communist associated with the event was Mériguet, and as chair he only introduced the session with brief comments and then presented each speaker. The FBI did not see any Communist Party attempt to dominate the event or to engage in "subversive activity of any kind." A reader, probably in the State Department, highlighted that final comment with a blue mark on the report, as if to underscore the FBI's misdirected dedication of resources into investigating Mériguet's activities.[103]

The FBI was more successful at uncovering a hidden communist hand in the organization of a provincial antifascist conference in Quito in September 1943. An FBI informant conveyed details of a private organizing committee that met a week before the conference was to start and provided information on the public events. The conference elected four subcommittees, with three people each, and according to the informant, Mériguet manipulated the process so that communists would control each subcommittee. As a result, communists chaired three of them in addition to the main organizational committee. Luis Maldonado Tamayo, secretary-general of the Socialist Party, chaired the fourth subcommittee. The FBI highlighted which organizers and speakers were communists and in particular singled out for attention the comments of the communist activist Primitivo Barreto, who eulogized the Soviet Union. A second informant identified delegates listed in the published proceedings from the conference with comments such as identifying Martínez, who represented the feminist AFE, as a "known Party member."[104]

Equally instructive as whom the FBI watched was whom agents ignored. The conference provided an opportunity to gather various, disparate organizing efforts into one, single centralized movement. Among those at the conference were the Indigenous leaders Dolores Cacuango and Jesús Gualavisí. In July 1943, Cacuango and her son Luis Catucuamba had gathered a group of fifty people in Cayambe to form the first rural antifascist committee. The following month, Gualavisí organized a similar committee in his community, Juan Montalvo. Both served as delegates to the provincial conference where they were singled out as a stimulating model for the rest of the country. Martínez observed, "In Kichwa Cacuango and Gualavisí condemned the fascism that they already had experienced."[105] The FBI, however, failed to mention their participation in the provincial conference.

An FBI informant reported on a private conversation after the conference in which Mériguet elaborated on his ideology. For him, the goal of an "evolution to Democracy" required the "suppression of the influence of Capitalism which prevents the development of a true Democracy." Mériguet contended that capitalism should be countered not with violence but, rather, by gradually "securing control over the masses of the people." Despite a strategic alliance with the United States in a battle against fascism, Mériguet confessed that he would not "trust anybody who works for the Yankees." FBI agents went out of their way to document anti–United States sentiments.

The FBI expressed more concern about communist domination of another group, the Anti-Nazi-Fascist Committee in Guayaquil, than it did about Mériguet's committee in Quito. An informant told the FBI that the communists had formed the committee to hide "the real nature of their activities." The source claimed that "practically all members" were communists and that anti-Nazism was of secondary importance to spreading communism. The author and Communist Party member Enrique Gil Gilbert was the secretary-general of the committee and "one of the shining lights" in guiding its organizational activities.[106] Even though the FBI was concerned with Gil Gilbert's communist affiliations, the local OIAA coordination committee had supported his antifascist organizing and publications for more than a year.[107] That relationship between the communist militant and the U.S. propaganda agency was inherently complicated. The OIAA's refusal to cooperate with the Anti-Nazi-Fascist Committee as fully as Gil Gilbert had come to expect led him to complain that the office had "seriously handicapped" the committee's efforts to assist the democratic cause.[108] That tension led the FBI to report—erroneously, as it turned out—that Gil Gilbert had become disillusioned with the committee and stepped aside from its leadership in the face of opposition to his efforts from the U.S. and Ecuadorian governments.[109] In fact, soon after the FBI's faulty report, Gil Gilbert gave a speech in Milagro in which he attacked fascism in Europe and then connected it to landowner abuses in Ecuador. According to an FBI informant, Gil Gilbert called the landowners "Nazis" and promised that when the communists terminated feudalism, the land would be given to the agricultural workers.[110] With or without backing from the OIAA, Gil Gilbert remained committed to the antifascist cause.

Whereas Mériguet largely restricted his criticism to fascist atrocities in Europe, Gil Gilbert connected those issues to economic exploitation in the Americas. Similar to the FBI, Quito's *El Comercio* reported on what it saw as the rise of a threat of subversive activity in Guayaquil organized under the guise of an antitotalitarian movement, a characterization that it did not use when discussing Mériguet's campaign in Quito.[111] A confidential FBI source declared, "The plans of the Communists are to gain sympathies and prestige among the masses, and especially among the small merchants and middle classes." In other words, the informant charged that the communists planned to exploit the OIAA coordination committee for their own, devious ends. Saad told an FBI informant that many merchants did not want to join the Anti-Nazi-Fascist Committee for fear that the United States would blacklist their businesses because of their collaboration with known communists. The FBI reported, with a certain amount of satisfaction, the problems that competing agencies faced. According to an agent, communists contemplated exploiting known tensions between the OIAA coordination committee and the U.S. consulate general to gain more favorable attitudes toward their work.[112] The only threat greater than communism was other intelligence-gathering agencies.

Whether or not the various U.S. agencies considered Mériguet dangerous, the Ecuadorian government still viewed his political activism as a security threat. In October 1943, Mériguet traveled to the Pacific coast to organize local antifascist committees in Guayaquil and Salinas and to investigate the possibilities of Nazi submarines' launching an attack on mining camps and refineries on the Santa Elena peninsula. Allegedly, Mériguet had permission to travel in the region only as a tourist, and the military arrested him on charges of engaging in communist activities.[113] The military released him, only to have the police rearrest him shortly thereafter. The government threatened to deport him but instead moved him around the country before finally confining him to the carabineros barracks in Tulcán, on the Colombian border. Mériguet's detention led to a concerted campaign to gain his freedom.[114] In an attempt to protect the activist, the PCE denied that he was a member of its party or that he had been involved in communist activities. The party found the revelation that Mériguet had been confined together with Axis spies particularly objectionable.[115]

The communists were not alone in calling for Mériguet's release. The PSE's Secretary-General Manuel Agustín Aguirre described the French activist as "one of the most active and sincere antifascist fighters whose activities and organizational capabilities have been placed at the service of the democratic cause." His imprisonment was a "shameful act" that revealed Arroyo del Río's fascist sympathies.[116] It was not until the Glorious May Revolution of 1944 that removed Arroyo del Río from power more than half a year later that the police finally released Mériguet from custody. During this entire time, the FBI monitored and reported on Mériguet and his location in the country, but not with an eye to gaining freedom for the antifascist fighter.[117]

In August 1944, in the context of political openings that the May revolution provided, Mériguet organized a new communist cell in Quito called "Dimitroff" that consisted only of foreigners. The FBI reported that a small group that included Charles Rapaport, Herbert Max Katz, and a man named Washsner gathered at the house of Heinz Alfred Stern. Stern, who sometimes used the alias Bobby Astor, was the president of the Free Germany Committee. Mériguet wanted a small vanguard cell with five or six members, while Stern advocated for a mass organization. Stern had contact with Saad, but to maintain security, local Communist Party members did not know any of the other members of the cell.[118] No other information on this cell remains, and it had little lasting effect. Nevertheless, the FBI maintained close and ongoing surveillance of Stern and his activities, as it did of other "free" Europe groups that it denounced as nothing more than communist front organizations.[119]

The FBI continued its surveillance of Mériguet throughout its sojourn in the country, including monitoring his meeting with the Panamanian communist leader Celso Nicolas Solano during a visit to Quito, reporting on Mériguet's alleged efforts to gather funds to launch a communist newspaper, and detailing regular meetings with the communist leader Ricardo Paredes.[120] Before the May revolution, an FBI informant had stated that Mériguet never attended Communist Party activities, but with a more relaxed and open political environment afterward, the FBI now asserted that he participated in Central Committee meetings. Mériguet also proposed to the communists the organization of a committee in solidarity with Spanish Republicans.[121] That committee held three meetings in October 1945, although the FBI noted that its members had not undertaken any activities "of an important nature."[122] In any case, Mériguet continued his political activism; FBI agents maintained their surveillance of his activities; and the Ecuadorian government persisted in its repression of the country's primary antifascist fighter.

Trotskyism

The initial FBI reports on communism in Ecuador reflected a fear that fascists and communists would make common cause against the United States. It should not be a surprise that the agents would make this assumption. Fred Ayer comments that during his training in 1941, the FBI emphasized to its new agents that little separated Nazis from communists.[123] While the termination of the Nazi-Soviet pact in June 1941 had made it more difficult to argue convincingly that communists were secretly conspiring with the fascists, suspicion now turned to Trotskyists who had become deeply opposed to Soviet policies. Leon Trotsky was a close collaborator of Vladimir Lenin in the Bolshevik Revolution of 1917 and the founding leader of the Red Army. After Lenin's death in 1924, Trotsky led a failed leftist opposition against the authoritarian and bureaucratic turn in Joseph Stalin's policies as head of the Soviet government. Stalin removed Trotsky from power in 1927 and exiled him from the country two years later. In 1938, Trotsky and his followers founded a new international communist organization denominated the Fourth International. Two years later, Stalin's agents assassinated Trotsky while he was living in exile in Mexico. From the U.S. perspective, if anyone had reason to make common cause with the fascists against a common enemy, it would be the Trotskyists. Although flawed, this logic informed FBI investigations in Ecuador.

Reflecting the FBI's fear of an alliance between fascists and Trotskyists is a report from May 1942 that included "a sample of the type of propaganda being circulated in Ecuador by the Fourth International." The FBI agents forwarded "a verbatim translation of a mimeographed circular which has been introduced into Ecuador allegedly by either the German Legation or the Spanish Legation," thereby implying an alliance of Trotskyist and fascist forces. The circular called for an intense study of the economic, social, and political situation to follow military and political developments in the context of the current war and to adopt political actions to the current situation. The document laid out different possible directions that the current international crisis could take and dictated the proper response to each. According to the circular, the United States intended to subjugate Latin America to its neocolonial control, and "only a communistic revolution [would] save [Latin America's] true independence and liberation from the imperialistic Yankee." Because Latin America was under the control and domination of the United States, the Soviet Union would not defend the region in case of a German or Japanese attack. The FBI appeared to read this document as a Trotskyist alliance with fascism to attack both the United States and its ally in the war, the Soviet Union.[124]

Charges that the Trotskyists had made common cause with fascists were common in the 1940s, even in Ecuador. In the context of the wartime alliance between the Soviets and Western capitalist powers, Stalinists painted any criticism of the Soviet Union as part of a Nazi fifth column and used the war as a justification to attack their opponents to their left. Unfortunately, Trotsky played into charges of collaboration with fascism in how he conducted his campaign against Stalin.[125] An article in the antifascist and generally pro-Soviet newspaper *Antinazi* in November 1942 characterized Falangists and Trotskyists as two enemies of democracy. Speaking in a global sense rather than specifically about Ecuador, the article charged that Trotskyists presented themselves as democrats and revolutionaries, but in reality they were demagogues and enemies of popular struggles. For Trotskyists, the article stated, "To support the American people, to support Roosevelt, the creator of the Good Neighbor policy, is to be a Yankee agent. To ask for the unification of the American people against the Nazi-Japanese threat is to be an agent of Yankee imperialism. To ask for worker unity, antifascist unity, and national unity is to be a Yankee agent." Falangists and Trotskyists opposed the Soviet Union and hence disrupted a unified front against Hitler; thus, the argument went, both were opposed to democracy. "No alliance can exist with Hitler's allies: Falangists and Trotskyists," the unsigned author (probably the newspaper's editor, Mériguet) argued. While the Falangists presented themselves as "fervent Catholics," the Trotskyists considered themselves "pure revolutionaries," and their "ultra-revolutionary" rhetoric was seditious and provocative. Although the Trotskyists claimed to defend popular interests, their actions undermined unity among workers. As a result, they functioned effectively as Hitler's agents. The Trotskyists presented themselves as opposed to fascism, but their actions sabotaged unity and for that reason they should be expelled from working-class organizations.[126]

The theme of "divisive maneuvers in the working class" translating into the Trotskyists functioning as de facto allies of fascism appeared multiple times in the pages of *Antinazi*. Half a year later, *Antinazi* defended Stalin's decision to close the Comintern and at the same time denounced the Trotskyists as "allies of Nazism" because their actions divided the working class, which allowed Nazism to strengthen. The world could see the role that communists had played in the struggle against fascism, the author (again, probably Mériguet) argued, and their actions highlighted the false nature of the Trotskyist accusations. The antifascist movement declared that it was "proud of the role that communists play alongside other Ecuadorian and foreign organizations."[127] Deep tensions existed between the Trotskyist and Stalinist wings of the global communist movement, to the point where those allied with the Soviet Union accused Trotsky's followers, even in remote areas such as Ecuador, of facilitating the rise of fascism.

The FBI's attention to the Fourth International's circular was also curious because Ecuador, unlike Bolivia, never had a strong Trotskyist movement. The renowned scholar Robert Jackson Alexander dedicates only three short paragraphs to the country in his book on Trotskyism in Latin America. According to Alexander, in 1934 an official with the Communist League of America mentioned the formation of a group in Ecuador but did not record its name, "and it seems to have disappeared without a trace." Alexander continues, "It was not until 1971 that there was again some indication of the existence of a Trotskyist group in Ecuador."[128] In his other writings on the Latin American left, Alexander, who assumed a strongly anticommunist social democratic position, does not mention a Trotskyist tendency in Ecuador, even though he interviewed political leaders and activists during his visits to the country in the 1940s. If Trotskyism had an organized political presence in Ecuador in the 1940s, Alexander would have mentioned it, or it would have surfaced in other documents.

The FBI continued to express concern about Trotskyism, despite evidence that this ideology had only a minor presence in Ecuador. The FBI reported that although there were few Trotskyists in the country—maybe no more than ten or twenty, with half of them foreigners—they were well organized. If that was the case, it is not entirely clear who these alleged Trotskyists were. One FBI source identified Arturo Eichler as well as Dr. Francisco Breth, Franz Wuerfl, Hans Wuerfl, and Kurt Sittenfeld, as the leading Trotskyists in Quito, ignoring that most were not native-born Ecuadorians. Breth was a Czechoslovakian Jew; Franz Wuerfl, the owner of Lucul Delicatessen Stores, was Austrian (Hans Wuerfl was his older brother); and Sittenfeld was a German Jewish dentist. Reportedly, Trotskyists held a meeting at Sittenfeld's house in early 1943, and Franz Wuerfl attended as the leader of the German-speaking revolutionary socialists known as Trotskyists or the Fourth International center. Wuerfl declared that they did not want to fight against Hitler in a way that would help U.S. imperialism. They were also opposed to Stalinist imperialism that was enslaving poor Russians, which naturally opened them up to charges of Trotskyism. According to the FBI source, although few Trotskyists lived in the city, this small group was gaining more converts through personal contacts. These leaders knew that the U.S., British, and local authorities were closely monitoring their activities and that officials of those governments would not be able to discover any significant information on their group. Once again, the intelligence-gathering operatives reported the irony that the targets of their investigation were aware of their surveillance. Political intimidation rather than documentation of subversive activity appeared to be the goal.

Eichler and Breth mentioned a visit to Ecuador in 1943 of a secret Trotsky-ist agent from the United States who posed as an expert on quinine, the medi-cation extracted from the bark of the cinchona tree found in Ecuador that was used to prevent and treat malaria. An unnamed U.S. government official, however, remembered a visit by only two quinine experts. One was Charles Cosse, president of the American Quinine Company in New York City, who was in Ecuador in June 1943 as part of a trip to Ecuador, Peru, and Guatemala with the Federal Economic Administration to advise on changes to quinine laboratories. The anonymous source characterized Cosse as a "four-flusher," a bluffer who did not know much about quinine and was subsequently dis-missed from his post. At the same time, there was no evidence that he was "communistically inclined." The second quinine expert was Lind Pettersen, a wealthy Norwegian citizen of Guatemala. He visited Ecuador in Novem-ber 1943 and "expressed no radical views whatsoever and appeared to be a most highly respectable citizen." The United States could not find a record in the immigration offices in Quito and Guayaquil of either man's arrival or departure from Ecuador. If a Trotskyist agent had indeed visited Ecuador, the United States could not confirm his identity. The FBI seemed to expend a lot of energy chasing dead-end leads.

Mériguet, whose *Antinazi* newspaper had previously condemned Trotsky-ists for their opposition to Stalin, reported that Trotskyism was strong in Ec-uador and that its base grew out of Bolivia, one of the few places in the world where that ideology did gain a significant foothold. Mériguet identified the main leaders as Dr. Gonzalo González, Julio Reyes, and Anastasio Viteri. All were writers for the liberal newspaper *El Día*, which would seem to put into question whether they were Trotskyist partisans. According to Mériguet, the Trotskyists advanced a five-point program:

1. Against Yankee Imperialism in South America;
2. Against Stalin for Free Russia;
3. To use British and American Interests against each other;
4. Against trenchorous (*sic*) United States paid agents (example, Lom-bardo Toledano); and
5. To promote revolution wherever possible in South America.

Mériguet also stated that the Trotskyist strategy "was to drive a wedge isolat-ing Russia from England and the United States" because "their purpose was to aid Russia in the war effort since they were not opposed to Russia but only to Stalin."[129] The FBI dutifully reported all of this information, even though its legal attaché had previously reported that Trotsky had few followers in Ecuador, with only a small and inactive group in Quito and no organized presence in Guayaquil.[130] Identifying writers for the liberal newspaper *El Día* as Trotskyist agents and including a charge that the Mexican labor leader and CTAL President Vicente Lombardo Toledano, who consistently took a pro–Soviet Union position, was a U.S. agent should have flagged the questionable accuracy of the intelligence.

The U.S. Embassy later reported on the presence of the "Czechoslovakian propagandist" Frantisek Hanus, an engineer at Skoda Works, who, according to immigration records that the embassy acquired, had arrived from Buenos Aires in June 1947 and left five days later for Cali, Colombia. Apparently not understanding the Stalinist nature of the PCE, the informant reported that Hanus "was well received by local Trotzkyite members who considered him a fellow member although not registered as a member of the Fourth International."[131] The desire of U.S. officials to identify Trotskyists says more about their imperial concerns than it does about Ecuador's domestic realities. Trotskyists viewed World War II as a war between imperial powers. While they defended the Soviet Union, unlike the Stalinists they did not support the Allies. Under the influence of the U.S. communist leader Earl Browder, the pro-Soviet communists supported bourgeois nationalist or democratic forces, whereas Trotskyists advocated for a permanent revolution. U.S. government officials may have feared the growth of Trotskyism among Latin American workers. Its strength in Bolivia certainly was not a comfort. Given the alternatives, U.S. policy makers may have seen the PCE as more palatable than possible alternatives on the radical left.

A possible source for the FBI's suspicion of Trotskyist activity in Ecuador was a charge that a naval attaché made in 1942 that the communist militant Nela Martínez "was receiving instructions from the 4th Internationale, lending further credence to her Communistic activities."[132] Martínez, however, was a longtime activist with the pro-Soviet PCE, and an imputation that she would receive instructions from a competing political tendency was clearly mistaken. Even so, years later the FBI still relied on this "intelligence" in its dispatches. An FBI memo from 1945 stated that in 1942 Martínez "was reported to have obtained instructions from the Fourth (possibly Third) International," seemingly attempting to correct the confusion as to where her ideological allegiances lay.[133] In any case, such inaccurate reports demonstrate the limitations of FBI surveillance.

Some political leaders whom Alexander interviewed during a visit to Ecuador in 1947 expressed a lingering fear of collaboration between fascist and communist forces. Alexander lumped the communist newspaper *El Trabajador* together with the conservative Catholic and allegedly pro-Nazi periodical *Voz Obrera* because in 1940 *El Trabajador* had followed the Comintern policy of supporting the Nazi-Soviet Non-Aggression Pact.[134] During the pact, communist policy shifted from advocacy of collective action against fascism to a denunciation of the war as an imperial conflict designed to divide up the world among capitalist powers, similar to what had been the socialist attitude toward World War I. From this perspective, workers should not support either side. While historians have long condemned the opportunistic nature of the pact, it is a stretch to argue that political support for it was the same as allying with the Nazis. Nevertheless, at the time it was common even among liberals in the United States to collapse Nazis and communists together with the term "Communazi."[135] A more accurate portrayal of political alliances, however, would be the civil rights leader Paul Robeson's observation, "Wherever I've been in the world . . . the first to die in the struggle against fascism were the communists."[136] Most leftists remained steadfastly opposed to fascist ideologies.

According to a memo dated 1943 from the assistant military attaché Vernet Gresham, Saad was concerned that Trotskyists had won some communists to their cause and that some of those remained in the PCE so as to report on internal developments to the Trotskyist headquarters. According to the memo, Saad did not know who the Trotskyists were because "they act with great discretion and do not reveal their identity," but their access to detailed information indicated their effectiveness. Saad estimated that there were twenty Trotskyists in Guayaquil. According to Gresham, "Trotskyists must be careful in all their activities because the Ecuadorian government has already stopped them from importing propaganda and is just looking for a good excuse to jail those they can prove are Trotskyists." For this reason, and seemingly contradictorily, the Trotskyists had asked communist sympathizers to use their post office box to import printed material from Argentina and the United States.[137] Eichler allegedly claimed that Trotskyists had planted members in the Communist Party with an appearance of cooperating but, in fact, with an intent to sabotage it. Furthermore, he maintained that a high government official who was well connected with the U.S. Embassy reported to the Trotskyist group anything he learned on investigations against the group.[138] What emerges repeatedly in these FBI reports is both a lack of a sophisticated understanding of divisions on the left and a superficial appreciation of how those global dynamics played out on Ecuador's local political landscape. Rather than erudite analysis, the political reports too often sunk to the level of conspiracy theories.

The FBI reported that Saad had considered expelling the longtime party militants Ricardo Paredes, Hermel Quevedo, and "others of this small 'radical' element from the Party due to their 'Trotskyite' tendencies."[139] Mériguet, who published the attacks on Trotskyism in *Antinazi*, worked closely with Paredes, however, and it seems unlikely that the antifascist fighter would conspire with Saad for his removal. One confidential source stated that communists complained that socialists, whom they derogatorily referred to as "Trotskyists," undermined their efforts in Guayaquil by sowing "disorder and anarchism among the organized workers." Saad stated that while Trotskyism was poorly organized, it was a growing threat because of Soviet cooperation with U.S. and British imperialists, leading some radicals to turn to Trotskyism as a better means to foster world revolution.[140] It appears that "Trotskyist" was a derogatory label used to criticize an opposing faction rather than a formally organized political tendency.[141] The comments, however, do highlight significant divisions on the left, no matter the label. Saad followed Browder in his call for a secession of attacks on capitalist countries in the context of the war in which the Soviet Union was fighting for its very existence. Saad's embrace of Browder's ideas, which meant a degree of support for U.S. imperialism in some guise, logically would be unpopular among more dogmatic leftists.[142] He may have perceived Paredes and Quevedo as sympathetic to Trotskyism simply because they maintained a more consistent and disciplined anti-imperialist line.

The FBI's anticommunism led it to focus on trends and themes that other analysts may not have thought worthy of detailed examination. The result is a mixed bag. On one hand, it is important to read the FBI reports through the lens of the bureau's ideological agenda and in light of the reason for its presence in the hemisphere, in addition to realizing that many agents had minimal language skills or understanding of South American politics. At the same time, the FBI did succeed in documenting trends on the left that might otherwise have been lost to posterity. Even with these shortcomings, the FBI reports do contribute new insights. Often the Communist Party took cautious and moderate positions that might otherwise not appear objectionable. One FBI report noted that the communists assumed "a pro-patriotic attitude." The party emphasized its anti-Nazi activity to gain support from Western capitalist powers. In addition, the PCE challenged the Ecuadorian government on the resolution of the border conflict with Peru to position itself domestically as a nationalistic force. The communists also highlighted the party's ongoing campaign for the United States to return its military bases at Salinas and the Galápagos Islands to accentuate its nationalist credentials. Rather than playing a disruptive role in society, the PCE emphasized positions that would gain it broad popular support.[143] The inadvertent result of the FBI surveillance is a more complete and deeper understanding of the Latin American left, including how it operated and why it took the positions that it did.

CHAPTER 3

Labor

NEPTALI PACHECO LEON
DIPUTADO POR LOS TRABAJADORES

NEPTALÍ PACHECO LEÓN was one of Ecuador's most important twentieth-century peasant leaders. He lived and worked in Milagro, located only fifty kilometers from the principal coastal city of Guayaquil. He owned and managed a cooperative farm called Ñauza, the subject of Enrique Gil Gilbert's prize-winning novel *Nuestra pan*. Pacheco León led a variety of local campaigns, including one to bring an electric light plant in Milagro under municipal control. He represented coastal peasants' concerns on several occasions in the National Congress, including in the 1944–45 Constituent Assembly. Source: León Borja, *Hombres de Mayo*.

Ecuador's small industrial base historically has hindered the development of strong working-class labor unions. Instead, in the late nineteenth century, artisans in the urban centers of Guayaquil and Quito organized mutual aid societies that provided social benefits for their members such as assisting with funeral expenses and aiding widows and orphans.[1] Many early working-class organizations were affiliated with the Catholic church and a conservative political party that emphasized individual morality rather than structural issues of class struggle. National worker congresses in 1909 and 1920, and the founding in 1938 of the conservative Confederación Ecuatoriana de Obreros Católicos (Ecuadorian Confederation of Catholic Workers; CEDOC), followed along these lines. An alternative anarchist tendency emphasized economic issues, culminating in a general strike in Guayaquil in 1922 that the military brutally suppressed in a bloody massacre that left hundreds of workers dead. That strike and massacre gave birth to the Ecuadorian left through a baptism of blood.[2]

In the 1940s, with militant working-class organizing on the rise, the FBI dedicated more resources to the surveillance of the labor leader Pedro Saad than any other communist in Ecuador. Many times FBI agents did little more than summarize newspaper reports or otherwise describe his very public activities as a labor leader and politician. On other occasions, FBI memos appear to include information from his close personal confidants. The surveillance raises the question of what the FBI was attempting to accomplish by observing labor movement activity. Apparently, this attention was a result of his visible international labor organizing work, particularly through his contacts in Mexico. The FBI was convinced that the Soviets passed instructions to Ecuadorian communists through labor leaders in Mexico and sought to document and interdict that flow of information.[3]

The FBI described Pedro Antonio Saad Niyaim as a white man; five feet and eight inches tall; 140 pounds with a slender build; with black eyes, black hair, a small black mustache; and a swarthy complexion, who resided at 209 Febres Cordero Street in Guayaquil.[4] He was born in 1909 to Lebanese immigrant parents, Kalil Boulos Saad and Celinda Niyaim. An FBI memo notes that his parents had come to Ecuador from Syria several years before his birth and owned "a moderately successful textile and clothing business" in Guayaquil. Their commercial endeavors provided him with class privileges. Saad graduated from the prestigious Colegio Vicente Rocafuerte and studied for a law degree at the University of Guayaquil. He did not submit his thesis for the degree because he thought establishing himself as a lawyer would hamper his work with the labor movement. Allegedly, Saad complained that if he finished the degree, he "would have had to spend the majority of his time defending poor people from whom the remuneration would be negligible." Instead, Saad's father employed him as an accountant in his clothing shop, and he possibly was a partner in the business and hence financially independent.[5] FBI agents repeated much of this basic biographical data almost verbatim in subsequent memos.[6]

U.S. officials monitored Saad's activities well before the arrival of the FBI. In 1931, he began teaching mathematics at his alma mater Vicente Rocafuerte.[7] Diplomatic officials complained that communism had spread throughout the University of Guayaquil and was openly tolerated at Vicente Rocafuerte. These ideological trends influenced Saad, and he encouraged their propagation. He joined the Partido Comunista del Ecuador (Communist Party of Ecuador; PCE) in 1931, and he repeatedly faced imprisonment and exile for his political activities. In April 1932, Minister William Dawson reported that the police had arrested Saad for spreading "communistic doctrines" while a university student and a teacher at Vicente Rocafuerte. The story of his arrest and exile to the provincial city of Manabí also made the pages of the *New York Times*. Reflecting the young communist's social connections, an outpouring of student protest quickly led to his release.[8]

In 1936, President Federico Páez expelled Saad to Panama for having participated in May Day protests against the rising cost of living. According to an FBI informant, Saad's father had registered him at the French consulate as a Syrian at birth, which allowed him to leave the country rather than face imprisonment.[9] From Panama, Saad moved to Costa Rica, where he wrote for the newspaper *Repertorio Americano* and collaborated in the launch of the PCE's *Vanguardia Popular*. After his return to Ecuador in 1938 he helped found the Confederación de Trabajadores de América Latina (Confederation of Latin American Workers;

CTAL), the Latin American trade union federation based in Mexico under the leadership of Vicente Lombardo Toledano. The U.S. diplomatic service identified Saad as a law student, an active communist, and an effective orator.[10] These skills made him a target of investigation.

Surveillance extended beyond the political realm and into his private life. In 1939, Saad married Isabel Herrería Herrería, and they had two children. According to the FBI, Saad and his "extremely loyal" wife, a teacher, were "very modest in their living and financial desires."[11] Saad divorced Herrería in 1951 and married Aracely Gilbert, with whom he had two more children. In 1952, Saad assumed the post of secretary-general of the PCE, a position he held for the next several decades. In 1968, Paul Reichler, a student at Tufts College who studied the communists in Ecuador, described the PCE as "the most bourgeois party in Ecuador," and Saad as "one of the country's biggest oligarchs."[12] Saad died in 1982 from complications from an aneurism.

The FBI paid closer attention to Saad than any other communist leader, including the party's secretaries general. During an eighteen-month period in 1944–45, FBI agents drafted at least ten reports based on information from "confidential and reliable" sources that detailed Saad's personal history and activities. The extent of surveillance could be a result of the convenience of having an informant willing to provide information, or alternatively as a true expression of concern for his activities. As a political leader, Saad represented the wing of the PCE most willing to collaborate with the United States and thus seemed less likely to present a threat to security concerns that would justify a sizable FBI presence in the country. If the FBI were truly concerned with Saad's activities, it highlights that the United States' underlying concerns were economic rather than political or ideological in nature and that organized labor provided a larger threat to the capitalist system than a small leftist political party. British diplomats similarly feared Saad's organizing skills. They considered him "typical of the Ecuadorean labour agitator." He was intelligent and knowledgeable about "social reforms in the United Kingdom, and in private conversation he [gave] the impression of complete sincerity and reasonableness." Nevertheless, according to British Envoy Leslie Hughes-Hallett, "These qualities desert him as soon as he stands before a working-class audience, and he becomes a rabble-rouser of the most unscrupulous and dangerous sort."[13] Political surveillance highlights the threat that labor activists presented to foreign economic interests in Latin America.

National Labor Congress

The first significant political surveillance of labor activism in Ecuador and Saad's role in those events came in the context of a failed attempt to form a national workers' federation. Labor leaders mobilized active support for a workers' congress in Quito in March 1943. Delegates from around the country gathered with the goal of creating the Confederación de Trabajadores del Ecuador (Confederation of Ecuadorian Workers; CTE). Despite an optimistic beginning, these efforts quickly ran into problems and soon fell apart. Under orders from President Carlos Arroyo del Río, some of the conservative labor leaders who initially had helped plan the congress changed their position and disrupted the efforts already in progress. The government, the oligarchy, and the Catholic church were opposed to any attempts to unify the working class, and that attitude became apparent in their move to impede the congress. Their actions eventually led to the cancelation of the planned congress and the convocation of a pro-government meeting instead. The exclusion of progressive leaders with an explicitly political agenda resulted in an assembly that failed to address the imperial penetration of foreign capital into Ecuador—nor did the resolutions from the congress challenge inequalities in the land tenure system. As soon as the pro-government congress finished, Arroyo del Río ordered a halt to any further labor organizing.[14] The May 1944 revolution a year later finally provided the necessary political openings that allowed leftist labor leaders to organize the CTE.

Throughout this entire failed process, the FBI maintained its surveillance of labor activists. In May 1943, FBI Director J. Edgar Hoover forwarded a pair of memoranda from a "confidential, reliable" source that outlined the history of the labor movement in Ecuador and, in particular, the role of the Mexican labor leader and CTAL President Lombardo Toledano in organizing the recent congress in Quito. This source recounted President Eloy Alfaro's support for founding the Confederación del Guayas (Guayas Confederation) on the coast in 1898 and the Sociedad Artística y Industrial de Pichincha (Artistic and Industrial Society of Pichincha; SAIP) in Quito in 1910 to provide a "center of culture and entertainment for all the workers." As long as the labor movement limited itself to cultural and entertainment matters, it made little progress. That changed in 1925 with the formation of socialist organizations. With that development, an "element of class consciousness entered into the Union's activities and a new union was organized along Marxian lines." In the report, the FBI highlighted political opposition that emerged against the socialist and communist leadership of strikes that advanced workers' demands.

Competition for control of the labor movement intensified during the first decades of the twentieth century. Socialists and communists maintained that the only way to advance their agenda was through strikes and engaging in a class struggle. Conservatives and Catholics, by contrast, aimed to preserve labor federations as merely social and cultural institutions and denounced leftists' efforts to convert "workers into instruments of hatred and social division which was contrary to Christian Brotherhood." According to these conservatives, "God Himself put rich and poor on the earth and they should not fight against the Divine Will, and the workers must try to improve their working conditions by appealing to the Christian hearts of the rich people and the union should be only a place for entertainment and enlightenment." Finally, governments also sought to control labor movements. In 1937, President Federico Paéz dissolved the SAIP because it was engaged in subversive activities, and the following year, the chief executive, Alberto Enríquez Gallo, approved a labor law to pull "workers away from Moscow domination." Similarly, Arroyo del Río urged labor activists to operate within the law and to refrain from making political demands. The FBI informant compared the struggle for control of Ecuadorian workers to battles between conservatives and leftists in the Spanish Civil War, with Catholics supporting Francisco Franco and communists advocating a class struggle. Opportunism also emerged, with José Elías Montenegro and Carlos Salazar assuming leadership of the SAIP, not because they were socialists or Catholics, but to retain their privileged positions in the labor movement.[15] All of these issues and conflicts that the FBI so astutely outlined underlay the collapse of the labor congress.

The plans for the congress of March 1943 grew out of Lombardo Toledano's visit in October 1942. At the CTAL's first general congress, held in Mexico in November 1941, labor activists resolved to send Lombardo Toledano on a tour of twelve Latin American countries to stimulate local organizing. He returned with the impression that "there is but one people in our countries, one fervor, one hope." He noted, "Mestizos, mulattoes, Indians, Blacks, whites, all those constituting the Latin America republics, regardless of their major problems, of their misery in some cases, their poverty or ignorance, have a free, indomitable spirit, and have circumvented prejudice that in other parts of the world divides men in a hopeless manner."[16] Lombardo Toledano was optimistic about the CTAL's ability to unify labor struggles across the Americas.

On October 6, 1942, Lombardo Toledano arrived in Tulcán, on Ecuador's northern border, from Colombia. Ten days later he departed from Guayaquil, in the south, for Peru. While traveling through the country, he stopped in communities that were home to militant organizing, including Cayambe, in the highlands, and Milagro, on the coast. In Cayambe, a large delegation of more than two thousand Indigenous peoples, including those with banners on horseback, received the Mexican labor leader. In a long and energetic meeting in the town square, local activists including Dolores Cacuango and Jesús Gualavisí presented their demands. Lombardo Toledano described revolutionary advances in agrarian reform and rural education that Mexicans had achieved.[17] Workers in Milagro similarly met Lombardo Toledano at the train station with signs and banners. The local leaders Neptalí Pacheco León, M. Raúl Rodríguez, and Antonio Ruiz Flores led Lombardo Toledano on a parade through the town before gathering in a solemn session where he was the honored guest. Lombardo Toledano departed the next morning duly impressed with the labor movement's unity.[18]

The primary purpose of Lombardo Toledano's stop in Ecuador was to encourage the formation of a local CTAL affiliate. Together with the Colombian labor leader Guillermo Rodríguez, the vice president of the CTAL, Lombardo Toledano met with local labor leaders in Guayaquil. Goals for the meeting included unification of the working class, development of a class struggle, advancement of a fight against fascism, and preparation of the country for the post-war world. To implement this agenda, those at the meeting agreed to organize a Congreso Nacional de Trabajadores (National Workers' Congress) and to form a countrywide labor federation. President Arroyo del Río and Carlos Dousdebés, head of the government's Department of Labor, promised funding and official support for the congress.[19]

In retrospect, and considering that government repression prevented the congress from taking place, official support might appear ironic. The Ecuadorian government, however, routinely supported these types of meetings, in part as a mechanism to control their outcome. Three years later and under equally difficult conditions, the CTE financed its second congress entirely with donations from individuals and labor unions and commented how rare that was.[20] In 1943, the CTAL had urged labor unity in support of the war against fascism and in defense of the Soviet Union. Its no-strike policy benefited both U.S. corporations operating in Latin America and local governments. The presidents of Bolivia, Peru, and Nicaragua, none of which were sympathetic to leftist ideologies, and Arroyo del Río met with Lombardo Toledano during his tours of Latin America. From that perspective, a loss of government support becomes a more important matter than explaining its initial encouragement.[21]

On February 19, 1943, a month before the planned congress was to start, Saad presented a talk to the Unión Sindical de Trabajadores (Workers' Trade Union) in which he outlined a history of the formation of the Ecuadorian nationality, the need for workers to organize, and issues that the forthcoming workers' conference should address. He examined Ecuador's economic situation and advanced an urgent program of action that the labor movement should undertake. Saad argued that the proposed labor federation must incorporate everyone, including peasants and Indigenous peoples, not just manual workers. Saad later distributed the talk in the form of a pamphlet—the first of his many published discourses on the pressing issues facing the labor movement. In the pamphlet's preface, Enrique Gil Gilbert described Saad as "a tireless, modest, energetic fighter, standing firm next to workers and peasants—Indians and *montubios*—the great masses of the people and all progressive forces." Together, they fought "against all the political, social, and economic manifestations of the feudal oligarchy, against the reactionary bourgeoisie that harms the development of our nation, and against imperialism that stands against our just and indisputable right to progress, freedom, and absolute independence." Gil Gilbert characterized Saad as "one of those fundamentally antifascist and mortal enemies of the hordes of fanatics who have smeared the entire world with blood, pain, and misery."[22] Saad appeared well positioned to organize a successful congress and launch an effective labor federation.

Meanwhile, four months had passed since the October meeting, and Rodríguez, who from his base in Colombia was to be in charge of the CTAL's South American efforts, had heard nothing from his colleagues in neighboring Ecuador. A week before the congress was to begin in Quito on March 1, Rodríguez sent a telegram to Dousdebés, the government labor inspector, that went unanswered. Rodríguez then received urgent telegrams from labor leaders in Ecuador and Lombardo Toledano in Mexico asking him to travel to Guayaquil to meet with the organizers. The Ecuadorian Embassy in Bogotá, however, refused to grant Rodríguez a visa for the labor congress, which forced him to travel on a tourist visa. Furthermore, the Panagra flights to Ecuador were full, which compelled Rodríguez to travel overland, further delaying his arrival.[23]

Growing government repression led to delays in the start of the congress. Two days before it was scheduled to begin, President Arroyo del Río backpedaled on his promises of support and imposed conditions on the meeting. He insisted that the congress include only manual laborers and exclude progressive political activists and foreign delegations, including the CTAL.[24] The organizers conceded to this political pressure and published a statement declaring that the meeting was not a project of the CTAL; that they had not invited the CTAL leaders Lombardo Toledano and Rodríguez; and that the congress would be limited to an exclusively national agenda, thereby implying that it would not be a communist meeting dedicated to an international working-class struggle.[25] The CTAL vice president Rodríguez responded harshly to this declaration, criticizing its passive and nationalist tone and its failure to address important topics such as the liberation of the Indigenous peasantry and the struggle against fascism. Furthermore, these concessions had not satisfied the reactionary and anti-worker forces that were dedicated to sabotaging the planned congress.[26] Because Lombardo Toledano allegedly received his instructions from the Soviet Union, Quito's Archbishop Carlos María de la Torre condemned the planned congress, labeled the organizers communists, and prohibited Catholic workers from attending.

During the first weeks of March, fierce debates took place inside the preparatory sessions over the shape and character of the proposed congress. A conservative dissident group advocated limiting attendance to manual laborers and excluding others, such as teachers and private employees. The group wanted to make the congress an exclusively Ecuadorian meeting and to bar the radical CTAL leaders Lombardo Toledano and Rodríguez from participating.[27] Contradictory newspaper reports alternatively indicated that the CTAL leaders would or would not attend the congress.[28] Similarly, it was never clear whether the conservative Catholic labor federation CEDOC would join the meeting.

Even as labor leaders organized the workers' congress, seemingly with the government's tacit support, the organizers faced repressive actions. On March 3, Rodríguez traveled to Guayaquil to meet with labor organizers in an attempt to salvage the congress. The secret police followed Rodríguez and monitored his communications. Saad and other labor leaders finally concluded that the congress could be successful only if Lombardo Toledano were in charge, because he would provide it with the necessary leadership and structure. The State Department, however, had asked the Mexican government to deny travel documents to Lombardo Toledano that prevented him from traveling to Quito, so he asked Rodríguez to preside over the congress in his stead.[29] On March 16, as Rodríguez was planning to travel to Quito for the start of the congress, the police arrested him in his hotel in Guayaquil. Rodríguez condemned the police for acting like the Gestapo and the police commander Carbo Paredes for acting like Hitler. From jail, Rodríguez sent a telegram to Arroyo del Río appealing to the previous support the president had lent the organizing efforts, but to no avail. According to the Ministry of Government, Rodríguez had come to Ecuador "to create divisions among the Ecuadorian workers." Rodríguez allegedly had intended to intervene in the workers' congress without being invited and with "the insidious task of insulting a respectable sector of Ecuadorian labor leaders." Rodríguez denied that he had ever intervened in the country's internal political affairs or acted in a subversive manner. Despite the government's claims, the same leftist labor leaders whom Rodríguez allegedly had insulted demanded that the government release him.[30] Instead, after holding him for three days in the carabineros' barracks, the government deported him to his native Colombia without even allowing him to return to his hotel to pick up his suitcase. The Catholic church hierarchy as well as conservative labor leaders applauded the government's actions against the Marxist labor leader.[31] Arroyo del Río claimed that he had not received any petitions in defense of Rodríguez, even though press reports indicated that both Colombian workers and their counterparts in Guayaquil had sent cables on his behalf.[32]

Even with Rodríguez's deportation, everything finally appeared to be firmly in place for the congress to begin. The inaugural session was scheduled for March 18 at the Deportivo Cóndor sports arena. The Ecuadorian president had agreed to attend, together with his ministers, local dignitaries, the diplomatic corps, important political and cultural figures, and the local press. *El Comercio* reported that the train from Guayaquil had arrived in Quito full of delegates and that organizers had worked with the government and transportation companies to modify bus schedules to facilitate the participation of workers.[33] With this level of official support and popular interest, the congress promised to be a success.[34] Unfortunately, those plans again quickly unraveled.

On the eve of the inaugural session, the militant Federación de Estudiantes Universitarios del Ecuador (Federation of Ecuadorian University Students; FEUE) organized a talk by Pedro Saad at Quito's Central University on the objectives of the congress. Unfortunately, at the last minute Julio Enrique Paredes, the rector of the university and one of the dignitaries who planned to attend the inaugural session the following day, canceled the lecture. Paredes argued that providing a platform for Saad to talk was not in the university's best interests.[35] The attacks on Saad and Rodríguez were part of a broader assault on communist participation in the labor congress.

At a final preparatory session on the day that the congress was to start, Luis Humberto Heredia, leader of the Sociedad de Carpinteros de Guayaquil (Society of Guayaquil Carpenters) proposed that rather than calling the meeting a Congreso Nacional Obrero (National Labor Congress), it should be denominated a Congreso Nacional de Unificación de Trabajadores (National Congress of Workers' Unification). Heredia advocated casting a broader net to include all workers in the country, including peasants, Indigenous peoples, laborers, proletariats, teachers, and private employees (*empleados privados*). He argued that he could see no good reason to exclude teachers and private employees from the meeting, because "the problems of the working class have a fair solution and are framed within the limits of justice."[36] In fact, newspaper reports from October 1942 indicated that organizers had included intellectuals and employees in their original plans for the congress. If the assembly were restricted to a narrow definition of the working class, it would eliminate delegates who were already present for the meeting, including the well-known Indigenous leaders Agustín Vega from Tigua and Jesús Gualavisí and Dolores Cacuango from Cayambe and the peasant leaders Neptalí Pacheco León and Antonio Ruiz Flores from Milagro.[37]

Heredia's proposal to broaden the scope of the meeting highlighted two opposing tendencies at the congress. The largest advocated the inclusion of all exploited classes, while a minority of more conservative pro-government leaders wanted to exclude leftist political activists and limit the congress to manual laborers. Finally, the minority dissident faction abandoned the meeting. The departing group released a statement that denounced communists for exploiting the meeting as "an opportunity to develop their passionate and anti-patriotic politics" that had created friction and divisions within the labor movement. According to the dissidents, delegates should participate freely in the congress without regard to their political affiliations or religious beliefs. Instead, the communists had attempted to subjugate workers to "the tutelage of international leaders, an attitude that earned the outright rejection of those of us who are proud of our nationality and sufficiently capable of finding our own way." They criticized the communists for attempting to broaden the congress away from a narrow focus on manual laborers (*obreros*) to include all workers (*trabajadores*), which would allow for the inclusion of teachers and intellectuals, and thereby would have provided leftists with control over the meeting. Instead, the conservative dissidents called for a congress of true and authentic manual laborers to allow them to organize around their class interests.[38] Decades later, Saad argued that what was at stake was not a simple question of whom to include in the congress but, rather, a much deeper issue of how to unify the entire working class in a struggle to address the problems that they and the country faced.[39]

Another organization from Guayaquil, the Frente Independiente Nacional de Trabajadores (Independent National Workers' Front), sent a petition to the Ministry of Government to request that the police evict members of political parties who had infiltrated the congress. They appealed to the government to maintain a strong police presence to preserve order and prevent further disruptions.[40] The signers of the statement, as well as of the previous one that had denounced communists, included labor leaders who had been involved in the original meeting with the CTAL in October 1942 out of which the idea for the congress had emerged. In fact, the Ecuadorian government paid for two of them—José Elías Montenegro and Alberto Torres Vera—to travel to Mexico in 1938 for the CTAL's founding congress. In his report on the failed congress, Rodríguez was particularly vicious in his criticism of these dissidents. He charged them with being traitors to their class, of being in the pay of the government, of working with the secret police to disrupt organizing, and even of hoping for a repeat of the November 15, 1922 massacre of striking workers in Guayaquil.[41]

In the midst of this repression and the chaos that the dissident delegation's noisy departure from the preparatory session had created, those who remained attempted to carry on with the congress. The majority faction that stayed convened an assembly on the afternoon of March 18 to inaugurate the labor congress. The ambassador from Cuba, Secretary-General Manuel Agustín Aguirre of the Socialist Party, and FEUE President Guillermo Lasso were present, but the Ecuadorian president and his ministers did not attend as originally planned. The assembly sent a delegation of workers to the presidential palace to invite Arroyo del Río, but he excused himself, citing the division among the organizers and the delay in the start of the assembly. He also made it clear that he had lent his support to a narrowly defined congress of manual laborers, not a broader unified congress of workers.

Without official government presence or support, the workers proceeded to elect leadership for the meeting. They selected Jorge Maldonado as president and Francisco Mora Guerrero as vice president. Delegates unanimously nominated Lombardo Toledano and Rodríguez as honorary members of the congress. Mora Guerrero stated that the delegates had not gathered to make a revolution, to conspire against the government, or to become tools of a political party. Rather, they would act with restraint so that the government would finally take the concerns of the working class into account in their policy decisions. He looked to the media to carry their message to the public. Reflecting the broad and inclusive nature of the meeting, Emperatriz Nazareno, an Afro-Esmeraldan, was present in representation of Tagua nut workers. Indigenous leaders also addressed the assembly, stating that they would unite with other workers to resolve underlying class problems and in the process construct a true Ecuadorian nationality.[42]

The following morning, March 19, the delegates descended en masse on the Deportivo Cóndor, where they were scheduled to begin their meetings, only to find that the government had sent the carabinero police armed with machine guns to block the doors. For a moment, the assembled activists feared they were about to witness a repeat of the famed massacre of November 15, 1922.[43] Facing this act of repression, the assembled workers sent a delegation of one representative from each province to persuade Arroyo del Río to allow them to meet. The president reiterated his claims of the previous day that he had permitted the convocation of a labor congress, but that what had gathered now was something entirely different. He said that those who wanted to return home could do so and the government would cover their transportation costs, but if they stayed in Quito they would have to pay their own way. In the face of these threats, some delegates left while others advocated remaining in Quito and searching for another venue where they could meet. Despite valiant effort, this attempt to found a national workers' federation collapsed under the pressure of the government's repressive force.[44]

The government, however, was not finished with its attempts to undermine leftist labor organizers. On the same afternoon, the secret police arrested the socialist leaders Juan Isaac Lovato and Ezequiel Paladines, as well as the worker David Villena, and held them incommunicado at the carabinero barracks. Maldonado and Mora Guerrero, the president and vice president of the planned workers' congress, were in hiding and facing threats of arrest. The detentions led Aguirre to send a petition to the Ministry of Government protesting the government's repressive actions. Secret police agents shadowed other labor and political leaders, seemingly using the tactics that they had acquired from the instruction that the carabineros' Commander Héctor Salgado had received during his recent FBI-sponsored visit to the United States. Salgado returned to Ecuador on the eve of the labor congress, and the police immediately employed their new skills to capture members of the PCE, including Saad, who had attended the congress as a representative of labor groups. The police did not present charges against Saad but said they were only following orders from above. Meanwhile, officials continued to insist on the possible negative consequences of what might have happened had the workers' congress been allowed to proceed as planned.[45]

The day after Saad was arrested, Arroyo del Río named Joaquín Córdova Malo assistant minister of government. At a press conference, the new government official claimed that the country was completely calm, despite all of the unrest surrounding the congress. He confirmed that Saad had been arrested for acting against the public order but mentioned that he did not have more information on Lovato and Paladines. Córdova Malo denied that any order to arrest other political leaders existed.[46] Labor unions and other groups, including Ecuador's antifascist movement, repeatedly sent petitions demanding the release of the prisoners, but the government claimed not to have received any communications on their behalf.[47] Meanwhile, from Colombia, Rodríguez denounced the Ecuadorian government for arresting and deporting him. He stated that his imprisonment was unjustified because he had traveled to Ecuador at the express invitation of the country's workers. During Lombardo Toledano's October 1942 visit to Ecuador when activists drafted plans for the labor meeting, the CTAL president had announced his intent to return for the congress. Since he was unable to attend, he had asked Rodríguez, as vice president, to appear in his absence. Rodríguez's only goal was to assist in the unification of workers' interests, but his protestations fell on deaf ears.[48]

Manuel Agustín Aguirre lamented the failure of the labor congress in his report to the Socialist Party's annual congress half a year later. It was only natural, he observed, that the "feudal capitalists who comprise the dominant class would view with extreme displeasure this serious attempt to organize workers, and would seek to suppress and disorient it." The government, with support of the Catholic church hierarchy, introduced reactionary workers lacking a class consciousness who sold out their colleagues for a pittance and thereby sabotaged worker unity. Aguirre highlighted the amount of organizing work that remained to make the necessary changes in the country.[49]

Meanwhile, the minority pro-government group that opposed holding a broader National Congress of Workers' Unification proceeded with plans for a National Labor Congress. According to Aguirre, Arroyo del Río had allowed this dissident effort to proceed as a show for Vice President Henry Wallace, who was traveling through South America and was scheduled to make a stop in Ecuador the following month, although Wallace was not fooled by the farce.[50] The conservative organizers delivered a message to Ecuador's president proclaiming that they had opposed the earlier, failed meeting at the Deportivo Cóndor because it was under the control of political leaders, and insisted instead that they were convoking a congress that would be composed entirely of "authentic representatives of laborers." Furthermore, unlike the previous attempt, their new effort would be open to Catholic workers. Unstated but implied was that communists would be excluded from the meeting. Arroyo del Río responded positively to this development and announced that he would support this new labor assembly. With this official support, this rump group proceeded to meet at the Casa del Obrero in a preparatory session to plan the inauguration of their congress.[51] The organizers requested a heavy police presence to maintain order and prevent the entry of "undesirable" delegates who would agitate for a leftist political agenda.[52] Despite claims that their meeting consist only of genuine laborers, it remained obvious that the government had sponsored the assembly and set its agenda. As a result, the congress would adopt a bourgeois and apolitical view of labor organizing.

At the preparatory session, delegates selected José Elías Montenegro, leader of the SAIP, as the president of the congress. Organizers proceeded to disqualify several delegates, allegedly because they were not manual laborers but obviously due to their leftist ideologies. Among those excluded was Luis Humberto Heredia, who several days before had proposed that the meeting be expanded into a National Congress of Workers' Unification. In addition, the credentials commission disqualified the renowned leftists Primitivo Barreto and Ernesto Endara from the Unión Sindical de Pichincha (Trade Union of Pichincha) with the excuse that they were *empleados* (employees). Conversely, they accepted Jorge Maldonado, the president of the previous, failed congress, as an "authentic laborer." The delegate Lope Lapuerta tried to have Carlos Proaño, representative of the Sindicato "El Pan" of Pichincha, excluded because of what he had written in the conservative Catholic newspaper *La Patria* against the congress. After other delegates objected, however, Proaño was allowed to remain.[53] The Ministry of Government declared unequivocally that it would "not permit that known subversive elements under the cover of calling themselves laborers or workers organize meetings or assemblies with clear political aims." Arroyo del Río would only allow workers to meet as long as they did not represent a challenge to his government.[54]

At 4:30 PM on March 21, 1943, the labor congress finally inaugurated its activities. After refusing to attend the original attempt to convene a congress, Minister of Social Welfare Leopoldo N. Chávez, along with several of his assistants, were present as government representatives. Initially, President Arroyo del Río and other dignitaries indicated their intentions to participate, but in the end they did not attend. Chávez, the only minister at the congress, proclaimed that the labor problem in Ecuador was not only an economic issue but also a cultural one and that the government should limit itself to addressing cultural concerns. His statement made it apparent that the conference would not engage structural or class issues. Chávez said he welcomed petitions from the congress to address concerns facing workers. As an indication of its limited goals, Alberto Torres Vera, the organizing committee's secretary-general, said that the assembled delegates were not visionaries but would work on practical concerns. He said that when organizers first considered calling the labor congress a "National Congress of Workers' Unification" they had not taken into consideration that this label would serve as a mechanism "to exploit the authentic working masses." From his perspective, the problems laborers faced were cultural rather than structural. Further indicating the conservative and apolitical orientation of the congress, David Checa Murillo, a delegate from Cañar, received applause when he proclaimed, "We workers do not know anything about politics or diplomacy, but we have a longing to march to the conquest of greatness and social welfare that will result in justice, welfare, and work." José Palma from Manabí added, also to applause, that "work is and will be freedom for the spirit and independence of man." The speakers' comments reflected the meeting's culturalist rather than class orientation.[55]

Despite the conservative orientation of the rump congress, delegates raised questions that inadvertently pointed to underlying political and economic issues. Palma asked why Ecuador exported cacao beans and not processed chocolate and why it sold tagua nuts but not finished buttons. In general, why did Ecuador export raw materials that were subsequently turned into manufactured products at great economic cost to Ecuador? This system of economic dependence of a marginalized periphery on an industrial core, of course, was part of a leftist critique to explain Latin America's underdevelopment. Palma, however, blamed a lack of democratic access to credit as preventing the agricultural and industrial development of workers. What he failed to recognize was how global capitalist economic structures limited Ecuador's ability to develop its internal economy.[56]

The issue of organizing a labor confederation on the basis of laborers (*obreros*) or workers (*trabajadores*) was slow to die, and two days later, with sessions in full swing, the assembly once again returned to this topic. The 101 delegates who were present voted on whether to form a National Labor Congress that would be limited to manual laborers or a National Congress of Workers' Unification that would permit the inclusion of those from other professions that leftists dominated. With leftists excluded from the meeting, the first and narrower option won by a wide margin of ninety-two to seven, with two delegates casting blank ballots.

The congress also passed resolutions calling on the government to expropriate haciendas and industries, not out of a desire to socialize the means of production but because the owners were on the U.S. and British blacklists. In practice, those productive units would pass to the hands of wealthy industrialists in the country. The assembly also requested that Ecuador declare war on the Axis powers, something that the government did not do until almost two years later, when the conflict was already largely concluded.[57] Soon the congress was receiving more petitions from the assembled delegates than the time allotted allowed for discussion. The leadership prioritized the most important petitions, which included calls to the federal government to address concerns with state monopolies for the production of matches and alcohol, to establish price controls over consumer goods to benefit workers, and to require haciendas to cultivate their idle land or otherwise face expropriation.[58] Interestingly, and in contrast to the agenda that the leadership had set, many of the resolutions that the delegates brought forward were progressive in their tone, even if they did not challenge government policies or the economic mode of production.

At the close of the final sessions, the delegates elected an Executive Committee to carry on the work of the congress for the next two years.[59] The president of the congress, José Elías Montenegro, continued on in that post and was charged with forwarding the petitions adopted at the meeting to the Ministry of Social Welfare. Of particular concern was the defense of the rights of those working for a U.S. company on the Galápagos Islands and the need for a development bank to provide credit to small agriculturalists and merchants to fuel economic growth.[60] Montenegro and the rest of the Executive Committee also presented Chávez with proposed statutes for a new Confederación de Obreros del Ecuador (Confederation of Ecuadorian Laborers; COE). The goal of this confederation was to work for the defense and economic improvement of manual laborers throughout Ecuador. In a reversal of previous attempts to exclude other workers, the organizers now stated that industrial workers, artisans, transportation workers, miners, and even peasants were welcome to join. Together, the statutes declared, they would raise the cultural, economic, moral, and material level of manual laborers and workers in general. They would form a united front for all of the workers and laborers in the country to struggle in defense of their common interests, including the right to petition the government.[61] The congress also created a legislative commission to press for laws that would benefit the social, economic, and cultural interests of workers.[62]

Despite all of these efforts, the planned labor federation was stillborn. Aguirre attempted to put a positive spin on the failure, claiming that the noble but ultimately futile attempt highlighted the consciousness, strength, and valor of the working class. He applauded the actions of the socialists, as well as of other leftists, for playing an essential role in the most important organizing effort to date in the country's history.[63] Subsequent scholars have generally been less charitable to the failed attempt. The labor historian Patricio Ycaza faults the organizers for assuming a passive vision of the labor struggle that was removed from international solidarity movements. As a result, the leaders were incapable of addressing fundamental underlying structural issues that directly influenced workers' roles in society.[64] The Marxist historian Osvaldo Albornoz further argues that it had been a mistake for the organizers to accept the government-imposed conditions. In order not to lose everything, they had attempted to hold the congress at all costs. This decision reflected the labor movement's ideological limits.[65]

FBI informants shared the concern of the government, the Catholic church, and the Conservative Party that Lombardo Toledano was a communist operative who, rather than mobilizing true laborers, collaborated with "intellectual workers," a code term for communist agitators. The Ecuadorian government feared that the labor congress would provide a medium for political agitation and for that reason sought to sabotage it. An informant recounted the Ecuadorian government's efforts to deny entry to Lombardo Toledano and its collaboration with the Colombian government to deport Rodríguez. According to this report, Rodríguez was opposed to "dying Anglo-American Imperialism," and "as soon as the war is over [the workers] should join with the North American workman to fight for the adoption of the Communist system to replace the capitalistic system of the Anglo-Americans." Fear of growing communist strength led Arroyo del Río's government to collaborate with the Catholic church and the Conservative Party to stop the labor congress, even though the nominally liberal administration typically would otherwise have stood in opposition to Catholic conservatives.

The FBI reports underscore points at which the perceived interests of the United States corresponded with those of the Ecuadorian government and when they diverged. U.S. officials were concerned that " 'Nazi' and anti-Communist elements" were working to organize a Catholic workers' congress that "would actually be controlled by the Totalitarians." Even as the United States was opposed to leftist organizations that challenged its economic interests, in the context of the war, officials were even more concerned with German penetration of the hemisphere under the guise of, and in collaboration with, the conservatives. In contrast, Ecuadorian officials and the country's upper class feared a communist-dominated labor movement more than they did the alternatives, and for that reason the government had cracked down hard on the leftist labor leaders. Even though the FBI thought that the Ecuadorian actions were misguided and wished that they had acted in a different fashion, they did little to ensure a different outcome.[66]

Labor historian Jon Kofas argues that in January 1943 the U.S. government began to plot with the pro-business American Federation of Labor (AFL) and anticommunist Latin American labor leaders to divide the CTAL. Rockefeller's OIAA invited the labor leaders to a secret meeting in the United States to challenge Lombardo Toledano's leadership of a hemisphere-wide leftist labor movement and replace the CTAL with a pro–United States organization. U.S. government and AFL officials were interested in the Latin American labor situation because wartime demand for raw materials had stimulated economic growth in the region. They assumed that this would translate into a surge in trade unionism and feared that organized labor historically had fallen under the influence of leftist political parties. Although the available documentation does not reveal a hidden imperialist hand behind the collapse of the Ecuadorian labor congress, it did take place in the context of this international political shift that may explain why Arroyo del Río withdrew his support.[67]

Despite the government repression that led to the failure of the March 1943 congress, leftist militants quietly persisted in their efforts. Although prevented from meeting on a national level, leftist labor leaders continued to mobilize in the provinces. Local groups selected delegates to join a coordinating committee to proceed with organizing.[68] The committee's composition reflected a loss of confidence in the labor movement's "old guard" leaders and the emergence of a new generation that employed new tactics. It operated in a clandestine fashion so that these new members might avoid arrest as had happened so often in the past.[69] Even in the face of repression that sent activists to prison, sometimes for months, the struggle continued.

Henry Wallace

In April 1943, only weeks after the implosion of the labor congress, U.S. Vice President Henry Wallace arrived in Ecuador as part of his goodwill tour of South America. Arroyo del Río was particularly interested in making a good impression on Wallace with the goal of reinforcing both domestic and international support for his government. Arroyo del Río mandated a mobilization of Quito's population to welcome Wallace and ordered that the visiting dignitary not meet with dissident labor leaders or, for that matter, anyone who might criticize government policies. In preparing for the visit, Arroyo del Río's perceptions of his country's security concerns corresponded with those of the United States, and the FBI worked hard to ensure that an opportunity for an embarrassing confrontation between labor leaders and Wallace, or even for the possibility of a friendly meeting in which labor unions could express their dissatisfaction with Arroyo del Río's policies, did not occur. A confidential FBI informant said that conservatives and those of the extreme right refused to take part in the visit because of their political opposition to Wallace's progressive policies, while leftists wanted to exploit his visit to demonstrate their opposition to Arroyo del Río's government.[70] After the Ecuadorian government rebuffed their efforts, labor leaders withdrew their support from joining an official demonstration to welcome Wallace.[71] The FBI and Ecuadorian government interests converged in their attempts to shelter the vice president from dissident voices. FBI surveillance created a documentary record of the left's failed attempts to meet with the vice president.

Even though leftists were barred from meeting with Wallace, they still warmly welcomed his visit. Ecuador's antifascist movement noted that the vice president was "much more than a tourist or a statesman on a courtesy call." Rather, his tour would "undoubtedly have a profound and transcendent importance" in terms of unifying the Americas in a struggle against fascism. They anticipated that his presence would push political sentiments in a leftward direction.[72] The British diplomat Leslie Hughes-Hallett, however, had a quite different read of Wallace's visit. He was distressed to observe that Wallace dressed and acted like a farmer rather than the vice president of the United States and devoted more time to reaching out to the working class than to the wealthy and governing upper class. As an example, he pointed to "his visit to Otavalo, where he spent the shortest possible time at the official reception in the municipal building, and proceeded to spend one-and-a-half hours in the house of an Indian couple, discussing with them their way of life, means of livelihood, &c." Illustrating the British diplomat's class and racial perspective, Hughes-Hallett reported that this was a strategic error "since the 'white' workers are apt to look with disdain on the pure Indians, who are almost entirely relegated to the heavier agricultural work."[73] It was, of course, Wallace's attention to working-class concerns that inspired the leftists, and led them to look hopefully to him as an ally to carry their concerns into the halls of power.

In preparation for Wallace's visit, the Legal Attaché's Office in the U.S. Embassy prepared three lists of Axis nationals in Ecuador. The first list was for internment; the second, for confinement to their homes; and the third, for surveillance. The embassy presented the three lists to Arroyo del Río, who ordered the minister of government to implement the request. The FBI reported that the Ecuadorian government was "fair" in the execution of the orders and that enforcement was "excellent." In fact, security forces under orders of the minister of government appeared to exceed the legal attaché's request and expelled rather than merely confined to their houses the Axis nationals in the provinces of Pichincha (Quito), Guayas (Guayaquil), and Imbabura (Otavalo) that Wallace was scheduled to visit. The FBI report indicates the level of control that United States officials maintained over Ecuador's domestic policies. In the end, the FBI succeeded in keeping Wallace separated from, and apparently blissfully ignorant of, the significant domestic discontent brewing in Ecuador.[74] Although President Roosevelt had mandated that the bureau play only an intelligence-gathering role in Latin America, in this case it successfully manipulated both Ecuadorian and U.S. policy decisions.

One exception to the isolation of leftists from Wallace that underscores the fears that the government and its supporters had of such contact was a letter from the communist activist Franklin Pérez Castro. Writing in the name of an antifascist committee on the Santa Elena peninsula, Pérez Castro sought to inform Wallace about working conditions at the U.S. military base at Salinas. The letter began with an appeal to a common struggle against the fascist threat. "We, genuine Anti-Fascists, believe that the Nazi regime is detestable," he wrote, "among other reasons because of the cruelty which it exercises towards workers in the concentration camps; the Nazis are the worst exploiters of workmen, the most cruel and the most brutal." Pérez Castro then proceeded to argue that a great difference should be immediately apparent "between the German concentration camps and the Democratic camps of Pan American collaboration." Reflecting a spirit of collaboration during the war effort, Pérez Castro maintained that Ecuadorian workers should be content and pleased with the presence of U.S. citizens in their country. "But the truth," he stated, "is that the wage workers of the U.S. Military Base at Salinas barely earn 5 sucres a day and are kicked about by the overseers and neither do they receive water to drink during the working hours in these arid deserts." The letter appealed to Wallace's "humanitarianism" and "Christian benevolence," and asked him to intervene with the Tucker McClure Company that held the contract and the U.S. government to improve working conditions on the base. The letter also included a data sheet that listed living expenses for workers, including the price of a dwelling, food, and fuel oil. Pérez Castro argued that the current salary of five sucres a day was not sufficient, and that workers needed to be paid at least eight or nine sucres a day to meet their expenses.

The appeal elicited a reply from Wallace in which he expressed his gratitude to the antifascist activists for having called his attention to the situation. "I wish to assure you that it is my desire that all workers employed in the project of my government in Ecuador receive a salary which will permit them to live decently," he wrote. Wallace pledged to "do everything possible so that matter presented by you shall receive a careful study in order to see what salary is necessary to permit the workers at the military base in Salinas to live more comfortably." Apparently when he returned to the United States, Wallace did contact the military and requested an investigation into the charges, although it is not clear whether anything came of the study or whether it was even conducted.

El Universo published this exchange with Wallace in its newspaper in Guayaquil, which led to no small amount of consternation from the government and its supporters in the business class. Representing Hoover's economic and political interests, the FBI director forwarded a letter he had received from a business owner in Guayaquil that highlighted the "considerable difficulties" that the demands for higher wages would present. The anonymous Ecuadorian capitalist declared that Wallace "was very well received" in Ecuador and had "made an excellent impression." The business community, however, was concerned that he had "addressed the workmen too much and stressed the labor situation perhaps a little more than he should have." The letter's author maintained that the unskilled workers were paid a legal salary and denied that they were mistreated. He declared, "Mr. Wallace has made a sad mistake in answering these communications and paying so much attention to them." He urged the vice president to first learn more about the situation in Ecuador "and the damage he might cause in the future through labor trouble." Pérez Castro was "doing nothing more than taking advantage of the laboring element to cause trouble to the present government of Ecuador." Furthermore, according to the business owner, U.S. government support for a wage increase would cause trouble because it would raise expectations "among the labor organizations and they will try to force everyone else in the country to increase salaries." Although the author conceded that the salaries were low, he argued that they were in line with what was paid elsewhere. The business owner reiterated a standard antilabor argument, one that has not necessarily been borne out in practice, that an increase in wages "would be very bad for the whole country and would cause the present Ecuadoran Government serious labor difficulties." Already Tucker McClure paid above-average salaries for skilled labor, which drew workers away from other companies. The letter writer requested intervention in the matter before Wallace inadvertently created more problems for business owners by pressing these labor demands.

The anonymous source, presumably an FBI agent in Quito who provided this information to Hoover, closed with a comment that Pérez Castro had become involved in this issue "because of pro-totalitarian motives," not bothering to make a distinction between his actual communist allegiances and his declared opposition to fascism. The source presented an alternative explanation that Pérez Castro sought to embarrass Arroyo del Río "for political reasons" and that going over the administration's head and gaining a wage increase without the Ecuadorian government's cooperation or intervention would provide such a blow.[75] The FBI did not seriously consider that Pérez Castro and his colleagues in the antifascist movement might be motivated by a serious concern for social justice and economic equality. While Wallace had a reputation for supporting progressive causes that benefited the working class, the interests of Hoover's FBI lay elsewhere.

Covert Surveillance

On July 5, 1943, the Ecuadorian government released Pedro Saad after holding him in prison since his arrest in Guayaquil on March 21 in the aftermath of the failed labor congress.[76] Just before his release, the naval attaché included a brief mention of Saad in a confidential intelligence report on leftist political parties. "Some years ago," the report read, Saad was part of a group of "40 Reds sent to the Galapagos Islands" who escaped and sought refuge in Costa Rica. The attaché described Saad as "an able agitator, intelligent and very thorough." The naval official acknowledged that Saad was opposed to the Nazis, had praised the United States, and was "imprisoned in Guayaquil on orders of the Ecuadoran Government."[77] Even though Saad seemingly did not represent a significant political threat to U.S. security concerns, the naval attaché's report represented the beginning of intense political surveillance of the communist labor leader.

In a lengthy report from June 1943, the FBI legal attaché observed, "The Communists have operated in the country freely among the masses with leaders of great talent and of proved honesty." Among the leaders were Saad, the "brain and nerve center of the Party in the Republic," whom the government had not hesitated to imprison on political charges. The FBI summarized a letter, apparently intercepted from the postal service, that Saad had sent to labor activists in Mexico stating an intent for the proposed labor federation to ally with the CTAL, as well as with the global struggle against the Axis powers. Saad also described plans to continue attempts to organize a labor federation in Ecuador.[78] In another letter to the State Department, Hoover identified the main labor agitators in Guayaquil. Saad was the only one in prison, but regardless, according to the letter, he was "the real adviser of the greater part of the laboring groups." Hoover noted, "His imprisonment has proved useful to his followers in helping stimulate discontent among the workers." The other labor leaders were Víctor Hugo Briones, who possessed "almost anarchistic ideas"; Luis Humberto Heredia, who was "a labor leader of considerable intellect"; Eusebio Moriel, who was "a person of extreme Communistic views"; Armando Cruz Bahamonde, who was "a student with communist connections"; and Neptalí Pacheco León, who was "a dangerous agitator of true Communistic viewpoint" in Milagro. Although all of the activists presented "serious problems" to the government through their efforts to incite the masses to action, officials were afraid to arrest them because "such an act would create a serious reaction among the workers under their influence." Even so, or perhaps because of the threat that they represented to U.S. economic interests, the FBI monitored the activities of these labor leaders.[79]

On July 14, a large group of workers and intellectuals gathered in Guayaquil to celebrate Saad's release. The FBI reported on those who gave speeches at the event. The first was the liberal leader Francisco Arízaga, whom, according to FBI intelligence, the Ecuadorian government had repeatedly charged with involvement in plots against the government. Despite Arízaga's attendance at Saad's party, the FBI had no evidence that he was active in explicitly communist affairs. The writer Joaquín Gallegos Lara, however, was an active PCE member and had published several articles denouncing Yankee imperialism. As evidence of Gallegos Lara's sympathies, the FBI noted that the Cuban communist Blas Roca had met with him during his visit to Ecuador in August 1942. The FBI did not have information about the identity or sympathies of a third speaker, Leonidas Caseras, a person who otherwise did not play a significant role in Ecuador's labor or leftist history.[80]

Much more surprising than the inclusion of this public meeting in the report was the information the FBI had on small private gatherings Saad convened with his comrades after his release from prison. An informant identified as "Confidential Source of Information S-2" reported that the first "secret meeting" Saad summoned with communist leaders in Guayaquil "was held at the home of Hermel Quevedo, Calle Chimborazo #1929, attended only by Saad, Quevedo and one Barrezeuea the last of whom is an employee of the Guayaquil Library at Calles Vera and Cia." The confidential source stated, "At this meeting Saad is reported to have instructed Quevedo to advise all Party members to abstain from celebrating his release from prison as it is in the interest of the Party to attract as little attention as possible, thus avoiding disclosing to the government the identities of Party members and sympathizers." Saad took this precaution because "it was learned that in the past secret government agents had taken the names of those attending similar celebrations and meetings," a quite ironic statement since the FBI source that reported this intelligence had recorded that information. According to Saad, "The position of the Party in Ecuador is delicate and consequently greatest care must be taken not to let the government know the PCE activities." He was keenly aware of the repressive situation in which the party operated and appeared to be preparing to move toward clandestine or otherwise illegal activity. While in detention "he had been able to make friends with some members of the Police force, especially among the Carbineros, and that many of these contacts may be counted upon in the future in 'emergency' cases." Those connections could play an important role if the party launched a coup attempt against Arroyo del Río's government.[81]

The FBI was not just aware of the PCE's strategic considerations and security concerns, but the level of intimate knowledge in the documents raises questions about how the bureau was able to acquire the information. The FBI seemingly had access to precisely the information that the communists did not want either the Ecuadorian government or the U.S. government to have. How, then, did FBI agents gain access to this intelligence? One extremely revealing piece of information on the agency's surveillance methods is contained in an annual report on the Special Intelligence Service (SIS) program. An abnormally highly redacted section of the report states, "The coverage of Communist activities in Ecuador has been unusually good because of [redacted] Pedro Saad, Communist labor leader of Guayaquil, Ecuador. This informant, [redacted] who has spent many years in Latin America and who was active in [redacted] which he in turn reports to the Legal Attaché."[82] That the informant's name would be redacted is not unusual. Sixty years after the closure of the sis program, the Society of Former Special Agents of the fbi interviewed aging agents about their experiences in the field and specifically instructed them to avoid identifying confidential sources or informants.[83] It would, however, appear that one of Saad's confidants was a double agent who participated in pce activities and reported the details of their private meetings to the fbi. This level of surveillance indicates a constant U.S. concern about who was a member of the pce and whether they opposed U.S. policies, even though the archival record does not include evidence that the U.S. government took action on this intelligence or passed it on to the Ecuadorian government.

Because of the fbi's practice of citing information from unnamed anonymous sources, it is difficult to determine how many informants provided intelligence on Saad, or to ascertain the legitimacy of their information. A source of "established reliability" complained that "the Communists offered no practical plans of their own, limiting themselves rather to criticizing the capitalistic system." The same source reported that in 1930 Saad maintained close friendships with other communist students such as Hermel Quevedo, Ricardo Paredes, and Neptalí Pacheco León at the University of Guayaquil, even though the others were not students at that time. This same informant recounts a private meeting with around thirty students in 1930 in which Saad "wildly accused the Government of Dr. Arroyo of 'Imperialism' though he made no constructive suggestions as to what should be done," even though Arroyo del Río would not be a president until a decade later. Without being able to crosscheck the identity of either the confidential informants or the fbi agents, it is difficult to know whether these factual errors were due to faulty memory on the part of the informants; misunderstandings on the part of the fbi agents, whose comprehension of Spanish may have been limited; or other failures in the intelligence-gathering process, including a tendency to exaggerate the importance of the information provided. Naturally, the intelligence from anonymous sources must always be read critically and with a grain of salt.

The fbi's informant proceeded to note that Saad hid in his house in 1935 during Páez's government to avoid arrest. Ironically, the same informant quoted Saad as bemoaning that many party members "could not be trusted" because they "were agents of the secret police," apparently a suspicion that applied directly to this source. Rather than attempting to increase the size of the party, Saad advocated organizing labor unions "in accordance with how they did it in Russia." Gil Gilbert reportedly "had the printed instructions from Russia, as to how labor organization must be done." Given the quality of the rest of

The Legal Attache's Office at Quito has assisted the Bureau's domestic field in many ways. In one instance involving a Selective Service fugitive from Alaska, it was possible to follow his activities and advise the Bureau of his departure from Ecuador in a home-made sloop in order that he could be taken into custody and held to answer the Selective Service charge pending against him. The fugitive, [   ] had not been heard from since January 25, 1941, until it was ascertained that he was sailing in the Pacific waters off the west coast of South America. X U   b7C

One of the principal exports of the Republic of Ecuador to the United States is balsa wood, which is vital to the Allied war effort in the production of airplanes. Many balsa wood mills have been surveyed by SIS representatives in Ecuador, and it has been necessary to constantly guard against activities which would indicate an endeavor to sabotage this strategic war industry. One instance of an attempt to sabotage a shipment of balsa wood from Ecuador to the United States was received in September, 1943, when an employee at the warehouse of J. H. Monteath Lumber Company in New Jersey stepped on a match which ignited the sawdust and shavings in the warehouse where the balsa wood was stored. It was reported that matches were found in the bundles of balsa wood. Inquiry undertaken in Ecuador with regard to this incident disclosed the act of placing matches among the bundles of balsa wood could not have occurred in Ecuador inasmuch as the matches in question were the common kitchen-type match which is not sold in Ecuador and is not available in that country. X U

Another questionable case involving a fire which destroyed the Kaufmann Balsa Wood Mill was thoroughly investigated by our representatives, and no evidence of sabotage was found in this instance. X U

The coverage of Communist activities in Ecuador has been unusually good because of [   ] Pedro Saad, Communist   b7C
labor leader of Guayaquil, Ecuador. THIS INFORMANT, [   ]   b7D
who has spent many years in Latin America and who was active in [   ]
[   ] which he in turn reports to the Legal Attache. The Communist Party in Ecuador was not recognized by the Government of Arroyo del Rio, which was overthrown by a revolt instituted on May 28, 1944. Because of the sympathy of the new Government established under Velasco Ibarra, it is   b7C
expected that the Party will play a much more important part in local   b7D
developments. A leading Communist, Jean Mariguet, who was imprisoned by the Arroyo Government, has already been released and Communist leaders including Pedro Saad and Enrique Gil have served in posts in the provisional Government. The Communist Party was affiliated with Alianza Democratica Ecuatoriana, which organization was responsible for the overthrow of President Arroyo del Rio. X U

118.

the information that this source provided, it is difficult to establish the credibility of these final statements.

A second source "whose reliability has at times been slightly questionable" recounted Saad's involvement in student strikes at the university. This source claimed to have trained in the military reserve (university battalion) with Saad in 1933. When ordered to salute the Ecuadorian flag, Saad and another student refused because they were communists and opposed any type of military training. The FBI memo also references private meetings with communist leaders in Quevedo's house after Saad's release from prison in July 1943, although it is not clear in the memo whether the informant is one of these two sources or the FBI agent simply recycled information from the earlier report, as they were wont to do on many occasions.[84]

The FBI was not the only counterintelligence agency to track Saad and his labor activities. In September 1943, Vernet Gresham, assistant military attaché and executive for special intelligence, prepared a secret memo based on information from a confidential source on communist activities in Ecuador. Gresham reported that the PCE had organized a secret congress of representatives of workers' unions in Guayaquil from August 13–15, 1943. Delegates elected Saad as the secretary-general of the Federación de Obreros (Laborers' Union). Among the topics delegates discussed was a decision that the unions should support José María Velasco Ibarra in the 1944 presidential election. Participants planned to draft a detailed list of living expenses to illustrate how workers' incomes fell far below the cost of living, and to distribute the information among workers to show "how much they are being exploited by capitalism." Gresham editorialized, "Undoubtedly, the real aim of the list is to encourage Communism among the laborers." He stated that the meeting was part of a dramatic increase in communist activity in Guayaquil. While the communists claimed that they were "a purely local group without international connections," he pointed to a six-sheet mimeographed pamphlet titled "Imperialistic Tendencies among the Democratic Governments" that a sailor had brought from Chile as evidence of international contacts. The pamphlet said that the Allied powers were defending capitalism and called for a workers' revolution as soon as Nazism was defeated. The memo closed with the concern that the communists were making headway in exploiting the local political situation to their benefit. Hoover forwarded a copy of this memo to the State Department, indicating both a certain amount of duplication and cooperation between the different intelligence agencies, as well as, perhaps, the FBI director's attempt to present himself as in charge of all surveillance activities.[85]

When Lombardo Toledano arrived in Guayaquil in late September 1943 after attending a workers' congress in Chile, the FBI reported that "the ostensible purpose of this trip is said to be the consolidation of labor unions of South America into a solid front and at the same time to disassociate in the minds of the public the fact that the labor unions are communistically controled [*sic*] and dominated." The FBI included information about a private meeting with Saad, Briones, and Quevedo in which Lombardo Toledano appointed Saad the Ecuadorian representative of the CTAL. Allegedly, Lombardo Toledano's plan was to organize communist activities on an international level but without using the word "communism." Saad explained to an FBI informant why the party emphasized syndicalism rather than communism. Nominally, it was not the PCE but the labor unions that maintained relations with communists in other countries. Since communists dominated these unions, labor leaders were often party members. Because governments were more willing to give union leaders than communists permission to travel internationally, the party used unions to maintain their connections with other countries.[86] Saad added, "Even though the name of the Communist Party will not be used, the primary ends of the Communist Party, that is social revolution, will still be the primary ends of the CTAL."[87] On other occasions, the FBI highlighted that "in their present activities, Communists make practically no mention of the word 'Communism.' They call it syndicalism."[88] Saad attempted to avoid red-baiting as much as possible. The FBI appeared to be fully aware of the logic behind the labor union's operations, but the documentation includes little indication that the U.S. government used this information to combat its activities in the same way that the CIA later would do.

U.S. surveillance extended to providing an English-language translation of a telegram from Lombardo Toledano to Saad regarding plans for an emergency congress of CTAL leaders in Montevideo, Uruguay, in February 1944. In response to Lombardo Toledano's query, Saad stated that he would need $600 to pay for the trip. Instead of sending money, Lombardo Toledano bought Saad a round-trip ticket on Panagra. Saad ultimately was unable to make the trip when the Ecuadorian government denied him a passport.[89] Other than citing an anonymous source of this intelligence, the documentation does not indicate how the FBI agent was able to access the information, although it may have come from a wiretap on labor leaders in Mexico.[90] Nor is it apparent whether the FBI pressured the Ecuadorian government to deny Saad his travel documents. The level of detail, however, does reveal the extent of penetration of the U.S. security apparatus into Ecuador, including the probable presence of moles in the telegraph and Panagra offices.

Most significantly, the FBI surveillance allows for a fuller understanding of the tensions and dynamics behind labor organizing in Ecuador in the 1940s. In the face of an antagonistic government, local organizers in Ecuador would have hesitated in their attempts to build a unified labor confederation had it not been for the encouragement of CTAL leaders in Mexico and Colombia. Despite U.S. opposition to communist-led organizing, the failure to hold a labor congress in March 1943 is best understood in the context of local political dynamics rather than as a result of external intervention. Nevertheless, the FBI surveillance documents illustrate that despite President Arroyo del Río's best efforts to halt the leftist labor activities, militants maintained their underground organizing campaigns. The networks that Saad and others created helped lay the groundwork for a mass uprising that soon removed Arroyo del Río from power and fundamentally transformed Ecuador's political landscape.

La Gloriosa

GUSTAVO BECERRA

DIPUTADO PROVINCIAL POR ESMERALDAS

GUSTAVO BECERRA operated a bookstore in Quito, and was elected to the 1944–45 Constituent Assembly as a representative of the province of Esmeraldas. Although Becerra was active in the Communist Party and served as its secretary-general from 1940 to 1944, the FBI did not draft a single memo on him and only included sporadic mentions of his activities in other reports. Source: León Borja, *Hombres de Mayo*.

"Revolution" is an oft-abused word. The term comes from the physical world to describe a rotation. In the political realm, it similarly means a change in which those who hold power are replaced with a previously dispossessed class of people. Scholars and politicians, however, often use the expression for any political disruption, even one that lacks an accompanying socioeconomic transformation of society. In the twentieth century, U.S. diplomatic officials commonly reported any disturbance in Latin America and even minor attempted palace coups, regardless of ideology or intent, as "revolutions." A U.S. consul noted that a "revolution" in Ecuador in 1924—in this case, a failed conservative revolt against a liberal government—would not achieve significant dimensions because it lacked a clearly defined political agenda, which is arguably a key element necessary for a successful revolution. In contrast, the consul noted, "A revolution which appealed to the masses, to the barefooted workmen (which this one apparently does not) would undoubtedly be a serious matter in this country."[1] Inadvertently, even the diplomat appeared to acknowledge his inappropriate use of the term.

Two decades later, the Glorious May Revolution (La Gloriosa) aroused mass social forces that threatened to transform Ecuadorian society. It was the closest Ecuador came to experiencing a true social revolution that would remove the ruling class from power and place previously dispossessed people in control of their fates. Workers, students, women, peasants, Indigenous peoples, and low-ranking military personnel revolted against President Alberto Carlos Arroyo del Río. His repressive and corrupt government had become deeply unpopular, particularly after he conceded half of Ecuador's territory to Peru following a 1941 border conflict. At the annual congress of the Partido Socialista Ecuatoriano (Ecuadorian Socialist Party; PSE) in November 1943, Secretary-General Manuel Agustín Aguirre declared that the country was living "under a totalitarian dictatorship vaguely disguised as a constitutional parliamentary system." All power was concentrated in the hands of one person, and all constitutional guarantees and freedoms had been suppressed. The result was an ultra-reactionary and fascist government that was the sworn enemy of the working class.[2] Half a year later, La Gloriosa ushered in a time of euphoric optimism that seemed to signal the emergence of new social relations and the end of economic exploitation and exclusionary state structures. That revolution, the creation of a leftist labor confederation, and the drafting of a new progressive constitution represented a high point of the political left's strength in Ecuador.

The May revolution emerged in the context of other popular revolts in Latin America. With World War II heading toward an Allied victory in Europe, activists leveraged the rhetoric of a global battle for democracy to defeat local dictatorships. Newspapers editorialized on the parallels between authoritarian governments in the Americas and the military dictatorships with which the Allies were at war in Europe, which provided further impetus to grassroots struggles.[3] On May 9, 1944, a general strike in El Salvador led to the downfall of the authoritarian leader Maximiliano Hernández Martínez. The removal of this dictator had repercussions throughout the region, leading to similar uprisings in Honduras, Guatemala, Nicaragua, and Costa Rica. The best known and longest lasting of these events was a massive strike of university students, teachers, and lawyers in Guatemala on June 23 that led to Jorge Ubico's resignation on July 1. This opened the way for Juan José Arévalo's and Jacobo Arbenz's progressive reforms that radically transformed Guatemalan society. Similar student strikes in Nicaragua attempted but ultimately failed to remove Anastasio Somoza García from power.[4] These popular uprisings reflected broad changes in Latin America that involved dramatic increases in working-class political participation, unprecedented labor militancy, and a significant shift to the left. By 1946, democratic and popular administrations governed almost all of Latin America. For a brief period of time, it appeared that the region would finally realize much needed and profound social and political changes.[5]

Political developments in Central America had a direct and unmistakable influence on how popular movements in Ecuador conceptualized their struggles. On the same day that Ecuador's newspapers announced Martínez's departure for exile in Guatemala, transportation workers published a manifesto threatening a similar strike in Ecuador if the government did not allow a presidential election planned for June to proceed without interference.[6] The manifesto caught the U.S. Embassy's attention. "Although talk of strikes was heard in Ecuador before the current situation in El Salvador had crystallized," Chargé d'Affaires James Gantenbein observed, "the idea appears to have gained strength as a result of the success of the recent strike in that country."[7] Assistant Military Attaché Vernet Gresham echoed reports from "fairly reliable sources" that Ecuadorian labor groups were "planning a general strike similar to the recent one in El Salvador which forced Dictator Martínez out of power."[8] The regional repercussions of Martínez's resignation were unambiguous. U.S. intelligence reports highlighted that many observers expected an imminent coup in Ecuador.

In the context of this unrest, the FBI highlighted U.S. economic interests in Latin America in its discussion of subversive political activities. "The solidarity of the Western Hemisphere has been threatened during 1943 by revolutionary movements," the bureau stated in its annual report on the Special Intelligence Service (SIS) program, "which have overthrown some of the governments of Latin American countries." The report observed, "While some such movements are local in nature, not inspired by outside elements, the removal of a government recognized by the United States in itself is detrimental to the Allied war effort in that it effects the flow of vital war materials being obtained from Latin America and causes a break in the present program as it concerns the security of the Hemisphere from Axis influence and penetration."[9] As surely would have been obvious to astute observers by 1944, the Axis powers represented no military threat to the hemisphere. Hence, the argument in favor of supporting dictators to defend the "security" of the hemisphere must be understood in financial rather than ideological or political terms.

Economic considerations not only involved "the flow of vital war materials," as the FBI report stated, but more broadly included an interest in maintaining control over Latin America as a source of cheap raw materials and as a market for finished industrial goods. Policy makers in Washington privileged commercial interests over democratic governance. They supported Arroyo del Río's pro–United States administration in Ecuador, even as critics compared his authoritarian government to the fascist powers in Europe and Japan. U.S. financial interests colored FBI intelligence gathering and highlight the limits of the agency's understanding of factors contributing to La Gloriosa. Nevertheless, despite these shortcomings, the FBI's effective penetration of the Communist Party and affiliated labor organizations provides unparalleled access to internal debates over what path to take to power that the La Gloriosa laid bare.

Military Socialists

Disagreements over the proper approach to follow to achieve true social revolution have long raged through the left. In the 1940s, debates in Ecuador fell out along the lines of whether to engage in a broad electoral front to contest for political office or to collaborate with progressive military officials in an attempt to gain power through what essentially would be a palace coup. Some dogmatic Marxists argued that the objective economic and political conditions were not yet right to take power and instead the left should organize at the grassroots to strengthen popular social movements and raise the class consciousness of its political base. The competing paths to power also reflected divisions within the left. Often the socialists were the most willing to collaborate with governments in power, including forming electoral fronts with the liberals to prevent a conservative victory and accepting ministerial posts to influence the direction of those governments. One wing of the Partido Comunista del Ecuador (Communist Party of Ecuador; PCE) also wanted to collaborate with liberals and socialists to influence government policies, while a more radical wing did not want to compromise on its ideologies and instead worked to organize a strong grassroots movement to raise the public's political consciousness.

In contrast to those who advocated for institutional paths to power or the mobilization of a mass popular movement, military officers organized under the guidance of Colonel Luis Larrea Alba of the Vanguardia Revolucionaria del Socialismo Ecuatoriano (Ecuadorian Revolutionary Socialist Vanguard; VRSE) were repeatedly implicated in armed actions against the current government. Some communists also advocated for direct armed action as the most effective path to power, to take power where power was held. Each option had its advantages and liabilities, and each path met with mixed success. In the 1940s, these debates were not simple theoretical exercises; they had real-life implications as the left first failed, then succeeded, in removing governments from office. Socialists, however, immediately ran into difficulties in collaborating with the administration they had helped place in power. Progressives faced an exceedingly difficult task in unifying the diverse tendencies within their ranks, and in the end many activists were not content with the outcome of the decisions they had made.

Since the colonial period, the military, Catholic church, and wealthy landholders formed a trilogy of conservative forces that controlled Latin America's political and economic structures. In the twentieth century, a dissident tradition in the military (and sometimes in the church) occasionally espoused socialist sympathies. Peruvian General Juan Velasco Alvarado took power in a military coup in 1968 and then implemented far-reaching social legislation that included a progressive agrarian reform program. Former Venezuelan President Hugo Chávez is one of the most celebrated recent instances of this leftist tradition in the Latin American military. Their examples illustrate that the Latin American military was not always a reactionary force but could also be used to command positive societal changes. In Ecuador, the VRSE reflected the considerable extent of socialist penetration into the country's armed forces. Rather than playing their traditional role of providing muscle for wealthy landowners, some low-ranking military officials allied with the working and peasant classes out of which they emerged. Although they never became the dominant tendency in the military, enough career officials joined the VRSE that it became a recognizable political force in the country.

In the 1920s, socialists viewed the military as a place ripe for recruits, which led to U.S. government preoccupation with potential leftist influences on military institutions. La Antorcha, one of Ecuador's first socialist organizations, saw strong potential for socialism emerging out of "the subordinate public employee, the worker of lands (the Indian), the labor apprentice, the common soldier, the school teacher."[10] In 1930, socialist organizing among the rank and file of the military caught the attention of U.S. officials. William Dawson, the U.S. minister in Quito, quoted a socialist handbill contending that "an immense majority of soldiers and lower officers have entered the Army because they are unable to find other means of livelihood." Because most of the soldiers came from a peasant background and would be just as happy working the soil, the Socialist Party urged the Ecuadorian government to provide them with land and tools so they could enjoy a rewarding and productive life. They demanded a raise in wages for common foot soldiers and low-ranking officers who remained in the military, with a commensurate drop in pay for the top brass. The socialists appealed to the soldiers to join them in a common class struggle. "You who have come from the laboring and peasant classes," the handbill stated, "who live in the midst of these classes which feed and clothe you, who have your brothers, your sons, your fathers, in the fields, factories, and workshops; you must not tolerate the impositions of the high chiefs who seek the military dictatorship; no more exploitation of the people; no more massacres of laborers and peasants." The handbill closed with a call for a government of workers, peasants, and soldiers. The State Department expressed concern with the socialists' growing presence in the military.[11]

In 1931, the U.S. Legation in Quito reported extensive communist attempts to organize among soldiers, although it characterized them as largely a failure and reported that the government no longer feared imminent trouble.[12] Nevertheless, PCE leader Ricardo Paredes continued to follow the Comintern line of calling for "the installation of a socialist government of the workers, peasants and soldiers."[13] When Paredes ran for the presidency of Ecuador in 1933, he campaigned as the "candidate of the workers, peasants, Indians, and soldiers," and promised bread, work, land, and liberty for the people. Among other demands, the Communist Party platform included a promise to reduce the salaries of high officials in the army and raise those of soldiers and police. The party also advocated granting military personnel "complete liberty both inside and out of the barracks to express opinions and organize themselves."[14] Whether successful or not, communists presented themselves as making common cause with soldiers.

Under Larrea Alba's guidance, the VRSE came closer to holding state power directly than any of the other leftist currents in Ecuador. Larrea Alba was chief executive for forty-five days after a coup removed President Isidro Ayora in August 1931. Among the socialists in Larrea's government was Ángel Modesto Paredes as minister of public education. Larrea Alba was ousted in October 1931 after attempting to establish himself as a dictator one week before scheduled elections. After leaving power, Larrea Alba moved further to the left and in 1934 ran as a presidential candidate on a socialist-communist popular front coalition ticket but came in a distant fourth. The conservative populist José María Velasco Ibarra won his first of five terms in office that year. That experience seemed to underscore that if the left wanted to take power—which would seem to be necessary to implement its political agenda—it would need to do so through military rather than electoral means.

A naval attaché investigation on political parties in Ecuador in July 1943 noted that Larrea Alba directed the VRSE and published a newspaper called *Vanguardia*. As an indication of the party's importance, the naval attaché reported that the present chief of the armed forces, General Ricardo Astudillo, was allegedly a member. "Even though the organization's members may not be numerous," the attaché concluded, "it is rumored that the organization, because of the military elements comprising it, has possibilities of assuming power by means of a coup d'état at the least suspected time."[15] Other intelligence-gathering agencies echoed these fears that even though the VRSE was small, it was potentially dangerous because it was composed largely of retired army officers, and its military connections provided it with the brute force necessary to overthrow a government.

Ecuadorian governments served at the will of the armed forces, and losing that support could mean their collapse.

The VRSE realized its height of power and prestige in the 1930s and 1940s. In 1960, the socialist Hugo Larrea Benalcazar reported that the VRSE had "died because its leader Larrea Alba was a coward. On several occasions he had the control of the country in his hands, but all of these times he ran away instead of really taking command of the situation as he should have done."[16] Underlying the VRSE's failures were the limits of both the authoritarian tendencies of its leadership and the weaknesses of a military path to a successful socialist revolution that shortcut a much longer and more difficult task of mobilizing grassroots support for a political project by raising the class consciousness of its working class and peasant base. Gaining power and implementing far-reaching social changes remained an illusive goal.

Ecuadorian Democratic Alliance

The left did not realize much more political success through the institutional means of electoral campaigns and collaborating with governments in power than it did through military coups. Leftist parties refused to participate in Ecuador's May 1941 congressional elections because of their disillusionment with the dictatorial and antidemocratic nature of Arroyo del Río's government, the perception of the inevitability of a fraudulent electoral process, and the literacy restrictions that excluded their base of support in the poor urban and rural masses from exercising the franchise. As a result of their abstention, voters' participation, which slowly had been rising throughout the 1930s, dropped noticeably.[17] The left's decision to abstain was perhaps a mistake, because as a result socialists were completely shut out of power. Isolated in its position of firm opposition and facing the twin threats of political repression and a rising cost of living, the left reversed course and decided to compete in the June 1944 presidential election. A confidential FBI source reported on discussions at a private meeting that Pedro Saad had convened that led to a decision to solicit funds from party members and sympathizers for the campaign.[18] Intriguingly, this surveillance reveals a particular preoccupation with the PCE's participation in institutional paths to power, even more so than with possible coup plotting that would have resulted in a break in the constitutional order.

By no means was the left unified in the idea that electoral campaigns were the proper place to dedicate limited resources. A confidential FBI informant who was close to communist leaders in Quito reported on bitter struggles that took place within the party over whether to collaborate with other parties in electoral campaigns. Due to a lack of public support for its candidates, the PCE had reached out to the VRSE. According to this source, the VRSE "rejects all connections with international groups, especially Moscow, under the theory that Moscow does not know the reality of local conditions and therefore cannot properly direct and instruct the Socialist and Communist parties." The VRSE followed a socialist program but was "politically passive, confining itself to propaganda." Unlike the PCE, the VRSE did not see itself as part of an international working-class struggle. The military socialists feared that too close an association with the communists would also subject them to political persecution.[19]

The naval attaché reported that in June 1943, leaders of the Communist and Socialist parties met in Quito to see whether they could unite behind a single presidential candidate, perhaps the perennial populist Velasco Ibarra.[20] According to the FBI, the communists reached out to the socialists despite "a great difference . . . in their doctrines and principles." Both parties were strongly anticapitalist and anti-imperialist, but "the Socialists were bitter enemies of Russia," although they had temporarily changed that position in the context of the war. Nevertheless, the PSE enjoyed legal recognition as a political party, and its advantage of being able to run candidates for office attracted communist attention. The PCE had made overtures to these socialist groups, as well as to independent liberals and other ideologically diverse groups that were united in their opposition to Arroyo del Río in an attempt "to gain popular sympathy and an opportunity to introduce more radical ideas among the people of Ecuador." The two parties and their leaders "experienced bitter controversy," which put the success of their plans of cooperation in doubt.[21]

The populist caudillo Velasco Ibarra was one of Ecuador's most notorious leaders, and he contributed his fair share of political instability to the country. He was a charismatic campaigner who declared, "Give me a balcony and the people are mine," but he had little luck holding on to power once elected. He assumed the presidency for the first time in 1934, but failed to complete a full year before popular opposition to his policies led to his removal. In fact, he finished only one of five terms in office (his third, 1952–56). An FBI agent commented on Velasco Ibarra's first election, "In ten months of administration he accomplished more than many presidents during four years in office." The statement led someone, presumably in the State Department, to quip in a marginal note, "How many Ecuadoran presidents (aside from major dictators) ever had a 4 year term?"[22] The 1930s was a particularly chaotic decade, with frequent extraconstitutional changes of government, which made it difficult to advance any coherent political agenda.

The Latin American left long faced the threat of populist movements that stole the thunder of leftist rhetoric but once in office ruled in favor of the oligarchy. In Ecuador, Velasco Ibarra rode waves of popular discontent to the presidency, but he largely excluded leftists from his administrations. Under his governance, the oligarchy quickly reestablished its financial and political control over the country. Ruling in favor of upper-class interests led to an erosion of his popular support. Although in his campaigns Velasco Ibarra promised popular reforms that appealed to the masses, he came from the privileged upper class and while in power implemented conservative policies that favored his class standing. As a result, Ecuador faced the irony of an environment that gave rise to strong and well-organized popular movements but also maintained a corrupt political system that repeatedly hampered the interests of the majority of the people from the impoverished and marginalized working class. Populist leadership styles fostered divisions on the left and undermined attempts to alter the country's economic and social structures.[23]

In July 1943, diverse political parties combined forces in the Alianza Democrática Ecuatoriana (Ecuadorian Democratic Alliance; ADE) to compete in the following year's election. The ADE grouped the broad opposition to Arroyo del Río's government that included socialists, vanguardists, independent liberals, and conservatives, as well as the newly formed Frente Democrático Nacional (Democratic National Front; FDN) and Unión Democrática Universitaria (University Democratic Union; UDE). In fact, the only party excluded from this eclectic coalition was Arroyo del Río's official Radical Liberal Party, and the desire to remove him from office unified all of his opponents. The ADE claimed to incorporate people from "all professions and religious faiths, all types of employment, all levels of wealth and culture, and all colors and races" to struggle for freedom, national unity, and economic development. Under the slogan "For the Restoration of Democracy and National Unity," the alliance defined itself as antifascist and in favor of a "true democracy" based on free elections with a constitutionally guaranteed right to organize. The ADE pledged to modernize the economy, extend agricultural credit to peasants, establish a minimum wage, and regulate prices. It also emphasized the importance of improving education, especially in rural areas, where the country suffered from 95 percent illiteracy rates that effectively excluded most people from participating in elections. The ADE championed the development of the military into a "democratic force, capable of defending national sovereignty," a not-so-subtle jab at Arroyo del Río's territorial concessions to Peru in the aftermath of the 1941 border war. The alliance would "defend the continent against totalitarianism," a direct statement of support for the Allies' fight against fascism in Europe.[24]

The Communist Party debated whether to support the ADE and at the end of July finally decided to do so, becoming the last party to join the alliance. According to the activist Francisco Pólit Ortiz, ultimately it was not communist hesitancy that delayed their entry but the opposition of conservative parties in the alliance that wanted to exclude the PCE. The conservatives had taken this measure even though the communists' popular front policies had inspired the formation of the ADE. Finally, due to popular pressure, the conservatives consented to the communists' participation.[25]

In explaining the decision to join, the PCE's Secretary-General Gustavo Becerra noted that the party had been engaged in a systematic and serious analysis of the country's situation. He pointed out that the party employed the scientific method of historical materialism to orient its political struggle. Key problems facing Ecuador included a feudalistic agricultural system and a lack of industrialization, both of which hindered economic development and left the country under the control of a small oligarchy. The PCE advocated taking advantage of the conditions that the war created, including accessing financial credit that the United States offered to encourage the development of industry and increase production. These actions would raise the standard of living in the country. For these reasons, the PCE looked to the ADE as the first step to unify forces from divergent sectors in Ecuador to draft a political program and propose a plan of action that would signal the beginning of a program of true national reconstruction. Becerra declared that the PCE was "willing to participate in a great movement that would guarantee a glorious and progressive future for Ecuador."[26] As a reflection of the surveillance agency's priorities, the FBI considered the statement sufficiently significant to translate it in full and to forward it to the State Department and other intelligence agencies as part of a regular report on communist activities in Ecuador. As was typically the case, neither the agents in Ecuador nor FBI Director J. Edgar Hoover in Washington added editorial comments to the translation. Despite the bureau's overt anticommunist agenda, it appeared content to concede analysis of the translation's contents to policy makers.[27]

After extensive discussion, in August 1943 the ADE decided to put Velasco Ibarra forward as its presidential candidate. The decision was not without dispute. With a certain amount of misgiving, the socialists reversed course on their earlier opposition to the populist caudillo and announced their decision to support him as well.[28] Communists made it clear that support for Velasco Ibarra's candidacy was only a mechanism to oppose Arroyo del Río's government. An anonymous FBI source reported that the socialists were "none to [sic] friendly toward Velasco whereas the Communists think he would be the transition candidate."[29] The socialist leader Ángel F. Rojas similarly acknowledged that a Velasco Ibarra presidency would not implement radical policies, but that his government would prepare the country for a passage to socialism.[30] The FBI reported that Saad characterized Velasco Ibarra as ideologically unwieldy and someone who could never fulfill all of the promises he had made.[31] As a consensus candidate, Velasco Ibarra was merely a tool to advance a common agenda.

In February 1944, the FBI reported that Arroyo del Río had become increasingly frightened of opposition activities and took "severe measures to check all possible subversive movements." He refused to allow Velasco Ibarra, who had gone into exile in Chile after leading a failed military insurrection when he lost the 1940 election, to return to Ecuador. Instead, Velasco Ibarra moved to Colombia and campaigned for the presidency from across Ecuador's northern border. Discontent was growing in the army due to the high cost of living and the government's inability to address issues of speculation, inflation, skyrocketing prices, and stagnating wages. In response, the president increased his reliance on the carabineros for security. The FBI noted that a large group of carabineros surrounded the presidential palace twenty-four hours a day. The strong police presence made the president's guests uncomfortable, and even Arroyo del Río's friends had begun to criticize him for his antidemocratic attitudes.[32] Dissent also ran through the governing Liberal Party with the selection of the longtime party stalwart and rabidly anticommunist Miguel Ángel Albornoz to stand for the presidency in the election scheduled for June 2–3, 1944. As the date approached, the ADE grew convinced that the ruling liberal party would not allow a free and fair vote to take place.

May Revolution

At 10 PM on May 28, 1944, only days before the planned election, the military moved against Arroyo del Río's government. The Army Artillery Unit in Guayaquil attacked the *cuartel de carabineros*, the barracks that housed the repressive police force that defended oligarchical interests and formed the president's main base of support. Francisco Arízaga Luque, the leader of the ADE, organized the revolt in collaboration with Captain Sergio Enrique Girón and other low-ranking army officers who had become disillusioned with Arroyo del Río's government after defeat in the war against Peru in 1941. Under Girón's leadership, the army surrounded the barracks of the carabineros and the secret police known popularly as the *pesquizas*. When the carabineros fired on their attackers, the army responded by arming the civilian population and encouraging them to assist in taking control of the city.[33]

Hundreds were killed and more were injured in the attack and subsequent street fighting. Full-scale battles involving army tanks and machine gunfire rolled through Guayaquil's streets. The army burned the carabineros' barracks, thereby forcing their surrender. By daybreak on May 29, most of the fighting was over and the insurgents controlled the city. With the elimination of the carabineros, students organized *guardias cívicas urbanas* (urban civil guards) to patrol the streets. The new police force reported that despite the intense fighting, the situation in the port city was surprisingly calm. From Guayaquil, the revolt spread to the highland cities of Cuenca, Riobamba, and Ambato and finally to the seat of government, in Quito, where comparatively little fighting took place. Protestors encircled government buildings in the capital and paralyzed their operations. Street demonstrations congregated on the Plaza de la Independencia in front of the government palace. Crowds cheered Velasco Ibarra, sang the national anthem, and made impassioned calls for social change. By the evening of May 29, about half of Quito's population was in the streets in support of the uprising. Aguirre noted that while the fighting in Guayaquil on May 28 provided the spark that initiated the revolution, this "extraordinary movement" was won in the capital thanks to the "admirably organized and disciplined people of Quito" who advanced their common agenda. The masses had determined the outcome of these historic events through their unmediated actions on the streets.[34] A general strike had brought success where elections and military coups had not.

Women's committees actively participated in the protests, even though their important roles tend to disappear in subsequent recounting of these events. Women organized a human enclosure around the government palace that forced the surrender of the men stationed inside. The writer, feminist, and communist leader Nela Martínez urged workers to stand firm in their general strike against the old regime and later assumed the role of minister of government in the transitional administration. In the countryside, Indigenous and peasant people joined the uprisings. The longtime activist Dolores Cacuango led Indigenous forces in an attack on the army barracks in Cayambe. Ecuador, one author observed, finally "was in the hands of its legitimate owners."[35] The country appeared to be experiencing a true social revolution.

Having lost virtually all of his support, at 7 PM on May 29 Arroyo del Río and his entire cabinet resigned and took refuge in various embassies and legations in Quito. In the early morning hours of May 30, the carabineros in Quito followed the lead of their counterparts in Guayaquil and surrendered to the army. The military leaders who had participated in the uprising claimed "the support of all the people, principally students, workers, and intellectuals" and declared that soldiers had rebelled "to put an end to the hateful tyranny of traitors whom we can no longer tolerate." The army denied that it desired to take over the government. Rather, power "will be placed in the hands of civilians who will guarantee an immediate return to normality." They promised that this would not be a traditional military or palace coup that had plagued much of Latin American history.[36] They immediately handed power to the ADE, which established provisional ruling juntas in Guayaquil and Quito to govern until Velasco Ibarra could return to the country from his exile in Colombia. A wide variety of people that included conservatives, independent liberals, socialists, and communists served in these juntas, representing the ideological diversity of the ADE coalition. The juntas announced a six-point political program that included agricultural, industrial, labor, and other reforms.[37] The military leaders asserted, "We, the men of the people, captured the government, and we set up a popular regime, the most democratic in this America."[38] The army presented itself as the defenders of the common people.

With the ADE firmly in control of the political situation, Velasco Ibarra returned from his temporary exile in Colombia. Men, women, children, Indigenous peoples, and others "from all stations in life" gave the leader a very warm welcome as he made his way to Quito.[39] On May 31, Velasco Ibarra arrived in the capital. The following day and before the left could present an alternative candidate, Julio Teodoro Salem, the liberal leader of the ADE, proclaimed Velasco Ibarra supreme chief of the republic, the country's seventeenth president in twenty years. Velasco Ibarra entered power with wide and diverse support that crossed all social classes, political persuasions, and sectors of society. As historian Ximena Sosa-Buchholz astutely notes, Velasco Ibarra appealed to many people because he appeared to be a "clean alternative" to the corrupt liberal and conservative parties.[40] The populist leader pledged to struggle for social justice and a transformation of the country's political structures.

Despite appearances that La Gloriosa was a spontaneous uprising, it emerged out of a long and organized struggle. The historian Enrique Ayala Mora recounts intense social movement mobilizations on the eve of the May revolution, with the carabineros shooting protesters simply for shouting "viva Velasco." The public quickly forgot the names of these "innocent victims," although at the time their funerals became an opportunity for students, workers, and other ADE members to denounce Arroyo del Río's excesses.[41] At one such event, the communist Nela Martínez gave a passionate speech at the burial of the young worker María del Carmen Espinoza.[42]

Aguirre declared that the revolution was much more than an armed revolt in Guayaquil. Rather, La Gloriosa was the outcome of "a series of conspiracies continuously made and dissolved, of dangerous and difficult clandestine organizing efforts that were developed over time and under the threat of violence from a tyrannical government." Activists needed to plant and awaken public discontent in a population that seemed to have lost hope for a better future. The work of unmasking the government was not one of days or even months, Aguirre proclaimed, but of years. The result, the socialist leader asserted, was that for the first time in history the popular masses formed the core of a revolutionary movement. The working class used its tools of a general strike to shut down an oppressive government and open the path toward revolutionary changes.[43] Aguirre overstated the uniqueness of the May revolution, but his description does offer a sense of the optimism and euphoria that it fostered. Hopes were high that the removal of Arroyo del Río would lead to a profound societal transformation, that this would be a true revolution.

U.S. Perspectives

At 1 AM on May 29, Harold Williamson, the U.S. consul general in Guayaquil, sent a telegram marked "urgent" to the State Department in Washington that stated, "Revolution has broken out in Guayaquil area. Situation serious. Americans apparently safe."[44] An hour later, the State Department received a second telegram from Ambassador Robert Scotten in Quito that also relayed the news of the outbreak of a revolution. The situation in Quito was calm, but communication had been cut off with Guayaquil.[45] At noon, Williamson communicated the content of a military proclamation defending the uprising. He reported that Guayaquil was relatively quiet but that he had no news from the rest of the country.[46] Throughout the course of the day, a flurry of telegrams

continued to pour into Washington from both Quito and Guayaquil with up-
dates on the progress of the May revolution.

The political unrest in Ecuador altered the standard practice that the FBI had
established for communicating information it had collected from its agents with
the State Department in Washington. Initially, most of Hoover's correspondence
entailed forwarding unsigned memos and reports that his field agents had assembled on internal political affairs in Latin America. As time went on, he would
include a brief summary in his cover letter highlighting what he saw as the key
points in the attached report. On the eve and in the immediate aftermath of La
Gloriosa, however, Hoover delivered a series of letters to the State Department
that lacked the customary attachments. Instead, the entire communication was
composed of his own letter, as if officials in the central FBI office were summarizing and elaborating on intelligence that they had received directly from the
field. Professional correspondence typically includes the initials of a typist, but
none of Hoover's letters carry any such indication, making it difficult to ascertain what type of assistance he might have received in drafting these missives or
even whether the reports are his own work. Some of his correspondence does
not carry his signature, further casting doubt on authorship. Hoover famously
employed an army of ghostwriters to draft not only his correspondence but also
his personal memoirs, and it is highly likely that an assistant was involved with
these communications as well. If that were the case, it is difficult to ascertain
what input Hoover had in drafting the correspondence or even what level of
awareness he had of political developments in Latin America.

The first letter, dated May 27—the day before La Gloriosa—was one page
long and carried the subject heading "Ecuadoran Government Fears Revolt
Prior to National Election, June 2 and 3, 1944." The FBI's "reliable sources"
reported that the Ecuadorian government had expressed "great concern over
the tense political situation" as the elections approached. Street disturbances
had resulted in four deaths, and more had been wounded. Rumors swirled of
a general strike in the face of what was widely believed would be a fraudulent
election. Because the government officials worried that they would not be
able to maintain control, bureaucrats began to draft plans to establish a triumvirate before the elections with Colonel Héctor Salgado in representation
of the carabineros along with an unnamed army officer and a civilian. Hoover
(or someone writing in his name) indicated that Arroyo del Río feared for his
life if he were to remain in Ecuador and had expressed interest in replacing
Colón Eloy Alfaro as ambassador to the United States as a path of escape. His
unpopularity, however, complicated his appointment to a diplomatic post.[47]

Five days before Hoover's letter, the embassy in Quito had already communicated to the State Department that "a source close to two members of the Cabinet" reported plans for a triumvirate "in order to avoid unnecessary bloodshed." The embassy identified the army officer who would participate in the junta as Defense Minister General Alberto Romero.[48] Hoover's information was neither new nor complete. An internal State Department memo reported receipt of information from the FBI on the cabinet meeting and added as an identifying annotation that Salgado was the "chief of civil police" who had "recently visited F.B.I."[49] In fact, for more than two months the embassy had been reporting rumors of a coup, possibly with Arroyo del Río's authorization, and the establishment of some sort of junta to stamp out growing resistance to his government and prevent an opposition victory in the June elections.[50] The embassy believed that the triumvirate could be successful only if the large pro–Velasco Ibarra element in the army approved of the unnamed civilian member.[51] Scotten reported that a previous attempt to establish a triumvirate of Salgado, Romero, and General Ricardo Astudillo, chief of the armed forces, had failed.[52] Despite a desire to stabilize the political situation, a lack of agreement among the conspirators led to the collapse of other attempts to form a triumvirate.[53]

Hoover's second letter was dated May 29, the day after the May revolution broke out, and was titled "Possible Revolutionary Action in Ecuador." It informed Assistant Secretary of State Berle that "information has been received from an outside confidential source to the effect that there exists a possibility of an armed revolution against the incumbent government in Ecuador." According to information from a member of the Acción Revolucionaria Nacionalista Ecuatoriana (Ecuadorian Nationalist Revolutionary Action; ARNE) and José María Plaza, a large number of machine guns were stored on one of the Plazas' haciendas, and the coup plotters were in the process of procuring more arms from Colombia. With this weaponry they would have the necessary military force to launch a general revolution. According to this source, Leonidas Plaza would lead the revolution, and its goal would be to bring Velasco Ibarra to power. The Plaza brothers (Leonidas, Galo, and José María) were not particularly interested in a Velasco Ibarra presidency, but they hoped to use his popularity to force Arroyo del Río from power. Furthermore, the ARNE hoped "to profit by the disturbance and produce a man of their own party who, with nationalistic tendencies, will embrace the Gran Colombia scheme and form an anti–United States bloc in this part of South America." Hoover closed the letter with a disclaimer that "the above data has not been verified by investigation," in essence acknowledging that what the FBI was reporting could amount to little more than wild rumor. In any case, as with all other correspondence, Hoover provided this information to the U.S. Embassy as well as to the War Department (in this case, to Assistant Chief of Staff Colonel L. R. Forney) and the director of naval intelligence.[54]

Several notable aspects of this letter stand out. Immediately obvious is the incomplete and inaccurate nature of Hoover's information. In particular, the Glorious May Revolution did not originate in the ARNE or with the Plaza brothers. The ARNE was founded on February 27, 1942, as a "third-way" movement that opposed both "Yankee imperialist capitalism" and "Bolshevik Marxist imperialism," as well as both conservative and liberal ideologies. Rather than assuming a centrist ideology, as later third-way movements sought to do, Spanish Falangist and Italian fascist movements strongly influenced its ideology. The ARNE drew its support from conservative Catholics, embraced *hispanismo*—a celebration of Hispanic culture—and assumed an extremely nationalist, authoritarian, hierarchical, and doctrinaire position. It opposed the Rio de Janeiro Protocol that ceded territory to neighboring Peru and the leasing of military bases to the United States, but as part of an extremely reactionary nationalism rather than a leftist critique of imperialism. U.S. policy makers feared the ARNE not because it was a leftist movement, but because it threatened to undermine their notions of the type of liberal democracy they sought to foster in Latin America. Members of the ARNE thought that liberal ideas of equality and democracy were absurd and instead favored rule by an enlightened minority. While conservatives denounced the ARNE as communist because of its talk of social justice, its most serious conflicts were with Marxist organizations that denounced it as reactionary, fascist, and totalitarian.[55] In this case, it was its fascist, not communist, tendencies that worried the State Department, although Hoover did not raise that concern in his correspondence. He may not have recognized its ideological proclivities.

The Plaza brothers whom Hoover had suspected as being behind the uprising were indeed independent liberals and strong opponents of President Arroyo del Río, but they also were not partisans of Velasco Ibarra. They followed in the footsteps of their famous father, the liberal General Leonidas Plaza Gutiérrez, who was president twice, from 1901 to 1905 and again from 1912 to 1916. Galo, the best known of the brothers, was born in New York City in 1906 while his father was in exile after running into conflict with Eloy Alfaro, the leader of the 1895 Liberal Revolution. The elder Plaza returned to office in 1912 after removing Alfaro in a military coup that degenerated into a lynch mob that killed Alfaro in Quito. In the 1940s, the brothers led several failed coup attempts against Arroyo del Río—most notably, an assault on May 28, 1942, on the Carondelet Palace that left five carabineros dead and a dozen more people injured. That coup attempt was designed to punish Arroyo del Río for having signed the Rio Protocol on January 28 of that year, although the brothers seemed to be driven as much by opportunism and a thirst for political power as any coherent political vision for change. According to the FBI, the Plazas opposed Arroyo del Río primarily because he did not include them in his government and supported Velasco Ibarra only because they believed they would receive powerful posts in his administration. As for Velasco Ibarra, the FBI had previously concluded that he would embrace "any party and its ideology to further his own political ends, be it Communist, Socialist or Conservative."[56] As a politician, Velasco Ibarra could be as opportunistic as the Plaza brothers.

Despite the FBI's statements, the Plaza brothers did not play a central role in La Gloriosa. The conspirators in Guayaquil allegedly informed José María Plaza of their plans the morning of the coup, but he was highly critical of those who put their hopes in the populist caudillo Velasco Ibarra. Rather than creating democratic openings, according to Plaza, his government degenerated into "primitive populist politics" that led to "prolonged political chaos."[57] Three months before the May revolution a confidential source in Guayaquil told the FBI that no significant organized opposition to Arroyo del Río existed and that any rumors to the contrary were a result of government propaganda designed to justify attacks on the president's opponents.[58] At the same time, a close associate of Velasco Ibarra reported that an uprising was imminent, that the army would support the general population against the current government, and that the Plaza brothers were likely to attempt to take political advantage of the chaos that would result from a coup attempt.[59] Ten days before the coup, the Assistant Military Attaché Vernet Gresham reported, "Prominently mentioned in connection with this strike are the Plaza brothers, Gustavo Becerra (Communist leader), and Amable Páez, leader of the chauffeurs' union."[60] Similarly, a *Newsweek* article declared—without providing supporting evidence to back up its claim—that the Plaza brothers were behind the coup that placed Velasco Ibarra in office.[61] The military intelligence and media reports turned out to be incorrect but may have influenced Hoover's initial assumptions.

In fairness to Hoover, May 29 was a very chaotic day, and in the midst of a coup it takes time to sort out what is happening on the ground. Even so, U.S. diplomatic officials in Ecuador were more quickly and more accurately able to establish the ideological orientation of La Gloriosa than were Hoover and his minions. At 9 AM on May 29, the Guayaquil consul had already sent a cable to the State Department correctly identifying Girón as the military leader and the revolution as being of "Velasco origin."[62] At 6 PM, the consul reported on the leadership of a new civilian advisory committee working with Girón in Guayaquil that was composed of the liberal Francisco Arízaga Luque, the vanguardist Alfonso Larrea Alba, the socialist Ángel F. Rojas, the conservative Efrain Camacho Santos, and the communist Pedro Saad.[63] That afternoon, Scotten had also concluded that the "revolutionary movement is of purely domestic political nature and has not (repeat not) been initiated through Axis influence," a point he reiterated on multiple occasions.[64] Ronn Pineo concludes from Scotten's concern that the uprising might be part of a Nazi plot that he "was close to the situation but far from understanding it."[65] Be that as it may, Hoover was both farther from the situation and farther from understanding it than the ambassador. In the aftermath of earlier coup rumors on March 6, the Legal Attaché's Office in Quito had submitted a twenty-page memo examining the current political conditions in Ecuador. The author surveyed possible sources of Axis financial support that "conceivably could be employed for subversive political activity, although there is no indication that such is the case." While Arroyo del Río's government inevitably would blame any political unrest on Axis influence, the report concluded, "At this writing there exists no factual evidence that would support such an anticipated accusation."[66] Even before the May revolution, the FBI's own intelligence sources in Ecuador clearly underscored that a revolution would have domestic, not foreign, roots, a point that apparently escaped their counterparts in Washington.

As a diplomatic official rather than part of an intelligence-gathering network, Scotten was more concerned in many of his communications with the legitimacy of the new government and whether the United States should recognize it than with its specific ideological orientation. The morning of May 30, Scotten reported from Quito that "the political situation is somewhat obscure." He was, however, the first diplomatic official to mention ADE, the coalition of opposition parties, in relationship to the uprising. He noted that they had published a manifesto and assumed executive power pending the arrival of Velasco Ibarra from Colombia.[67] "Velasco Ibarra is in no sense a constitutional president," the ambassador reported, "although he has been put into power by the will of the vast majority of the population." At present, "Velasco Ibarra in a legal sense could be termed either a dictator or a provisional president with no basis under the law for holding power."[68] Scotten concluded that even though Velasco Ibarra was "an illegal President," since he "came into power with the support popularly estimated at over 90 percent of the people, it would not only do us no harm to give speedy recognition to the new government but on the contrary a prolonged delay in recognition would create an unfriendly atmosphere generally throughout Ecuador which would work against our best interests." To underscore his argument, Scotten noted that the entire staff, as well as the British, Brazilian, and Belgian diplomatic representatives, endorsed this position.[69] Once the U.S. government had convinced itself that neither the Axis nor any other foreign power had inspired the coup, it quickly recognized Velasco Ibarra's government, even though he had not come to power through liberal democratic means.[70]

Hoover's third letter on La Gloriosa, with the subject line "Revolutionary in Ecuador," came several days later, on June 2, and was two pages long—twice as long as the previous one. Instead of mentioning the ARNE, this time the letter simply began "As you know, the revolutionary forces sponsored by the Alianza Democrática Ecuatoriana have been successful in overthrowing the Ecuadorian Government." The letter proceeded to report that Arroyo del Río was in asylum at the Colombian Embassy, and most other members of the cabinet were seeking shelter at various embassies in Quito. (The Associated Press had erroneously reported that Arroyo del Río was at the U.S. Embassy, which caused a certain amount of consternation among State Department officials in Washington.[71] Scotten corrected this misinformation with the explanation that the minister for foreign affairs had inquired whether the disposed president might be granted asylum in the U.S. Embassy, but the ambassador informed him that his government did not recognize the right of asylum.[72]) Velasco Ibarra had arrived in Quito and announced his intention to form a government and call for elections for a constitutional assembly. The new president "would support the Allies, seek to better Latin American relations, and . . . support the Gran Colombian political theory" that favored steps toward a customs union and regional integration among the northern South American countries. Hoover reported that conservatives would support Velasco Ibarra, but evidence emerged of dissension among the parties of the ADE. In particular, the Socialist Party would not be loyal to Velasco Ibarra. The archbishop of Quito also opposed Velasco Ibarra because of his divorce and remarriage.[73] After a communication plagued with incorrect facts three days earlier, this letter finally transmitted largely accurate information.

It is noteworthy that Hoover took it upon himself to report these events to the State Department, and apparently after the State Department's own officials

in its embassy and consulate had already communicated the news directly. Although Hoover does not indicate his sources, he apparently drew on the same
intelligence as the embassy in Quito, even though he introduced dated and
incorrect information into his reports. Consul Williamson reported that on
May 30 the legal attaché in Guayaquil had "informally interviewed members
of the Junta" who informed him that Velasco Ibarra's de facto government supported democracy and the Allied war effort. It would promptly hold elections,
and—reflecting the diplomatic mission's central purpose—the new government would respect U.S. property rights.[74] The following day, Ambassador
Scotten reported on Velasco Ibarra's arrival in Quito. He emphasized that the
new president would follow a "Gran Colombia" policy, possibly the source for
the mention in Hoover's letter.[75]

On June 2, Hoover's office sent the State Department an additional letter, this time following the standard format of a short cover letter followed
by a seven-page, unsigned report titled "Revolution in Ecuador" that provides
much more detail on the events of May 28. That document, presumably drafted
by SIS personnel in Ecuador, observed that Velasco Ibarra "does not enjoy the
confidence of the more educated anti-administration elements and politicians,
but he is the only available candidate who possesses political appeal among
the great percentage of the voting public." Pointing to an underlying purpose
for watching internal political developments so closely, the anonymous author
acknowledged a lack of "evidence indicating organized Axis subversive elements
to be currently influencing or leading any of the Ecuadoran political parties."
Ironically, the FBI's own reports undermined their purported justification for
conducting surveillance in the rest of the hemisphere. A cover note from the office of Foreign Activity Correlation in the State Department embraced the report
"as being quite clear, and it contains some biographical data on several of the
revolutionary leaders which may be of interest." Drawing on text from previous dispatches and including misspellings in names, the memo provided brief
sketches of the central "revolutionary personalities" that reflected the ideologically eclectic nature of the May revolution.[76] Noticeably absent is any mention
of the ARNE or the Plaza brothers, who Hoover assumed in his first letter were
behind the revolt. That intelligence failure was quietly dropped without explanation or apology.

Hoover's shortcomings are also significant because the transmittal of diplomatic reports that proved to be more accurate than what he provided was built
directly on the backbone of the political intelligence and surveillance networks
that the FBI had constructed in the country. In an annual report on the SIS

program, Hoover boasted that the background information that the FBI had prepared on the people involved in revolutionary movements was "of valuable assistance to the State Department" in deciding how to respond to a newly established government.[77] In the case of Ecuador, the agency claimed, "Investigation by our representatives disclosed no subversive elements to be controlling the revolutionary movement," even though this is not what Hoover initially reported.[78] In addition, Hoover highlighted the "vital importance" of the radio facilities that the legal attachés had installed in embassies for transmitting information on political developments to Washington. In most cases, he stated, as if to justify his activities, "no other means of communication has been open while the revolutionary movement was in progress."[79] The value of the radio equipment in the Legal Attaché's Office became apparent, he reported, when "during the revolutionary movement of May 1944, it was the only contact between Quito and the outside world. At that time, it was the only means of rapid communication available to the Ambassador and the Military and Naval Attaches as well as to the Bureau's representatives."[80] The irony, however, is that while that communication passed through the FBI's hands, the bureau apparently was not able to make use of it to provide more accurate information on the political upheaval coursing through the country.

At the time Hoover bragged, "The Bureau's radio facilities at Quito were used exclusively by the American Ambassador in communicating with the State Department, which enabled the Ambassador to forward information while the revolution was in progress." Furthermore, Hoover stressed, "The Legal Attaché advised that practically all information forwarded by the Ambassador to the State Department had been furnished by the Legal Attaché's office."[81] The FBI repeated these claims in its history of the SIS. Because of "the Bureau's many contacts and confidential informants, it was possible for Bureau representatives to keep abreast of the many and varying revolutionary intrigues and plots." That book further states, "During the revolution of May 28–29, 1944, practically all of the information concerning the revolution and its ramifications which was reported by the Ambassador had been furnished by the Legal Attaché's Office. It was sent by the Ambassador to the State Department via Bureau radio facilities." According to the FBI, Ambassador Scotten "was at all times kept informed for which he verbally expressed his appreciation to the Director on November 2, 1945."[82] And indeed, as events unfolded at the end of May, Scotten did acknowledge the bureau's key logistical role in facilitating communications when he needed guidance on appropriate diplomatic action. The ambassador had specifically requested that the

State Department "telegraph approval immediate instructions through the FBI."[83] Hoover successfully positioned the FBI as a key information broker for U.S. concerns that extended well beyond the original antifascist justification for the agency's presence in the region.

Not only did the embassy use the FBI's radio to communicate with Washington, but the State Department also used those same facilities to send messages back and forth between the embassy in Quito and the consulate in Guayaquil. Soon, however, the embassy and consulate were communicating with each other through a private Panagra wire, a connection that an undercover FBI agent working with the airline likely facilitated.[84] Nevertheless, the embassy continued to rely on the FBI's infrastructure to send messages from the military and naval attachés in Ecuador to their respective departments in the United States.[85] The embassy also used the FBI's radio facilities to assist diplomatic officials from other countries. On the afternoon of May 29, Scotten forwarded a request to the State Department from the Cuban minister to inform his government in Havana about the political situation in Ecuador. The State Department complied with the request with a telegram to the embassy in Havana and instructions to forward the message to the Cuban Ministry of State.[86] The diplomatic officials even used the communication network to inform financial institutions in the United States about the status of their businesses in Ecuador, underscoring the central role of the embassy in facilitating commerce.[87]

A year after the May revolution, Hoover's assistant Edward Tamm emphasized to bureaucrats in Washington that on two occasions (the other being during similar events in Paraguay) the FBI's radio system was the only channel of communication between the embassies and the State Department.[88] Despite his intelligence failures, Hoover never hesitated to champion statements in favor of his agency that would justify an expansion of his empire. Without the intelligence-gathering structures Hoover had established, the United States would not have been able to maintain such close surveillance of political developments in Latin America. Notwithstanding occasional shortcomings, the FBI agents also provided key insights into internal discussions that led up to the revolt.

In the immediate aftermath of the May revolution, the U.S. Consulate General in Guayaquil sent the FBI's legal attaché Raymond O'Mara to interview the ADE's civil-military committee to verify its information on recent events. U.S. Consul Williamson sent O'Mara because "it would have been inappropriate for the Consulate General directly to approach the de facto authorities," and the legal attaché's "position is more or less independent of the Consulate." In the weeks after the May revolution, the Guayaquil consulate continued to rely on O'Mara to maintain contact with the leaders of La Gloriosa. The ADE conspirators informed the legal attaché that they had planned simultaneous uprisings throughout the country, but, their carefully laid plans were accelerated when the carabineros attacked a truckload of army conscripts as the insurgents were moving into their positions. According to Scotten, most people in Quito learned of the revolt only through a fragmentary story on the front page of *El Comercio* on the morning of May 29. In Guayaquil, reflecting the State Department's key concerns, the junta leaders satisfied the FBI officer that U.S. property and economic interests in Ecuador would be protected. Support for democratic governance and the Allied war efforts were of only secondary concern.[89]

The FBI also helped document the role of the communists in the uprising. Apparently drawing on O'Mara's collaboration with the Guayaquil consulate, the FBI reported that Saad had no knowledge of the planned coup until the afternoon of May 28—hours before it was to begin. Rather than involving the communists in the planning and execution of the coup, the ADE leadership wanted to know whether they would support an uprising if the army backed it. The ADE messenger promised to let the communist leader know of plans as they developed, but Saad found out about the coup attempt only when he heard shooting in the streets. At that point, the insurgents asked the Communist Party to send anyone with military training. The communists apparently joined the uprising only after it was in progress and later attempted to guide its direction.[90] If true, this would alternatively highlight attempts within the ADE to isolate the communists or provide an example of the ideological incoherence of the May revolution that ultimately led to its failure.

A year earlier and at the height of World War II, the FBI's legal attaché reported that many PCE members were opportunists. He cautioned that the communists might be allies during the war but would present a real danger afterward.[91] This perception would explain why the ADE might have wanted to exclude the communists from its plans. Nevertheless, as Ecuador returned to normal after the May revolution, Consul Williamson reported from Guayaquil, "The Communist labor leader Pedro Saad has personally appealed to workers to go back to jobs and turn in arms."[92] An FBI report echoed, "That there have not been as many political demonstrations and riots as expected may be due in large part to the policy of labor and Communist leaders."[93] Despite initially viewing the communists as dangerous opportunists, such statements came to characterize some FBI field agents' interpretations of the PCE's actions.

In a letter to the State Department dated June 6, Hoover highlighted information from unnamed "confidential and reliable sources" that in the aftermath of the May revolution "the Communists are reported to have demanded, and will probably obtain, the right to legalize the Communist Party, which will enable them to spread Communist propaganda among the people." Hoover expressed this as his primary concern, despite acknowledging the decidedly anti-leftist nature of Velasco Ibarra's new government. The cabinet featured the prominent presence of two strongly conservative politicians (Camilo Ponce Enríquez as minister of foreign affairs and Mariano Suárez Veintimilla as minister of agriculture) who historically had demonstrated pro-Axis and Falangist sympathies. In a position that was somewhat out of step with State Department policy and even the attitudes of some FBI agents on the ground, Hoover was not as bothered by their presence in the government as he was by that of two leftists: the socialist Alfonso Calderón Moreno, who was in charge of public welfare, and the communist sympathizer Carlos Guevara Moreno, the secretary-general of the administration. (On July 28, Velasco Ibarra also appointed the communist Alfredo Vera as minister of education.) While the conservatives actively supported Velasco Ibarra, the socialists demanded that Calderón Moreno resign his post because of the party's lack of control over the government's policy. If Hoover were truly concerned about fascist penetration of Latin America, he could have expressed more sympathy for the leftists who offered the most consistent and reliable support for the Allied cause.[94] In contrast, Hoover was more relieved that leftist influence in Velasco Ibarra's cabinet had been temporarily bypassed than he was concerned with the presence of Falangist and anti-Allied elements that provided the original justification for the FBI's presence in the hemisphere.[95]

A later FBI report "from a confidential and reliable source" indicated that the Communist Party had been legalized and Saad's influence with Velasco Ibarra had greatly increased. Saad briefly served in the Consejo Administrativo Revolucionario (Revolutionary Administrative Council) until Velasco Ibarra arrived in Quito to assume power. Saad urged the revolutionaries to maintain control of the situation and encouraged the public to resume their normal labors. He exercised a great deal of influence in the government due to his leadership position in the workers' movement and his personal friendship with Velasco Ibarra. According to the anonymous FBI informant, Saad refused a cabinet post as minister of government to remain active in the labor movement and instead became a deputy in the assembly.[96] Such reports of growing communist influence alarmed Hoover.

Ambassador Scotten presented a different interpretation of leftist participation in Velasco Ibarra's government. According to "a reliable source close to Socialist circles," the leftist parties had originally barred their members from accepting posts in the new government because "Velasco Ibarra's dominating character" would limit and compromise their effectiveness. The socialists, however, permitted the "very bourgeois" Calderón to join the administration to prevent the portfolio of social welfare from ending up in conservative hands and thereby strengthening the control of "nationalistic rightist elements" over the government. At the same time, according to Scotten, the left was concerned that open opposition to Velasco Ibarra would permit Arroyo del Río's supporters to reorganize before they could be completely destroyed. In particular, leftist student leaders expressed concern about the direction of the new government and warned Velasco Ibarra that they could bring down his government just as easily as they did Arroyo del Río's.[97] The embassy betrayed more concern about a strong conservative and potentially pro-Axis presence in the government than Hoover, who consistently embraced anticommunist paranoia.

Scotten reported that the political left had emerged from La Gloriosa in a significantly strengthened position. He worried, "Once it becomes evident that the Communist Party can work openly without fear of persecution of its members, many who are now only sympathizers and hangers-on will affiliate themselves with it." Furthermore, with the dissolution of the Comintern a year earlier, the youth wings of the various leftist parties believed that the principal dividing issue between them had been eliminated, and they advocated for a move toward a unified organization. An older and more established generation, however, sought to retain their separate institutional identities. Saad betrayed suspicions that the socialists would attempt to sabotage communist organizing. Scotten noted that in the absence of recent honest elections, it was hard to judge the left's true strength, but if the PCE, PSE, and VRSE were able to unify their forces, "the three parties could presumably constitute an impressive political force."[98] The embassy understood that the political winds in Ecuador had shifted and sought to adopt its positions to that new political reality.

Dating back to the first FBI agent Edgar Thompson's original mission to Ecuador in 1940, the bureau had maintained a long and close relationship with the carabineros that ended up on the losing side of the May revolution.

In particular, the FBI preserved this association with the carabineros' Commander Salgado, who was imprisoned in the immediate aftermath of the uprising. Shortly before La Gloriosa, the Guayaquil consulate reported that a legal attaché just "happened to be present" when Salgado instructed the carabineros to "watch out for the Velasquistas but not interfere with the supporters of Sr. Albornoz," the government's heir apparent to the presidency.[99] The statement intended to report the nature of political tensions a month before the planned elections but inadvertently reveals the close nature of the FBI's collaboration with the repressive police forces. The carabineros were central to FBI intelligence work in Ecuador, and they did not want to give up that advantage.

On June 6, 1944, Velasco Ibarra signed a decree that transformed the carabineros into a civil guard. He justified this action by saying that they had failed to comply with their original mission to maintain order in society and "instead were responsible for criminal attacks on democracy and against the rights of citizens." He charged that Arroyo del Río had placed the carabineros "at the service of an electoral fraud and political oligarchs who had spread terror and corruption in the country."[100] Williamson reported that the new force was "ill-trained and undisciplined," in part due to a lack of adequate pay and qualified leadership. The army stepped in to fill the gap until an appropriate police force could be established.[101] With the disappearance of the carabineros, the FBI considered moving its police liaison agents to Bogotá because they would no longer have a useful role to play in Ecuador. Scotten, however, had acquired a positive view of the bureau's counterintelligence activity and objected to this transfer. With the ambassador's urging, the FBI left its officials in Ecuador. The FBI agents quickly secured contacts in the new Ecuadorian police force that replaced the carabineros, and the police-training program proceeded as before. The FBI continued its surveillance of leftist activists without skipping a beat.[102]

In the weeks after La Gloriosa, FBI agents continued to draft lengthy narrative summaries of recent political developments. The reports contained surprisingly little interpretive analysis or indications of an underlying ideological agenda. Nevertheless, the concerns of a security apparatus could emerge almost inadvertently. Toward the end of one such twenty-one-page report, the unnamed author inserted a brief description of communist participation in a march in support of Velasco Ibarra. Included among the mass of ten thousand people was a small contingent "of roughly 40 individuals who identified themselves as Communists by carrying the Soviet flag," apparently a reference to the red communist hammer-and-sickle banner. Seemingly highlighting both the communists' weakness and strength, the report noted, "This small group was the only section in the entire parade that marched in unison." The FBI report conceded that the march reflected a total absence of "Axis subversive political activity or suspicion thereof," and agents had found only isolated and insignificant expressions of anti–United States sentiments. The effort to generate such detailed reports did not seem to match the bureau's stated security concerns and objectives of countering Nazi infiltration into the hemisphere. Instead, their investigations demonstrated that the May revolution was of a purely domestic nature and did not represent a threat to the international order or the Allied war effort.[103]

In another twenty-page report, which included mention of the nomination of potentially pro-Nazi officials to office, Hoover highlighted in his cover letter to the State Department only PCE attempts "to gain minor government positions and capitalize on the part they played in the revolution." The FBI director was concerned that the communists had been in contact with "[CTAL President] Lombardo Toledano in Mexico for advice and instructions and [would] attempt to change and enforce the labor laws, develop agricultural cooperatives, revise terms of foreign concessions to nationalize such enterprises, and will endeavor to establish contacts with army personnel."[104] The same concern emerges in the FBI's annual report on the SIS program. "Through informants," the bureau reported, "the Office of the Legal Attaché maintains efficient coverage of Communist developments." In particular, agents continued their surveillance of Saad and especially of his relations with Lombardo Toledano.[105] In the midst of a global battle against fascism, Hoover retained an overriding fixation on communists.

Unlike the FBI, the State Department was concerned with Nazi rather than communist influence in La Gloriosa. Consul Williamson provided a detailed and graphic description of the insurrectionary events as they unfolded in Guayaquil. He reported that no Nazi or foreign influence was apparent in the junta, but "what is apprehended by the more stable classes is the distinctly leftish caste of many of those in power in Guayaquil." He noted that the "strong men" of the Guayaquil junta that took power were the ADE's liberal leader Arízaga; VRSE's representative Alfonso Larrea Alba; and, "of course Sr. Pedro Saad the 'communist' labor leader." The consul observed, "Saad has shown considerable ability as a leader during the emergency; in many instances he has prevented his followers from looting as well as having at length induced the laborers to go back to work when the time came." Nevertheless, Williamson feared that as a result Saad had "cemented his position and it may well be that later on he will demand as labor's reward some concessions from capital." Even so, in a memo attached to Williamson's report, a State Department official echoed with some relief the consul's observation that "certainly no Nazi or foreign influence [was] apparent before, during or after the revolution."[106] Former Ambassador Boaz Long reported from his new post in Guatemala that although he had been gone for more than a year, in his assessment "the recent rebellion had little to do with communism or any Soviet activity." Instead, he interpreted La Gloriosa in light of a recent pattern of rapid political changes in the country.[107] With the collapse of Jorge Ubico's regime, Long had reason to view events in Latin America through a quite different lens from Hoover's. His perspective generally reflected that of the diplomatic corps in Latin America.

In Scotten's own report to the State Department, drawing in part on Williamson's comments, the ambassador observed, "There is no evidence whatever that Axis influences played a part in the revolution, and there is every reason to believe that it was an exclusively internal movement." He reiterated the new government's intention to collaborate with the Allied war effort and its desire for warm relations with the United States. Unlike Hoover, Scotten was most concerned with the potentially disruptive actions of the most conservative members of Velasco Ibarra's cabinet. Minister of Agriculture Suárez Veintimilla had been the editor of the conservative newspaper *El Debate*, which the ambassador characterized as pro-Nazi, and Foreign Affairs Minister Ponce Enríquez "has been associated with activities of totalitarian ideology."[108] Suárez Veintimilla in particular was eager to meet with U.S. officials to justify his pro-Franco attitudes and the use of the German Transocean news service in *El Debate*, even as he denied holding pro-Axis perspectives.[109]

In contrast to Scotten's relief at the absence of direct Axis influence in the new government, he expressed concern about the inherent weaknesses of the new government. Among the ambassador's apprehensions were the heterogeneous nature of Velasco Ibarra's coalition, the caudillo's "unstable temperament," his failure to consult with the ADE or include more people from Guayaquil in his government, and the marginalization of leftist voices. These factors were already leading to a fall in the new president's popularity. Velasco Ibarra's speech in Quito "was too rightist to suit his leftist following," the ambassador observed. Labor and leftist organizations were already pressing for the president to address urgent economic issues. Scotten had little doubt that popular disillusionment with the government would quickly grow.[110]

A week before the July 23 elections for a constituent assembly that would write a new constitution, Vice Consul Juan Gorrell drafted a memo for Scotten on Ecuador's internal political situation that was at least as critical of the right as it was the left. Gorrell interviewed Manuel María Pólit Moreno, a conservative Catholic cleric and director of the Catholic newspaper *La Patria*, who described the country as very politically polarized. Pólit Moreno called for U.S. intervention to maintain that country's influence and avoid political chaos. He pledged that the right was the only sector that could be counted on to cooperate with the United States. Gorrell did not appear to reciprocate these warm feelings entirely to the conservatives. Rather dismissively, he reported Pólit Moreno's repetition of "the usual Rightist claims that the Left was simply a minion of Moscow, bent on eliminating American influence in South America, commercial and other."[111] Neither Gorrell nor Scotten expressed as much alarm concerning the political course that Ecuador was taking as did the Catholic cleric or, for that matter, the director of the FBI. In the context of collaboration with the Soviet Union in the battle against fascism, communism did not appear to be that serious a threat.

The political uses of information flowing from Ecuador to Washington during La Gloriosa reflect the contrast in perceptions and attitudes between the State Department and the FBI. While Hoover remained steadfast in his anticommunist positions, diplomats were willing to work with leftists if that would mean a more congenial and stable atmosphere for U.S. business interests. Despite the FBI's undercurrent of anticommunist paranoia, its field reports highlight that the PCE was unprepared to take maximum advantage of the disruptions that La Gloriosa provided. While the May revolution was not of their making, party leaders now scrambled to catch up with the dramatic political shifts surging through the country. The FBI's preoccupation with communism provides a rare window into the thinking and actions of those leftist militants.

CHAPTER 5

Constitution

MANUEL AGUSTÍN AGUIRRE
DIPUTADO POR LOS TRABAJADORES

Daniel
León B.

MANUEL AGUSTÍN AGUIRRE represented a left wing of the Socialist Party that often took political positions close to the Communist Party. He served as secretary-general of the Socialist Party on multiple occasions. Aguirre taught economics at Quito's Central University and was a leading socialist intellect. Labor unions designated Aguirre as one of their representatives in the 1944–45 Constituent Assembly, and the assembly selected him as its second vice president. Source: León Borja, *Hombres de Mayo*.

La Gloriosa introduced a period of high expectations for deep changes in Ecuador. Leftists thought May 28 was the beginning of a social revolution. The Partido Comunista del Ecuador (Communist Party of Ecuador; PCE) emerged from La Gloriosa with more legitimacy than it had previously enjoyed but ended up weaker than ever before. It was a curious dilemma. Seemingly objective conditions should have played to the left's advantage. With Carlos Arroyo del Río's repressive governing apparatus gone, popular organizing flourished. Workers, peasants, Indigenous peoples, and others who formed the left's base held congresses and outlined far-reaching policy proposals. The Alianza Democrática Ecuatoriana (Ecuadorian Democratic Alliance; ADE) also pressured José María Velasco Ibarra to draft a new constitution to codify the changes they anticipated making in society. In July 1944, the electorate gave the left a majority in the Constituent Assembly, and the resulting constitution was the most progressive in Ecuador's history. Even U.S. officials applauded the communists for their moderate and respectable policies. Why was the PCE unable to leverage these factors to its advantage? The reason, in part, was that the large communist presence in the assembly and the redirecting of resources into electoral campaigns came at the expense of taking some of the party's best organizers off the streets, where they had been building mass popular movements. Leftist participation in the assembly highlights the tradeoffs of attempting to legislate political change, as opposed to creating new political structures through mobilized social movements on the streets.

The left's support for Velasco Ibarra ultimately undermined its political position. Velasco Ibarra was not a leftist but a populist who excelled at mobilizing the masses through large political gatherings and moralistic rhetoric. His style of campaigning broke from the previous highly exclusionary nature of electoral politics, with participation rates that hovered around 3–5 percent of the population. Even so, the policies that he implemented once in office primarily benefited upper-class economic interests. His personalistic style meant that he failed to build the institutions that would help sustain him in power or extend a political project beyond support for his person. Velasco Ibarra's pop-ulism limited the implementation of the social transformations that the ADE had promised in its electoral platform.

A lack of ideological coherence in the ADE coalition grounded in the con-cerns and demands of Ecuador's popular movements allowed for populist rather than leftist rhetoric to emerge as the dominant discourse after the May revolution. Missing from the governing juntas were the voices of work-ers, peasants, women, and other marginalized people, leaving instead sym-pathetic members of the dominant classes to represent their concerns. The initial presence of competing governing juntas in Guayaquil, on the coast, and Quito, in the highlands, reflected the fractured regional nature of Ec-uadorian politics. Military and political leaders in Guayaquil resented their marginalization when their counterparts in Quito formed a new government without consulting them. Since those in Guayaquil were responsible for the political rupture that removed Arroyo del Río and allowed for Velasco Ibar-ra's return, they believed that the new president should have conferred with them before naming government ministers. Furthermore, some members of the ADE were disappointed that Velasco Ibarra assumed dictatorial powers, especially since preserving constitutional structures had been one of their primary objectives. Activists in Guayaquil, according to the U.S. consul, did not trust the caudillo's "hot-headed and autocratic tendencies." In addition, labor leaders feared that the new administration's policies would not justify the sacrifices that they had made to realize these political changes.[1] Rather than unifying the diverse tendencies in the ADE, Velasco Ibarra alienated many of its members. Ultimately, these factors would limit the depth of the reforms that the new government would be able to implement.

A certain amount of political intrigue surrounded Velasco Ibarra's return to power in the aftermath of the May revolution. Manuel Agustín Aguirre, leader of the Partido Socialista Ecuatoriano (Ecuadorian Socialist Party; PSE), placed the blame for this development squarely at the feet of the communists. Because of conservative opposition, the PCE had been the last to join the ADE, but they were also among the most enthusiastic supporters of Velasco Ibarra. In 1943, the PCE had declared that *el gran ausente* (the great absent one, referring to Velasco Ibarra's frequent exiles) was the only person capable of carrying for-ward the ADE's program of liberating the toiling masses.[2] By all rights, accord-ing to Aguirre, the ADE's presidential nomination belonged to the independent liberal Francisco Arízaga Luque, the founder of the alliance, not to the popu-list caudillo. Because of petty rivalries and opportunism, the PCE forced the candidacy to go to Velasco Ibarra, and that resulted in an opening to the right and a closing of the possibilities of agrarian and other reforms.[3] The communists sensed a historic opportunity to grab power and were hesitant to reverse course and oppose the president. Velasco Ibarra, however, was not committed to social, economic, or racial justice, much less to class struggle. Meanwhile, the unwieldy political forces that had brought the ADE together in the Glorious May Revolution began to unravel. Conservatives broke off into the Frente Electoral Velasquista (Velasquist Electoral Front; FEV), which further limited the coalition's ability to achieve reforms. These competing and divergent interests tore at the unity that had made the May uprising possible.

Despite problems in holding the ADE together, the next several months witnessed an explosion of popular organizing. Groups that had been prevented from gathering under Arroyo del Río's repressive government capitalized on this political opening to put forward their political agendas. Students, workers, women, peasants, Indigenous peoples, agriculturalists, and others all held meetings during the months of June to August. With the ADE's shrinking ability to push through reforms, more of the impetus for social change came from the growing force of popular movements.

The most significant of these grassroots movement meetings was a labor assembly that resulted in the formation of the Confederación de Trabajadores del Ecuador (Confederation of Ecuadorian Workers; CTE), Ecuador's first national leftist labor confederation. More than a thousand workers, artisans, peasants, Indigenous rights activists, intellectuals, and socialist and communist political leaders, as well as anarcho-syndicalists, gathered at the beginning of July 1944 to draft a platform to "better workers' economic and social situation and defend their class interests."[4] The CTE sought to improve the living conditions of the masses through industrializing the country, raising salaries, shortening the workweek, protecting the right to strike, eliminating feudal trappings in agriculture, defending democracy, and embracing other elements that favored the proletariat within the framework of an international working-class struggle. Delegates elected the prominent communist labor leader Pedro Saad as president of the CTE and the socialist lawyer Juan Isaac Lovato as vice president. The CTE established close relations with the communist-dominated Confederación de Trabajadores de América Latina (Confederation of Latin American Workers; CTAL). After the aborted attempt in March 1943, the successful creation of the CTE was one of the most significant and concrete achievements of the May revolution.

Velasco Ibarra agreed to support the CTE congress in exchange for the socialist Alfonso Calderón assuming the portfolio of social welfare in his government.[5] According to Ambassador Robert Scotten, leftist leaders had rushed to organize the CTE before Velasco Ibarra had gained sufficient strength to prevent them from doing so. At the same time, the Catholic church had not opposed the labor organizing, as it had done the previous year. Conservative opposition to the organizing of 1943 had backfired in that it strengthened the ability of leftist labor to mobilize workers to support their agenda. Some Catholic observers maintained that fewer frontal or direct attacks on communism could prove to be more effective in curtailing their actions.[6] The global environment also provided a propitious occasion for the formation of a leftist labor federation. The United States still maintained collegial relations with the Soviets in a common battle against fascism, and the onset of the Cold War was still several years off on the horizon.

Diplomatic officials recognized that Velasco Ibarra's government was torn between its conservative and progressive supporters, and in this context the left was growing in strength. The communists came out of La Gloriosa, and in particular the founding of the CTE, in a strengthened position. The embassy in Quito reported that the socialists and communists were locked in competition for control of the labor movement, and currently the communists were in a more dominant position in both labor and broader political activism. The communists had become so powerful that the socialists considered withdrawing from their alliance to avoid being absorbed into the communist movement. The military socialists organized into the Vanguardia Revolucionaria del Socialismo Ecuatoriano (Ecuadorian Revolutionary Socialist Vanguard; VRSE) had less support and did not present serious competition to the other two. The conservatives had lost much of their influence, and Ambassador Scotten feared that the entire country might come under communist control. At least in the short term, the communists leveraged the May revolution to their benefit.[7]

Constituent Assembly

On July 23, 1944, the Ecuadorian electorate (literate men and women, about 5 percent of the population) picked delegates for an assembly to write a new constitution. Leading up to the vote, U.S. diplomats in Ecuador noted rising tensions, particularly between the left and right wings of the movement that had removed Arroyo del Río from power. In the end, the election passed largely without incident. The 1930s had been a time of growing strength for the left, and together with their significant participation in the events of May, socialists led the ADE to victory in the elections. Of the parties grouped into the ADE coalition, socialists held thirty-one of the assembly's ninety-eight seats and communists had nine more. In comparison, the liberals held twenty-nine seats, and the conservatives held twenty-four. It was one of the left's highest points of electoral strength in the country's history. Communist leaders played active roles in the assembly and helped push through reforms that benefited the rural and urban working classes. Socialists intended to use this opportunity "to write a revolution" because, as Aguirre later commented, a "revolution is not only the triumph of arms, but more than anything it is changing the fundamental bases of the socio-economic organization" of state structures.[8] This large and significant leftist presence in the assembly resulted in the most progressive constitution that Ecuador had implemented.

Consul Harold Williamson maintained that the left fared better than predicted because "the so-called better families" who would have voted conservative stayed away from the polls out of fear of violence. As a result, in Guayaquil the ADE easily elected its full slate of candidates, with the liberal Francisco Arízaga Luque gaining the top number of votes, followed by Alfonso Larrea Alba of the VRSE, Enrique Gil Gilbert of the PCE, and Alejandro Herrería of the PSE. Williamson claimed, "The communists never expected to gain a majority in their own name, but in combination with the socialists and other leftist factions they would appear to have obtained a decided voice for the laboring man and workers' organizations." The consul noted disappointment among the conservatives that they did not perform better and could not establish a bulwark against "radical extremes."[9] From the embassy's perspective, the biggest danger was a polarization into both radical left and right extremes with no moderate party to hold the center.[10]

The provision of "functional" representation for special interest groups that had been codified into the 1929 constitution further inflated leftist domination in the assembly. Elected deputies and functional representatives had the same power in the assembly; the only difference was their method of selection and the constituency they represented. Elected delegates traditionally represented propertied interests, whereas functional delegates reflected the growing corporate power of grassroots movements. Some of the functional delegates represented wealthy commercial and agricultural interests, but ten served a variety of educational interests; eight represented workers; and one was delegated for Indigenous peoples. Socialists and communists held more than half (seventeen) of these seats, whereas the conservatives held only three (those for the Catholic workers and for private schools, which were also largely in Catholic hands). During July and August of 1944, a variety of organizations gathered to select their functional representation for the Constituent Assembly. At the end of the CTE's founding congress, workers selected six delegates (four socialists and two communists) to represent their interests. They included Saad and Aguirre, who was later also elected as the first vice president of the Constituent Assembly.[11] On August 10, as the assembly was engaged in its opening formalities, activists at the founding congress of Ecuador's first national Indigenous organization, the Federación Ecuatoriana de Indios (Ecuadorian Federation of Indians; FEI), announced that they had selected Ricardo Paredes, founder of the Communist Party and longtime advocate of Indigenous demands, as the functional representative for the Indigenous race to defend their interests in the assembly.[12] It was the only time Indigenous organizations had direct control over their representative to the congress and the closest they had come to having a voice in government.

Despite this functional representation, all of the delegates who gathered in Quito to draft the constitution were men from Ecuador's privileged, wealthy white-mestizo class. Notably absent from the assembly, as with the juntas that had taken power in May, was the unmediated participation of Indigenous peoples, women, and other members of marginalized sectors of society who had played important roles in the Glorious May Revolution. Although the Alianza Femenina Ecuatoriana (Ecuadorian Feminist Alliance; AFE) met on July 29 to select a new governing board and subsequently disseminated a document describing societal changes it wished to see in the country, women were denied functional representation in the assembly.[13] Since the nineteenth century, Ecuador's constitutions had never mentioned race as a condition of citizenship, but literacy restrictions excluded most Indigenous peoples, peasants, and poor workers from citizenship and, hence, from engaging in electoral politics or exercising a direct role in the National Congress. In addition, voters had to return to their home districts and pay a fee for each election, which further discouraged poor people from participating in this activity. A small but growing literate middle class brought more people into the electorate who were willing to voice working-class concerns, but the ruling classes continued to exclude the large rural Indigenous masses, urban poor, workers, and women from political discourse. They still had to rely on their urban, male, and often communist allies to petition for their concerns.

Leading up to the election, FBI Director J. Edgar Hoover remained fixated on the presence of several minor communist sympathizers in Velasco Ibarra's government. He was relieved, however, to receive reports that conservatives would win the election.[14] It was with a certain amount of disappointment that Hoover reported a week later that what he characterized as the "extreme left" (the PSE, PCE, and VRSE) had won a majority of seats in the assembly.[15] Even though no documentary evidence has emerged that the U.S. government attempted to influence the outcome of these elections, Hoover fomented anticommunist sentiments. For example, he highlighted the detention of the wealthy industrialist brothers Ramón and Oscar González Artigas for their financial dealings with the previous government of President Carlos Arroyo del Río. Hoover blamed the "communist" Minister of Government Carlos Guevara Moreno for their arrests. While the working class applauded their prosecution, the upper class "deplore[d] the illegal and vindictive policy of the present government." Hoover also repeated unconfirmed rumors "that numerous wealthy Ecuadorians [were] attempting to liquidate their properties and transfer their wealth outside of the country because of fear of further reprisals." He expected these retaliations to lead to a "tense internal financial situation." Hoover argued that "no government can maintain itself in power without the support of the local capitalists." In addition to anticommunist ideologies, economic interests lay at the heart of Hoover's actions. He feared that the U.S. presence in the region would be diminished.[16]

The Constituent Assembly convened on August 10, 1944, the anniversary of Quito's failed 1809 declaration of independence from Spain; declared the liberal 1906 constitution to be in effect; and formally named Velasco Ibarra president of the republic. In the inaugural session, the liberal leader Arízaga Luque, as president of the congress, stated that the new constitution that they were to write needed to be simple, straightforward, and democratic. Delegates did not expect the congress to stay in session for more than two months, with the first month allocated to approving a new constitution and the second month devoted to addressing other important legal reforms.[17] This was not to be the case, however, as highly contested issues such as citizenship rights and construction of state structures led to lengthy debates. In one of the longest constitutional deliberations in the country's history, it took seven months to complete work on Ecuador's fifteenth constitution before it was formally promulgated on March 6, 1945.

The debates in the constitutional assembly began with a tone of congeniality and consensus. The independent delegate Carlos Zambrano noted that the

May revolution belonged to the Ecuadorian people, and not to the left or the right. Leftist delegates acknowledged that people had participated in the May revolution to address problems of unbearable poverty and misery and not to write constitutions. They proclaimed their dedication to national unity and harmony and promised not to use the congress as a platform to organize a social revolution. Saad, in representation of workers' interests, claimed that the communists did not "want to make a revolution of the extreme left, as people are saying on the street."[18] To calm fears over reports in *El Día* that the assembly planned to pass laws breaking up large estates, the socialist delegate David Altamirano from Chimborazo noted that there was no cause for alarm because the assembly would not promulgate any agrarian reform laws.[19] Agustín Vera Loor, a communist delegate from Manabí, observed that the legislators were less interested in a revolution of ideas than a judicial and political transformation that would benefit the general public.[20] From the beginning, the left's desire not to alienate conservative colleagues in the ADE and to maintain themselves in power ultimately would mean a failure to incorporate working-class concerns fully into the body polity.

FBI informants kept close tabs on communist participation in the constituent assembly, but if the reports that Hoover filed with the State Department are any indication, there was little reason for concern. The memos specified that the communists would not propose any radical changes. In the context of World War II, Saad wanted to cooperate with the United States as the leader of democratic countries, even as he agitated for diplomatic recognition of the Soviet Union.[21] In August 1945, the FBI reported that the only item that it had to report regarding the communist attitudes toward the United States was a private comment Saad had made in opposition to the appointment of South Carolina Senator James Byrnes as secretary of state because of his reactionary views on the Congress of Industrial Organizations (CIO), a view that organized labor in the United States shared.[22] Notwithstanding such comments, the embassy's Second Secretary James Gantenbein echoed the FBI informant's observation that communist leaders "have been among the most conspicuous defenders of the United States," even as they blamed the United States for blocking Ecuador's moves toward diplomatic recognition of the Soviet Union.[23] The communists moved cautiously so as not to lose the political advantages that they had gained from the May revolution.

Gil Gilbert expressed optimism that the Ecuadorian government would soon recognize the Soviet Union. If that happened, he had been asked to travel to Moscow as secretary to the Ecuadorian representative. Gil Gilbert told an anonymous FBI informant that he was "very much interested in getting acquainted with conditions in that country, and in learning more about Communism as it is working there." He acknowledged, however, that it was more important for him to stay in Ecuador to continue the socialist struggle. "An Ecuadoran Communist is so urgently needed these days in his own country," he purportedly said. "We do not yet know which of our comrades can be spared for the job in Moscow." In any case, he did not believe that recognition of the Soviet Union would significantly change how the party operated in Ecuador, because it already maintained contact with Russian officials in Mexico and Colombia. Recognition would mean only that it would be easier to sustain those connections.[24]

Saad recounted to a "reliable, confidential source" who had multiple conversations with the communist leader and communicated their substance to the FBI that he had a long argument with Velasco Ibarra regarding recognition of the Soviet Union. The president feared alienating the United States, whereas Saad argued that recognition would play to Ecuador's advantage because the United States would offer more financial assistance to counter Soviet influence. The communists also requested changes in the labor code and land ownership structures. Otherwise, their strategy was to go slow and play it safe.[25] Confidential FBI sources reported that Saad was the only person in the assembly with any constructive ideas and criticisms, and this had led to an increase in the power and prestige of communism in Ecuador.[26] Throughout the assembly, anonymous sources reported on international travelers and their contact with Saad, even as they acknowledged that the communist leader advocated for restraint among labor groups.[27] FBI agents reported on all of these steps toward moderation, even though they did little to calm the agency's underlying anticommunist paranoia.

Different U.S. agencies expressed contrasting attitudes toward a perceived communist threat in the Constituent Assembly. In November 1944, with the work on the constitution dragging out and seemingly nowhere near completion, Ambassador Scotten reported, "The general political picture remains obscure and confused," with ongoing challenges to Velasco Ibarra's hold on power. Scotten forwarded to the State Department a copy of a memorandum that Legal Attaché Charles Higdon had prepared on communist activities in Guayaquil. The FBI agent reported on threats of protest and armed occupations of land and concluded, "The slightest incident may precipitate an uprising ending with looting and ransacking of stores." Scotten was rather dismissive of Higdon's concerns, characterizing them as "unduly alarming."[28] Even though

State Department officials and FBI agents worked together in the U.S. Embassy in Quito, that did not mean that they necessarily shared similar interpretations of events.

An FBI informant reported Gil Gilbert as stating that communists "recognize that the country is not yet ripe for an exclusive Communist order of things." As a result, the party focused its efforts on the political education of the masses rather than attempting to take executive power. Gil Gilbert argued that the balance of power was on the side of the communists. In all of Latin America, Ecuador had the largest number of communists in the assembly (twelve—the number varied depending on who was identified as a socialist or a communist), and after the formation of the CTE in July, the labor movement was coalescing. Daily meetings with labor unions helped set the basis for future organizational activities, as well as the formulation of specific proposals for legislative actions. Not having to face government repression further facilitated the realization of communist goals.[29] Scotten echoed reports, probably drawing from the same informants, that Saad and Gil Gilbert represented a moderating influence on communist policies on the coast, but the ambassador added a concern that the two leaders "are finding it difficult to maintain their leadership." He feared the situation could change if less reliable (by which he perhaps meant more radical) activists gained control of the party. Militant grassroots activists pushed cautious leaders in a leftist direction, and their demands for more immediate and concrete action eventually led to divisions in the party.[30] The FBI appeared to understand better than the PCE where the left's biggest threat to the established order lay, and that was through its involvement in mobilizing the masses into a powerful popular movement for social change.

The 1945 constitution contained extensive checks against executive power, and functional delegates ensured permanent leftist representation in the government. At the time, the political scientist George Blanksten characterized these provisions as part of a document that was utopian, unworkable, and "divorced from reality."[31] In contrast, supporters termed it "the most perfect and advanced" of the various constitutions that had governed Ecuador and glorified its emphasis on equality and embrace of the Kichwa language and women's rights.[32] The constitution extended legal guarantees to marginalized people, defended freedom of assembly and political organizations, declared education to be free and secular, and restricted military and religious participation in political activities.

Despite the constitution's progressive tinge, the FBI concluded that the left's organizational weakness limited its effectiveness. Notwithstanding the success of the communists in gaining representation in the assembly, "at the closing of this Assembly on March 10, 1945, the Communist Party had suffered a considerable loss of prestige and influence in the political life of the nation." In an observant comment, the FBI noted, "Since the majority of Communist leaders were occupied during these months in the Constitutional Assembly, Party organizational work suffered and Party progress insofar as the recruiting of new members was concerned, was at a standstill." As a result of dedicating resources to constitutional debates rather than mobilizing popular forces on the streets, "as of March, 1945, the Communist Party's influence and power had declined from the high mark it attained in September, 1944."[33] The left should have emerged out of the assembly with power consolidated in its hands, but this was not to be the case. The period after the promulgation of the constitution represented a slow unraveling of the strength that the left had gained during La Gloriosa.

Aguirre, the socialist vice president of the assembly, provided an analysis similar to that of the FBI. He noted that moving so quickly to a constituent assembly was the first misstep of the May revolution. "Every revolution means a transformation," he wrote, "not a simple change of chips on the same old political board. Destruction needs to precede reconstruction." Revolutionary concepts must first be clarified before freezing them in a judicial mold. The members of the assembly set out to "write a revolution that had not yet been accomplished." Aguirre claimed that although leftists provided the primary impetus behind the May revolution, it was not a socialist revolution—nor did they intend to promulgate a socialist constitution. "It was a democratic revolution," the socialist leader declared, "with a deep sense of social reform." As such, the constitution was "eminently Ecuadorian," because the deputies had based it on an analysis of the country's national reality. From Aguirre's perspective, revolutions were much more than armed struggle; they required a fundamental transformation in society's socioeconomic structures. These changes would require slow and difficult work, because the socialists could not transform overnight a country that the oligarchy had spent years destroying.[34]

Scholars subsequently interpreted the Constituent Assembly in similar terms. The sociologist Silvia Vega characterizes the magna carta as "tepidly reformist" in terms of how it addressed issues of property, labor, and social welfare. It defended private property, outlawed expropriations, and retained large landholdings (the *latifundio*) as the basis of the country's agricultural system. Although it incorporated elements of the progressive 1938 labor code, including outlawing child labor and preserving the right to strike, the constitution failed to establish a minimum wage. In retrospect, Vega regards the assembly as yet another lost opportunity for popular forces to challenge the fundamental assumptions underlying the social and economic organization of Ecuador's state structures.[35]

Most of the people Velasco Ibarra named to his cabinet were from the more conservative wings of the ADE. The two exceptions were the socialist Alfonso Calderón Moreno, who served as minister of social welfare, and the communist Alfredo Vera, who served as minister of education. Neither was a prominent member of his party. Ambassador Scotten identified Vera as "known to be closely identified with the extreme Left" and reportedly "affiliated with the Communist Party."[36] According to the FBI, four years earlier Vera had formally resigned from the Communist Party after accusations surfaced that his brother-in-law was a Nazi, even though he personally remained sympathetic to communist principles. Velasco Ibarra forced both leftist ministers out of office on January 30, 1945, before the new constitution was even finished. The president claimed that the ministers were incompetent, although it was clear that his actual reason was to lessen leftist influence in government. A day after the dismissals, the PCE accused the administration of moving to the right and announced that it would no longer collaborate with the government. The Central Committee ordered all of the party's members to resign their government positions and to form a leftist political bloc with the socialists. FBI agents reported that a goal was to force Velasco Ibarra from power and replace him with Arízaga Luque, the assembly's liberal president.[37] Tellingly, even in the midst of crisis the communists looked outside their ranks for leaders to guide them forward.

Political divisions in the assembly also played out in street battles. In January 1945, leftist and conservative Velasquist forces clashed on the streets in Quito and Guayaquil, injuring several people, including the communist delegates Pedro Saad and José María Roura. The FBI reported that Saad was "badly mauled and would have been killed had he not been able to gain refuge in a nearby banking institution." According to *El Comercio*, the González Artigas brothers, the same wealthy industrialists whose properties Saad had advocated nationalizing because of their relationship with Arroyo del Río, owned the building in which he sought refuge.[38] Throughout the highlands Indigenous communities protested for better wages and access to land, the May revolution having raised their expectations for a better life. In Chimborazo, police killed one person and injured several more when they attempted to arrest

Feliciano Pilamunga and Toribio Chacaguaza, whom they accused of leading an uprising. The government mobilized two army units, thirteen tanks, and two planes to Cayambe under the pretext of suppressing another alleged revolt.[39] Showing his true colors, Velasco Ibarra sided with the wealthy landholding class, blamed outside agitators for the unrest, and told the Indians to quit causing trouble and go back to work. Despite his populist rhetoric, Velasco Ibarra remained clearly and deliberately allied with the conservative oligarchy. His reforms never fundamentally altered political and economic relations in Ecuador. The Glorious May Revolution appeared not to have solved any of the country's problems, and the moderate reforms the communists favored seemed to be impotent in changing that situation.

Moderating Force

At May Day celebrations in 1945, Gil Gilbert contended that communists did not need to push their cause through violent means because it would "advance automatically as a result of events in Europe." He believed growing communist influence in Europe would be reflected immediately in Latin America. "It is a law of human nature to subject to power," he argued, "and in noticing the growth of Communism elsewhere, many people in this country calculating upon the likeliness of future similar developments in Ecuador will want to become our friends with a view to gain thereby." Even though the Communist Party lacked financial resources at the moment, its cash flow would increase with its growing prospects for assuming power.[40] As with most communist parties in the Americas, in the 1940s the PCE was far from launching a violent or revolutionary movement. It consistently opposed extraconstitutional changes in power and argued that a coup attempt would only lead to a dictatorial regime and bring more repression to the working class.[41] Communists favored no-strike pledges so as not to undermine wartime production. The Ecuadorian party's political position reflected broader shifts in global attitudes toward communists that grew out of the Soviet Union's collaboration with Western capitalist powers in a common battle against fascism.

The fortunes of communists across the Americas improved when, in May 1943, Joseph Stalin dissolved the Comintern as a gesture of goodwill to the Allies. The British mission reported that Stalin's action "did much to remove, to some extent, the latent fear of communism, which was an obstacle to the fuller co-operation of Ecuador in the war effort."[42] The communists returned to a popular front policy that had been in place since the Comintern's seventh congress in 1935 and attempted to put the memories of the Nazi-Soviet Non-Aggression Pact behind them. From November 28 to December 1, 1943, Stalin met with Franklin D. Roosevelt and Winston Churchill, representing the "big three" Allied powers (the Soviet Union, the United States, and the United Kingdom), at the Teheran Conference to strategize in their war against Germany and to build postwar agreements. The Teheran Conference was part of a series of meetings between the wartime allies, with subsequent summits held at Yalta and Potsdam in 1945. These collaborative efforts contributed to international feelings of goodwill toward communists who had previously been seen as threatening the established order.

With a warming global political environment and communists in Ecuador holding important positions in government without disrupting the current political and economic system, some State Department officials began to view the communists as a tempering force in the country's politics. In July 1945, Consul General Joseph Burt observed, in a "personal and secret" communication to Henry Dearborn at the Ecuador desk in the State Department, that "the Communists are still acting as the principal moderating influence in Ecuador."[43] As evidence for his assertion, Burt pointed to a recent declaration of the communist-dominated CTE that defended Velasco Ibarra's government against external threats.[44] Rather than an ideological commitment to the institutional order, Burt claimed that the communists thought they could still work with the president—or, at least, that they saw his government as preferable to any foreseeable alternative options. Burt's comments influenced the State Department to take a more open position toward the communists than what one might otherwise expect. Gaining legitimacy, however, had a downside and came at a cost. As with the CIO in the United States, a desire to gain public acceptance from government officials and capitalists weakened radical influences among workers and undermined the left's broader goals.[45]

Dearborn read Burt's memorandum on communist activities in Latin America "with great interest." In reference to Ecuador, Dearborn asked his superiors whether they had "noticed that our consul General in Guayaquil believes that the communists have been the principal moderating influence in Ecuador during the current wave of unrest." Because of that characterization, Dearborn inquired, "Do you think that we would be justified in putting Ecuador under the title 'Countries where the communists are a major political party with an important influence in public affairs'?" From his perspective, "The Party is 'a major political force' in Ecuador at this time." The correspondence does not contain a direct reply to the query, although an unsigned handwritten note at the bottom of the memo adds, "I believe you will find that the Constitutional Assembly of 1944 had a total membership of 95 of whom at least 12 and possibly 16 were Communist Party members."[46] The tone of the remark indicates that the State Department did not seem to be overly concerned with the communist presence in the assembly. U.S. foreign-policy makers were still operating in the glow of the warm relations with the Soviet Union in the common battle against Hitler's Germany. As Thomas Leonard notes, "Until 1947, Americans viewed communism in Central America as an internal matter."[47] The same attitude was at play in Ecuador.

In September 1945, the State Department sent a "secret mimeographed instruction" presumably to all of its embassies in Latin America asking for comment on a draft study on communism in Latin America. From Quito, Chargé d'Affaires Ad Interim George P. Shaw responded with "a memorandum written as a result of study of the Department's instruction and based on intimate knowledge of communist activities in the Republic of Ecuador."[48] According to Shaw, embassy officers collaborated on their response and believed it represented a fair evaluation of the State Department's memo. They concluded that the memo was "relatively accurate," even though it tended to understate the PCE's political strength. Depending on the State Department's intended purpose for the memo, however, the embassy cautioned that "insufficient use was made of information available in Washington," perhaps a subtle jab at bureaucrats sitting at their desks who were out of touch with local realities.

Embassy officials in Quito questioned the State Department for classifying the Communist Party of Ecuador as "not a major political factor." Although the diplomats in Quito acknowledged that the PCE was not as strong as its counterparts in Cuba, Chile, Costa Rica, and Mexico, they argued that such a categorization minimized the importance of the party. Even though historically the Conservative Party was the strongest in Ecuador, the left's forceful presence in the constitutional assembly of 1944–45 had revealed a shifting balance of power. While the socialists were stronger than the communists, the latter had made convincing gains. Furthermore, the State Department memo had under-counted communists in the constitutional assembly. Rather than three deputies, the communists had nine—four elected representatives (Enrique Gil Gilbert, Gustavo Becerra, Manuel Medina Castro, and Agustín Vera Loor) and five functional representatives for workers and Indigenous peoples (Pedro Antonio Saad, Neptalí Pacheco León, Franklin Pérez Castro, Eloy Velásquez Cevallos, and Ricardo Paredes)—roughly a tenth of the assembly. In addition, the embassy pointed out, communists had held posts in Velasco Ibarra's government, including Alfredo Vera as minister of education, Enrique Barrezueta as sub-comptroller, and Enrique Gil Gilbert as a member of the *tribunal de garantías constitucionales* (Tribunal of Constitutional Guarantees), a provision of the new constitution designed to place a check on executive power. Moreover, at the close of the assembly, Saad held a seat on the *comisión legislativa permanente* (Permanent Legislative Commission) that served as a watchdog on the president and further curtailed his executive power. Communists had a significant presence in government, and they were acting in a responsible fashion.

The embassy personnel in Quito added that, since the founding of the CTE and FEI in the aftermath of the May revolution, the labor movement could no longer be characterized as weak, as stated in the State Department memo. The CTE claimed a total membership of 101,606, but the embassy pointed out that this number included "negative groups from a political point of view, such as the Indian cooperatives and Comunes organized under the Federación Indígena." Even with that "negative element," by which the FBI presumably meant groups without access to formal political power, the CTE was "relatively strong in comparison with other political groups." Of additional importance was Saad's role in the organization of the CTAL, including his participation at its assembly in Cali, Colombia, in December 1944.

Despite the PCE's growing electoral power and presence in organized labor, it did not have sufficient financial resources to publish a newspaper, which limited its ability to spread its message. The embassy had "ascertained reliably" that the party was to receive fifty copies of Karl Marx's complete works from Russia via Mexico, and the PCE hoped to generate a profit from the sale of these books. Saad was also attempting to negotiate communist control over the distribution of Russian films in Ecuador, which would provide another source of revenue. The embassy reported unconfirmed rumors that the party received money from the Communist Party of the USA (CPUSA).[49] The U.S. government was determined to document foreign sources of communist funding, even as the party's constant search for financial substance cast doubt on the presence of such revenue streams.

The British Foreign Office also requested information on communist strength in Latin America, although British Envoy Leslie Hughes-Hallett painted a picture that was somewhat different from that of his U.S. counterparts. Hughes-Hallett reported that although the Communist Party had been present in Ecuador for years, it had gained strength only after the May revolution. Even so, most of its work remained on "a clandestine, extra-political" level. Hughes-Hallett stated that it was difficult "to know who the genuine Communists are, because the term is wont to be used loosely to denote the more turbulent element of the extreme Left." Furthermore, in direct contradiction to what the U.S. government believed and endlessly sought to document, Hughes-Hallett claimed, "No evidence that regular direct communication with Moscow has ever existed." His communist informants reported that, instead, instructions arrived indirectly through their comrades in Mexico. He cautioned, however, against overstating a centralized coordination of communist activity in Latin America. "Communist activities in different countries are bound to derive a semblance of co-ordination from the fact that the aims and tenets of communism are the same the world over," Hughes-Hallett observed, but this was not the same as "a concerted Communist plan of action." He saw no need to exaggerate a communist threat, and misrepresenting the nature of an alleged international communist conspiracy could lead to mistaken policy initiatives.[50]

Hughes-Hallett's comments mirrored the general attitude of the British Foreign Office that a communist threat in Latin America was too innocuous to bother conducting a campaign against it. The Soviets were too focused on Europe to dedicate much attention to the Americas, which limited the extent of their influence in the hemisphere. Many Latin American communists had adopted Marxism to fit local conditions rather than adhering strictly to an international party line. A bigger threat, from the British perspective, was a reactionary Catholic church that favored authoritarianism over democracy and as a result held a strong inclination toward fascism.[51] As with the State Department, the British found little to fear from Ecuador's communist movement. In contrast, the FBI's fixation on a communist threat was more a reflection of Hoover's paranoia than a manifestation of Latin American realities.

Browderism

Perceptive observers recognized that the global left had long been divided into an older reformist social democratic tendency and a newer revolutionary communist one that the Bolshevik Revolution had influenced. These ideological fractures existed before the founding of the PCE in 1926. Those divisions reflected broader political disagreements among Marxists, anarchists, and utopian socialists over the role of government structures in addressing economic and social inequality. Over time, fissures would develop along different lines. One of the most hotly contested issues at the formation of the Ecuadorian party was whether to join an international communist movement. By World War II, the debates had shifted once again, and one of the central disagreements concerned whether to build alliances with liberals and other leftists against a common conservative enemy.

In the 1940s, one of the most serious divisions within international communist movements concerned Earl Browder's class-collaborationist policy. Browder, the general secretary of the CPUSA, interpreted Soviet collaboration with the British and United States at the 1943 Teheran Conference to mean that peaceful collaboration between the Soviet Union and the major capitalist powers would characterize the postwar world.[52] Browder envisioned that this new world order would transform U.S. relations with Latin America, including representing an end to imperial exploitation of colonial and semicolonial countries.[53] Browder's position had repercussions throughout the Americas. Despite common protestations that local parties operated independently, instructions continued to flow from Moscow through the United States to the rest of the parties in the hemisphere, even though local activists often had to reinterpret the directives in creative ways to make them applicable to local realities. Browder supported Roosevelt's New Deal and advocated a popular front strategy of building alliances with other social classes. After the collapse of the Nazi-Soviet Pact and with Germany threatening the very existence of the Soviet Union, Browder argued that the historical antagonisms and contradictions between the bourgeoisie and the working class had disappeared. Communists should unite behind their governments and support the Allies in the war effort to defeat fascism in Europe. Because of this position, Browder gained a reputation as a revisionist who advocated socialist collaboration with the United States and capitalism rather than direct confrontation between classes, as had been the Comintern policy before its seventh congress in 1935.

In 1944, Browder dissolved the CPUSA and formed a Communist Political Association in its stead, which led to intense opposition from those to his left. The U.S. communist activist Dorothy Healey charged that Browder had made the same mistake in interpreting the Teheran declaration as the party had made in following the Nazi-Soviet Pact. Diplomatic positions that held a certain amount of rationale for a sovereign government (the Soviet Union) lost political effectiveness if converted into a political line for a domestic party, as the CPUSA had done. "There's no reason why the Party itself had to abandon all sense of complexity in its analysis," Healey later argued. She maintained that critical thought and reflection were the key to building a revolutionary organization and that Browder's collaborationist position had lost that component.[54]

With the end of the war, Browder's position came under increasingly harsh criticism from the rest of the international communist movement. In April 1945, the prominent French communist Jacques Duclos published an article in *Cahiers du Communisme* denouncing Browder's policies. Duclos criticized Browder for converting the Teheran declaration from a diplomatic document into a political platform that called for an end to class conflict. The article stated that Browder's erroneous interpretations of the postwar world flowed from a failure to apply a Marxist-Leninist analysis to the current political situation.[55] Even though the Comintern no longer existed, many observers understood that the contents of Duclos's article were prepared in Moscow.[56] The "Duclos letter" indicated that Browder's position had fallen out of favor with the Soviet Union, and William Z. Foster soon replaced Browder as head of the CPUSA.[57] With Duclos's denunciations, the international communist movement began to disavow Browderism, although it took a while for the shift in policy to filter down to Latin America. Even in neighboring Mexico, the embrace and then repudiation of Browderism did not penetrate very deeply into the party. Responding to local conditions, the Mexicans had already followed some of Browder's policies on their own. Barry Carr suggests that one aspect of Browderism that may have been incorporated usefully into Mexico was an "opening to national traditions," which could have created more space for independent Marxists, thereby avoiding intense sectarianism and political purges.[58]

Duclos observed that most communist parties did not approve of Browder's position, and several, including those in Australia and South Africa, had come out openly against it. However, several Latin American parties followed Browder's lead. In fact, the Chilean Communist Party adopted policies at a meeting on August 1944 that were consistent with Browder's preference for class collaboration rather than class conflict.[59] In his history of the Comintern, Manuel Caballero points out that the Colombian, Cuban, and Venezuelan communist parties were the ones most eager to accept Browder's ideas and were left to engage in self-criticism of their "deviations" after the Duclos letter had made it clear that these ideas had fallen out of favor with Moscow. Furthermore, Caballero argued that it was not entirely correct to interpret Browder as misleading the parties toward a class-collaborationist strategy, as aspects of advocating for national unity were already part of the Comintern's united front strategy rather than an innovation of the CPUSA leader.[60] Venezuelan communists debated whether to denounce Duclos's charges and worried that accepting his critique would lay the party open once again to accusations that it followed foreign instructions. Even before Duclos's article, some already questioned whether it made sense in Latin America to follow Browder's collaborationist position into the postwar period.[61] Some leftists questioned whether Browderism really represented anything different from an extension of the popular front policy initiated at the seventh Comintern congress. Unlike in neighboring Chile and Argentina, Browderism had minimal influence in Brazil.[62] The varying responses to Browder's policies highlight that rather than following a hegemonic hemispheric pattern, the policies of each country's communist party must be understood within its own, specific context. Ecuador's responses to Browderism were unique, as were those of other countries.

Ecuador

Communist parties, including the one in Ecuador, suffered internal divisions over the issue of whether or not to follow Browder's line. Several key members of the PCE's Central Committee, including Ricardo Paredes, Joaquín Gallegos Lara, Nela Martínez, María Luisa Gómez de la Torre, and Gustavo Becerra, energetically battled Browderism. They advocated for a more radical and combative position against capitalism to achieve a proletarian revolution. According to historian Jorge Nuñez, Gallegos Lara was the first to oppose Browderism, and he was expelled from the party for his open attack.[63] In contrast, militants grouped around Saad in Guayaquil favored following Browder's reformist line of conciliation with capitalism as the best path forward to improve the party's fortunes.[64]

Years later, the communist militants Isabel Herrería and Ana Moreno recounted that Blas Roca, the secretary-general of the Cuban Communist Party, introduced Browder's ideas into Latin America in a brochure that he distributed throughout the region. In Ecuador, many communists embraced his political line with a great deal of enthusiasm. According to Herrería and Moreno, only Gallegos Lara and Paredes opposed his position. They met with students, workers, and other sectors of the party's base to defend Marxism in the face of Browder's actions. Herrería and Moreno condemned Browder for having "lost all of his ideological structure, departing from Marxist methodology, dismissing the class struggle, and finally dissolving the Communist Party and replacing it with committees where anyone could have their say." At the time, however, other party leaders viciously attacked both Paredes and Gallegos Lara, even though Paredes was the secretary-general of the party.

Gallegos Lara filled his copy of Browder's writing on Teheran with marginal comments in which he critiqued the accommodationist position. "It was a reckless liberal trend within the Marxist parties," Herrería and Moreno argued. "Gallegos and Paredes deserve fair recognition for being the first in the world to point out such an error, one later recognized by Jacques Duclos." Herrería and Moreno contended that Browderism was not easily defeated, and its policy of class collaboration helped undermine revolutionary impulses that otherwise would have flourished during La Gloriosa.[65]

The dissolution of the Comintern in May 1943 contributed to Browder's line gaining strength. On June 2, 1943, the PCE issued a resolution supporting the dissolution of the Comintern. The statement, signed by the PCE's current Secretary-General Gustavo Becerra, states (in translation by the FBI's Legal Attaché's Office), "The PCE considers just the attitude of the Communist Internationale, because the PCE regards it as the most efficient way to carry out the unity of effort of all peoples and governments which fight Nazi-Fascism." The Communist Party "declares that the decision of the Communist Internationale strengthens its struggle for the liberation of the Ecuadoran people and does not modify at all its position towards the economical [sic] transformation of Society." The PCE further proclaimed that "it has no foreign directives or instructions" and that it was committed to "the establishment of a democratic regime in Ecuador." It declared its support for the antifascist struggle and paid "homage of admiration and gratitude to the Soviet Nation in its most legitimate representative, Comrade Stalin."[66] As with communist parties elsewhere, the PCE exhibited an ideological flexibility in its official proclamations that allowed it to adhere to the twists and turns of policies emanating from Moscow. Among the ramifications for Latin American communists was a lessening of the intensity of frontal attacks against U.S. imperialism in the region.

Even party members who did not support Browder eventually fell in line behind party positions. Mériguet claimed that Moscow had not meddled in local communist affairs since even before the Comintern's seventh congress in 1935 that represented a shift from a class against class to a popular front strategy.[67] This subsequently became the formal line to which the PCE adhered. While the party openly acknowledged its admiration and support for the Soviet Union because it was the first socialist country and defended freedom for other countries, "in no way have, do, or will we communists obey instructions from the Soviet government." Instead, the PCE defined its own program of building a new social and political structure that would benefit

Ecuador.[68] Saad similarly declared, "The Communist Party of Ecuador has absolutely nothing to do with the Communist Party of the Soviet Union." He proclaimed, "Our party is a purely Ecuadorian party."[69] Rather more accurate might be the dynamics that Barry Carr discovered in Cuba in which party members struggled to apply the spirit rather than the letter of specific directives, rather akin to the Spanish colonial adage "Obedezco pero no cumplo" (I obey but do not follow through).[70] Because of Browder's key position in a hierarchical organization, loyal militants struggled to follow his leadership even when they questioned the wisdom of his positions.

In the political context of wartime collaboration, socialists (who were not subject to Comintern dictates) also backed off of their criticisms of the United States. In November 1943, PSE Secretary-General Aguirre, who represented the left wing of the Socialist Party, clarified, "To fight against English or U.S. imperialism does not mean to fight against England or the United States but, rather, to fight for the liberation of the people in England and the United States who constitute the true nation subjugated and oppressed by imperialism." Aguirre declared that to be an anti-imperialist did not mean hating England and the United States; rather, it meant "to love them dearly and work with them for true liberation." Aguirre called on Latin American socialists to join with the English and North American people in a common anti-imperialist struggle against the yoke of capitalism wherever it existed, whether in England, the United States, Nazi Germany, or imperial Japan.[71]

In recounting the history of the PCE, the FBI claimed that with the dissolution of the Comintern, communists in Ecuador rapidly began to gain support from the broader public. Communists "claimed that their politics were of local character only, and that since they were legitimate citizens of a democratic country they were entitled to being officially recognized." They campaigned primarily for raising the country's education levels and forming new labor unions under communist leadership. Particularly after the May revolution, the communists made their presence and power felt in the new government, including in the civil guard that replaced the hated carabineros, in government ministries, and in the assembly tasked with drafting a new constitution. The communists agitated for higher wages and more control over the universities. The author of the FBI memo believed that this new strategy of exhibiting "a rather exuberant lot of local patriotism" was more dangerous than when the PCE had functioned overtly as a communist force that might otherwise alienate potential supporters. The PCE could become a significant political force if it functioned in a respectable and responsible manner.[72]

The Office of Strategic Services (oss) provided a similar type of analysis of the pce's role. That agency characterized Velasco Ibarra's administration as "a left-of-center coalition government which may well seem extremely revolutionary against the background of the country's history and feudal institutions, but which can hardly be called extremist in any other sense." Contributing to that moderation were the actions of communist leaders such as Saad who had "considerable training and discipline." Without naming Browderism, the oss situated the pce within that tendency. Its actions paralleled communists elsewhere in stressing "cooperation with other labor factions as well as middle class parties under general democratic and pro–United Nations slogans." The party "puts aside the issue of socialism in favor of early social reforms within the framework of a private enterprise economy." The oss observed that "under such a program boundary lines between Communists and other parties tend to become obscure, and distinctions between the various genuine Independents and Liberal, Socialist, or Communist sympathizers become extremely hazardous." At present, the communists cooperated with the popular front policies of the Velasco Ibarra government, and their true strength would emerge only if they became estranged from the rest of the coalition. Until that point, communists could be distinguished from others primarily "by the general zeal and discipline of their adherents, their sympathy for Russia, and paradoxically, by the relatively more moderate and more pro-United States language of their leaders." The oss cautioned, however, that the pce could change its pro-democratic political positions in the future.[73]

Despite Browder's influence in Latin America, his positions were not automatically accepted in Ecuador. In October 1944, Saad recounted internal party conflicts to an fbi informant. "My position in the Party is stronger in the interior than it used to be, but here on the coast things are going against me," he stated. "Many believe that I am not sufficiently radical, but they do not know how hard it is under the circumstances to keep going." Saad complained, "There seems to be trouble brewing in the Party, but it will be recognized sooner or later that I always did the best I could and therefore the opposition does not worry me." Resistance to Saad continued to grow, however, with some local activists advocating for his replacement. Finally, pce Secretary-General Paredes traveled to Guayaquil to assess the situation. He called for a meeting, in which Gil Gilbert defended Saad's policies. Saad was forced to respond to charges that he had been too conservative in party policies, and both Saad and Gil Gilbert were compelled to promise a more radical party program in the future. In particular, pressure from workers extorted

Saad to reverse his earlier policy of holding off on demands for wage increases until the new government could consolidate its political control.[74] While party leaders might follow Browder's collaborationist agenda, grassroots opposition was strong enough to force leaders to alter that policy.

In February 1945, the FBI reported that some members in Guayaquil were still dissatisfied with the leadership of Saad, Gil Gilbert, and Pacheco León because of their failure in the constitutional assembly to achieve concrete measures such as recognition of the Soviet Union, reduction in the cost of living, and greater influence on the direction of Velasco Ibarra's government policies. The largest faction in Guayaquil was known as the "Toledanistas," and was grouped around Saad and Gil Gilbert. A more radical wing of the party supported Paredes and Quevedo, and the FBI optimistically reported that "it is possible that this radical element within the Party will cause a split in Party ranks in coming weeks."[75] No such split, however, was imminently forthcoming. Nor does the archival documentation include evidence that the FBI actively intervened to foster internal fractures, as the bureau later did to the Black Panthers and other radical groups in the United States through its counterintelligence program known as Cointelpro.[76] At this point and in this context, Hoover appeared willing to limit his activities to gathering information on subversive groups.

After the completion of work on the new constitution in March 1945, Gil Gilbert returned to Guayaquil and assumed control over the party while Saad remained in Quito as a member of the Permanent Legislative Commission. FBI agents reported that Saad continued to advocate for moderation among labor groups. He urged workers to provide Minister of Social Welfare Santiago Roldós Soria with "an opportunity to prove his ability." An informant told the FBI that he did "not quite understand Saad's attitude of trying to calm the populace and hold them in check unless Saad feels that this is not the opportune time to incite trouble." The FBI also quoted Saad as proclaiming in a public speech, "Workers should not oppose foreign capital but should fight for their rights; that profits made by foreign capital invested in the country should remain in the country."[77] Saad's statements stood against a more radical critique of imperial penetration of Latin America that others to his left in the party had made. His position, however, followed what Lombardo Toledano had communicated to the U.S. Embassy in Mexico, that he was not against foreign investment as long as it followed the guidelines of government regulations. Furthermore, the true opponents of the United States were not leftists but conservatives.[78] Some U.S. officials agreed that conservatives represented more of a barrier than liberals and leftists to the development of capitalism in the region, and the communists played that sentiment to their advantage.

Along these same pro-capitalist lines, Saad accompanied Roberto Levi, a wealthy German Jew who had come to Ecuador thirty-six years earlier and had a son who worked with the Rockefeller Foundation, to the office of the South American Development Company to discuss labor problems. The FBI informant described Saad as "quite cooperative" and declared that he understood the problems that the company faced. Saad "did not want to force foreign capital out of country, although he does want labor to obtain its just dues." The confidential source expressed surprise at Saad's accommodating stance and his relationship with a wealthy industrialist. Saad also advocated for the elimination of the labor commissioner as a step to avoiding "continuous labor difficulties" while being "fair to both employer and employee." The source stated that Saad's cooperative attitude was consistent with his recent statement that "you cannot develop the proletarian class until you have industry developed" and as a result advocated "cooperation with 'progressive capitalism,' that is, capitalists who believe in fair dealings with their personnel."[79] Without mentioning Browder, Saad's position was consistent with his collaborationist attitudes. He argued for a delay in attempting to move to socialism because the objective economic conditions were not yet ready. In opposition to a more militant rank-and-file that wanted to press their class demands now, the communist labor leader urged moderation and patience in the building of a respectable party apparatus.

United for Democracy and Progress

Despite Paredes's opposition, the Communist Party continued to advocate collaboration with Velasco Ibarra's government. This collaborationist line was most clearly manifest in a May 1945 pamphlet titled "United for Democracy and Progress—Position of the Communist Party of Ecuador at the Present Time." At the time the pamphlet was released, the Duclos-Browder debate had not yet reached Ecuador. With the defeat of the Nazis in Europe and the collapse of the Japanese empire on the horizon, the PCE Central Committee, which included Paredes and others opposed to Browderism, released the statement laying out the position of the party in the face of the meetings of the Allied powers at Dumbarton Oaks, Teheran, and Yalta to establish a postwar global political order. According to the FBI, "The Communists are relying on information received from Earl Browder and Lombardo Toledano to the effect that there might be a number of Communist surprises in Europe which would have considerable influence on Latin America." The party attempted to position itself in the context of that international political environment.[80]

The pamphlet reflected the thinking behind a speech that Saad gave in January 1945 to a large audience at the University of Guayaquil on the Teheran and Dumbarton Oaks conferences. Drawing on Browder's ideas, Saad argued that international politics should not be the subject of secret discussion but be opened to debate among the general public. He contended that the current war was different from previous ones in that it was fought for the preservation of liberty and security rather than imperial advances. Potential postwar problems should be addressed immediately, and if applied correctly, the resolutions of Teheran and Dumbarton Oaks could solve many of those problems. Saad thought that these resolutions were more important than the Atlantic Charter in defining a peaceful postwar world. He maintained that it was utopic to think of absolute national autonomy, and the major power brokers would necessarily need to define the nature of the future world and guarantee its peace. Saad argued that the Soviet Union was strong enough to prevent the United Nations from becoming an instrument for the advancement of imperialism. To realize this goal, Ecuador needed to change its foreign policy away from support for Falangist governments in Argentina and Spain. It should break diplomatic relations with those countries and recognize the Soviet Union instead.[81]

Following the current Browderist line, the pamphlet similarly called for "a firm and constructive alliance of all progressive and democratic forces" to defeat their reactionary opponents that impeded Ecuador's progress and international cooperation. Most fundamentally, this meant collaboration with the current government of Velasco Ibarra. The party pointed to the May revolution as an example of national unity that had defeated a "shameful regime" and opened a path toward national reconstruction with the seating of a constituent assembly that drafted the "most democratic and progressive constitution in our history." The gains for workers, including the organization of the CTE—which, the PCE proclaimed, contributed to economic progress—were examples of the "victories of national unity, realized within the spirit of Teheran." An attitude of accommodation with capitalism as eventually leading to a triumph of communism underscored the pamphlet's political philosophy.[82]

Despite these positive developments, Ecuador still faced challenges that threatened to turn back this progress. For example, the conservative Foreign Minister Ponce Enríquez favored the Falangists, and he followed international policies that delayed the country's decision to join the United Nations and recognize the Soviet Union. His reactionary actions threatened Ecuador's sovereignty. Only an alliance of the country's progressive forces that included workers, members of the middle class, progressive capitalists, and wealthy agriculturalists committed to national development could implement the program of the May revolution and save the country from certain disaster. Conservative domestic forces holding to a feudal past represented a larger threat to the party's goals than international liberal capitalism.[83] In an echo of Browder's policies in the United States, the PCE statement declared that "it is not time for socialism in Ecuador." Rather, it was necessary to fight for individual political freedoms, economic progress, improvements in standards of living, and a just and democratic foreign policy—all of which were liberal rather than socialist goals. The party called for a battle against anticommunism, as well as a "fight against unnecessary provocation and violence," thereby positioning itself as a responsible force in the postwar period.[84]

The party laid out a program of economic reforms it wanted to see implemented in Ecuador, including promoting industrialization, enabling modern forms of cultivation in agriculture, and fighting feudalism that held back capitalist production. In addition, the party called for measures that would improve standards of living such as price controls, increases in salaries, collective bargaining agreements, expansion of social welfare programs, improvement in housing, bettering the lives of Indigenous peoples and peasants, raising the level of the popular culture and technical abilities of workers, and putting a stop to speculation. The party also called for international cooperation against all forms of aggression and support for national sovereignty, including the return of land that Ecuador had ceded to Peru under the Rio Protocol during the war in the name of continental solidarity. International policies, the party argued, should focus on the destruction of fascism in all of its forms and the establishment of diplomatic relations with the Soviet Union—one of the party's most constant demands. The communists promised to support all of Velasco Ibarra's democratic and progressive measures that would contribute to national progress. The party proclaimed that its program synthesized the patriotic aspirations of all Ecuadorians. These goals would be realized, in part, with the organization of a strong unified labor federation (the CTE) to carry the masses forward to victory, and would open up the path to future progress and social conquests. Following Browder's line, the pamphlet closed with a proclamation that the communists were "the most loyal and fervent supporters" of taking the steps necessary to carry the country forward.[85]

An FBI informant spoke with Gil Gilbert, the general secretary of the coastal region for the PCE, about the contents of the pamphlet. The party leader stated that the communists were not opposed to Velasco Ibarra, although he acknowledged that they had not cooperated with him "for some time." The president, however, was slowly becoming aware that it was better for him to ally with the left because conservative cooperation had not been sincere and would use him opportunistically only to carry out its own agenda. Gil Gilbert presented an image of the party as a responsible political force. He argued, "We do not have to push our cause violently as we know that it would advance automatically as a result of events in Europe." He believed Latin America would inevitably follow a global growth of communist power. In the meantime, Gil Gilbert still advocated supporting Velasco Ibarra because doing so would help strengthen the Communist Party. The PCE pursed a two-track policy: they supported the president publicly while covertly challenging his policies. Gil Gilbert did not think Velasco Ibarra would survive in office to the end of the year. Privately, he confided to a confidential FBI informant that he anticipated dramatic political changes on the horizon, which left him feeling optimistic about the prospects of the party. In playing it safe and not challenging capitalism or imperialism directly, Browder's supporters expected to advance communism's prospects.[86]

The FBI highlighted an issue of the communist newspaper *Bloque* from July 1945 as adhering to the party's collaborationist line, indicating the delay in the full significance of the Duclos article reaching into the Ecuadorian party. The newspaper declared that the party's call "for national democratic unity in support of the constitution and government, has met with great national enthusiasm." Even while calling for national unity, FBI agents pointed to divisions in the international communist movement that echoed through the PCE. Because of Saad's close identification with Lombardo Toledano, who had followed a similar collaborationist line, the Guayaquil branch of the party felt the fallout of the Duclos-Browder dispute before its counterpart in the capital. One of the FBI's sources said that "Paredes spoke openly and with considerable emphasis" about the mistakes that PCE had made in collaborating with other parties and Velasco Ibarra's government. He advocated "a return to Marxism." Saad countered with a defense of collaboration and said that he would submit a written reply to Paredes in support of his position.[87] Slowly but surely, the international ramifications of the challenges to Browder's line filtered to Ecuador.

According to the FBI, the Duclos-Browder debate finally came out into the open at a Central Committee meeting in August 1945. Paredes purportedly observed that "the task of organizing cells within the trade unions had fallen more and more exclusively to Pedro Saad" and "Saad had done very good work in that respect, but that considering the importance of such work to the Communist movement, it could not be left entirely to any one individual." The remark appears to be a backhanded compliment designed to undermine the labor leader's strength and at the same time push him away from a collaborationist position. Those comments were preliminary to a discussion of the Browder-Duclos controversy, in which "Saad was the spokesman for the Browder collaboration point of view" while Paredes "tend[ed] toward a strict interpretation of revolutionary Communism." According to an FBI source, "Saad won out in this matter inasmuch as the final resolution as drafted was in favor of holding to a line of collaboration as the best policy for a Communist Party in 'a semi-colonial nation such as Ecuador.'"[88] If the FBI was still hoping for an open break in the party, that did not appear to be an imminent danger. Despite deep internal disagreements, a common agenda and goals still bound the communist militants together.

In a subsequent memo, the FBI described Paredes as "an old line Communist leader" who supported Duclos. The memo also reported that Saad's promised statement in defense of a collaborationist position was not forthcoming, but at a Central Committee meeting the following day, Paredes presented a tentative resolution to the disagreement. The FBI informant did not have precise details about the resolution, but the general plan was to follow "Duclos's recommendations as closely as possible, and yet try to obtain a practical, advantageous political position." Almost as a quid pro quo, Paredes proceeded to applaud Saad for his work within the labor unions and characterized it as the party's most important activity.[89] Dropping a conciliatory wartime stance, as Steve Ellner notes in the case of Venezuela, allowed parties to move to the left, although that did not eliminate friction among different factions.[90] In Ecuador, party leaders sought to bridge those divides and remain united, as their May pamphlet proclaimed, for democracy and progress.

Decades later, Saad's association with Browderism and the divisions it created in the party were still visibly present. The compromises that these reformists had made contributed to the support that Maoism and Fidel Castro, both of whom were not tainted by those associations, received in Latin America. In 1968, the communist militant Nela Martínez published an essay in the leftist magazine *Mañana* criticizing Saad for not acknowledging his error in following Browder's collaborationist line and for failing to recognize that others in the party opposed that line. Martínez denounced Browderism as "one of the worst and crassest revisionisms in the service of Yankee interests in Latin America." She criticized Saad for playing into a colonial mentality in highlighting that criticism of the shortcomings of this line came from France and the United States, and ignoring the open opposition to his position that existed within his own party. Martínez complained that the same problems with an inability to engage in critical reflection still existed in the party.[91] Martínez acknowledged in her autobiography that while searching for sympathetic allies might be an appropriate and necessary strategy to win a war, it would only weaken the working class if applied to an internal political practice inside a party and leave both the party and the country in a vulnerable situation.[92] A sense of inferiority and aversion to challenging the leadership of what Latin American communists regarded as one of the most influential parties was a problem throughout the region.[93] The divisions that Browder's position created never disappeared and contributed to splits in the 1960s, with some militants continuing to advocate in favor of more radical party positions.

Local Elections of November 1945

A detailed FBI monthly summary of communist activities for October 1945 reviewed communist plans for the upcoming November municipal elections. The communists had been able to build a leftist electoral alliance with the PSE and VRSE throughout the country, except in Guayaquil. In the coastal port city, the PCE in alliance with independent liberals selected the former Education Minister Alfredo Vera as their candidate for mayor, with the PSE supporting Antonio Mata Martínez and the VRSE backing Carlos Ayala Cabanilla. FBI agents reported that the PCE had been very active in Guayaquil. The party disseminated mimeographed and printed campaign propaganda that, in addition to information on the candidates, included explicit registration and voting instructions. Apparently, the communists assumed that their target demographic would have minimal experience with voting. Although on other occasions Paredes had participated in electoral campaigns, this time he chose to remain in Tigua, a communist-controlled Indigenous cooperative, rather than return to Quito. From his perspective, "Work among the Indians was far more important for the Party than the elections."[94] Paredes believed that the PCE needed to build a stronger and politically conscious grassroots movement to realize its objectives and that electoral contests in the current environment were a distraction from more important political tasks.

In Quito, the PCE unified with the PSE and VRSE behind the mayoral candidacy of the socialist Juan Isaac Lovato, with the communists having two candidates in the list of ten for the City Council: Primitivo Barreto and María Luisa Gómez de la Torre. Barreto was a member of the Central Committee of the PCE, and Gómez de la Torre was the secretary of an active women's Communist Party cell known as La Pasionaría. Communist substitutes included Modesto Rivera (responsible for communist infiltration of the shoemakers' union), Manuel Oña (a student), Rafael Almeida Hidalgo ("comparatively inactive"), and Newton Moreno (in charge of legal matters).[95] The candidates described their coalition as one of workers and students. Rather than engaging in political propaganda or making doctrinaire statements, they promised to work on behalf of the public, "without hateful preferences or petty discrimination." They pledged to engage in a democratic reform of the city government. In an attempt to gain respectability, the party adhered to moderate positions in its platform.[96]

The conservatives soundly trounced both the liberals and the leftists in the election, seemingly putting into question whether the campaign was the best use of the party's resources.[97] Consul Burt reported that the conservative victory in the municipal elections left the PCE "greatly disheartened." Following an institutional path to power did not have the expected outcome. An informant said that the party faced both financial difficulties and problems in convincing members to attend meetings. The electoral defeat had made collaboration with the socialists and the VRSE even more difficult. It would appear that engaging in the election had been a strategic error.[98]

Despite the communist emphasis on elections, the (unnamed) author of an FBI memo on communist activities repeated rumors from unspecified sources of what ultimately was an ungrounded fear of violence. The report warned, "With respect to violence to be expected during the elections initiated by the Communists, enemies of the Communist Party have alleged that that Party could be expected to provoke violence during the elections." The FBI stated, "It was reliably reported that the Communist Party, both in Guayaquil and Quito, considered the reestablishment of an armed group known as the 'Fuerza de Choque,' which operated prior to and during the revolution of May 1944."[99] The FBI had long been concerned about this communist-organized paramilitary organization also known as the *guardia de choque* (shock troops) or *brigadas de choque* (shock brigade), even as party leaders denied that they represented a subversive threat to the country's political stability.[100]

During February and March 1944 in the context of the repressive Arroyo del Río government, the PCE allegedly had charged Franklin Pérez Castro and Simón Zambrano with organizing groups of civilians into an armed force. Their mandate included training its members in the use of firearms to act as bodyguards and protect the party's meetings and parades from government attacks. From this position, Pérez Castro and Zambrano helped lay plans for the May revolution, including negotiating agreements between the military barracks and revolutionary forces and acting as couriers between Guayaquil and Quito. At the time, Gil Gilbert claimed that labor and student leaders were working to check the desire of "the masses to engage in street rioting." He observed, "They *do* want to fight, and they make all possible efforts to get into possession of whatever firearms can become available." While Gil Gilbert understood the preference to die fighting rather than starve, he believed that such a strategy did not provide a path to political change. Rather, the communist strategy was to continue organizing labor to be prepared when a proper opportunity presented itself. "Ecuador resembles a powder keg," Saad observed. "So does all Latin America—and it is going to blow up some day." The party leaders considered it irresponsible to encourage that chaos. Instead, they sought to channel it toward effective and positive political changes.[101]

After the triumph of the May revolution, the shock troops received additional arms and ammunition from the Ecuadorian army and initially protected the city of Guayaquil until formal police forces reestablished their control. The armed bands never returned their weapons to the military, and the guns presumably remained in Pérez Castro's possession. The FBI has a well-established tradition of exaggerating threats of leftist violence, and without corroborating evidence it is difficult to know how accurate their reports of armed communist groups were. With relief, the FBI noted, "It was reliably reported that in the course of a meeting of the Communist Party in Quito on October 31, 1945, it was definitely decided to abandon for the time being plans for the reestablishment of these armed groups." The party refrained from violence because "it was the opinion of the Communist leaders present at that meeting that such a group would be too difficult to control during election excitement." The FBI reported, "Prominent members of the Communist Party have been reliably reported to express the viewpoint that under the present regime the Communist Party of Ecuador has complete freedom to organize and operate effectively, and that therefore they must avoid any violence or other activity on their part which might jeopardize its present status."[102] Such statements appear to reflect accurately the cautious and moderate position of the party as it favored functioning within a constitutional system.

Perhaps the FBI's fear of communist violence came from statements Gil Gilbert had made a year earlier when he argued in favor of stockpiling arms and building support in the military in preparation for a potential counter-revolution against the gains of La Gloriosa.[103] A year later and in a different political environment with Velasco Ibarra well established in power, turning to extraconstitutional measures would not be in the party's interest. The FBI reports appear to have been sensationalistic and alarmist in nature to justify further surveillance. The PCE did not move toward military action, but the FBI surveillance hints at the presence of hidden narratives. In reflecting back on La Gloriosa forty years later, the party members Herrería and Moreno noted that the "heroic participation" of comrades in these shock brigades remained a story yet to be told.[104]

In contrast to the FBI's exaggerated preoccupation for the potential of communist violence, the British diplomatic mission in Ecuador highlighted the left's shortcomings. In a report on the political events of 1945, the diplomat J. H. Wright claimed that the left's behavior in the Constituent Assembly had caused a pronounced swing of public opinion away from support for its position and in favor of Velasco Ibarra, who was moving rightward. From Wright's perspective, the left's failures "resulted in a sweeping success for the Conservative Party" in November's municipal elections. While the electoral outcome "reflected the clerical influence among the people of Ecuador," it also, in Wright's assessment, "constituted a positive sign that opinion had swung away from the Left." The British diplomat applauded that development as serving his government's imperial interests.[105]

Aguirre recognized the fragility of the left's hold on power in the aftermath of La Gloriosa. In his report to the PSE congress of November 1945, he noted that Ecuadorians still held on to the freedoms they gained in the May revolution, but that they must not forget that these advances were thanks to the constitution of 1945. Among its benefits were the Tribunal of Constitutional Guarantees that moderated the excesses of executive power, the superior electoral tribunal that stood guard against corruption in the voting process, and a Permanent Legislative Commission that drafted laws to address urgent economic problems. If the constitution were to be revoked, they would lose their freedoms. Leftists needed to defend these institutions to preserve the country's democratic future, but resorting to violence might result in an upending of all of their hard-earned gains.[106]

At about the same time as the PSE congress in November 1945, the communists released a short pamphlet that laid out the party's ideological orientation and political program that seemed to place it to the right of its rivals in the Socialist Party. The PCE declared that it was a party of the working class, peasants, and popular sectors and that it drew on the country's democratic, revolutionary, and progressive traditions. The country's problems could be solved only through socialism that would create a society without classes. Nevertheless, in the party's assessment, "In the country's current historical state the immediate establishment of a socialist regime is not possible." While Ecuador had a capitalist system of social organization, feudalism and imperial intervention had stopped its economic development. For that reason, Ecuador needed to develop its economy and work for national liberation in the context of unifying all of the country's democratic and progressive forces. The PCE proceeded to define a program that was more liberal than socialist in its orientation, including promoting freedom of religion.[107] British Envoy Leslie Hughes-Hallett described the pamphlet as "surprisingly moderate" in its acknowledgment that "in the country's present stage of development it is not possible to contemplate the immediate establishment of a Socialist regime, although that is its final goal."[108] The PCE reiterated on multiple occasions its belief that the country was not ready for socialism and instead called for a democratic reconstruction of the country. All of this was part of an attempt to position the party as a moderate and unthreatening force in the country.[109]

The FBI's penetration of the Communist Party, together with State Department and British Foreign Office reports, underscores the fact that in the aftermath of La Gloriosa the Communist Party operated in a constitutional and responsible manner. Emphasizing electoral paths to power limited the party's effectiveness, even as alternative paths to government were not readily apparent—nor would they necessarily have led to more success. What the FBI surveillance does reveal, however, is the presence of a healthy and lively debate over a range of issues of ideology and strategy that have long beguiled the left. Disagreements over whether to collaborate with other progressive forces, whether to invest resources into electoral contests, whether to contest class enemies head on, and whether to assume an antagonistic attitude toward the government currently in power would continue to divide the left. FBI surveillance inadvertently provides an opportunity to gain a more complete understanding of those disputes as they played out inside the Communist Party.

CHAPTER 6

Coup

Daniel
León B.

ENRIQUE GIL GILBERT
DIPUTADO PROVINCIAL POR GUAYAS

ENRIQUE GIL GILBERT was a novelist best known for his 1940 book *Nuestro pan*, which critiqued problems that the lower classes faced, especially rice growers in Milagro. The book won several prizes, including honorable mention in a literary contest that led to its publication in English in 1943 as *Our Daily Bread*. He worked actively in labor unions and on antifascist committees and was the secretary-general of the Communist Party's coastal branch. He won election to the 1944–45 Constituent Assembly as a representative of the province of Guayas. Source: León Borja, *Hombres de Mayo*.

Before the May revolution, Enrique Gil Gilbert characterized the populist politician José María Velasco Ibarra as "a great international intellectual" who "understands the necessities of the masses and is a bridge from capitalism to communism." After the May revolution, the FBI said that Gil Gilbert had been more active than anyone else in the party in the formation of new "Velasquista" clubs, which they feared were nothing more than communist cells. Gil Gilbert visited the clubs to give orders and direct their course of action. While communists could expect little from Velasco Ibarra, Gil Gilbert thought that the party had better chances of flourishing under his government than with any other immediately apparent alternative. For that reason, they exploited the formation of clubs to their advantage.[1] The left initially made significant advances after the May revolution, he noted, but within two or three months the situation changed, and capitalism in all its aspects came back to the position of power it formerly had held. The left had lost the initiative. Gil Gilbert argued that the Partido Comunista del Ecuador (Communist Party of Ecuador; PCE) must provide leadership in the struggle to regain the ground that the left had previously won in La Gloriosa.[2] While communists supported the May revolution and participated in Velasco Ibarra's government, policy differences meant that leftists eventually broke with the administration and resigned their positions. FBI surveillance of labor and leftist activists charts the breakdown of this relationship between Velasco Ibarra and his supporters.

Communists throughout Latin America have vacillated in their positions toward populist movements and governments, from Jorge Eliécer Gaitán in Colombia to Juan Perón in Argentina. Too often these politicians mimic the rhetoric of leftist parties, but rather than following through on promises of a structural reform of society, they consolidate power in their own hands and for their own purposes. The onset of the Cold War introduced additional complications for communist collaboration with elected governments. In Chile, for example, Gabriel González Videla won election in 1946 with Communist Party support and initially rewarded several of its members with cabinet positions. Once in office, however, González Videla quickly turned rightward and repressed labor movements that challenged his economic policies. Communists left his government rather than acquiesce to his conservative policies. At the same time, the State Department pressured González Videla to break his ties with the party, which he eventually outlawed. Leftist goals of achieving positive policy reforms through collaboration with moderate governments typically reached dead ends.[3]

Velasco Ibarra followed similar patterns of accepting leftist backing when it served his interests but then turning against his former supporters when they pushed his government in a progressive direction. His assumption of dictatorial powers on March 30, 1946, and proscribing the Communist Party, foreshadowed a swing away from popular governments and toward authoritarian administrations in 1947 and 1948 across the region.[4] This shift occurred in the context in a change in U.S. policy from support for democratic governments during the war to an emphasis on anticommunism with the outbreak of the Cold War.[5] That policy also emboldened conservatives in Latin America to launch counteroffensives against the left and organized labor. After coming to power based on promises he had made to the left, Velasco Ibarra's swing to the right following La Gloriosa intensified schisms within the PCE over whether to adhere to institutional forms of governance. Similar to what Andrew Barnard describes in the case of Chile, "The Cold War had the effect of exacerbating existing factionalisms and encouraging already established tendencies rather than that of initiating novel departures."[6] The FBI reports cast light on the dilemmas and frustrations that the Velasco Ibarra administration created for labor and leftist activists who first looked to him with hope but then became deeply disillusioned as he turned rightward.

Reaction

In a speech at the Plaza Arenas in Quito on June 11, 1944, two weeks after the May revolution, Velasco Ibarra famously proclaimed to prolonged applause, "I am not a man of the right. My soul is purely leftist." He compared La Gloriosa to the French Revolution and promised that together all Ecuadorians, including secular communists and conservative clergy members, would build a new and progressive country.[7] Even as those on the left rallied to Velasco Ibarra's cause, U.S. Consul Harold Williamson had a much soberer assessment of the political currents running through the country. Velasco Ibarra never embraced socialist ideals, Williamson observed, and he saw his rise to power as his own personal triumph. Only a week after the May revolution, William-son reported that the communist labor leader Pedro Saad was "a trifle dis-appointed that trial balloons which he had launched in favor of such radical projects as nationalization of essential industries were very guardedly viewed by Dr. Velasco, who seems anxious to present a conservative front to capital."[8] Williamson noted, "Preliminary indications are that, despite his visionary characteristics, Dr. Velasco Ibarra is fundamentally conservative in his politi-cal tenets." Most government appointments "generally represent the capitalistic point of view." The president attempted to placate socialists and communists with policy reforms rather than administrative posts, which limited their true political power. As the president's honeymoon with popular forces quickly ended, Williamson recognized that a struggle between the left and the right would make it difficult to govern the country.[9] Whatever Velasco Ibarra's po-litical attitudes before May 1944, he deliberately moved to the right after the Glorious May Revolution.

As part of the PCE's bid to collaborate with Velasco Ibarra, Gil Gilbert at-tempted to persuade the president to visit the cooperative farms at Milagro. Velasco Ibarra finally scheduled a trip for September 17, 1944, and Gil Gilbert convinced local activists to take advantage of the president's visit to gain his support. He encouraged them to open a new road to facilitate Velasco Ibarra's arrival and arranged for six hundred men on horseback to accompany the president from the train station to the farm. The populist leader failed to show up as promised, and the communists proceeded with their program without him.[10] According to an FBI informant, Velasco Ibarra's refusal to appear in Milagro caused "a considerable amount of consternation and bitterness" from both communist leaders and local cooperative workers. Saad's father told the informant that Velasco Ibarra and Saad did not speak to each other for two weeks because Velasco Ibarra was "jealous of Pedro because he knows him to be very strong." An FBI informant who apparently was very close to Saad related that the labor leader remained on friendly terms with Velasco Ibarra, but the president had held him "responsible for the unwise attitude of some of the syndicates." Velasco Ibarra blamed Saad "for their bothering him so much for their being so greedy." In response, Saad urged party members to moder-ate their positions so as not to alienate the president and lose their access to power. Despite this overture, Velasco Ibarra actively conspired to undermine, or at least control, Saad's support base.[11] Coming only months after the May revolution and shortly after the start of the Constituent Assembly that was to draft a new and progressive constitution, the failure of the Milagro visit foreshadowed what would eventually be a complete break between his government and the left.

It was not long before Gil Gilbert condemned a conservative reaction that was betraying the goals of the May revolution. "Capitalism, both foreign and local," he stated, "has opened battle against us and we must defend our stand." In contradiction to other statements he had made regarding a peaceful path to power, if the FBI informant who provided this information is to be believed, Gil Gilbert argued that the only way to prevent a reversal of communist gains was through "bloodshed because those who cannot be made to understand by good must be forced by bad." He called for the extermination of conservative forces because no other alternative to preserve progressive gains existed.[12]

Saad clung longer than Gil Gilbert to the illusionary promise of exploiting Velasco Ibarra's presidency to advance leftist aims. Eventually Saad also grew despondent at Velasco Ibarra's conservative trajectory, even as he told the president that his best hope for survival was cooperation with the left. Saad maintained that Velasco Ibarra's worst enemies were not the communists but conservatives like his minister of foreign relations, Camilo Ponce Enríquez, and minister of government, Carlos Guevara Moreno, whose political positions had shifted significantly to the right during his time in office. Saad denied Velasco Ibarra's accusations that he had fostered strikes against his government.[13] When the government offered the communist leader a position as a legal adviser in its embassy in Washington, Saad turned it down to remain politically active in Ecuador.[14] Saad's relationship with Velasco Ibarra became increasingly estranged, and as a result, his influence with the president slowly declined. In February 1945, Saad failed to negotiate an agreement with the president regarding aspects of the new constitution that he opposed. Saad finally concluded that Velasco Ibarra had made a definite turn to the right and no longer trusted him.[15]

Although at that point in Ecuador's history 70 percent of the population embraced leftist sympathies, socialist leaders, due to a lack of vision, political experience, sophistication, and the vanity of its leaders, had allowed liberals and conservatives to gain control of the assembly. As leader of the leftist Confederación de Trabajadores del Ecuador (Confederation of Ecuadorian Workers; CTE), Saad made demands that were more reformist and corporatist than structural in nature. Some progressive groups, including the military socialists grouped in the Vanguardia Revolucionaria del Socialismo Ecuatoriano (Ecuadorian Revolutionary Socialist Vanguard; VRSE), retained more of a caudillo and authoritarian style of leadership than an ideological leftist formation that favored democratic participation. These political strategies limited the democratic transformation of society. Saad expressed skepticism at the left's ability to unite in opposition to the president. He confided to an informant that the left had learned two lessons from the failures of the May revolution: that they needed more unity, and they needed more administrative experience.[16] Minister of Education Alfredo Vera similarly described the left as "poor in political experience, but rich in idealism and naivety."[17] Their technical and strategic deficiencies undermined the realization of their goals.

Velasco Ibarra proudly proclaimed that all Ecuadorians, "the red with the conservative, the priest with the soldier, the woman and the man, the student and worker," united their forces to overthrow Carlos Arroyo del Río and make the glorious May revolution.[18] But it became impossible to solidify these diverse forces into a common front to transform the country after the ouster of the former president. As the historian Pablo Ospina Peralta notes, Velasco Ibarra quickly marginalized the communists and only the conservative priests remained.[19] Many of the initial apparent gains of this "revolution" were limited and short-lived and failed to result in profound or long-lasting changes. Leftists were unable to alter literacy restrictions that excluded Indigenous peoples, peasants, and the urban poor from citizenship and, as a result, prevented the bulk of the left's constituency from exercising the franchise. Although these marginalized sectors of society had played important roles in bringing down the Arroyo del Río regime, after La Gloriosa they were soon excluded from participation in government affairs. Meanwhile, the economic situation in the country continued to decline, with the cost of living rising dramatically during the 1940s and real wages falling.[20] The change in administration did not create a fundamental or conceptual shift that would address the underlying structural problems resulting from exclusionary state structures. Rather than solving the country's problems, the new government only exacerbated a worsening situation.

In retrospect, many participants in La Gloriosa noted the conservative outcome of the events. The military leader Colonel Sergio Enrique Girón called the revolution "stillborn."[21] Others called it a "revolution betrayed" and observed that while the events of May should have been glorious, they had devolved into little more than a barracks revolt with a reactionary result.[22] Vera commented that Velasco Ibarra was never committed to the revolution but only wanted to restore democracy to preserve the privileges of the oligarchy of which he was part.[23] Secretary-General Manuel Agustín Aguirre of the Partido

Socialista Ecuatoriano (Ecuadorian Socialist Party; PSE) noted that his first meeting with Velasco Ibarra left him feeling disillusioned, not only because of the leader's cold and distant personality but also because of his conservative and opportunistic political stance that could only mean limited political outcomes.[24] He called Velasco Ibarra "the number one traitor," who entered the revolution as a Trojan horse. In retrospect, Aguirre declared, the counter-revolution had already begun on May 30 when Velasco Ibarra assumed power and set democratic and revolutionary forces against each other. Rather than placing the revolution's leaders in positions of power, he marginalized them in favor of a reactionary old guard. His policies left previous political structures intact rather than fomenting a fundamental transformation of society.[25] Velasco Ibarra's second period in office, much like the other four times he was the chief executive, resulted in a re-entrenchment of the exclusionary nature of Ecuadorian politics and the denial of a voice to women, workers, peasants, Indigenous peoples, and popular movements in general.

Barely a month into the Constituent Assembly, the communist delegate Gustavo Becerra declared that even though Velasco Ibarra "came to serve the Ecuadorian people who put him in power, he has not been able to free himself from landholder and reactionary influences."[26] Even before the Constituent Assembly was done with its work, Velasco Ibarra vocally expressed his disapproval of the direction that the drafting of the constitution had taken. He opposed the system of functional representation and restrictions on executive power because they limited "the sovereignty of the people."[27] As a result, Velasco Ibarra found the 1945 constitution too radical and criticized it for being "barbaric, absurd, utopian, and impossible, a typical example of the idiotic *criollo* Communism that congratulates itself for filling theaters and lecture halls with illiterate Indians."[28] His disdain for those to his left and below him was unmistakable.

In the context of strained communist relations with Velasco Ibarra's government, FBI agents expressed concerns about a leftist-inspired military coup. According to their reports, "The Communists have developed a considerable number of sympathizers within the Army," particularly "among the privates and low ranking officers." The agents complained that "Communist elements" dominated the civil guard police in Guayaquil that had replaced the carabineros the FBI had trained.[29] Ricardo Paredes told a confidential FBI source that the present government placed the civil guard on a lower plane than the military, while the Arroyo del Río administration had privileged the carabineros over the military. As a result, under current conditions the civil guard was more easily brought against Velasco Ibarra than the army, whereas under Arroyo del Río the reverse was true.[30]

The embassy similarly reported that Captain Carlos Egas Llaguno, a "well-known communist," had been named head of the civil guard police in Riobamba. The informant "assumed that Egas [would] contact other communists in Riobamba which has been the scene of various communist meetings and subversive movements in the past."[31] Embassy officials repeated rumors of communist penetration of Ecuador's armed forces and at one time attributed that influence "as a result of intrigues of the Communist Ministers of Government and Education" in Velasco Ibarra's government.[32] On the surface, such rumors and reports might appear to be the exaggerations of an obsessive security apparatus's overactive imagination. Nevertheless, some truth exists behind a fear of individual military personnel breaking with their traditional alliance with the Catholic church and wealthy landholders and instead embracing a leftist vision for a more egalitarian and inclusive political system, one that would not necessarily be in the economic and political interests of the United States.

The unnamed author of an August 1945 FBI report surmised, "the Communists feel that they might be able to produce a coup d'état in Ecuador, placing in power perhaps Pedro Saad or perhaps an army officer controlled by them." The report listed Captain César Montufar and General Luis Larrea Alba as possible coup leaders. The U.S. intelligence apparatus feared the possibility of a coup, despite the fact that its own reports reiterated that the PCE was committed to maintenance of the existing institutional order. That contradiction might be due either to faulty intelligence or, more likely, to a divergence of opinion within the Communist Party. The same report concluded, "The communists can best achieve their aims by prolonging the term of Velasco Ibarra in spite of the fact that the latter is opposed to them."[33] This followed a detailed report from several months earlier in which Saad expressed his lack of "confidence in the plan to unite all Leftist groups in opposition to Velasco." Rather, Saad advocated "that by cooperating with Velasco and gaining his confidence the Communist Party will also gain the support of the Army and thus of the people in general." From Saad's perspective, the communists should make common cause with the military in support of Velasco Ibarra and against their mutual conservative enemies to "secure power where power is."[34]

The FBI documented tensions between Paredes and the provincial party leadership in Riobamba. One local leader, Arsenio Veloz, accused Paredes of being careless in his management of party affairs and stated that Paredes was "not the type of man who should head the PCE under present difficult circumstances."[35] The PCE lost ground as Velasco Ibarra's government swung to the right and struggled to remain politically active. In Ambassador Robert Scotten's estimation, Velasco Ibarra's opposition "may have stimulated its efforts." Scotten pointed to evidence that the communists might support General Alberto Enríquez Gallo if he were to attempt a coup. Internationally, Scotten observed, "The Communist line has changed decidedly since the end of the war and . . . the United States as a capitalist nation is being openly and covertly attacked." In particular, the communists played up the presence of U.S. troops at a military base on the Galápagos Islands "to make anti-American propaganda."[36] Mobilizing opposition to the base became a key component of the PCE's nationalist credentials now that defeat of the Axis powers was no longer a prime concern.[37]

Enríquez's alleged involvement in coup conspiracies highlights the complicated relationship that the left maintained with charismatic but ideologically undefined leaders. According to an FBI monthly report on communist activities, "It was well known that Enríquez, if he came to power, would not tolerate the Communist Party, stating that he would declare it without legal status." The general was negotiating with the communists to gain access to the arms they had acquired during the May revolution "to neutralize the group as a factor in the revolt." The PCE headquarters in Quito had repeatedly repudiated Enríquez's overtures, believing that the party's fortunes would be best served with a continuance of constitutional rule under Velasco Ibarra. Some party activists in Guayaquil, however, argued that Enríquez would be preferable to the growing conservative presence in Velasco Ibarra's government.[38] That attitude was by no means unanimous. Ana Moreno, a member of the PCE's Central Committee, complained that socialists favored Enríquez, but the communists did not want to return to a dictatorship, which he almost certainly would promote. "It would do us no good to remove Velasco and place another dictator in his stead," she reportedly stated. "We are fighting for a government that respects law and the constitution of 1945 and for a government which will give us something to eat when we are dying of hunger; which gives us a better life, which gives liberty to the people and which will not take from us the rights that we fought for in the May 28 (1944) revolution."[39] Gil Gilbert expressed a similar attitude, cautioning against replacing Velasco Ibarra with an equally disagreeable authoritarian leader such as Enríquez.[40]

Communist opposition to the socialist support for Enríquez led to mutual "hatred" between Enríquez and communist leaders and fear that the army would annihilate the PCE if they took over the government.[41] Despite these tensions and disagreements, an informant told U.S. Embassy officials that Enríquez had promised the communists support in a public demonstration against the CTE's potential affiliation with the American Federation of Labor (AFL). The ambassador read this advance as "a bid on his part for future Communist political backing."[42] As a populist and caudillo, Enríquez seemed ready to make whatever pacts were necessary to keep him in power. As the FBI and embassy surveillance highlighted, socialists and communists responded to those openings in a variety of contradictory fashions. Militants continued to debate whether they should take armed action against the government, organize a general strike, or engage in electoral contests. Each option had its advocates and its tradeoffs.[43]

Autogolpe

Rather than the left initiating a coup, on March 30, 1946, Velasco Ibarra launched an *autogolpe*, or coup against his own government. He took this action to quash institutional mechanisms that the opposition might use to challenge his hold on power. He dissolved the Constituent Assembly that had been elected in July 1944 and was scheduled to remain in office until August 1946. He abrogated the progressive 1945 constitution that had been in effect for only a little more than a year and reinstated the liberal 1906 constitution. As justification for his action, Velasco Ibarra accused progressive military officials of plotting a coup against his government and ordered Enríquez and the VRSE members Guillermo Burbano Rueda and Aurelio Olarte arrested and expelled from the country.[44] In response to Velasco Ibarra's move, a group of socialists left the government. They included Alfredo Pérez Guerrero, the attorney-general and president of the Constitutional Court; Benjamín Carrión, the president of the National Institute of Social Welfare; Comptroller-General Ángel F. Rojas; and Jorge Carrera Andrade, Ecuador's ambassador to Venezuela.

Velasco Ibarra had come to power in La Gloriosa during a period of rising labor and leftist influence throughout Latin America. Now, less than two years later, with the war over and in the context of George Kennan's February 1946 "long telegram" from Moscow that launched the Cold War policy of containment, the international situation appeared much dimmer for Latin American leftists. Over the course of the next two years, labor activists faced increased repression and were excluded from political positions. Formerly reformist or progressive parties moved to the right, and governments outlawed communist parties. The May 1944 democratic spring had been reversed, along with opportunities for much needed and profound political and social changes.[45]

Velasco Ibarra's self-coup triggered street protests that spread across Quito and in particular were concentrated in front of the Central University and presidential palace, even as the police cracked down on the demonstrators.[46] For the most part, Guayaquil remained calm, although the civil guard police broke up a meeting of liberals and leftists as part of a crackdown on those opposed to the president's authoritarian move. The police arrested Franklin Pérez Castro and other communist activists. The VRSE's Clotario Paz and the PCE's Simón Zambrano were in hiding.[47] Galo Plaza, Velasco Ibarra's ambassador to the United States and a future president, nevertheless, stayed in his post in Washington and claimed not to know what was happening in his country.[48] Such ruptures are periods of intense confusion, and Plaza sought to play it in a way that would advance his political fortunes. The coup led British Minister Colin Edmond to summarize 1946 as "another year of tumult in the history of Ecuador," leaving "the country no respite from political unrest."[49]

Velasco Ibarra restricted the freedom of the press and ordered the arrest and expulsion of Héctor Vásconez, a liberal congressional deputy who should have enjoyed legal impunity. The president would tolerate no opposition to his government. In response to these and other actions, PSE Secretary-General Aguirre, PCE Secretary-General Becerra, and Sergio Lasso Meneses, president of the Pichincha provincial Radical Liberal Party, issued a proclamation that accused the president of exceeding his constitutional authority and in effect implementing a totalitarian regime. The political leaders argued that the 1945 constitution provided sufficient facilities for a democratic government to preserve order without disrupting the institutional process and assuming dictatorial powers.[50] That statement led Velasco Ibarra to arrest and deport Aguirre to Peru, along with the military officials the president had accused of plotting a coup.[51] With Aguirre in exile, Emilio Gangotena assumed leadership of the Socialist Party. Gangotena issued a series of statements demanding the secretary-general's release and calling on Velasco Ibarra to recognize constitutional guarantees.[52] Aguirre regularly sent communiqués from Lima with instructions for political action.[53]

The PCE distributed its own statement that called on the entire left, as well as progressives in the Liberal Party, to join a struggle against Velasco Ibarra's dictatorship and fight for the restoration of democratic order under the 1945 constitution. The statement proclaimed, "Leftist political parties, and in particular the Communist Party, have ardently struggled in defense of the constitutional order and for the rights of workers and people in general." The communists called for the restoration of constitutional institutions, including the Permanent Legislative Commission and the Tribunal of Constitutional Guarantees on which Saad and Gil Gilbert had sat. Once again, the party emphasized that the time was not right for socialism. Rather than assuming power, the communists proclaimed that they only wanted to restore institutional governance as established in the 1945 constitution. The PCE called for a defense of territorial integrity and repeated its opposition to the U.S. military occupation of the Galápagos Islands. The communists took advantage of the break in power to reiterate, in contrast to Velasco Ibarra, their patriotic and anti-imperialist credentials.[54]

Luis Maldonado Tamayo, a member of the Constitutional Court and the editor of the socialist newspaper *La Tierra*, also directly challenged the government's actions. He claimed that if the government had brought evidence of an imminent coup attempt to the court, it would have studied the situation and perhaps granted the president the extraordinary powers necessary to confront the challenge to the institutional order. Since the government had failed to follow those legal provisions, it had violated the constitution. The loyal sub-secretary of government, José Rafael Terán Robalino, countered that government officials had not violated the constitution and would not accept Maldonado Tamayo's insults and slander.[55] Although Terán Robalino claimed that the government continued to respect freedom of the press, early in the morning on April 2 he sent armed police to shut down *La Tierra*. The police trashed the newspaper's office and arrested those present, including the socialist lawyer Juan Isaac Lovato. The police tore that day's edition off the press and lit a bonfire with it in front of the building. To avoid arrest, Maldonado Tamayo sought refuge at the Venezuelan Embassy.[56] One of the items to be published in that day's issue was a statement from the Federación de Estudiantes Universitarios del Ecuador (Federation of Ecuadorian University Students; FEUE) denouncing Velasco Ibarra's actions. Without a place to publish its manifesto, the FEUE declared an indefinite strike.[57] When *La Tierra* finally reopened two weeks later, it remained as defiant as ever.

A month later, in its annual May Day statement, the CTE called on workers to fight against Velasco Ibarra's authoritarian measures and for democracy, freedom for political prisoners, the return of exiles, and the retention of gains in the 1945 constitution.[58] Several weeks later, the Federación de Trabajadores de Pichincha (Pichincha Workers Federation; FTP) held its third congress in Quito. Among its proclamations was an expression of admiration for the media for its defense of human rights in the face of Velasco Ibarra's assumption of dictatorial powers. Similar to the CTE, the FTP denounced the government's repressive actions, expressed its solidarity with all who worked in support of the constitutional order, and called for freedom for all political prisoners.[59] In the midst of all of this protest and repression, labor activists commemorated La Gloriosa's second anniversary. The CTE called on workers to defend the ideals of the May revolution and to fight for the return of constitutional rule.[60]

The March 30 coup represented a definitive break between Velasco Ibarra's government and leftist forces, and the political repression extended to various sectors of society. The police arrested the student activist Gustavo Buendía and held him incommunicado. The government also threatened to deport the French antifascist fighter Raymond Mériguet to Colombia for having intervened in Ecuador's internal politics.[61] The police arrested the Indigenous rights activist Luis F. Alvaro as he planned a trip to Riobamba to help the workers at the Tipin hacienda settle their accounts with the assistance of the labor inspector's office.[62] Even the government's Ministry of Labor protested his arrest, stating that Alvaro was not a terrorist but simply complying with his obligations as a member of the Indigenous congress to facilitate the payment of workers' wages.[63] As the arrests piled up, La Tierra published an occasional column with the names of political prisoners that was ironically titled, "Who Is a Terrorist."[64]

Velasco Ibarra's self-coup did not come as a surprise to many observers. A month earlier the U.S. Embassy had reported a turbulent political environment and open threats from the president to abolish the Tribunal of Constitutional Guarantees and Permanent Legislative Commission. Doing so, the embassy noted, would imply "the setting up of a virtual dictatorship." The socialist Manuel Agustín Aguirre as the vice president of the Constituent Assembly was next in line to succeed the president. According to the embassy's informants, if Velasco Ibarra were to establish a dictatorship, Aguirre would convoke a congress to unseat the president.[65] If that was indeed Aguirre's plan, Velasco Ibarra deported him before he had a chance to act.

Similarly, the British diplomatic mission claimed that Velasco Ibarra had exaggerated the significance of the challenge to his government in order to scare people, discredit the opposition, and rally support for his administration. The mission concluded that the allegedly planned coup of progressive military officers that the president used to justify his actions "was neither imminent nor of any serious proportions."[66] The mission's First Secretary J. H. Wright reported, "The fact that the plot had little or no support in the army, which must be the breeding ground of all revolutions, shows how little progress it had made." As long as the government enjoyed the military's support, it would be very difficult to remove it from power. Furthermore, the mission contended that the conservatives were committed to proceeding with the midterm elections because they were better positioned to regain power than at any time since Eloy Alfaro's 1895 liberal revolution. Finally, Wright maintained that Velasco Ibarra still largely enjoyed the support of the general public—or, at least, the public did not see an attractive alternative. The most likely option was "a Government of the extreme Left," which, according to Wright, was "a source of dread to the average middle-of-the-road Ecuadorean." The diplomat claimed that the obstructions that leftists had thrown up in the face of the smooth functioning of society had led to an erosion of their popular support and, in general, to their being discredited in the public eye.[67]

FBI surveillance provides more details about the difficulties that "the extreme left" confronted in the face of the coup. While previously the FBI had largely ignored female activists in the Communist Party, agents now drafted a comparatively long and detailed report on Nela Martínez's activities. The surveillance offers insights into communist responses to the coup. Less than two months before the coup, the government canceled the program for which Martínez worked in Manabí, and she returned to Quito unemployed. A "reliable source" advised the FBI that "although Nela Martínez has never been known to have been in possession of any appreciable sum of money, . . . since her return to Quito she has made a point of the fact that she now has fifty thousand sucres ($3,800) which she wishes to invest in a house." The FBI informant commented that the origin of the money was not known, although the source speculated that Martínez was attempting to purchase a house for Saad, who had faced difficulties in obtaining residence in the capital. Even before the coup, Velasco Ibarra's former allies faced increased repression.

While Martínez was in Manabí, "her close friend María Luisa Gómez de la Torre, a Quito schoolteacher who has long been active in Communist matters," took over her work in the party. The FBI cited from "sources who are in regular attendance at communist meetings" that Martínez had not participated in party activities since her return from the coast. That changed, however, as soon as Velasco Ibarra assumed dictatorial control and drove the party underground. Immediately, Martínez "began to lend enthusiastic support to the Party's endeavors." She visited factories to encourage adherence to a general strike that the CTE called for April 3. The strike failed, and many labor leaders were arrested or forced into hiding, but "Martínez has remained entirely at liberty." As with women in wartime, her gender and privileged class status afforded her a certain amount of protection. Saad, however, was underground. Martínez moved into his room at the Savoy Hotel to accompany his spouse, Isabel Herrería. A week later, a car hit their five-year-old son and left him with a serious head wound. Martínez claimed that the injury was part of a government conspiracy to force Saad out of hiding.[68]

The FBI translated the text of an open letter to Velasco Ibarra that Martínez and other female activists published in *La Tierra* to denounce the self-coup. The women proclaimed that at one point they had supported the populist leader, but he had betrayed the promises of the May revolution. He had violated both their trust and the constitution and should resign. "You are no longer the friend of the popular majority," the letter declared.[69] With many of the male leaders lying low, the women's very public protest finally brought them to the attention of the FBI.

Female activists were not entirely immune from repression. Gómez de la Torre's signature on the letter led to her dismissal from the Colegio Mejía. Gómez de la Torre was widely renowned as the first woman to earn a teaching position at the prestigious all-male school. In response, fifty "leftist ladies" held a tea at the Savoy Hotel in her honor. According to an article in *El Día*, Mrs. Saad spoke at the event in the name of Guayaquil women; Mrs. Ester de Castrejón spoke for schoolteachers; Miss Clemencia Salazar spoke for the Alianza Femenina Ecuatoriana (Ecuadorian Feminist Alliance; AFE); Mrs. Lucrecia de López spoke for working-class women; and Miss Nela Martínez spoke for the national university. A similar story in *El Comercio* stated that Martínez expounded on women's juridical and constitutional advances. The FBI report quoted from both articles but apparently did not have corroborating informants who could confirm which version of the story was correct, once again underscoring that much of the bureau's so-called intelligence apparently came from publicly available sources. The protest was successful, and the women forced the school's rector to reinstate Gómez de la Torre in her job.[70]

The women gathered at the Savoy Hotel formed a committee to defend human rights to prevent future abuses. One of their first actions was to ask *La Tierra* to publicize their demands. Despite coming from more privileged sectors of society, the female activists highlighted the needs of working women.[71] Although speaking out in defense of lower-class women could be seen as betraying a touch of paternalism, it also highlights the types of structural changes they envisioned in society.

An FBI "investigation" of Paredes following the coup exhibited little more interest in the PCE secretary-general's activities than in those of Martínez and the other leftist women. The bureau's probe primarily involved summarizing reports from mainstream newspapers. One of those was a statement Paredes published in *El Comercio* declaring that no division existed between the Quito and Guayaquil branches of the party, and that the PCE had only one line, and that was support for constitutionality against Velasco Ibarra's dictatorship. He declared that the communists were ready to ally with all political parties, including the Radical Liberal Party, for the restoration of democracy in the country.[72] Paredes had initially gone into hiding after the coup, but when he became convinced that the police were not looking for him, he returned to his residence in Quito. Apparently, the police were no more interested in the party leader than was the FBI.

Elections

Velasco Ibarra launched his March 30 coup as Ecuador was preparing to hold congressional elections. The electoral law stipulated that the electoral tribunal was to issue a call on April 5 for the elections that would be held a month later, but that institution disintegrated as officials resigned rather than collaborate with Velasco Ibarra in his authoritarian move. Velasco Ibarra's ally Alberto Acosta Soberón attempted to step in as a member of the Tribunal of Constitutional Guarantees, but opponents stopped him from doing so.[73] In this vacuum, Velasco Ibarra issued an executive decree calling for legislative elections for the first Sunday in May, an action that elicited howls of protests from his opponents, who complained that they would not be able to compete under the existing conditions.[74] In turn, the liberal and various leftist parties announced that they would not participate in what they considered a sham designed to legitimize Velasco Ibarra's hold on power. The protests delayed the elections for a month but did not alter the conditions under which they would be held. In fact, the situation was now worse, as Velasco Ibarra announced an election in June to choose a new constitutional assembly. Again, the left protested the president's proposal. The PCE declared the planned elections "spurious, because it will only serve to perpetuate the reactionaries' hold on power, and thereby provide them with a mask of legality."[75] When the PSE publicized its intention to abstain, the government arrested Gangotena, the party's acting secretary-general.[76]

With the election a month away, Paredes condemned Velasco Ibarra's regime and called for a boycott of the vote. He proposed a new democratic coalition government that would work for the development of the country's economy, improve the lives of the workers, fight corruption, and defend Ecuador's territorial integrity and national sovereignty. Paredes called for liberal-left unity to defeat Velasco Ibarra's despotic government and to advance the communists' democratic agenda. Before the coup and in light of the left's defeat in the November 1945 municipal elections, Saad had advocated building a similar liberal-left coalition to compete in the upcoming congressional race. The Communist Party, however, had been largely unsuccessful in gaining support from other political parties to form an electoral alliance. Now, the PCE even appealed to Catholics, the Conservative Party's traditional base of support, to join their struggle. Paredes declared, "The Communist Party has fought, and always will fight, for [the Catholics'] economic and cultural interests." He denounced as false the charges that the communists sought to abolish religion, massacre priests, and burn churches. He pointed to the party's support for freedom of religion in the 1944 Constituent Assembly as firm evidence against these charges.[77] Paredes's statement caught the attention of both the media and the FBI. *El Comercio* referenced the call for leftists, liberals, and Catholics to unify in a struggle for democratic restoration, and the FBI summarized the manifesto's main points.[78]

While previously both the FBI and the Ecuadorian government had largely ignored Paredes, his public statements now led to a police raid on his house. An FBI informant said that in response party members removed Paredes's essential belongings and moved him to a new location. The police also arrested Gustavo Araujo for printing his statement. FBI agents conveyed newspaper reports to Washington of police surveillance of leftist politicians, which is odd because the bureau's police trainers presumably would have had direct contact with the security officials conducting the investigations. The two forces probably shared information on suspected subversives, although the available sources do not document such activities. In all likelihood, had the FBI so desired, it could have reported Paredes's new location to the police. That it did not do so either reveals that the bureau did not view the communist leader as representing a significant threat or, perhaps, the agents took seriously their mandate to be a service agency that limited itself to collecting information rather than acting on it.[79]

Despite the repression, Paredes continued to publish statements in the name of the PCE's Executive Committee that denounced Velasco Ibarra's repressive actions and called for respect for the 1945 constitution. He demanded the release of all political prisoners, including Mériguet and Vásconez, and implored that Aguirre be allowed to return from exile.[80] The French minister in Ecuador refused to intervene on Mériguet's behalf when the government threatened to exile him, which led the antifascist fighter to begin a hunger strike. As the pressure mounted on the government, Velasco Ibarra finally released both Mériguet and Vásconez.[81] It was not until the end of August, however, that the government finally allowed Aguirre to return to Ecuador. The socialists organized a large welcome for the return of their secretary-general, complete with oversize headlines in their newspaper La Tierra.[82]

Leftist parties debated reconstituting the Alianza Democrática Ecuatoriana (Ecuadorian Democratic Alliance; ADE) to compete in the congressional elections. The PCE sent Martínez and Gómez de la Torre as their representatives to a meeting to discuss what shape such collaboration might take, but the socialists objected to the Communist Party sending women instead of the male leaders Paredes and Saad.[83] The FBI reported that the communist militant Francisco Mora Guerrero similarly complained that women were distributing orders for the party.[84] Women may have been used in this situation because many of the male leaders were in hiding or prison—or, perhaps, because of a perception that under the repressive conditions, the women could move about more easily in society. If that was the case, the assumption was not entirely correct. The FBI recounted that Martínez was an organizer of a protest in Quito on June 3 to denounce the death of a student in Loja the preceding day. The police broke up the protest and arrested Martínez but released her after interrogating her for an hour. An informant reported that Martínez continued to be unemployed and was living with Gómez de la Torre. Because of her well-known communist activities, she was unlikely to find a job. That possibility did not deter her from continuing with her political activities.[85] Both Martínez and Gómez de la Torre were political militants in their own right, despite the overt sexism that they faced.

The planned congressional elections were repeatedly delayed and finally held on June 30 in a spirit of what critics characterized as complete popular indifference. Given the Liberal Party's numerical electoral advantage and almost hegemonic control over the country for the previous half-century, the British diplomatic mission depicted its abstention as "one of the most ridiculous and unaccountable episodes in the complicated politics of Ecuador."[86] Only conservative parties participated in what Aguirre portrayed as a totalitarian attempt to legalize Velasco Ibarra's dictatorship.[87] Similarly, Paredes denounced the elections as a "farce" because only the most conservative and reactionary elements participated. The communists pledged to continue fighting against those enemies of progress and for "an authentic democracy." Paredes called on "all free and patriotic Ecuadorians" to join in a struggle against Velasco Ibarra's dictatorship and for the restoration of democracy.[88] Several weeks later, the PCE repeated its calls for people to take to the streets to overthrow Velasco Ibarra's government and for the socialists and liberals to join the communists in establishing a new coalition government that would respect democracy, reconstruct the country's deteriorated economy, liquidate feudalism, liberate Indigenous peoples, advance social programs, and defend the country's sovereignty and territorial integrity.[89]

FBI agents reported that the PCE had become more active in its clandestine operations under Velasco Ibarra's authoritarian regime than it had been out in the open. The party began publishing its first paper since *Bloque* disappeared in late 1945. The new weekly paper *Combate* (Combat), was appropriately subtitled, "Clandestine Organ of Struggle against the Dictatorship."[90] The newspaper was short-lived; a more successful and long-lasting effort was the subsequent weekly newspaper *El Pueblo* (The People). Martínez, Gómez de la Torre, and Herrería were the principal collectors of funds for what would become the party's main propaganda organ for the next several decades. In this case, their success caught the FBI's attention.[91] It also gained the disapproval of others who saw a need to operate in a more cautious manner. Gil Gilbert indicated that a shortcoming of his counterparts in Quito was that they "put all of their interest in papers, and tell everybody what they do, think and plan." In Guayaquil, in contrast, communists "think, plan and act without letting the general public know, and we are much stronger than our group in Quito." The claim of working effectively in a clandestine fashion was quite an ironic statement to include in a confidential surveillance report and reflects the gains the FBI had made in penetrating the Communist Party's inner circles.[92]

On August 10, 1946, Velasco Ibarra convened a constitutional assembly tasked with drafting a new magna carta that was more to his liking. Leftists refused to participate in the writing of a new constitution, favoring instead adherence to the one that they had implemented the previous year. As a result, conservatives dominated the assembly and dictated the contents of a document that governed the country for the next twenty years. Just before the assembly met, Ecuador's political police engaged in another round of arrests of leftist dissidents, including imprisoning once more the acting PSE Secretary-General Gangotena.[93] The assembly proceeded to declare a general amnesty for political prisoners that included Gangotena.[94] Even so, the PSE accused the government of continuing to persecute its members.[95] Velasco Ibarra's Minister of Government Benjamín Terán Varea called for national harmony, which led Paredes to point out that the communists had defended the constitutional order in the face of Velasco Ibarra's repressive and dictatorial action. National harmony could be reestablished only if the country returned to the political conditions that existed before Velasco Ibarra's March 30 coup. The communists called for an institutional solution to the country's problems.[96] The socialists similarly responded that the country had been at peace until Velasco Ibarra disrupted the constitutional order, and they found the call for reconciliation from the offending party to be an empty gesture.[97]

Liberals and leftists denounced the 1946 constitution for rolling back the democratic advances embodied in the preceding document.[98] The PCE condemned the new constitution for facilitating the economic and political dominance of the oligarchy over the country, including providing a legal basis for the continuation of the large landed estates, or latifundio, as the primary mode of agricultural production. The communists complained that the new constitution removed government control over subsoil rights and in the process sacrificed Ecuador's independence and territorial integrity and opened the country to imperialist penetration. They also protested the concentration of power in the executive.[99] The socialists similarly criticized the removal of working-class participation in such organisms as the Permanent Legislative Commission and Tribunal of Constitutional Guarantees that provided the earlier constitution with its democratic characteristics.[100] The conservative delegates also struck the limited functional representation that Indigenous peoples and peasants enjoyed in the 1929 and 1945 constitutions, although wealthy agriculturalists and merchants retained their representatives. The new constitution failed to acknowledge the importance of ethnicity and removed the reference to Kichwa and other Indigenous languages that delegates had included in the previous constitution. The new document eliminated the right of divorce and secular education. The PCE characterized public education as "one of the fundamental democratic conquests of the 1895 liberal revolution." The party reiterated its defense of religious freedoms but argued that a return to religious control over education would be a serious blow to the country's progress. The communists called for "all democratic forces to fight against the consummation of this monstrous crime" of rolling back the liberal gains in secularizing society.[101] The VRSE similarly denounced the document as a return to dark depths of the conservative caudillo Gabriel García Moreno's 1869 Catholic constitution. "It is time for action," the military socialists declared.[102]

Not everyone, of course, was unhappy with the new text. British Minister Colin Edmond found the new constitution "more acceptable and appropriate" to his country's imperial interests than the previous one, although "its merits are due less to the Assembly than to the body of lawyers whom the President invited in May last year to draft it."[103] The assembly, it turned out, was little more than a choreographed exercise designed to provide a veneer of legitimacy to an authoritarian endeavor to concentrate wealth and power in the upper class. These reversals indicated a determined effort on the part of wealthy conservatives to exclude from political discourse those whom they believed were unworthy of that activity. The ruling classes made little effort to meet the general demands that the working class had been pressing with the government.

With the codification of Velasco Ibarra's conservative policies in the new constitution, leftist and labor groups reflected on how best to advance their struggles. Internal divisions spread throughout the PCE over how to respond to Velasco Ibarra's swing to the right. An FBI agent interviewed a confidential source about César Andrade Meneses, a relatively minor member of the party who was charged with establishing a communist-controlled food-processing cooperative and running the PCE's November 1945 municipal election campaign. Neither was successful, although Andrade would not say why, and the failures led to his falling out of favor with the party's Central Committee. As a result, Andrade was "bitterly antagonistic" toward Paredes and was part of a group of discontented party members who had grown close to Saad. Their strategy was to refuse to cooperate with Paredes and, they hoped, replace him with Saad at the next party congress.[104]

Divisions had always existed in the PCE, and Velasco Ibarra's coup only made them more visible. At the CTE's May Day celebration in Quito in 1946, Primitivo Barreto read Saad's speech in which he argued that the leftist movement in Ecuador should be made up entirely of workers. Nela Martínez responded in the name of the PCE with Paredes's argument that, because of a lack of industrialization, a working class had not developed to the point where a movement could be built solely on laborers. In the meantime, a movement must be constructed on a broad base that included Indigenous peoples, artisans, and progressive individuals. In addition, Martínez argued that the movement should seek cooperation with progressive-minded industrialists.[105] Saad's position encouraged growing unhappiness among workers in Guayaquil with the party's "intellectual" leadership, including both Saad and Paredes. Party members attempted to remove the entire Central Committee of the coastal party and replace its members with workers, and their preference was to do the same with the entire party.[106] The anti-intellectual bloc in Guayaquil turned against Gil Gilbert, secretary-general of the coastal regional party, in part because he had spent most of his time dedicated to the Tribunal of Constitutional Guarantees rather than party activities. Saad, however, successfully used his clout as president of the CTE to regain working-class support for himself and Gil Gilbert.[107]

Whereas during the war U.S. diplomats occasionally had treated the communists as a legitimate political force, those attitudes changed with the onset of the Cold War. In mid-1946, the State Department requested assistance from the AFL to stem communist advances in Latin America, as well as to export U.S. political values and institutional styles to the region. Government officials turned to the AFL for this task because it favored liberal economic measures of unrestricted trade that played to the advantage of U.S. corporations. In contrast, its competitor, the Congress of Industrial Organizations (CIO), backed the CTAL's policy recommendations of protectionist tariffs and government-directed development of basic industries designed to advance domestic Latin American interests. The AFL selected the strongly anticommunist Serafino Romualdi as its representative to advance its agenda in Latin America. Romualdi had established contacts with pro–United States union leaders while working as an OSS agent in Brazil during the war, and he expanded on them as an AFL representative. Secretary of State James Byrnes instructed embassies to provide assistance to Romualdi as he developed a new hemispheric labor organization to counter the communist-dominated CTAL.[108] Some scholars regard the AFL's actions in 1946 as the beginning of U.S. Cold War intervention in Latin America.[109]

Romualdi contended that government repression and a lack of political freedoms hindered the development of a vibrant labor movement in Latin America, which forced workers to live in miserable conditions. He expressed concern that communists manipulated this exploitative situation to their own political benefit. He pointed to a pattern of communist leaders rising to positions of leadership in trade unions even though they were not workers. Pedro Saad, for example, was a businessman. Romualdi criticized the CTAL for promoting protectionist policies to defend nationalist industries, even though that might mean denying workers access to cheaper and better products imported from industrialized countries.[110] Romualdi was not concerned with larger structural issues.

In August 1946, Romualdi traveled to Ecuador with the specific goal of pulling the socialists away from collaborating with the communists.[111] In his memoirs, Romualdi characterizes his visit as "inconclusive" because of the futility of the socialists' "naive and indecisive" tactics.[112] At the time, however, the AFL representative thought his trip was successful. Romualdi cheered when, at the second CTE congress several months after his visit, the communists lost control of the labor federation to the socialists.[113] After the congress, the CTE's new President Maldonado Jarrín described in a private conversation with the State Department how the socialists controlled the Credentials Committee to defeat communist candidates for leadership positions. Maldonado pledged to work with the AFL and to take the CTE in an anticommunist direction.[114] Henry Dearborn at the State Department's Ecuador desk portrayed the communists' loss as "consistent with the continued decline of the Ecuadoran Communist Party since 1945."[115] Romualdi selected the socialist lawyer Lovato as the AFL's "confidential" correspondent in Ecuador and specifically tasked him with breaking from the CTAL. Lovato, however, came from the left wing of the Socialist Party, which was willing to work with the communists, as well as the CTAL. Despite the apparent momentary victory, decades later Romualdi criticized the CTE's socialist leadership for being too "cautious." He regarded his work in Ecuador as a failure because the labor federation maintained its affiliation with the communist-dominated CTAL.[116]

The left's diminished strength corresponded with an increase in effective FBI surveillance. An open question, however, is how much of that decline was due to internal divisions—which had always been present in the party as part of ongoing policy debates—and how much it was due to external interventions. Romualdi's work represented the beginning of Cold War collaboration between the U.S. government and the AFL to counter independent leftist union initiatives, and to extend U.S. imperial reach into Latin America.[117] In this new political environment, the PCE struggled to regain the initiative it had enjoyed in the immediate aftermath of La Gloriosa. Its history would be one of both advances and reversals.

Party Congress

For years, the communists had attempted without success to organize a national congress. According to party statutes, the PCE was to hold a congress every two years. The party, however, had not convened one since 1931, when the PCE, which was founded as a socialist party in 1926, formally changed its name to "Communist." Internal divisions tore at the party. The Guayaquil cells that were unhappy with Quito's leadership agitated for a congress to elect new leaders and change the party's political line. Some of those members refused to pay their dues. Leaders kept pushing back the date for the congress, most recently in 1945, from October to November, then to December, and then to some unspecified date in the future.[118] The socialist newspaper *La Tierra* reported at the end of September 1946 that the PCE's Executive Committee had instructed local committees to name delegates for the national congress scheduled for October 1–6. The congress was to define the party's structure, receive reports on activities, and plan future actions.[119] After further delays, the party finally convened the congress on November 16, 1946.

The PCE meeting ran parallel to the weeklong thirteenth congress of the PSE, which faithfully met every November 15 on the anniversary of the 1922 massacre of striking workers in Guayaquil. At the same time, the VRSE announced plans for its third national congress in Cuenca in December.[120] In contrast to these other meetings, the communist congress received little public attention. One exception to the media blackout was three articles in *La Tierra*, and in the absence of party archives, this newspaper coverage provides one of the few documentary records of the congress. The first article announced that the longtime party activist Antonio Ruiz Flores served as the president of the congress. Unlike other political parties that were exclusively affairs of men from privileged, European-descended classes, the communists opened up spaces for representatives from marginalized communities. At this congress, the Indigenous activist Dolores Cacuango joined Paredes and Saad on the congress's presidium. The Cuban communist Blas Roca presented a global political overview to the congress. As had become common during the war, Roca emphasized that the Cuban party was essentially a national party and denied that it received international orders. The Cuban delegate emphasized the pro-communist CTAL's important role in advancing workers' interests and denounced the AFL's anticommunist campaign. Representatives of fraternal organizations typically address such congresses, and in this case it was members of the PSE and VRSE who called for a return to the unity that had led to the successful May revolution. PCE Secretary-General Paredes presented his report to the congress. Finally, Saad closed the inaugural session with a call for a democratic front of leftist parties to address the political and economic issues facing the country.[121]

La Tierra also reported that among the resolutions to come out of the PCE congress was one defending the Indigenous community of Urcuquí in its long-running struggle for water rights from the conservative landowner and amateur archaeologist Jacinto Jijón y Caamaño. Fifteen years earlier, the community had petitioned the governor of Imbabura for access to an irrigation canal.[122] Two years earlier, Paredes had convinced the Constituent Assembly to expropriate the canal for the community.[123] The day before the communist congress gathered, representatives from Urcuquí published a letter in *El Comercio* in which they pointed out that since 1582 the community had had rights to the irrigation canal. Now that conservatives were back in control of the assembly, the wealthy landowners were once again attempting to deprive them of their rights.[124] The PCE resolution called on its members and sympathizers, as well as the CTE, PSE, VRSE, and Liberal Party, to mobilize all popular and progressive sectors in defense of Urcuquí in the face of the attacks of a "conservative feudal reaction."[125] In response, a variety of labor and left organizations issued letters in support of Urcuquí, including the Cuban peasant federation, which reflects the international attention that Roca's presence at the congress brought to the issue.[126] Even though the communist congress received little media attention, the party did help bring Indigenous demands to public consciousness. Without a direct presence in the National Assembly, however, the communists had trouble stopping the conservatives' legislative attack on the community's rights.[127]

The last article on the congress in *La Tierra* reported that the communists paid special attention to Indigenous problems and the economic situation in their closing session on November 23. The party also decided to build a progressive democratic front to combat Velasco Ibarra's dictatorship by any means necessary. The final task was to select party leaders. Although Paredes had declared that he did not want to remain as secretary-general, the party reelected him anyway. Gil Gilbert continued as leader of the coastal regional committee. In marked contrast to the socialists who did not include Indigenous or female representation in their congress, delegates elected both Nela Martínez and María Luisa Gómez de la Torre to the party's Executive Committee. Dolores Cacuango joined them on the Central Committee.[128] That the socialist newspaper would report on the communist congress in a largely objective fashion would seem to indicate that the possibilities of active collaboration between the two leftist parties had not entirely disappeared.

In contrast to the mainstream media's indifference, with the onset of the Cold War the U.S. intelligence apparatus paid significant attention to the communist congress. From the State Department's Ecuador desk in Washington, Henry Dearborn drafted a two-page confidential memo on the congress drawing on information from a military attaché's report from Quito. The State Department estimated the party's membership at 3,500–4,000, but only about fifty delegates attended the congress. The memo stated that this small number "was indicative of the weakness of the Party and its lack of funds," without acknowledging that it would be rare for a party's entire membership to attend a congress. Dearborn observed, "Cells in distant parts of the Republic could not afford to send delegates," but such a geographic reach beyond urban areas where most parties focused their efforts was characteristic of a communist desire to organize among marginalized communities. Dearborn recognized as much by noting, "The Party anticipates making gains in the near future through promising among agricultural workers that the lands upon which they now work will become theirs upon the materialization of the Party program." The memo warned that while "previously, the Party's program had called for socialization of means of evolution," at the November congress the party "adopted a more radical policy by sponsering [sic] plans to win over the general masses and organized labor by means of revolution." State Department personnel also flagged parallel communist policies of attempting to build leftist electoral unity while competing with socialists for control over labor organizations.

The State Department memo reflects a shift from a wartime collaborationist model toward Cold War concerns. Dearborn highlights that at the congress, Roca was "especially vocal on the subject of U.S. imperialism in Cuba and on its eventual penetration into Europe and Latin America." A reader underlined references to communist policy statements against U.S. and British imperialism and the mention of a possible war between the United States and the Soviet Union. The reader was particularly alarmed that speakers at the congress "emphasized that all Communists must be on the side of Russia in such a conflict." Allegedly, plans at the congress included sabotage and the sinking of ships transporting vital raw materials to the United States that could be used in a war effort, although such sensationalist claims would appear to be more of a reflection of paranoia than reality.[129]

Half a year later, the embassy transmitted a transcribed copy of the PCE statutes adopted at the congress. George Shaw, the chargé d'affaires ad interim at the embassy, noted that the statutes had been "distributed surreptitiously among Party members and fellow travelers." Few copies of the statutes remain, and even at the time the embassy had acquired only one copy and, as a result, made a typewritten duplicate to forward to Washington rather than sending the original. "A presumably reliable source" told the embassy that the party was in the process of printing ten thousand copies of the statutes to be sold for fifty centavos each. Although the embassy doubted that changes would be made to the draft, the embassy decided to delay translation until it received the final printed version. A copy of these statutes—either in draft or final form, if indeed a final version was ever published—is not readily available in Ecuador, and the embassy seemingly never did translate them into English for the State Department. As a result, the embassy's typewritten copy provides a rare opportunity for a glimpse into the party's thinking and priorities at the dawn of the Cold War.

The PCE statutes began with a declaration of principles that asserted it was "the political party of the working class, based on the principles of scientific socialism, on Marxism-Leninism-Stalinism." The party "defends the immediate and vital interests of the workers and peasants and of all manual and intellectual workers." To advance that goal, it "fights for the development of an anti-imperialist agrarian revolution, for national independence, and for the transformation of the bourgeois-democratic revolution into a socialist revolution." The communists advocated "for the establishment of collective ownership of the basic means of production; for the elimination of the exploitation of man by man and the suppression of antagonistic classes in the process of building a socialist society." A successful class struggle would be "the first step towards the definitive establishment of communism." The party imagined the revolution to be agrarian and nationalist in character.

The statutes declared that the party was "the heir and successor of the country's struggles for independence, freedom, improvement of the living conditions of the masses, and progress and national greatness." Militants pledged to follow "in the footsteps of the best revolutionary and progressive democratic traditions of our history." The statutes defined members as anyone willing to accept the party's program, submit to its discipline, and actively join in its efforts. The party was a collection not of individuals but of organisms, and its structure was based on the principles of democratic centralism. As before, the statutes declared that the party was to have a national congress every other year, although in practice it never met that often. In between congresses, the central committee was in charge of making decisions. The control of a few individuals over party decisions reveals that in practice the party functioned in a more hierarchical than democratic fashion, though, as the FBI surveillance highlights, internal debates could be quite intense.

The party statutes also set dues, beginning with an obligatory but voluntary amount for the unemployed and hacienda workers known as *huasipungueros*. Housewives, unskilled workers, and students were to contribute two sucres monthly, and others were to pay a percentage of their salaries. Government officials were required to donate 20 percent of their salaries. The expectation was that everyone would contribute something—from each according to their means—with a premium placed on those who collaborated with the government. Members could be expelled from the party for a variety of reasons, including betraying the working class, creating dissent within the party, drunkenness and other immoral behavior, terrorism, or otherwise acting in a way that impinged on the reputation of the party. Communist parties are notoriously strict and moralistic, and the Ecuadorian party was no exception. Finally, the PCE was committed to an international proletarianism, and that would be expressed through the maintenance of relations with fellow communist parties in other countries. Even though the party did not take instructions from Moscow, it was part of a movement that disseminated out of that core.[130] FBI Director J. Edgar Hoover's fear of communists advocating for a global revolution was not entirely off the mark.

A week after the PCE congress, a football match for Ecuador's national championship that pitted teams from the provinces of Pichincha and Guayas against each other led to a riot that left one person dead. On the evening of Sunday, December 1, 1946, fans of the losing team marched through the streets of their hometown of Guayaquil and began to loot and burn commercial establishments. The police rounded up thirty people whom they deemed responsible for the violence and destruction. Unexplainably, however, conservative politicians—including both President Velasco Ibarra and deputies in the National Assembly—began to point to a dark hidden hand behind the disturbances.[131] Based on these charges, the police first arrested the coastal communist leaders Saad and Gil Gilbert, and then began to engage in a general roundup that netted about half a dozen more communist activists.[132] Perhaps the reason for the repression was a statement that Paredes had issued in the name of the Communist Party denouncing police aggression against the football fans.[133] If Velasco Ibarra thought the repression would silence the communists, he was sorely mistaken. The party's Central Committee immediately assembled a commission that demanded answers from the Ministry of Government for the arrests. The ministry denied knowledge of the detentions and acknowledged their presence only when the communist militants threatened to launch an international campaign for the prisoners' freedom.[134]

Several days later, Paredes issued a lengthy statement in the name of the PCE's Executive Committee that denounced a new round of terror that Velasco Ibarra had launched against the left and called for the release of their comrades from prison. The communist leader denied that his party was behind the unrest at the football match and instead accused Velasco Ibarra of fostering regional divisions in the country with the goal of undermining opposition to the government. Paredes declared that the president was attempting "to sweep away with blood and fire all opposition to his government." At the time of the May revolution, Velasco Ibarra had applauded the efforts of the "shock troops" for keeping order and preventing acts of vandalism, but now he had imprisoned these same leaders. Paredes noted that Adolf Hitler had quashed the Communist Party in Germany to consolidate his control, and now Ecuador's "Führer criollo" was following a similar strategy to maintain himself in power. The communists criticized the president for his support of "feudal sectors that starve, kill, and rob Indians and *montuvios* [coastal peasants]," including backing landowners who stole land from Indigenous peasants at Panyatug and Shacundo. All of his actions were leading to a new dictatorship, and the party exploited any opportunity to attack the president.[135]

The communists argued that the only way to avoid the chaos that Velasco Ibarra had introduced into the country was to build a broad and powerful liberal-left coalition that included worker, student, peasant, and Indigenous organizations with a clear program of struggle. The Indigenous federation FEI seconded the call for the release of the imprisoned communists who had fought for the realization of the aspirations of Indigenous communities. The FEI called on their member organizations to write the president and other government officials to demand their release.[136] Coastal labor organizations made similar demands, and a group of leftist lawyers formed a legal defense committee for the political prisoners.[137] Finally, in an early Christmas present, on December 22 the Ministry of Government announced that Saad and Gil Gilbert had been released from prison.[138] The communist mobilization had successfully forced the government to back down.

The Communist Party congress and the riot in Guayaquil came as the FBI was closing down its operations in Latin America and transferring surveillance of potential leftist subversives to State Department officials. With the Cold War starting to heat up, the potential for peaceful collaboration with the United States and capitalist forces quickly evaporated. Throughout these transitions, information from U.S. intelligence-gathering operations—regardless of who ran them—help chart internal debates on the left over how best to respond to an authoritarian government that acted against their class interests. Militants discussed whether to continue to engage in electoral contests, invest energy into building a mass movement, or resort to armed action. Without a clearly defined strategy or path forward, activists shifted their plan of action and sometimes engaged in contradictory and conflictive approaches. Within only a couple of years, all of the hopes and aspirations that leftists had placed in Velasco Ibarra melted away. Despite very high initial aspirations, the effort invested in La Gloriosa appeared to be for naught.

CHAPTER 7

Departures

ALFREDO VERA
MINISTRO DE EDUCACION

ALFREDO VERA served as minister of education after the May 1944 revolution. Vera worked closely with the Communist Party but was not a formal member. After half a year, President José María Velasco Ibarra forced him out of his cabinet as his government moved in a conservative direction. Vera subsequently ran for elected office as a member of leftist coalitions. Source: León Borja, *Hombres de Mayo*.

In June 1947, Ecuador held midterm elections under José María Velasco Ibarra's new conservative constitution. The Legislative Assembly was not scheduled to be seated until August 1948, but the vote was held more than a year in advance to prevent the possibility of reconvening the conservative-dominated Constituent Assembly in case the need for an extraordinary session of congress arose. Once again, the left debated what was the best way to remove a repressive government from power and how to usher in more progressive and transformative changes in society. Should activists engage in elections, dedicate resources to the mobilization of their grassroots, or resort to extra-constitutional methods to gain political power? The choices were not necessarily mutually exclusive and each option had its benefits and drawbacks, but the underlying contradictions of the alternatives tore at the left's unity and coherence.

The elections came in the immediate aftermath of the FBI closing its intelligence-gathering operations in Latin America and passing its surveillance contacts on to its institutional competitors in the State Department and newly formed CIA. Only two months after the congressional elections and a year before the new body was to be seated, a military coup forced Velasco Ibarra from office. By then, these twin departures (Velasco Ibarra and the FBI) had minimal effect on Ecuador's left. The hopes and aspirations of profound changes that the May 1944 revolution had precipitated had dissipated. The onset of the Cold War closed political spaces that communists had enjoyed as a result of joining a battle with capitalist powers against a common fascist enemy amid World War II. Those broader Cold War geopolitical realignments also tore at the possibilities of building unity among Ecuador's diverse leftist parties. The surreptitious surveillance of the U.S. security apparatus survived these shifts, and persisted in the provision of insights that assist in understanding leftist strategies to advance struggles for social justice.

Electoral Contests

The Communist Party long debated whether it was worth the effort to engage in electoral contests, an issue that remained at the forefront of political discussions even after Velasco Ibarra's overthrow. Some communists attempted to build a leftist electoral front with the socialists and vanguardists to prevent the trilogy of threats of the perpetuation of Velasco Ibarra's dictatorship, a conservative electoral victory, or a return of the liberal oligarchy to power. These militants argued that the three leftist parties shared similar ideological perspectives and political platforms, and for this reason should combine their forces in an electoral campaign. Sectarian divisions, however, tore at leftist efforts to unify their struggles. The communists complained that some progressives were more willing to ally with declared enemies of the left rather than to join forces with the Partido Comunista del Ecuador (Communist Party of Ecuador; PCE). The start of the Cold War had only heightened this problem. In particular, the PCE cautioned the socialists against joining an anticommunist campaign, because ultimately the same imperialist propaganda would also target their political projects. Distancing themselves from the communists only meant digging their own tomb.[1]

The PCE called on the Ecuadorian public to support leftist and progressive candidates in the 1947 congressional elections to prevent a return of the ruling class to power because that would mean more hunger, economic disorganization, and political repression. The communists laid out a political platform that included an embrace of truly democratic governance. It advocated for an agrarian reform program to break up both domestic and international monopolies, deliver land to those who worked it, and in the process improve agricultural production. The platform also called for the industrial development of the country's economy, the termination of commercial speculation, improvements in health care and housing, the expansion of education and literacy campaigns, and an increase in worker salaries. The party yet again defended the country's sovereignty and territorial integrity and called for a revision of the Rio Protocol that ceded land to Peru. Underlying the entire document was a call to break from U.S. imperial control over the country.[2]

In the month before the elections, the three recognized political parties (conservative, liberal, and socialist) scrambled to define their candidate lists. In the province of Pichincha, the socialists entered into an alliance with the Movimiento Cívico Democrático Nacional (National Democratic Civic

Movement; MCDN) that also included independent liberals and other progressives. Galo Plaza, Jorge Carrera Andrade, and Benjamín Carrión led the slate of candidates. The communists denounced the socialists for separating themselves from other leftist forces and joining an alliance with "frankly reactionary elements who are bitterly opposed to social reforms." In particular, the communists opposed working with the wealthy landowner Plaza who as Ecuador's ambassador to the United States had functioned as an "agent of Yankee imperialism" in facilitating the U.S. occupation of military bases at Salinas and the Galápagos Islands.[3]

As a midnight deadline for the registration of electoral lists quickly approached, the PCE formed a Frente Popular de Izquierda (Leftist Popular Front) in Quito. Partisans paraded to the Pichincha Electoral Council with the required petition and signatures of two hundred supporters. Communists dominated the candidate list, with the PCE's Secretary-General Ricardo Paredes and the party militant César Endara leading the slate of candidates. The communist militant Rubén Rodríguez from the canton of Cayambe and Diógenes Paredes were alternatives. The list also included such well-known communist militants as Primitivo Barreto, Newton Moreno, and Tirso Gómez.[4]

About a month earlier, shortly after the FBI left Ecuador, a "fairly reliable source" conveyed the text of a conversation with Pedro Saad to the U.S. Embassy. According to the transcription of the conversation, Saad noted that the election placed the Communist Party "in a most delicate position." The new electoral law required each party to register two thousand names with the electoral board to qualify for ballot access. (The Leftist Popular Front needed only two hundred signatures because it was registering candidates rather than a party.) Although the party could easily register five thousand, Saad asked, "Would we not endanger all those whom we would register?" Saad proceeded to observe, "The present world situation commands greatest care on our part, inasmuch as we consider ourselves already at war with occidental capitalism." Whereas previously, under the influence of Browderism, Saad's wing of the PCE had advocated for peaceful existence with the United States, with the commencement of the Cold War that period had passed. Saad noted that in a previous election, when the party registered five hundred members, the U.S. Embassy easily obtained the list. "If we now register 2,000," the transcription states, "the Americans will obtain those names also, and this would constitute very bad policy on our part."[5] Saad's concerns became reality when the U.S. Embassy promptly acquired the Leftist Popular Front's registration list from the Electoral Council and forwarded the names of Communist Party members to the State Department in Washington.[6]

Saad emphasized the need to protect Communist Party members from political surveillance. Furthermore, he did not think the current political climate was conducive to electoral participation. "Whatever the results of the elections," Saad stated, "this is no time for Communists in Ecuador to expect anything good. We have not the slightest chance for changing the political plans of our government simply because the latter is being dominated by the United States." The threat of exposure would be minimized if the communists entered into a coalition with other leftist parties, but he did not find the formation of such an alliance likely because the "socialists are on the side of United States imperialism," whereas the PCE was allied with the Soviet Union. Further hindering collaboration with the socialists was that its leftist Secretary-General Manuel Agustín Aguirre required medical attention and was to be replaced by the "reactionary" Luis Maldonado Tamayo and other intellectuals who were "cowards." Maldonado Tamayo led a strongly anticommunist minority within the Socialist Party who, while opposed to collaborating with the conservatives, favored warm relations with the United States. Instead of engaging in electoral contests, Saad advocated preparation for moving the party underground.[7]

A week after registering the electoral lists, the Pichincha Electoral Council annulled the Leftist Popular Front's registration with the charge that they had not met the minimal requirement of two hundred signatures.[8] According to officials, forty-six names that the party had submitted were not on the electoral rolls and other details had been entered incorrectly on the petition. Given the demographics of the Communist Party's working class and peasant support, the elimination of names may have been a result of literacy restrictions on citizenship. The communists appealed, and had their electoral list reinstated on the ballot.[9] According to the U.S. Embassy, the conservatives had used their influence to reinstate the communists, not because they supported their right to campaign but as an opportunist move to split the left-liberal vote and make it easier for them to win congressional seats in the election.[10] In the face of these difficulties, while the conservatives, liberals, and socialists ramped up their campaigns in advance of the election on June 1, *El Comercio* reported that the communist campaign in Quito did not show many signs of life.[11] The *New York Times* similarly claimed, "The Communists have little popular backing," which was largely a reflection of the institutional barriers to their electoral participation.[12]

In a public manifesto, the Leftist Popular Front complained that Velasco Ibarra's new conservative constitution destroyed many of the social and political conquests gained under the previous progressive document. Despite the Communist Party's best efforts, the left was deeply divided in the face of Velasco Ibarra's dictatorial regime and the resurgence of conservative political forces. Even so, the leftist electoral coalition laid out a political platform that was the product of a deep study of Ecuador's reality. The platform began with a call for agrarian reform and demanded attention to other social issues such as raising salaries and improving the standard of living for the working class. The statement declared strong support for freedom of religion but also adamantly argued against clerical influence in politics and for the necessity of secular education to build a democratic culture. Foreign economic investment must be subjugated to the interests of the Ecuadorian state and must respect its sovereignty. Similarly, the manifesto called for a revision of the Rio Protocol that had harmed vital Ecuadorian interests. "What Ecuadorian who truly wants progress for the country could be against this program?" the manifesto asked, positioning itself as a nationalistic force. The statement proclaimed that the leftist coalition was the best guarantee of its success.[13]

The Vanguardia Revolucionaria del Socialismo Ecuatoriano (Ecuadorian Revolutionary Socialist Vanguard; VRSE), for their part, resolved not to support any of the congressional candidates for the province of Pichincha. Instead, the party recommended that their members "vote for the lists in which left and progressive elements are participating that will strengthen civic anticonservative thinking that will bring honor to the Marxist doctrine that our party professes."[14] Like some communists, the VRSE had hesitations about engaging in electoral contests. Meanwhile, in Guayaquil on the coast, a broad leftist coalition with the independent liberal Carlos Zevallos Menéndez, the vanguardist Alfonso Larrea Alba, the socialist Agustín Freire Núñez, and the communist Segundo Ramos heading the list appeared to be more active than their counterparts in the highlands. As was typically the case, the two regions followed different rhythms and logics.[15]

A week before the elections, police arrested the communist leaders Segundo Ramos and Simón Zambrano, as well as several military officers in Guayaquil, and charged them with launching a revolution against Velasco Ibarra's government. The revolt apparently started with workers at the electric plant in Guayaquil clamoring for an increase in wages. Other leftists rallied in solidarity with their demands, and members of the military joined in under the leadership of the retired Major Eduardo Silva. From there, the rumors and panic quickly ran out of control. According to the embassy's report on the incident, Zambrano and Raúl Soria organized and trained hundreds of communists in the use of rifles, hand grenades, and machine guns. Even though much of the weaponry was obsolete, Enrique Gil Gilbert allegedly expected the Soviet Union to supply an "Ecuadoran Red Army" with modern weaponry in case of the breakout of war with the United States.[16] The government charged that provocateurs had attempted to launch a "Sergeant's Revolution" similar to the civil-military coup in Cuba that placed Fulgencio Batista in power in 1933.[17] The *New York Times* reported that the government had "leaders of the extreme Left groups . . . under strict surveillance." The newspaper expected more arrests of military troops and labor leaders.[18] Unlike in Cuba, the Ecuadorian attempt failed.

A United Press wire story published in *El Comercio* concluded that the "subversive movement" lacked much importance, but apparently it served as an opportunity for Velasco Ibarra to crack down on leftist opposition to his government.[19] The following day, press reports indicated that all was calm in Guayaquil, although the left had been forced to suspend its electoral campaign. Leftists demanded guarantees from the government that it would be allowed to participate in the upcoming elections.[20] The PCE petitioned the Council of State for the release of Ramos and Zambrano in light of the electoral campaign currently under way, although the council failed to act on the petition in time to free the two before the election took place.[21] The repression of the communist leaders backfired, however, and when Ramos was finally released in June the public greeted him as a hero and martyr. With his heightened stature, the embassy acknowledged that he was situated to gain a seat in the new senate as a functional senator for labor.[22]

Even with the political unrest and tensions leading up to the election, the vote itself proceeded relatively quietly. The *New York Times* reported that although women had the right to vote since 1929, few actually did so.[23] In contrast, literate men were required to vote and faced severe sanctions, including a loss of employment and fines, if they failed to comply with their civic duty. The MCDN soundly defeated the conservatives who had won the previous election, and the liberals came in second place. For the socialists in alliance with independent liberals and other progressives, the elections were a resounding success. The socialist newspaper *La Tierra* warmly embraced the results.[24] In contrast, the communists did not fare well. The Leftist Popular Front placed last in Pichincha and failed to win a single seat in the new congress.[25] On a federal level, the communists were situated to hold two seats in the new congress—one that Gil Gilbert won in the province of Guayas, and a second that Saad would probably hold as a functional senator for coastal labor. In any case, this would be an increase over the last assembly in which they had no representation. According to the embassy, a primary reason why the communists did not do better in the election was because of internal discontent with Paredes's leadership of the party.[26] The dismal return on investment raised questions as to whether the communists could best achieve their vision for a more equal and just society through electoral means.

Grassroots Mobilizations

Despite the communists' poor showing in elections, after the FBI's departure the U.S. Embassy continued to report on their activities to the State Department and expressed concern at their possible actions. "The relatively small but effective Communist Party," a report stated, "is a potential danger whose force will be felt the moment there is chaos in the country or should an opportunity present itself to embarrass or to actually harm the interests of the United States." The communiqué did not define what the actual interests of the United States were, or how exactly the communists would damage them, but a paranoia of communism always provided an undercurrent of concern for surveillance reports. U.S. officials were anxious that the communists might make better progress organized as a social movement than as a political party.[27]

Paredes allegedly told a "reliable informant" that "we must not attack the Americans too much through the press; they should even be praised on occasion in order that we not attract too much attention upon ourselves and in order to keep them from knowing our real strength." Paredes added, "We must be extremely careful not to allow our new party members to become known. The older members are already well-known [sic] and therefore easily watched." The informant remarked that the comments were "in line with the party's efforts in the past six months to work underground as much as possible to avoid attention in anticipation of possible repressive measures by the government." The embassy's Chargé d'Affaires Ad Interim George Shaw simply stated "no comment" in his cover letter with which he forwarded the interview to the secretary of state, seemingly implying that the interview quotes spoke for themselves in terms of the types of underhanded tactics in which communists could be expected to engage.[28] Another informant also observed that while the former Minister of Education Alfredo Vera was an avowed communist, he had "never publicly stated disapproval of the United States Government."[29] The embassy struggled to understand what political position the PCE might take in the context of the new and emerging Cold War environment and how they could best counter it.

Embassy officials reported repeatedly on Paredes's plans to resign his position as secretary-general of the party and move to Manabí to take up a private medical practice. In July 1947, a "reliable informant" told the U.S. Embassy that Paredes planned to "leave Quito in the immediate future and that Saad has been designated to replace him." Ambassador John Simmons claimed that public visibility was not Saad's desire; he preferred instead to work quietly in the background.[30] The embassy asserted that this "discord should seriously impair the Communist cause" because Paredes had "provided an aggressive and intelligent leadership."[31] The debates over what strategy to follow tore at Paredes's leadership of the party.

In August 1947, a "reliable informant" told the U.S. Embassy that the Cuenca cell of the party was unhappy that the party headquarters in Quito had been negligent in keeping in touch with them; as a result, their numbers had dropped from thirty-five to twenty-two members. The cell pressed to be transferred from Quito to the jurisdiction of the coastal regional headquarters in Guayaquil. The informant noted that the discontent in Cuenca was reflective of a broader state of affairs in the party as Paredes planned to leave the post of secretary-general and his replacement had not yet been named. The state of neglect would probably not change until the party named a new and forceful leader. Ambassador Simmons added a comment that "it would seem natural that Cuenca should be linked up with Guayaquil as regards communist affairs, since this would follow the already existing commercial tendencies in the Cuenca region." The Cuenca cell had been grouped with the highland party because of its geographic location in the Ecuadorian sierra. Simmons's comment reveals that he interpreted Ecuador through a financial rather than cultural or historical lens, and that he sought to exploit communist weaknesses to the U.S. advantage.[32]

Nor would everyone be happy with Saad's leadership. Vera stated that he was ideologically opposed to Saad's pro-Soviet line. He was of the opinion that Ecuador was not ready for communism and first must progress through a stage of capitalism to create a prosperous middle class. An informant to the U.S. Embassy identified Vera as the leader of a "separatist" line in the PCE, in opposition to Saad's "Unionist" line. Although Vera enjoyed a good deal of support for his position on the coast, the informant found it unlikely that Vera and his followers would "attempt to disrupt their connections with Saad, because no practical benefit could be gained." Nevertheless, "It is clear that there is a spiritual split existing within the Ecuadoran Communist Party." This could lead to a rift between the leaders if the Soviets attempted to extend their influence into Ecuador. The informant stated that this was "the only evidence of divergent sentiment within the Ecuadoran Communist Party," but that "a split is unlikely at this time."[33] Unlike their Venezuelan counterparts, the Ecuadorian militants, despite internal disagreements, did manage to remain united in one party.[34]

The Cold War began in 1946 with the resurgence of conservative forces domestically and with the Truman Doctrine advancing an anticommunist agenda on an international scale. In this context, the PCE lashed out at U.S. imperialism. "In Latin America we are not surprised at the stance of the United States because of previous experiences," the party proclaimed. The recent wartime experiences were only the latest episode that was reflective of a much longer history. During the war, the United States called on other American republics to rally against fascism in Europe. While the countries willingly joined, the United States paid them lower prices for commodities than they otherwise could have received on the open market, which as a result distorted their economies. After the war, the United States stopped buying products from Latin America, even as the prices of imports from the United States continued to rise.

In reality, the communists charged, under Harry Truman's presidency the United States had turned away from Franklin Roosevelt's Good Neighbor policy and the progressive policies that Vice President Henry Wallace represented and turned the concept of Pan-Americanism into an empty catchphrase. Rather than following the anticolonial rhetoric of "America for the Americans," as codified in the Monroe Doctrine, Pan-Americanism had become a mechanism for the United States to subjugate Latin America to its political and economic interests. Any warm feelings that might have existed between capitalism and communism during the war against fascism quickly dissipated in the postwar period. "Once again imperialism, and now with more intensity than ever, reemerges as a colonizing force in Latin America," the PCE declared. In this context, the Latin American independence leader Simón Bolívar's idea of unifying Latin America to withstand U.S. imperial pressure assumed undisputed importance for the region. The Communist Party called on all of the continent's progressive forces to unify in a struggle for peace, progress, democracy, and national independence.[35]

Extraconstitutional Means

At the end of the 1940s, the State Department's Office of Intelligence Research (OIR) observed that since the May revolution Ecuador had witnessed "a striking growth of leftist thinking which has not yet been reflected to its actual extent in elections." The OIR claimed, "This growth has been largely at the expense of liberalism and has resulted in a strengthening of the extreme left and, in reaction thereto, of the extreme right in Ecuadoran politics." The report noted, "Leftist sentiment today is particularly strong among the working and lower middle classes, intellectuals and student circles, and in the ranks of the Army." The OIR was especially concerned with the increase of leftist influence in the military and what that might mean for Ecuador's political future. This confidential report complained that "the militant attitude of the Army and the Church have tended to retard rather than promote the orderly progress of the country," particularly in terms of fostering a constitutional democracy. Given a choice, OIR analysts believed that the growth of a progressive and constitutional left was preferable to the entrenched traditional and feudalistic tendencies in the country.[36] In contrast to the stereotype of the U.S. government working hand in glove with conservatives in Latin America, these State Department officials looked to liberal and democratic forces as their natural allies.

Some diplomats appealed to progressive socialism as a welcome alternative to reactionary conservatism that held Latin America back or to communism that they believed Moscow controlled through the Communist International, even though that body had been disbanded in 1943. As ambassador to Argentina in 1945, the longtime Latin American diplomat Spruille Braden made this argument in favor of working with local progressive forces. Other ambassadors, including John Simmons, after leaving his post in Ecuador for El Salvador, agreed with Braden. As assistant secretary of state for inter-American affairs in 1947, Braden once again warned that "to join with Fascists and ultra-reactionaries in 'common cause' against Communism is against principle, foolhardy and will greatly weaken us in the struggle to defeat totalitarianism of every variety." Allan Dawson, the U.S. consul in Venezuela, drew a distinction in 1947 "between communism and the native socialistic parties which are friendly to the United States." He was willing to work with the second, but not the first. As the communists feared, the embassy worked to divide the left and weaken the Communist Party. The CIA also echoed this perspective. In the 1947 Venezuelan elections, the agency contended, "An active non-Communist progressive party constitutes one of the best guarantees against a strong Communist movement."[37] An implication was that both the extreme left and the extreme right would resort to extraconstitutional methods to change political structures. Indeed, it took such extraconstitutional measures to remove Velasco Ibarra from office when seemingly no other viable alternative existed.

Velasco's Second Exit

Velasco Ibarra promulgated his new constitution on December 31, 1946, but he did not remain in power long to enjoy its advantages. Velasco Ibarra's conservative populism alienated both those to his left and those to his right. On August 23, 1947, Defense Minister Colonel Carlos Mancheno arrested Velasco Ibarra on charges of economic mismanagement, forced him to resign, and expelled him from the country.[38] Unlike the popular acclaim that had placed Velasco Ibarra in power in May 1944, few people now came to his defense as he once again left for exile in Colombia.

Neftali Ponce, Ecuador's ambassador to the United States, defined the cause of the coup as a "personal dispute" between Velasco Ibarra and Mancheno rather than political in nature.[39] In fact, previously Mancheno had been one of Velasco Ibarra's longest and most loyal military supporters. Velasco Ibarra had appointed Mancheno as Defense Minister after taking office in 1944. The Colonel had participated in Velasco Ibarra's "self-coup" the previous March, and in August had forced the Constituent Assembly to confirm his designation as president. As Defense Minister, Mancheno had engaged in a thorough house cleaning in the army, but resigned in January 1947 over a disagreement with the president on military promotions. The squabble appeared to have been smoothed over, as Velasco Ibarra had only recently on July 2 reappointed Mancheno to his previous post as Defense Minister.[40] The British Legation echoed Ponce's interpretation that political issues did not underlie the coup, and added that the public's "hopeless apathy" should not be mistaken for active support. The majority was weary of Velasco Ibarra and welcomed his departure.[41]

Ambassador Simmons observed that Mancheno had consolidated "opposition to Velasco among various civilian groups including Conservatives, Liberals, Socialists and more particularly Communists," notably a similar type of coalition that the Alianza Democrática Ecuatoriana (Ecuadorian Democratic Alliance; ADE) had formed several years earlier to bring Velasco Ibarra to power. Simmons cited an anonymous source who claimed that the "only condition of Communist support was a promise that if [the] coup [was] successful [Foreign Minister José Vicente] Trujillo would be recalled from Rio Conference" as part of the PCE's nationalist campaign in favor of Ecuadorian sovereignty. Despite this range of civilian support, Simmons maintained that army support was "the chief determining factor" in the struggle between Mancheno and Velasco Ibarra.[42] Civilian governments always served at the will of the military.

Paredes greeted Velasco Ibarra's fall with the declaration that the president had become a victim of his own contradictions. The government had left its popular base behind to rule on behalf of wealthy landholders and conservative clerics. The former president had undermined a secular system of education; attacked the rights of workers; persecuted and massacred Indigenous peasants; and subjugated the country to foreign imperial interests. "The struggle of the Ecuadorian people against the shameful regime of Velasco Ibarra could have become a popular insurrection, the only type of authentic constructive revolutionary action," Paredes wrote. Instead, Mancheno had taken advantage of this popular discontent. While understanding the military's motivation, Paredes called on the army to correct its mistake of not collaborating with popular movements and to return Ecuador to a civilian government as quickly as possible. For Paredes, a people's government did not necessarily mean one that came to power through elections but one that reflected the popular will.

Paredes claimed that the Communist Party was "the political force that with the greatest energy, clarity, and consistency has fought against Velasco's errors and crimes." The communists called for a return to the 1945 constitution, the convoking of a new Constituent Assembly, and the drafting of a new electoral law that would expand representation for marginalized peoples and eliminate that of the clergy, the historical ally of the conservatives. In addition, the PCE called for agrarian reform, the expansion of industry, and control over foreign investment. The government should build affordable housing and raise salaries for workers. Internationally, the party repeated its demands that the government should defend the country's sovereignty and territorial integrity through the removal of military personnel from the Galápagos military base and the revision of the Rio Protocol. Paredes described the communist program as moderate. "It is not a socialist or communist program," he wrote, "but a broad democratic platform that postulates economic, political, and social progress."[43] In fact, these policies would not alter the mode of production; they would simply shift more resources to the lower classes. Despite rhetorical calls for revolutionary change, the communists limited themselves to demands for rather limited reforms.

Mancheno was implicated in multiple coup attempts, both before and after he took power in August 1947. When U.S. recognition of Mancheno's government arose, Acting Secretary of State Robert Lovett quipped that his "revolution did not seem to have any special significance, being similar to 40 or 50 others in Ecuador's history."[44] Several years earlier the British diplomat Leslie Hughes-Hallett echoed Lovett's sentiments that "there is always the possibility that a revolution may break out in this country." Rumors of such "impending revolutions are a recognised part of the daily diet of newly-arrived diplomats," and seasoned officials had become somewhat desensitized to the significance of such gossip.[45] For example, Colin Edmond, Hughes-Hallett's replacement, reported only "for completeness" on "a very tame subversive attempt" that former army officers had led in Santo Domingo de los Colorados in February 1947. Edmond observed, "Revolutions mark the only rhythm in Ecuadorean life."[46] President Galo Plaza appeared unfazed when two years later Mancheno once again attempted to overthrow his government. "I am witnessing a demonstration of the national sport," he quipped in response to the failed coup.[47] Political instability was part of the being of the country.

Mancheno's new government did not signal a significant shift in policy. Most government employees remained at their posts, and Mancheno announced that his political and economic policies would closely parallel those of the United States. In fact, Ambassador Simmons expected the new government to be friendlier to the United States than that of Velasco Ibarra. The new chief executive promised to form a strong central government with capable men, but he excluded both conservatives and communists. Simmons reported that Mancheno "refused to talk to the Communist delegate who went to the meeting for the formation of the Cabinet in the hope that a Communist member of the government could be appointed."[48] Communists' attempts to present themselves as a moderate and patriotic force in the country to gain legitimacy and a role in government had been for naught.

After holding power for less than ten days, another military coup of "constitutionalist" troops overthrew Mancheno. Highlighting his political preferences, Mancheno sought asylum in the U.S. Embassy, but the diplomatic mission refused protection based on its general policy against providing such a right.[49] Turned away, Mancheno took refuge instead in the Venezuelan Embassy. In light of Mancheno's removal from office, the PCE proclaimed that the only option for leftist and progressive forces was to fight for "a genuinely popular government, in which all political sectors except for conservatives and reactionary groups would be represented." The party urged leftists to stand firm in their defense of democracy, progress, and national dignity in the face of conservative forces that were responsible for hunger and chaos in the country.[50]

A leftist triumvirate composed of Luis Larrea Alba, Humberto Albornoz, and Luis Maldonado Tamayo briefly took power before passing the office of chief executive to Velasco Ibarra's Vice President Mariano Suárez Veintimilla, the first time in half a century that a conservative had held that office.[51] On September 16, 1947, an extraordinary session of Congress named the wealthy Guayaquil banker Carlos Julio Arosemena Tola to serve out the final year of Velasco Ibarra's term. Rather than signifying a political break, through all of these changes in office the same political class representing propertied interests remained in control of the country. Once again, a palace coup had failed to alter Ecuador's political configuration. To the surprise of the British Legation, dissidents did not launch any more coup attempts before presidential elections the following June, which the pro–United States candidate Galo Plaza won.[52] Representatives of the dominant society that had long controlled Latin America returned Ecuador to a path of institutional governance, but not one that prioritized the class interests of the most marginalized sectors of society.

Departure of the FBI

In August 1946, just as Velasco Ibarra's conservative Constituent Assembly began its work, Ambassador Scotten wrote to FBI Director J. Edgar Hoover in distress over the decision to recall the legal attaché from his embassy, "especially at the present time" with the political situation in flux. Scotten claimed that the FBI agent had "proved invaluable" because in his three years in the country "he ha[d] come to know all sides of Ecuadoran political life, including all of the Ecuadoran officials in key positions." Scotten, not realizing that Velasco Ibarra would manage to hold on to power for another year, expected serious trouble in three to six months. Recalling the agent at this point, Scotten declared, "would be like cutting off my right arm, and I do hope you will find it possible to leave him here for the time being." Hoover underscored the "high regard" in which Scotten held the Special Intelligence Service (SIS) program and the "perfectly splendid job" that the FBI had done with its surveillance work in Latin America to argue that it was a mistake to curtail his endeavors.[53]

Despite all of the accolades, the war was over, and the original justification for the bureau's presence had vanished. Even with all of the surveillance and searches for divisions on the left, the FBI's own reports indicated that communism presented little cause for alarm. By the time the SIS program closed in 1947, the FBI had concluded that "the Communist Party of Ecuador had become one of the weakest and most ineffective in the Western Hemisphere, according to Bureau coverage close to the Party." The FBI noted, "It had no newspaper or propaganda medium and depended on its control of labor for its existence."[54] Regardless of this situation, and apparently with little serious justification, the FBI still actively maintained surveillance of its allegedly subversive activities. These patterns of surveillance continued with State Department officials and the CIA after the FBI departed. If the U.S. government played a role in weakening the party, no such indications have been located in the available archival record. As first the FBI and then embassy surveillance reveals, the party's own internal divisions and shortcomings, rather than external factors, explain its relative weakness. Communists, together with other leftist and labor activists, continued to struggle in the face of the overwhelming power of the existing political structures to find the most effective way to implement their vision of a more inclusive and socially just society.

With the FBI gone, the U.S. Embassy kept up a constant stream of reports on communist activities in Ecuador similar to what the FBI had previously submitted. During World War II and in the context of a common battle against a fascist threat, diplomatic officials betrayed a willingness to collaborate with communists. Now with the deepening of Cold War tensions and the Soviet Union as an adversary rather than ally, the State Department assumed the anticommunist positions that Hoover's FBI had taken during the war. Similar to the FBI, embassy staff in Quito quoted from anonymous informants and rated them in terms of their perceived reliability. Embassy reports reflected a newfound concern with any leftist labor organizing. When Vicente Lombardo Toledano's emissary Francisco Arechandieta Ortega arrived in Ecuador to organize oil workers, an informant exaggerated the visit to include plans to organize industrial sabotage.[55] The embassy also related the U.S. labor organizer Serafino Romualdi's ongoing efforts to draw the Confederación de Trabajadores del Ecuador (Confederation of Ecuadorian Workers; CTE) out of the communist orbit and into affiliation with the American Federation of Labor (AFL).[56] The State Department took the cables from Quito seriously. A report on the fabrication and sale of PCE and CTE insignia led the State Department to query all of its embassies in the Americas about whether such emblems were being manufactured and distributed elsewhere in the hemisphere.[57] On the surface, in terms of political surveillance little appeared to have changed with the FBI's departure.

Among the issues the embassy's reports highlighted was Saad's plan to step aside from his post as functional representative for coastal labor in the 1948 National Assembly so that either Segundo Ramos or Marco Tulio Oramas could take over his position. The embassy's informant reported that Ramos had gained support due to his "martyr complex, because of his recent imprisonment" just before the June 1947 election. The source considered Ramos "an opportunist and not one who is interested in immediate overthrow of the Government."[58] The collection of intelligence on internal conflicts on the left continued in much the same vein as before the FBI's departure.

The embassy continued to express concern about potential communist infiltration into the government. Alejandro Valdéz, whom a reliable informant identified as "at one time a well-known communist" (even though he had never played a significant role in the national organization), allegedly dropped all connections with the party upon orders from the leaders to prepare for infiltration into the government. The "very confidential source" who relayed this conspiratorial information claimed that Minister of Government Aurelio Cordovez recruited Valdéz as secretary to the director of national security to investigate communism, and subsequently he operated as a double agent. The informant charged that Valdéz's presence in the government functioned as a defensive technique for the Communist Party to have advance knowledge of, and time to prepare a response to, repressive measures that the government might implement.[59] The archive is mum on whether the embassy communicated this information to the Ecuadorian government.

Fears of leftist rather than rightist subversion within the military also continued after the FBI's departure. An informant reported to the U.S. Embassy that the military sports society Los Comandos was probably a communist front organization. It was founded in Guayaquil in November 1944 as a nationalist organization designed "to provide the civilian population with military and physical training" to defend the country. The informant feared that the organization was a cover to recruit university students to communism. In turn, Ambassador Simmons expressed concern with the vocal criticism of U.S. military bases that the organization had published in *La Tierra*.[60] A second "reliable" informant claimed that Los Comandos was "a nationalist organization supported by the Conservatives, Socialists and Communists," an assertion of an unwieldy alliance that Simmons labeled "somewhat questionable." He disputed that the society included conservatives but instead found it to be "extreme left-ist" and "probably communist dominated."[61] Nationalist sentiments and the populist politicians who appealed to them were often ill defined ideologically, which could lead in a variety of directions. As a result, paranoia rather than accurate intelligence sometimes drove U.S. policy concerns.

In January 1948, Major Sergio Enrique Girón, who had played a leading role in removing President Carlos Arroyo del Río from power in May 1944, made known his desire to attend the U.S. Army Command and General Staff School. Simmons labeled him a communist and a troublemaker and noted that the current president, Carlos Julio Arosemena Tola, wanted him out of the country. Arosemena attempted to have him assigned as military attaché to Chile, but Girón continued to emphasize his wish to go to the United States instead. This put Simmons in a difficult situation, because Foreign Minister Antonio Parra Velasco would strongly back his visa application, and it would prove embarrassing for the embassy to refuse the visa.[62] Parra Velasco supported all visa applications for travel to the United States, including one for the communist labor leader Pedro Saad. The U.S. Army also opposed Girón's designation because of "his communist associations and generally intense political activities." Secretary of State George Marshall asked the embassy in Quito whether it would be possible to have Ecuadorian authorities set aside his designation to avoid the diplomatic complications of denying him a visa.[63] The problem was solved when Defense Minister Miguel Adrian Navarro canceled the list of officer candidates and issued a new one without Girón's name. According to Simmons, Navarro knew about Girón's communist affiliation, but his chief of staff, VRSE leader Luis Larrea Alba, placed his name on the list anyway, apparently part of an ongoing conflict between the two military men.[64] The incident highlights the degree of influence that socialists maintained in the military and, by extension, the political power that VRSE leaders held in the country. Despite the military's roots in conservative political ideologies, the U.S. government feared the role it could play in challenging its economic interests in the hemisphere.

Unlike what had been the pattern with the SIS program, which theoretically functioned as a "service agency" that limited itself to gathering information during the war years, during the Cold War the embassy was continually on the watch for information that it could use as propaganda against the PCE. The embassy received a report that the party opposed plans by the commercial firm of González Artigas to construct homes for its employees in Quito. An informant claimed that the party opposed the "action as detrimental to its cause and that it would impair its hold over the workers," leading laborers to "become sympathetic toward their employers." Ambassador Simmons found this report to offer "a striking example of what might be termed the deception of the Communist Party as regards the difference between its alleged objectives and actual objectives." Furthermore, it provided evidence that "the Party is willing to sacrifice the true interests and welfare of the working classes on the altar of the communist concept that discontent among workers with their present lot is the key to future communist success." Finally, Simmons found it contradictory that while communists claimed to favor good housing, "such high objectives do not apply, in their thinking, to countries where communist ascendancy has not yet asserted itself."[65] Strikingly, such editorial comments were largely absent in FBI reports, including in the cover letters from the famously and rabidly anticommunist Hoover. The onset of the Cold War had visibly and pointedly altered the purpose and function of U.S. intelligence-gathering operations.

The embassy also tracked the movements of U.S. citizens in Ecuador who might be involved in subversive activities. The embassy had received information that a doctor named Rubin Lewis, stationed in Guayaquil, was "believed to be Communist and possibly a member of the Communist Party," but further investigation "revealed that although Lewis is a believer in Marxism, he is not considered a Communist nor a member of the Communist Party of Ecuador."[66] The embassy was also concerned that a Dr. Wilburn Ferguson advocated the sending of the known communist Captain Carlos Egas Llaguno to the United States for police training. Simmons was unclear about why Ferguson was taking an interest in the issue—whether Ferguson was "merely a well meaning citizen interested in public affairs" or was being used by Egas as a tool for some nefarious purpose. Curiously—and seemingly contradictory, if he was indeed a communist agent—Ferguson also asked for the renewal of a police-training program that had existed before the FBI closed the Legal Attaché's Office in the embassy and withdrew its officials from Latin America. The ambassador did not attempt to explain this contradiction.[67] Chasing down such phantom leads on its own citizens highlights the expanding presence of the U.S. security apparatus.

Much of the information that the embassy reported to the State Department was of questionable validity. In one such example, two informants presented conflicting information about the identity of Jorge Adalberto Estupiñan Tello: he was alternatively introduced as a psychology student and a biology professor at the Central University who had received either a scholarship or an invitation to study or lecture in Chile with a plan to continue on to Argentina, Uruguay, and, finally, Brazil, with the goal of delivering a letter from the PCE to the Brazilian communist leader Luís Carlos Prestes. Using similar techniques as the FBI, and probably the same contacts, the embassy had one of its moles check with travel agencies but could not find any evidence that the subject had made any reservations to travel by sea or air.[68] Despite its extensive reach, the embassy's intelligence gathering suffered from the operation's seemingly random, partial, and problematic nature.

The most notable example of intelligence paranoia came in April 1948 with a visit to the U.S. Embassy of Subsecretary of Foreign Affairs José Antonio Baquero de la Calle. He called on Ambassador Simmons with a concern that communists, under direction from Moscow, might "instigate acts of sabotage, insurrection or even assassination." Baquero de la Calle was particularly interested in any information that the embassy might have collected on communists' activities, including lists of party members and names of secret Soviet agents. Simmons expressed his desire to help but indicated that the Ecuadorians probably had as much information on subversive activities in the country as the embassy.

Whether or not the embassy did indeed have access to the requested information, Simmons feared that ulterior motives might underlie the inquiry. "I have information," Simmons confided to the secretary of state, "that the Ecuadoran Government is well aware of the names of Communists in this country, and it is possible that the Foreign Office may wish to obtain information as to how much the Embassy knows in regard to these matters." Despite the Arosemena administration's friendly attitude toward the United States, Simmons found himself in a delicate balancing act, "wishing to be cooperative but at the same time not wishing to enlighten the Ecuadoran Government, in an undue manner, in regard to our possession of certain types of information or as to the means by which such information might have been obtained." If anything, the U.S. surveillance apparatus had expanded and become more entrenched with the FBI's departure.

Simmons agreed to present Baquero de la Calle with "a secret and informal memorandum, written in somewhat general and cautious terms," outlining the embassy's views and attitudes toward the communist situation in Ecuador. Simmons explained to the secretary of state that he mentioned only one name in the memorandum of a person suspected of communist activities, and that was a name Baquero de la Calle had already provided. "It was therefore true," Simmons emphasized, "that I actually furnished him with no names of

Communists or Communist suspects." The diplomat wished to sidestep the compromises of intervention in the sovereign affairs of a friendly country.

Simmons in fact mentioned two names in the memorandum: that of the maverick military leader Enríquez and a Mr. Wengerow. The party, Simmons wrote, "appears to have thrown its weight behind the Enríquez campaign, not openly, but covertly," in the upcoming presidential election. The communists controlled labor federations in the provinces of Guayas and Pichincha, and "although grievances apparently exist for strikes . . . the communists counsel patience in the hope that Enríquez will solve their problems and in turn they will support Enríquez." For this reason, it was important that communists not be allowed to assume positions of leadership in labor unions. As for Wengerow, Simmons stated that it was "reasonable" to believe that the Soviets had an agent in Ecuador, even though "this Embassy is not aware of the true identity of such a person." Wengerow was a photographer and a Russian citizen who was reportedly a communist, but the embassy did not have confirmation of that fact.

The memorandum noted the embassy's endeavors "to remain cognizant of the dangers of Communism in Ecuador as a matter of hemispheric security," although it claimed to lack "an investigative body to explore this subject." Simmons stated that the Communist Party had an estimated four thousand members, with five thousand more sympathizers. "Despite favorable factors for the growth of Communism," Simmons observed, "it has not been very successful in increasing its strength." Although small, "even a minority party becomes dangerous if permitted to use innocent groups to support its objectives." Simmons particularly objected to the "slanderous propaganda" that the communists carried on against the U.S. government, including spreading a "program of hate propaganda" among university students.

Despite the dangers of communism, Simmons stated his opposition to outlawing the party. He maintained this position even while Gabriel González Videla had banned the communist party in Chile in 1947, in spite of the fact that it had endorsed his presidential candidacy. In Venezuela, conservative hard-liners favored doing the same and criticized Rómulo Betancourt for not proscribing the party. In contrast, Simmons claimed that U.S. government officials "hold the view that legal suppression of the Party, per se, is contrary to our principles of democracy; further, such action would only result in increasing the danger due to forcing same into illegal channels, which would become extremely difficult to follow." Rather, because "all Communists, whether knowingly or unknowingly, are working in the interests of World Communism,"

Simmons advocated that, for security, anyone suspected of communist affiliation be excluded "from positions within the government where they may have access to information that would be harmful to the nation." Simmons closed this secret memorandum to Ecuador's Foreign Office with an emphasis on the confidential and personal nature of his observations. "I am not aware," he stated, "of any immediate threat to the stability of your Government although the latent factors are present just as they are in many governments of the world today." Baquero de la Calle read Simmons's memorandum "with great interest and expressed his deep appreciation of [Simmons's] cooperative attitude," and assured the ambassador that it "would be treated with great confidence."[69] Rather than an open and collaborative relationship, however, attempts to gain an upper hand characterized the diplomatic interactions. A certain amount of Cold War paranoia underlay the embassy's response to the request.

Instead of sending his subsecretary, Acting Minister of Foreign Affairs José Miguel García Moreno met with Simmons a week later about the same purported communist threat. García Moreno was concerned that Mancheno's and Enríquez's political ambitions might encourage a "subversive movement." The government was alert to this threat, García Moreno confided, but the danger had diminished since Baquero de la Calle's previous meeting with Simmons. García Moreno remained concerned, however, that communists "being well organized and determined" would take advantage of any political disruption to carry out "acts of violence, arson or assassination [against] one or more prominent persons in Quito or Guayaquil." Political rivalries, particularly between Mancheno and Enríquez, meant that in the event of a crisis the army would not be entirely reliable. García Moreno requested tear gas from the United States in case of such an eventuality.

The conversation then took a turn that startled the ambassador. As Simmons described in his report to the State Department, "Dr. García Moreno then made the surprising request that, if possible, I undertake steps to 'reinstate' the intelligence service of this Embassy, which he described as having existed up to the early part of the year 1947." García Moreno argued, "In these critical times, such a service had become more necessary than ever before." Simmons explained that while the FBI had indeed left a year earlier, "all officers of our Embassy were interested in securing information of all types in regard to Ecuador paralleling the interests and duties of Ecuadoran diplomats in connection with their daily work in all other countries of the world." Simmons acknowledged that the embassy did "make frequent reports to Washington, and that these reports cover[ed] a wide variety of subjects, commercial, social, cultural, political and others." The ambassador dodged the specific request to renew foreign surveillance, though, with the argument that with limited resources he did not believe "the United States Government would be in a position to take the action [García Moreno] suggested." The Acting Minister of Foreign Affairs "repeated his request towards the end of our interview, and I told him once more that I saw no prospect of favorable action although I would report to my Government the views which he had expressed."

Highly revealing are Simmons's statements in this secret correspondence to the secretary of state. The ambassador confessed, "It seems surprising that Dr. García Moreno would act upon the assumption that we have no intelligence service now which might be considered as comparable to that which existed a year ago" when the FBI still operated in the country. Simmons assured the State Department, "I naturally did not elucidate on this subject." He was worried that García Moreno was on a fishing expedition about the nature of current operations. If so, Simmons wrote, "He certainly received no enlightenment as regards our organization, although I expressed to him my appreciation of his discussing with me, in such a frank manner, various confidential matters of mutual interest." Furthermore, the ambassador reiterated to the minister, "It would be difficult for me to undertake any general exchange of information of this type, since such action might be considered as contrary to our basic concepts of non-intervention in the internal affairs of other countries."[70]

In this secret correspondence, despite his public claims to the contrary, Simmons acknowledged the presence of ongoing intelligence gathering in Ecuador after the withdrawal of the FBI and even indicated that little had changed with the agents' departure. Presumably, U.S. Embassy officials continued to use the same tactics and informants that the FBI had employed. Administrative battles in Washington among different intelligence agencies remained far removed from the political realities on the ground in Latin America. At the same time, Simmons claimed that these were only intelligence-gathering enterprises, not secret operations designed to alter Ecuadorian government policy. The nature of Simmons's conversation with the officials also reveals that U.S. informants did not penetrate so deeply into the Ecuadorian government; otherwise, the ambassador would have been able to ascertain more easily and directly the intent of the minister's request. The embassy did not appear to be engaged in a sophisticated spying operation against the Ecuadorian government. If anything, U.S. officials were more interested in private individuals involved in leftist political and labor organizing endeavors than in public policy makers.

The presence of ongoing intelligence gathering had been brought to the attention of the Ecuadorian minister through a column titled, "U.S. Agents in Latin America," which the journalist Drew Pearson had published in his syndicated Washington Merry-Go-Round newspaper column in December 1947. Pearson proclaimed that it was no longer a secret that U.S. intelligence agencies were operating out of U.S. embassies in Latin America. "Latin American governments have become accustomed to the presence of undercover operatives" in embassies, Pearson wrote, since FBI agents had been stationed at diplomatic missions since 1940, and with the war, the number of agents had reached almost seven hundred. A year and a half earlier, Central Intelligence Group (CIG) agents began to replace Hoover's men in Mexico City, Havana, Rio de Janeiro, and Montevideo. Now no FBI agents remained in Latin America. The biggest difference between the FBI and CIG, Pearson stated, was that FBI agents were technically independent of the embassies, even though they worked closely with the diplomatic and military missions. In contrast, CIG agents were an integral part of embassy and consular staffs, from the lowest clerical employees to the highest levels of leadership. During the Cold War, the CIG (as well as the subsequent CIA) became an agency to advance U.S. imperial concerns in a manner that State Department officials and FBI agents previously had not undertaken. Pearson claimed that one of the current ambassadors in a Latin American capital was in fact a CIG agent. The main qualifications to be a CIG agent, according to Pearson, were to have wartime intelligence-gathering experience, to be educated, and to have knowledge of other languages. Most of the agents in Latin America were military veterans. Finally, the principal responsibility of these agents was surveillance of communist activities and to monitor the "loyalty" of U.S. citizens living in Latin America.[71]

Simmons expressed concern that Pearson's columns could damage the State Department's mission to project a positive image of the United States in Latin America. In particular, he was perturbed by Pearson's "detailed description . . . of the secret intelligence service which has been established in all of our Embassies abroad." Pearson's columns provided "an unfortunate influence which certainly does not help us in our efforts to improve our informational services abroad."[72] The ambassador would have preferred that information on covert intelligence gathering not be publicly broadcast, as it threatened to reveal its true purpose and extent.

The reason for Simmons's hesitance to provide too much information to Ecuador's Foreign Ministry is revealed in a confidential letter to the secretary of state describing his response to a request for assistance from two private individuals, Enrique Ruata and Humberto Custode, who wanted to form an anticommunist movement in Ecuador. Simmons reported that he "naturally told them that the Embassy could not be directly involved or interested in any way in a movement of this type, although we were of course interested in hearing of their plans." Although he did not consider the matter of particular significance, he reported it "merely as a matter of record." Vice Consul Lynn Olson told the two men that the embassy "could do nothing because it would violate the long-established American policy of non-intervention in the internal affairs of another country." Olson emphasized, "This prohibition covered recommendations as well as contributions of any kind."

Vice Consul Olson dismissed the men's request for assistance because "they have no information of value to offer and no apparent organization to pursue their alleged aims." He concluded that their main goal was to collect a bit of cash and surmised that they were "crackpots, small-time swindlers or possibly even inept Communists seeking anti-American ammunition." While embassy officials were ready to dismiss them as crackpots, a handwritten note on Simmons's letter, most likely from someone at the State Department in Washington, states "Suppose the [Communist Party] put them up to this."[73] A certain amount of paranoia emerges in these communications that, despite public claims to the contrary, the fact might surface that the U.S. government was indeed deeply involved in covert surveillance designed to intervene in Ecuador's internal affairs. For the Ecuadorian left, the sis program that functioned as a service agency to gather intelligence was less damaging to its political and ideological interests than the tools of explicit imperial intervention that characterized the U.S. role in the region during the long Cold War.

Cold War

Self-portrait of artist **DANIEL LEÓN BORJA**, who drew the caricatures that precede each chapter in this book. Source: León Borja, *Hombres de Mayo*.

The historian Valeria Coronel considers the conservative reaction against La Gloriosa to be "one of the first Cold War counterrevolutions in Latin America."[1] La Gloriosa emerged in the same context as the Guatemalan Spring that led to a flourishing of economic and social opportunities before being brutally suppressed in a 1954 military coup that represented the end of the Good Neighbor policy. A combination of domestic conservative opposition and international imperial concerns brought an end to reforms in Ecuador long before they had the possibility to evolve to the level that Jacobo Arbenz had achieved temporarily in Guatemala. Popular aspirations for such radical aspirations, however, never disappeared from either country.

The former CIA officer Philip Agee in his book *Inside the Company* provides one of the earliest and most prominent exposés of U.S. political tactics in undermining leftist organizing in Latin America during the Cold War. Agee is most notorious for revealing the names of agents who worked with the CIA in Ecuador and elsewhere in Latin America in the 1960s. For most readers, Agee provided the first detailed insights into the inner workings of the U.S. intelligence apparatus in Latin America.[2] Following Agee's lead, other former CIA officials released memoirs that were openly critical of the agency, followed by academic tomes that analyzed U.S. security operations in Latin America and elsewhere.[3] After these revelations, the WikiLeaks documents subsequently released in 2006 were less surprising for their contents than for highlighting the extensive, ongoing, and deeply institutionalized nature of such intelligence-gathering operations.

As this book illustrates, an equally significant intelligence-gathering operation predated Agee's actions by two decades, although in the 1940s the FBI rather than the CIA ran it. In fact, different U.S. government agencies had collected and reported information on Latin America's internal affairs dating back to the nineteenth century. The underlying purpose and configuration of the surveillance, however, always remained quite similar. As Ambassador John Simmons observed in the case of Ecuador, many countries use their diplomatic personnel to spy on the internal affairs of another country and report that information back to their home countries so international policies can be drafted and implemented appropriately. It should hardly be surprising that a powerful empire would have the political reach such as that which the WikiLeaks documents illustrated.

It can be tempting to view Franklin Roosevelt's Good Neighbor era as a positive aberration, as a model for more constructive relations between the United States and Latin America. The World War II period examined in this book can be interpreted as an embodiment or extension of that policy. From this perspective, the onset of the Cold War disrupted what might otherwise have been harmonious relations among the American republics. The United States, however, has always acted as an empire and sought to control the rest of the hemisphere to its benefit. These policies are inherently embodied in the Monroe Doctrine and Manifest Destiny and draw on an earlier Doctrine of Discovery in which fifteenth-century papal bulls provided European explorers with a legal "right" to colonize and exploit land in the Americas that for millennia had provided subsistence to its original inhabitants.

The debates, including those that emerged so visibly in the interagency institutional battles over control of information in the 1940s, never interrogated the Doctrine of Discovery and its intellectual descendants. Rather than questioning whether to engage in imperialist undertakings, the debate concerned how to advance that imperial agenda most efficiently. Specifically, in the case of the 1940s, some diplomatic officials argued in favor of progressive reforms to enable the flourishing of a capitalist world order that would contribute to conditions that would foster the U.S. extraction of resources from a periphery. FBI Director J. Edgar Hoover's fear of communist doctrines that advocated a downward redistribution of resources to benefit the most disadvantaged members of society is the perspective that won out in the Cold War. In a sense, it is tempting to view the FBI's surveillance activities in the 1940s as a foreshadowing of the CIA and the Cold War and a loss of a more humane model for international relations.

The FBI represents a positive prototype for how the United States should conduct its international surveillance only in the sense that the sixteenth-century Dominican Friar Bartolomé de las Casas envisioned a more peaceful conquest when his ultimate goal was entirely consistent with the fundamental underlying precepts of the Doctrine of Discovery. If our options are las Casas or Christopher Columbus, an argument from a humanist perspective can be made for las Casas. If we are interested in human liberation and the rights of self-determination, they are equally objectionable. Rather than looking for more effective or less objectionable forms of imperialism, we need to build new and better worlds.

A More Effective Imperialism

The WikiLeaks revelations came in the context of powerful social movement challenges to neoliberal hegemony in Latin America in the 1990s that led to a wave of leftwing electoral victories across the continent. Those documents reveal that despite diplomatic claims that the U.S. role in the hemisphere is benign and non-interventionist, Washington continues its interference in Latin America's internal political affairs in order to support its friends and subvert its enemies. The fundamental gist of the Monroe Doctrine had not changed throughout World War II and the Cold War.[4]

Rafael Correa was elected the president of Ecuador in 2006 as part of the "pink tide" of leftist governments that swept the region. Correa and his supporters were always aware of potential U.S. attempts to undermine his government. During his reelection campaign in 2013, Correa characterized reported threats of a CIA plot to kill him as "credible" because of previous actions in Latin America. "There are many cases of [the CIA] interfering" in Latin American, Correa stated. "These are credible [reports] because this has happened before in Latin America." In response, Adam Nann, the U.S. ambassador to Ecuador, denied that the United States would interfere in the Ecuadorian elections or other internal political issues. According to the Russian news agency RT, "Although Correa conceded that he believed the statements of the U.S. ambassador, he warned that agencies such as the CIA often follow their own agenda and maintain links with organizations representing the extreme right in the countries in which they operate." Correa feared rogue elements in the CIA more than official U.S. policy as formulated in the legislative and executive branches of government.[5]

Correa's statements in 2013 echoed his interpretation of the role of the U.S. government in a police mutiny of September 30, 2010, that threatened to destabilize his government. Correa blamed CIA infiltration into Ecuador's intelligence services for what he presented as a failed coup attempt, but he contended that U.S. policy makers were not behind the uprising. On multiple occasions Correa unequivocally declared, "I honestly believe that neither President [Barack] Obama's government or the State Department had an intervention in the coup attempt on September 30."[6] In fact, Correa claimed that Obama called him personally to assure him that the United States was not involved in the failed coup. Correa stated that he had no reason to doubt the president's word.[7] Despite strong rhetoric and even Correa's refusal to renew the U.S. lease on the Manta Airbase in 2009, the expulsion of U.S. Ambassador Heather Hodges in April 2011 over WikiLeaks revelations, and Julian Assange's request for asylum in Ecuador's embassy in London and the withdrawal of Ecuador from the School of the Americas in June 2012, Correa acted as if he had little to fear from official U.S. actions against his government.

Secretary of State Hillary Clinton helped foster the perception that the United States would not attempt to undermine the Correa administration. On the afternoon of the 2010 police uprising, Clinton issued a strongly worded statement in which she declared, "The United States deplores violence and lawlessness and we express our full support for President Rafael Correa and the institutions of democratic government in that country." Her statement urged "all Ecuadorians to come together and to work within the framework of Ecuador's democratic institutions to reach a rapid and peaceful restoration of order."[8] For those who closely follow Ecuadorian politics, Clinton's statement came as no surprise. In June 2010, she had a very warm visit with Correa that was designed to pull his government away from radical leftist trends in South America and into her orbit of influence. Correa told Clinton that the new left that he represented was not "anti" anything: not anticapitalist, anti–United States, or anti-imperialist. His comments led the Ecuadorian leftist Guido Proaño to retort, "A left that is not anticapitalist and anti-imperialist is not left."[9] The leftist newspaper *Opción* declared in an editorial, "Yes, in Ecuador we are anti-imperialists."[10] Correa's leftist opponents criticized the president for responding so positively to overt pressure to move in a reformist direction and away from the revolutionary policies that his electoral campaigns had promised. They urged him to take a stronger anti-imperialist and anticapitalist stance in the face of empire.

Clinton's discussion in *Hard Choices* of her years as secretary of state in the Obama administration highlights the nature of ongoing U.S. imperial interest in Latin America. Similar to Roosevelt's Good Neighbor policy, little immediate danger existed of a direct and overt U.S. military intervention in Latin America. Clinton's memoir, however, highlights the subtle but much more damaging and ongoing nature of attempts to maintain economic control over Latin America. Clinton does not discuss Ecuador in her book, but the broader policies she advocates directly contradict those she articulated while in Ecuador in June 2010. During that visit, she left the impression that the Obama administration had backed away from the brutal neoliberal economic policies of the previous George W. Bush administration. Instead, she claimed that their government embraced the importance of social, racial, and gender justice as a path to greater equality and fairness that would lead to better economic performance and a reduction of poverty. This attitude resonated with the social democratic policies that Correa was pursuing in Ecuador.

While in *Hard Choices* Clinton discards a 1960s Cold War view of Latin America that informed decades of U.S. policy in the region, she does remain wedded to the neoliberal policies of Bill Clinton's administration in the 1990s that so ravaged the poor of Latin America. The dramatic turn leftward in South America in the twenty-first century was largely a result of grassroots mobilization that rejected those ideas and in the process fundamentally shifted the dominant discourse and political ideologies in the region. Rather than embracing progressive concerns for social justice or even liberal ideas of equality, Clinton primarily emphasizes a continuing belief in discredited neoliberal economic policies that were designed to benefit the growth of corporate profits at a cost to the impoverished majority. Once we look beyond the highly derogatory comments that Clinton makes about the leftist leaders Fidel Castro and Hugo Chávez and a surprisingly anachronistic and paternalistic depiction of Latin America as being part of the U.S. "backyard," we are left with much more significant underlying economic policy objectives of extracting wealth and resources to the benefit of wealthy corporations and the weakening and underdevelopment of local economies.[11] Similar to las Casas in the sixteenth century and to some diplomats in the 1940s, Clinton simply seeks a more effective imperial intervention in the internal, sovereign affairs of another society.

Without a question, individual rogue elements and loose cannons that might advocate for assassination hit squads to take out Latin America's popular progressive leaders probably do exist within the extensive U.S. intelligence and security apparatus. At times, such actions have risen to the point of formal policy, as with Operation Mongoose, which sought to assassinate Castro in the 1960s. But progressive change in Latin America is not about individual leaders who can be killed or co-opted, and the actions necessary for a fundamental shift in the mode of production extend far beyond a change in the current administration in power, either in the United States or in Latin America. Instead, a much more significant and longer-term concern is who controls and who benefits from the natural resources and economic wealth of Latin America. In January 2015, U.S. Vice President Joe Biden announced plans to extend the policies of Plan Colombia, which he had drafted in the 1990s under Bill Clinton's presidency, to Central America. "For the first time," Biden stated, "we can envision and work toward having the Americas be overwhelmingly middle class, democratic and secure." His goals echoed those of some U.S. diplomats in the 1940s who opposed Hoover's bluntly anticommunist agenda. Seemingly well-meaning liberal policy statements hide much more onerous underlying objectives of preventing radical alterations to fundamentally unjust structures. The harmful effects of imperial economic policies are less imme- diately obvious than overt military interventions, but they have much more significant and longer-term ramifications than a military coup that captures the public's attention.

In a sense, Correa had his concerns and priorities backward in fearing that rogue elements in the CIA might plot to assassinate him while claiming that official U.S. policy makers wish him no harm. It is not unconfirmed rumors and conspiracy theories that have the potential to undermine Latin America's move to the left but, instead, the continuance and deepening of neoliberal economic policies. The U.S. government has learned that its imperial concerns are most effectively achieved not through military coups or by directly dictat- ing economic policies but, instead, by quietly negotiating in the background to ensure maintenance of control over the region. These actions do not grab sensationalist headlines and are much more difficult to see and understand, but their long-term ramifications are potentially much more damaging than overt and political actions that might trigger a strong negative reaction.

On the Counter-Hegemonic Use of Documentation

Most scholars who examine foreign intelligence-gathering operations empha- size governments and official policy-making decisions, with particular atten- tion paid to their effect on the United States. María Emilia Paz Salinas, for example, concludes, "Interagency jurisdiction difficulties handicapped a more efficient counterintelligence work." The lesson that she extrapolates is one of "the need for a more efficient intelligence service . . . that would permit the U.S. government to anticipate the problems they must deal with in the future."[12] Typically, these studies with an eye toward policy relevance examine national security and military concerns, which in the context of World War II neces- sitates a concentration on the Nazis and translates into a concern for the eco- nomic competition that Germany presented to the United States. The goals of such investigations tend toward either a consideration for how to foster a more effective U.S. presence in Latin America or a pointed critique of those same imperial projects.

The same intelligence documents that scholars use to critique U.S. policies, however, can also serve a counter-hegemonic purpose to document and understand the aspirations of popular movements. Most scholars will read U.S. surveillance documents through a Cold War lens that focuses on a perceived communist menace. It is easy to discount the validity of this documentation for the shortcomings and misunderstandings of foreign intelligence officers who lacked a sophisticated understanding of the milieu in which they operated. They brought in their own stereotypes, political agendas, and intellectual baggage. The limits of innocence and naivety, however, can also provide openings to new insights. Particularly in situations with a dearth of domestic records on labor and leftist organizing, international surveillance can fill in gaps in our understanding and highlight themes that otherwise would not be available to scholars. Archival records that are more commonly used for foreign policy and international relations studies can assist in the writing of a rich social history. These documents facilitate a project of uncovering a previously unrecorded legacy of a class struggle for a more just and equal society.

As this book has established, the FBI's original excuse of combating Nazism in Latin America does not explain the extensive surveillance of communist activities. Neither did Ecuador's small Communist Party warrant the dedication of such resources. Even though the potential threat of Axis infiltration in the hemisphere provided the original rationale for the agency's activities, the pace and quality of the surveillance increased after it became apparent in 1943 that fascism did not present a serious threat to Latin America. Field reports, together with FBI agents' subsequent testimony, highlight that throughout this period the bureau remained more preoccupied with communists than fascists. In Ecuador, the FBI's intelligence gathering rose noticeably in the aftermath of the 1944 Glorious May Revolution, when leftist activity intensified, even as the policy makers in Washington began to curtail the bureau's activities in the region as the war in Europe wound down.

It can be tempting to commend Hoover for recognizing, even at the height of the war against fascism, of the importance in taking strategic action against communism in anticipation of the Cold War in which the Soviet Union would be the primary enemy. That thinking gives Hoover too much credit. Rather than being percipient of future events, the FBI director's policies can more logically be understood as consistent with his anticommunist attitudes dating back to the 1919 Palmer raids in which the Department of

Justice captured, arrested, and deported leftists from the United States.[13] The intent and tactics of his surveillance in Latin America formed a logical extension of the types of political repression he had employed domestically during the previous two decades. Unfortunately, for both the United States and Latin America, Hoover's "hard" line on the Soviet Union and international communism that degenerated into McCarthyism in the 1950s won out during the Cold War over a more rational "soft" line that the State Department advocated during World War II, even as their policy objectives were essentially the same.

The FBI dedicated an impressive quantity of resources to the surveillance of Latin American communists. The result is that for a brief period of time, the FBI created an especially rich trove of documents that chronicle the actions and attitudes of Ecuador's leftist movements at one of its most vibrant and important moments. Even though the agents' reporting was not always accurate and could miss significant events, it also documented aspects of the Latin American left for which no other sources of evidence are readily available. As a result, we gain a more complete understanding of the internal debates, positions, and dynamics within labor movements and the political left as the activists confronted important issues of the day. The left did not speak or act with one voice; competing interests were often at play. Regional and ideological disputes divided the Communist Party, with the PCE's leader, Ricardo Paredes, in Quito taking more dogmatic positions than the labor leader Pedro Saad in Guayaquil. The intelligence reports reveal the willingness of the novelist Enrique Gil Gilbert and antifascist activist Raymond Mériguet to collaborate with the United States and the Allied powers in their war against the Nazis. The agrarian activists Neptalí Pacheco León and Jesús Gualavisí, by contrast, were more concerned with local events in Milagro and Cayambe than global issues. These diverse activists together constructed a movement to extend social rights to broader sectors of society. Thanks to the FBI's counterintelligence activities, we gain a better appreciation of their activities. The lessons that they leave for future generations are invaluable.

NOTES

Acknowledgments

1. The papers from this conference are published in Cabrera, *La Gloriosa ¿revolución que no fue?*

Introduction

1. Hoover to Berle, September 11, 1943, Record Group (RG) 59, 822.00B/69, NARA.

2. FBI, *History of the Special Intelligence Service Division*, 1.

3. Bethell and Roxborough, "Conclusion," 328–32.

4. See, e.g., Blum, *Killing Hope*; Grandin, *Empire's Workshop*; McPherson, *The Invaded*.

5. James Reston, "Priorities Threatening Good-Neighbor Policy," *New York Times*, October 19, 1941, 103.

6. "Pan-American Labor Urged to Fight U.S. Trusts," *Daily Worker* 22, no. 279 (November 21, 1945): 8.

7. Central Intelligence Agency, "Military Junta in Ecuador," July 15, 1963, http://www.foia.cia.gov/sites/default/files/document_conversions/89801/DOC_0000437007.pdf.

8. Good introductory studies of the Ecuadorian left include Páez, *Los orígenes de la izquierda ecuatoriana*; Rodas, *La izquierda ecuatoriana en el siglo XX*. Páez examines an earlier period of anarchism in *El anarquismo en el Ecuador*, and Bonilla analyzes the subsequent 1960s in *En busca del pueblo perdido*. Ibarra provides very close and careful readings in his many works. In particular, see Ibarra, "Los idearios de la izquierda comunista ecuatoriana." See also the masterful studies by Coronel, "A Revolution in Stages"; Ospina, "La aleación inestable."

9. Becker, "La historia del movimiento indígena escrita a través de las páginas de Ñucanchic Allpa."

10. Political police and spy archives have provided rich sources of documentation elsewhere in Latin America. In particular, see Weld, *Paper Cadavers*. Similar to what the research for this book discovered for Ecuador, the historian Aaron Navarro notes that "the bureaucracies of the Central Intelligence Agency, Federal Bureau of Investigation, Military Intelligence Division, Office of Strategic Services, and State Department produced voluminous and sometimes very cogent reports

detailing economic, social, and political developments in Mexico": Navarro, *Political Intelligence and the Creation of Modern Mexico*, 5. Alexander Stephan and Jan van Heurck characterize the sheer bulk of material that the FBI collected as a result of the agency's "combination of high efficiency with grotesque overkill": Stephan and van Heurck, *"Communazis,"* xii. Tanalís Padilla and Louise Walker edited the special dossier "Spy Reports: Content, Methodology, and Historiography in Mexico's Secret Police Archive," which documents the potential for using police archives to write twentieth-century history. The dossier provides an excellent critique of the "methodological challenges regarding accuracy, bias and motivation" that arise in reading such documents: Padilla and Walker, "In the Archives," 4.

11. Society of Former Special Agents of the FBI Inc., *Society of Former Special Agents of the FBI*. Interviews with some SIS agents are also available on the FBI Oral Histories page at the National Law Enforcement Museum's website, http://www.nleomf .org/museum/the-collection/oral-histories. I thank Miguel Tinker Salas for bringing this resource to my attention.

12. A partially redacted PDF of *History of the Special Intelligence Service Division* is posted on the FBI's website, http://vault.fbi.gov/special-intelligence-service. I thank Miguel Tinker Salas for bringing this publication to my attention.

13. Among the most significant recent books that create a broader context for this work are Medsger, *The Burglary*; Rosenfeld, *Subversives*; Weiner, *Enemies*. The best known study is Whitehead, *The FBI Story*. Hoover authorized its publication; thus, it presents an internal history of the agency on which many subsequent books have drawn.

14. Kessler, *The Bureau*, 69.

15. Among the works that offer a good interpretation of the FBI's role in Latin America are Friedman, *Nazis and Good Neighbors*; Galvis and Donadío, *Colombia nazi, 1939–1945*; Newton, *The "Nazi Menace" in Argentina*; Paz Salinas, *Strategy, Security, and Spies*; Rout and Bratzel, *The Shadow War*.

16. Andrew Barnard, for example, mentions the FBI as "intermittently active in Chile," even though at its height in October 1943 the bureau had forty-three agents in the country and a total of more than one hundred during the 1940s: Barnard, "Chile," 67.

17. Among the most significant of these works are Donner, *The Age of Surveillance*; Huggins, *Political Policing*; Ratner and Smith, *Che Guevara and the FBI*.

18. See, e.g., Sadlier, *Americans All*, 200.

19. Raat, "U.S. Intelligence Operations and Covert Action in Mexico," 620; Paz Salinas, *Strategy, Security, and Spies*.

20. Society of Former Special Agents of the FBI, "Interview of Former Special Agent of the FBI John J. Walsh (1938–1953)," May 19, 2003, http://www.nleomf.org /museum/the-collection/oral-histories/john-j-walsh.html.

21. "Exposed: FBI Surveillance of SOA Watch," *¡Presente!* 21, no. 1 (Spring 2016): 2, 11.

22. Whitehead, *The FBI Story*, 159. See also Donner, *The Age of Surveillance*, 56–57; Goldstein, *Political Repression in Modern America from 1870 to the Present*, 215, 247.

23. Huggins, *Political Policing*, 55.

24. Raat, "U.S. Intelligence Operations and Covert Action in Mexico," 622.

25. Whitehead, *The FBI Story*, 167.

26. Society of Former Special Agents of the FBI, "Former Special Employee of the FBI William Horan," July 23, 2003, http://www.nleomf.org/museum/the-collection /oral-histories/william-horan.html.

27. FBI, *Report of the Director of the Federal Bureau of Investigation John Edgar Hoover for the Fiscal Year 1942*, 4.

28. Stuart, *The Department of State*, 410.

29. Batvinis, *The Origins of FBI Counterintelligence*, 214. One of the first SIS agents describes the functioning of this confidential fund in Society of Former Special Agents of the FBI, August 14, 2003, "Telephone Interview of Dallas Johnson," http:// www.nleomf.org/museum/the-collection/oral-histories/dallas-johnson.html.

30. When the State Department sent its Ecuadorian records to NARA in 1977, thirty years after the FBI program in Latin America closed, a "declassification review project" separated almost all of these field reports from the rest of the diplomatic correspondence. The FBI documents were placed in manila envelopes at the back of the corresponding archival box and were marked "Screened, do *not* refile," "Screened to remain classified do not refile," or "FBI—privileged material." The FBI has consistently delayed action on Freedom of Information Act (FOIA) requests, refused to turn over documents to NARA, and even destroyed field office records. See Stephan and van Heurck, *"Communazis,"* 283.

31. John Speakes, "Memories," http://www.nleomf.org/museum/the-collection /oral-histories/john-speakes.html.

32. Bratzel, "Introduction," 6.

33. Hoover to Berle, March 13, 1942, RG 59, 822.20/218½, NARA; "Named to Ecuadorean Cabinet," *New York Times*, January 29, 1942, 3.

34. Paz Salinas, *Strategy, Security, and Spies*, 202.

35. Johnson, *The Sorrows of Empire*, 10.

36. See, e.g., Tewksbury to Secretary of State, December 28, 1944, RG 59, 822.00/12–2844, NARA.

37. Webb, "Intelligence Liaison between the FBI and State."

38. Berle, *Navigating the Rapids*, 404.

39. FBI, *History of the Special Intelligence Service Division*, 614.

40. Raat, "U.S. Intelligence Operations and Covert Action in Mexico," 617.

41. Paz Salinas, *Strategy, Security, and Spies*, 192.

42. Society of Former Special Agents of the FBI, "Interview of Former Special Agent of the FBI Charles E. Higdon (1940–1945)," August 11, 2004, http://www.nleomf .org/museum/the-collection/oral-histories/charles-e-higdon.html.

43. Isserman, *Which Side Were You On?*, 182–83.

44. Healey, *California Red*, 131.

45. Coordinator of Information, "Preliminary Analysis of Elements of Insecurity in Ecuador," 1, 14.

46. The Council of National Defense created the OIAA with the cumbersome title of the Office for Coordination of Commercial and Cultural Relations between the American Republics (OCCCRBAR). In July 1941, the agency was renamed the Office of the Coordinator of Inter-American Affairs (OCIAA) and finally became the OIAA in March 1945. For more on the OIAA, see Office of the Coordinator of Inter-American Affairs, *History of the Office of the Coordinator of Inter-American Affairs*; Rankin, *¡México, la patria!*; Cramer and Prutsch, "Nelson A. Rockefeller's Office of Inter-American Affairs"; Cramer and Prutsch, *¡Américas Unidas!*; Tota, *The Seduction of Brazil*.

47. Society of Former Special Agents of the FBI, "Interview of Former Special Agent of the FBI Allan Gillies (1940–1964)," August 4, 2004, http://www.nleomf.org /assets/pdfs/nlem/oral-histories/FBI_Gillies_interview.pdf.

48. Williamson to Secretary of State, March 22, 1944, RG 59, 822.00/1612, NARA.

49. Williamson to Secretary of State, March 27, 1944, RG 59, 822.00/1614, NARA.

50. See Agee, *Inside the Company*.

51. Barnard, "Chilean Communists, Radical Presidents and Chilean Relations with the United States," 363.

52. FBI, *History of the Special Intelligence Service Division*, 340.

53. McIntosh, *Sisterhood of Spies*, 12–13.

Chapter 1. SIS

1. Society of Former Special Agents of the FBI, "Interview of Former Special Agent of the FBI Richard E. Crow (1941–1947)," August 2, 2006, http://www.nleomf.org /museum/the-collection/oral-histories/richard-e-crow.html.

2. Society of Former Special Agents of the FBI, "Interview of Former Special Agent of the FBI Harold Judell (1939–1944)," March 30, 2005, http://www.nleomf.org /museum/the-collection/oral-histories/harold-judell.html.

3. Society of Former Special Agents of the FBI, "Interview with Former Special Agent of the FBI James C. Kraus (1941–1976)," May 5, 2009, http://www.nleomf.org /museum/the-collection/oral-histories/james-c-kraus.html.

4. Society of Former Special Agents of the FBI, "Recollections of Roy Britton as Told to Stanley A. Pimentel from February 2003 to November 2006," 2006, http:// www.nleomf.org/museum/the-collection/oral-histories/roy-britton.html.

5. Society of Former Special Agents of the FBI, "Interview of Former Employee of the FBI Ronald J. Sundberg," November 1, 2005, http://www.nleomf.org/museum/the -collection/oral-histories/ronald-j-sundberg.html.

6. Many former agents mentioned a lack of awareness of the SIS program. See, for example, Society of Former Special Agents of the FBI, "Interview with Former Special Agent of the FBI James C. Kraus."

7. Society of Former Special Agents of the FBI, "Interview of Former Special Agent of the FBI William J. Bradley (1940–1945)," August 6, 2003, http://www.nleomf.org /museum/the-collection/oral-histories/william-j-bradley.html.

8. Society of Former Special Agents of the FBI, "Interview of Former Special Agent of the Federal Bureau of Investigation Thomas Gaquin (1941–1945)," March 14, 2007, http://www.nleomf.org/museum/the-collection/oral-histories/thomas-gaquin.html.

9. Society of Former Special Agents of the FBI, "Interview of Former Special Agent of the FBI Richard E. Crow."

10. Society of Former Special Agents of the FBI, "Interview of Former Employee of the FBI Ronald J. Sundberg."

11. Paz Salinas, *Strategy, Security, and Spies*, 147, 185.

12. FBI, *Report of the Director of the Federal Bureau of Investigation John Edgar Hoover for the Fiscal Year 1947*, 11.

13. Society of Former Special Agents of the FBI, "Telephone Interview of Dallas Johnson," August 14, 2003, http://www.nleomf.org/museum/the-collection/oral-histories/dallas-johnson.html.

14. Society of Former Special Agents of the FBI Inc., *Society of Former Special Agents of the FBI*, 173, 181, 212.

15. Society of Former Special Agents of the FBI, "Recollections of Roy Britton as Told to Stanley A. Pimentel from February 2003 to November 2006."

16. Society of Former Special Agents of the FBI, "Interview of Former Special Agent of the FBI Woodrow P. Lipscomb (1941–1966)," August 6, 2004, http://www.nleomf.org/museum/the-collection/oral-histories/woodrow-p-lipscomb.html.

17. Society of Former Special Agents of the FBI, "Telephone Interview of Dallas Johnson"; Paz Salinas, *Strategy, Security, and Spies*, 162, 181.

18. Raat, "U.S. Intelligence Operations and Covert Action in Mexico," 629.

19. FBI, *History of the Special Intelligence Service Division*, 143–63.

20. Huggins, *Political Policing*, 56; Whitehead, *The FBI Story*, 212, 224.

21. Rout and Bratzel, *The Shadow War*.

22. Friedman, *Nazis and Good Neighbors*, 68.

23. Society of Former Special Agents of the FBI, "Interview of Former Special Agent, Federal Bureau of Investigation Robert P. Gemberling (1941–1976)," May 7, 2004, http://www.nleomf.org/museum/the-collection/oral-histories/robert-p-gemberling.html.

24. Ayer, *Yankee G-Man*, 108.

25. FBI, *History of the Special Intelligence Service Division*, 28.

26. Society of Former Special Agents of the FBI, "Interview of Former Special Agent of the FBI William J. Bradley."

27. Society of Former Special Agents of the FBI, "Interview of Former Special Agent of the FBI Wade E. Knapp (1941–1965)," July 19, 2004, http://www.nleomf.org/museum/the-collection/oral-histories/wade-e-knapp.html.

28. Society of Former Special Agents of the FBI, "Interview of Former Employee of the FBI Ronald J. Sundberg."

29. FBI, *History of the Special Intelligence Service Division*, 27. Britton remembered the names of a couple of women (whom he called "girls Friday") who worked for the SIS, but said he did not know how to contact them: Society of Former Special Agents of the FBI, "Recollections of Roy Britton as Told to Stanley A. Pimentel

from February 2003 to November 2006." I have not located interviews or writings of women who were stationed in Latin American with the SIS similar to what Elizabeth McIntosh wrote about her experiences in Asia with the OSS in *Undercover Girl* and later treated in broader detail in *Sisterhood of Spies.*

30. Society of Former Special Agents of the FBI, "Interview of Former Special Agent of the FBI Richard E. Crow."

31. Society of Former Special Agents of the FBI, "Interview with Former Special Agent of the FBI James C. Kraus."

32. FBI, *History of the Special Intelligence Service Division*, 141.

33. Batvinis, *The Origins of FBI Counterintelligence*, 65.

34. Huggins, *Political Policing*, 59.

35. Huggins, *Political Policing*, 53.

36. Batvinis, *The Origins of FBI Counterintelligence*, 66, 208.

37. Huggins, *Political Policing*, 56.

38. Society of Former Special Agents of the FBI, "Telephone Interview of Dallas Johnson."

39. Bratzel, "Introduction," 6.

40. Society of Former Special Agents of the FBI, "Interview of Former Special Agent of the FBI John J. Walsh (1938–1953)," May 19, 2003, http://www.nleomf.org /museum/the-collection/oral-histories/john-j-walsh.html.

41. Cueva, *The Process of Political Domination in Ecuador*, 24.

42. Long to Secretary of State, June 19, 1940, RG 59, 822.105A/2, NARA; Berle to Hoover, June 21, 1940, RG 59, 822.105A/2, NARA; Berle to Quito American Legation, June 21, 1940, RG 59, 822.105A/2, NARA. Long incorrectly rendered Campanole's name as "Nicholaus Campanoli."

43. Hoover to Berle, July 1, 1940, RG 59, 822.00N/63, NARA.

44. Hoover to Berle, July 18, 1940, RG 59, 822.00N/66, NARA.

45. Hoover to Berle, August 12, 1940, RG 59, 822.00N/71, NARA.

46. Office of Intelligence Research, "A Survey of the Principal Newspapers of the Other American Republics," 22.

47. Wright to Bevin, September 8, 1947, AS 5445/1151/54, in *British Documents on Foreign Affairs*, series D, pt. 4, vol. 4, doc. no. 82, 366.

48. Hoover to Berle, August 8, 1940, RG 59, 822.00N/68, NARA. Also see Hoover to Berle, August 6, 1940, RG 59, 822.00F/16, NARA.

49. Hoover to Berle, August 12, 1940.

50. Paz Salinas, *Strategy, Security, and Spies*, 34, 182; Raat, "U.S. Intelligence Operations and Covert Action in Mexico," 629.

51. Hoover to Berle, July 18, 1940.

52. "Misión militar italiana vendrá al Ecuador," *El Comercio*, December 2, 1936, 1.

53. FBI, *Ecuador . . . Today*, 65.

54. Coordinator of Information, "Preliminary Analysis of Elements of Insecurity in Ecuador," 5.

55. Long to Welles, August 9, 1940, RG 59, 822.00N/82, NARA.

56. Lauderbaugh, "Estados Unidos y Ecuador durante la Segunda Guerra Mundial," 282.

57. Russell B. Porter, "Usual Nazi Tactics Tried on Ecuador," *New York Times*, August 11, 1940, 14.

58. Ciro Luis Tinajero C. and César A. Stornayola, "Un yanqui ultraja al Ecuador," August 24, 1940, BEAEP.

59. Alexander and Parker, *A History of Organized Labor in Peru and Ecuador*, 166.

60. Núñez del Arco Proaño, *El Ecuador y la Alemania Nazi*, 209.

61. Hoover to Berle, September 7, 1940, RG 59, 822.00N/85, NARA.

62. Porter, "Usual Nazi Tactics Tried on Ecuador."

63. Russell B. Porter, "Germans Maintain Losing Airline inside Panama Canal Defense Zone," *New York Times*, August 10, 1940, 6.

64. Edward Tomlison, "Ecuador es uno de los tres países vitales para la defensa de América," *El Comercio*, July 30, 1941, 1, 8.

65. Secretary of State to Long, April 25, 1940, RG 59, 822.796/112, telegram, in *FRUS*, 1940, 5:831; Long to Secretary of State, April 26, 1940, RG 59, 822.796/114, telegram, in *FRUS*, 1940, 5:831–32.

66. Friedman, *Nazis and Good Neighbors*, 56.

67. Secretary of State to Long, July 3, 1940, RG 59, 822.796/183a, telegram, in *FRUS*, 1940, 5:835–37.

68. Secretary of State to Long, July 6, 1940, RG 59, 822.796/183a supp., telegram, in *FRUS*, 1940, 5:838–39.

69. Hoover to Berle, August 6, 1940; Hoover to Berle, August 23, 1940, RG 59, 822.796/215, NARA.

70. Long to Secretary of State, July 22, 1941, RG 59, 822.796/375, in *FRUS*, 1941, 7:277–79.

71. FBI, *Ecuador . . . Today*, 44.

72. L. C. Hughes-Hallett, "Political Situation in Ecuador," January 3, 1942, A 1597/574/54, in *British Documents on Foreign Affairs*, series D, pt. 3, vol. 4, doc. no. 48, 95.

73. Secretary of State to Long, May 14, 1940, RG 59, 822.796/121, telegram, in *FRUS*, 1940, 5:832.

74. Randall, "Colombia, the United States and Inter-American Aviation Rivalry."

75. Long to Secretary of State, October 26, 1940, RG 59, 822.796/247, telegram, in *FRUS*, 1940, 5:846.

76. Long to Secretary of State, November 6, 1940, RG 59, 822.796/258, telegram, in *FRUS*, 1940, 5:848–49.

77. Norweb to Secretary of State, September 26, 1941, RG 59, 822.796/470, NARA.

78. Long to Secretary of State, July 22, 1941.

79. "Contract between the Government of Ecuador and the Defense Supplies Corporation," October 1, 1941, RG 59, 822.24/121, in *FRUS*, 1941, 7:285–90.

80. L. C. Hughes-Hallett, "Annual Report on Heads of Foreign Missions in Ecuador," June 26, 1942, A 6558/1718/54, in *British Documents on Foreign Affairs*, series D, pt. 3, vol. 5, doc. no. 105, 129.

81. Hughes-Hallett to Eden, January 2, 1944, AS 525/525/54, in *British Documents on Foreign Affairs*, series D, pt. 3, vol. 8, doc. no. 100, 183.

82. Tomlison, "Ecuador es uno de los tres países vitales para la defensa de América."

83. Pineo, *Ecuador and the United States*, 117.

84. Porter, "Hitler's Shadow over South America," *New York Times Magazine*, September 1, 1940, 3, 14.

85. "La política de buena vecindad debe consistir en respetar soberanía de los pueblos," *El Comercio*, February 25, 1944, 10.

86. Long to Welles, August 9, 1940.

87. FBI, *History of the Special Intelligence Service Division*, 408.

88. Hull to Quito Amembassy [American Embassy], November 19, 1942, RG 59, 822.105A/25A, NARA.

89. Bonsal to Keith and Melby, October 30, 1942, RG 59, 822.105A/26, NARA.

90. Nester to Secretary of State, November 23, 1942, RG 59, 822.105A/27, NARA.

91. FBI, *History of the Special Intelligence Service Division*, 409.

92. "Coronel Salgado ensayará en el Ecuador los métodos de la Oficina Federal de Investigaciones de los Estados Unidos," *El Comercio*, March 5, 1943, 10; "Coronel Salgado traerá un equipo moderno de identificación y dactiloscopia," *El Comercio*, March 15, 1943, 10.

93. "El Cnel Salgado ha terminado su visita a los Estados Unidos," *El Comercio*, March 2, 1943, 1.

94. Hull to Quito Amembassy [American Embassy], February 1, 1943, RG 59, 822.105A/25, NARA.

95. Hoover to Berle, August 30, 1944, RG 59, 822.00/8–3044, NARA.

96. Bonsal to Bacon, October 16, 1943, RG 59, 822.105A/32, NARA.

97. FBI, *History of the Special Intelligence Service Division*, 416–17.

98. FBI, *Annual Report, Special Intelligence Service, Federal Bureau of Investigation, United States Department of Justice, 1941–1942*, 36.

99. Hoover to Berle, June 13, 1944, RG 59, 822.00/6–1344, NARA.

100. "Investigaciones sobre actividades de los Nazis en los Estados Unidos," *El Comercio*, August 13, 1938, 6; "Actúan libremente varios núcleos Nazis en Estados Unidos," *La Tierra*, December 21, 1945, 1.

101. Donald Daughters, interview by Anton Daughters, 1998, transcription of an interview in Anton Daughters' personal possession.

102. FBI, *Annual Report, Special Intelligence Service, Federal Bureau of Investigation, United States Department of Justice, 1942–1943*, 69.

103. FBI, *History of the Special Intelligence Service Division*, 125.

104. Society of Former Special Agents of the FBI, "Interview of Former Special Agent of the Federal Bureau of Investigation Thomas Gaquin."

105. Society of Former Special Agents of the FBI, "Interview of Former Special Agent of the FBI Richard E. Crow."

106. FBI, *History of the Special Intelligence Service Division*, 73.

107. Society of Former Special Agents of the FBI, "Interview of Former Special Agent of the Federal Bureau of Investigation Thomas Gaquin."

108. Society of Former Special Agents of the FBI, "Interview of Former Special Agent of the FBI Fred C. Woodcock (1941–1975)," September 14, 2004, http://www.nleomf.org/museum/the-collection/oral-histories/fred-c-woodcock.html.

109. Society of Former Special Agents of the FBI, "Former Special Employee of the FBI William Horan," July 23, 2003, http://www.nleomf.org/museum/the-collection/oral-histories/william-horan.html.

110. Society of Former Special Agents of the FBI, "Interview of Former Special Agent of the FBI Charles D. Dickey, Jr. (1942–1943)," January 8, 2008, http://www.nleomf.org/museum/the-collection/oral-histories/charles-d-dickey-jr.html.

111. See, e.g., the memories of John J. Walsh in Medellín, Colombia, in Society of Former Special Agents of the FBI, "Interview of Former Special Agent of the FBI John J. Walsh."

112. Society of Former Special Agents of the FBI, "Interview of Former Special Agent of the FBI Allan Gillies (1940–1964)," August 4, 2004, http://www.nleomf.org/museum/the-collection/oral-histories/allan-gillies.html.

113. Society of Former Special Agents of the FBI, "Interview of Former Special Agent of the FBI Woodrow P. Lipscomb."

114. Society of Former Special Agents of the FBI, "Interview of Former Special Agent of the FBI Wade E. Knapp."

115. See, e.g., FBI, *History of the Special Intelligence Service Division*, 355–56.

116. Society of Former Special Agents of the FBI, "Interview of Former Special Agent of the FBI William J. Bradley."

117. Society of Former Special Agents of the FBI, "Interview of Former Special Agent of the Federal Bureau of Investigation John Paul Larkin (1941–1966)," March 13, 2007, http://www.nleomf.org/museum/the-collection/oral-histories/john-paul-larkin.html.

118. Society of Former Special Agents of the FBI, "Interview of Former Special Agent of the Federal Bureau of Investigation Thomas Gaquin."

119. FBI, *History of the Special Intelligence Service Division*, 45.

120. Society of Former Special Agents of the FBI, "Interview of Former Special Agent of the FBI Edward S. Sanders (1940–1965)," January 2, 2004, http://www.nleomf.org/museum/the-collection/oral-histories/edward-s-sanders.html.

121. Society of Former Special Agents of the FBI, "SIS Phone Interviews 5/30/06 of Former Special Agent of the FBI John Diesing (1941–1946)," May 30, 2006, http://www.nleomf.org/museum/the-collection/oral-histories/john-diesing.html.

122. Society of Former Special Agents of the FBI, "SIS Phone Interviews 5/30/06 of Former Special Agents of the FBI Donald Roney (1940–1967)," May 30, 2006, http://www.nleomf.org/museum/the-collection/oral-histories/donald-roney.html.

123. Society of Former Special Agents of the FBI, "Interview with Former Special Agent of the FBI James C. Kraus."

124. Society of Former Special Agents of the FBI, "Interview of Former Special Agent of the FBI Richard E. Crow."

125. Society of Former Special Agents of the FBI, "Interview of Former Special Agent of the FBI Richard S. Leahy (1941–1952)," May 9, 2007, http://www.nleomf.org/museum/the-collection/oral-histories/richard-s-leahy.html.

126. Daughters interview.

127. Society of Former Special Agents of the FBI Inc., *Society of Former Special Agents of the FBI*, 198.

128. Moore to Vázquez, February 5, 1942, Ministerio del Interior, Gobernación Pichincha, box 163, folder February 1942, ANE.

129. Long to Duggan, "Memorandum for the Under Secretary of State," October 31, 1942, RG 59, 822.105/19, NARA.

130. FBI, *History of the Special Intelligence Service Division*, 408–10.

131. Society of Former Special Agents of the FBI, "Interview of Former Special Agent of the FBI William J. Bradley."

132. Society of Former Special Agents of the FBI Inc., *Society of Former Special Agents of the FBI*, 258.

133. Ungar, *FBI*, 224.

134. Society of Former Special Agents of the FBI, "Interview of Former Special Agent of the Federal Bureau of Investigation Thomas Gaquin"; Society of Former Special Agents of the FBI, "Interview with Former Special Agent of the FBI Francis E. Grimes (1939–1946)," August 6, 2003, http://www.nleomf.org/museum/the-collection/oral-histories/francis-e-grimes.html.

135. Society of Former Special Agents of the FBI, "Recollections of Roy Britton as told to Stanley A. Pimentel from February 2003 to November 2006."

136. Society of Former Special Agents of the FBI, "Telephone Interview of Dallas Johnson."

137. Society of Former Special Agents of the FBI, "Interview of Former Special Agent of the FBI John J. Walsh."

138. Society of Former Special Agents of the FBI, "Interview of Former Special Agent of the FBI Fred C. Woodcock."

139. Society of Former Special Agents of the FBI, "Interview with Former Special Agent of the FBI James C. Kraus."

140. Leslie Bethell and Ian Roxborough, for example, identify legal attachés as "almost always FBI agents," without recognizing that the office by definition was FBI: Bethell and Roxborough, "Introduction," 25–26.

141. Daughters interview.

142. Creeden to Director, Havana, Cuba, December 19, 1945; Clifford to Director, Managua, Nicaragua, August 11, 1944; Martin to Director, Montevideo, Uruguay, January 24, 1944; Hulbert Jr. to Director, Asunción, Paraguay, January 24, 1944, all in "FBI Record: The Vault," http://vault.fbi.gov/J. Edgar Hoover/J. Edgar Hoover Part 8 of 22/view.

143. "Ecuador condecora a Hoover," *El Comercio*, January 27, 1944, 1. See also Suttler to Jones, July 7, 1944; Wiley to Director, Barranquilla, Colombia, January 27,

1944; Brown to Director, Caracas, Venezuela, January 27, 1944, all in "FBI Record: The Vault," http://vault.fbi.gov/J. Edgar Hoover/J. Edgar Hoover Part 8 of 22/view.

144. Ungar, FBI, 225.

145. FBI, History of the Special Intelligence Service Division, 408–10.

146. Long to Duggan, October 31, 1942.

147. FBI, History of the Special Intelligence Service Division, 408. The SIS radio operator James R. Wilson describes the Quito station in "Memoir of Former Special Agent James R. Wilson (1941–1975)," http://www.nleomf.org/museum/the-collection /oral-histories/james-r-wilson.html, 2006.

148. FBI, Annual Report (1941–42), 37.

149. Federal Bureau of Investigation, Annual Report, Special Intelligence Service, Federal Bureau of Investigation, United States Department of Justice, 1944–1945, 86.

150. Scotten to Secretary of State, August 3, 1943, RG 59, 822.00/1531, NARA. In the weeks before the start of the congressional session on August 10, Hoover forwarded several anonymous and confidential memos to the State Department, presumably with information from Blue that predicted an armed uprising against Arroyo del Río: see Hoover to Berle, July 31, 1943, RG 59, 822.00/1547, NARA; Hoover to Berle, August 7, 1943, RG 59, 822.00/1535, NARA. A memo dated July 8 from the military attaché, however, indicated that feuding between General Alberto C. Romero and General Ricardo Astudillo and opposition from Colonel Héctor Salgado, head of the carabineros, made a coup d'état at the present time "very unlikely": see memo attached to Hoover to Berle, July 31, 1943.

151. Hoover to Berle, December 1, 1943, RG 59, 822.248/12–143, NARA.

152. Scotten to Secretary of State, December 24, 1943, RG 59, 822.248/520, NARA.

153. FBI, History of the Special Intelligence Service Division, 143–63, 171, 408, 416–17.

154. FBI, Annual Report (1942–43), 69–70.

155. Hoover to Berle, September 10, 1942, RG 59, 822.00/1460, NARA.

156. Hoover to Berle, July 8, 1943, RG 59, 822.50/251, NARA.

157. FBI, History of the Special Intelligence Service Division, 416–17.

158. Batvinis, The Origins of FBI Counterintelligence, 83.

159. FBI, Report of the Director of the Federal Bureau of Investigation John Edgar Hoover for the Fiscal Year 1942, 7.

160. FBI, Ecuador . . . Today, 1–2.

161. FBI, Report of the Director of the Federal Bureau of Investigation John Edgar Hoover for the Fiscal Year 1947, 11.

162. Wilson, "Memoir of Former Special Agent James R. Wilson."

163. FBI, History of the Special Intelligence Service Division, 143–63, 171, 408, 416–17. Unfortunately, two final reports from the FBI to the State Department, dated January 14, 1947, and February 14, 1947, have been removed from NARA. In their place, a withdrawal notice states "access restricted" because the documents contain "security-classified information." The withdrawal authorization is signed "FBI/Post '45" and dated November 1, 1977.

164. Society of Former Special Agents of the FBI, "Interview of Former Employee of the FBI Ronald J. Sundberg."

165. John Edgar Hoover, "Memorandum from the Director of the Federal Bureau of Investigation (Hoover) to Attorney General Clark," Washington, DC, August 29, 1945 in U.S. Department of State, *Emergence of the Intelligence Establishment*, 24–25.

166. Ameringer, *U.S. Foreign Intelligence*, 83.

167. U.S. Department of State, *Emergence of the Intelligence Establishment*, 4; Troy, *Donovan and the CIA*, 267.

168. Dean Acheson, "Memorandum from Acting Secretary of State Acheson to the Members of the National Intelligence Authority," Washington, DC, August 5, 1946, in U.S. Department of State, *Emergence of the Intelligence Establishment*, 286–87.

169. John Speakes, "Memories," http://www.nleomf.org/museum/the-collection /oral-histories/john-speakes.html.

170. Acheson, "Memorandum From Acting Secretary of State Acheson to the Members of the National Intelligence Authority"; J. Edgar Hoover, "Letter from the Director of the Federal Bureau of Investigation (Hoover) to the Assistant Secretary of State for American Republic Affairs (Braden)," Washington, DC, July 22, 1946, in U.S. Department of State, *Emergence of the Intelligence Establishment*, 285.

171. Hoover, "Letter From the Director of the Federal Bureau of Investigation (Hoover) to the Assistant Secretary of State for American Republic Affairs (Braden)"; J. Edgar Hoover, "Memorandum from the Director of the Federal Bureau of Investigation (Hoover) to Attorney General Clark," Washington, DC, August 8, 1946, in U.S. Department of State, *Emergence of the Intelligence Establishment*, 291–94.

172. Hoyt Vandenberg, "Letter from the Director of Central Intelligence (Vandenberg) to the Assistant Secretary of State for American Republic Affairs (Braden)," Washington, DC, October 9, 1946, in U.S. Department of State, *Emergence of the Intelligence Establishment*, 304.

173. FBI, *Report of the Director of the Federal Bureau of Investigation John Edgar Hoover for the Fiscal Year 1947*, 11.

174. Society of Former Special Agents of the FBI, "Interview of Former Special Agent of the FBI Fred C. Woodcock."

175. Society of Former Special Agents of the FBI, "Recollections of Roy Britton as told to Stanley A. Pimentel from February 2003 to November 2006."

176. Hoover, "Letter from the Director of the Federal Bureau of Investigation (Hoover) to the Assistant Secretary of State for American Republic Affairs (Braden)"; Hoover, "Memorandum from the Director of the Federal Bureau of Investigation (Hoover) to Attorney General Clark."

177. Daughters interview.

178. Society of Former Special Agents of the FBI, "A Memoir of Francis Stephen Milovich, Jr.," http://www.nleomf.org/museum/the-collection/oral-histories/francis -stephen-milovich-jr.html.

179. Society of Former Special Agents of the FBI, "Interview of Former Special Agent of the FBI John J. Walsh."

180. Society of Former Special Agents of the FBI, "Interview of Former Special Agent of the FBI Fred C. Woodcock."

181. FBI, *Report of the Director of the Federal Bureau of Investigation John Edgar Hoover for the Fiscal Year 1947*, 11–12.

182. Society of Former Special Agents of the FBI, "Recollections of Roy Britton as Told to Stanley A. Pimentel from February 2003 to November 2006."

183. "Legal Attaché Offices," http://www.fbi.gov/contact-us/legat.

184. Theoharis, *From the Secret Files of J. Edgar Hoover*, 194; Ungar, *FBI*, 241.

185. Huggins, *Political Policing*, 61; Langguth, *Hidden Terrors*; Rout and Bratzel, *The Shadow War*, 40, 455–56; Whitehead, *The FBI Story*, 230.

Chapter 2. Communism

1. Federal Bureau of Investigation, *Annual Report, Special Intelligence Service, Federal Bureau of Investigation, United States Department of Justice, 1945–1946*, 65.

2. Federal Bureau of Investigation, *Annual Report, Special Intelligence Service, Federal Bureau of Investigation, United States Department of Justice, 1941–1942*, 36–37.

3. Society of Former Special Agents of the FBI, "Telephone Interview of Dallas Johnson," August 14, 2003, http://www.nleomf.org/museum/the-collection/oral-histories/dallas-johnson.html; Stephan and van Heurck, *"Communazis,"* 228.

4. Society of Former Special Agents of the FBI, "Interview of Former Special Agent of the Federal Bureau of Investigation John Paul Larkin (1941–1966)," March 13, 2007, http://www.nleomf.org/museum/the-collection/oral-histories/john-paul-larkin.html.

5. Society of Former Special Agents of the FBI, "Interview of Former Employee of the FBI Ronald J. Sundberg," November 1, 2005, http://www.nleomf.org/museum/the-collection/oral-histories/ronald-j-sundberg.html; Federal Bureau of Investigation, *History of the Special Intelligence Service Division*, 423.

6. Society of Former Special Agents of the FBI, "Interview of Former Special Agent of the FBI Harold Judell (1939–1944)," March 30, 2005, http://www.nleomf.org/museum/the-collection/oral-histories/harold-judell.html.

7. Society of Former Special Agents of the FBI, "Interview of Former Special Agent of the FBI John J. Walsh (1938–1953)," May 19, 2003, http://www.nleomf.org/museum/the-collection/oral-histories/john-j-walsh.html.

8. Society of Former Special Agents of the FBI, "Interview of Former Special Agent of the FBI Wade E. Knapp (1941–1965)," July 19, 2004, http://www.nleomf.org/museum/the-collection/oral-histories/wade-e-knapp.html; Society of Former Special Agents of the FBI, "Interview of Former Special Agent of the FBI Richard S. Leahy (1941–1952)," May 9, 2007, http://www.nleomf.org/museum/the-collection/oral-histories/richard-s-leahy.html; Society of Former Special Agents of the FBI, "Interview of Former Employee of the FBI Ronald J. Sundberg."

9. Society of Former Special Agents of the FBI, "Interview of Former Special Agent of the FBI Wade E. Knapp (1941–1965)." Knapp's report is probably the one at

Scotten to Secretary of State, August 14, 1943, RG 59, 822.00B/67, NARA. It is included in an electronic appendix for this book at http://www.yachana.org/fbi.

10. Federal Bureau of Investigation, *History of the Special Intelligence Service Division*, 7.

11. Thanks to Kris Lane (personal communication) for this insightful parallel.

12. Ayer, *Yankee G-Man*, 7–8, 111.

13. R. M. de Lambert to Secretary of State, August 14, 1925, RG 59, 822.00/614, NARA.

14. Aguirre, *Una etapa política del socialismo ecuatoriano*, 84.

15. Aguirre, *El Partido Socialista en la Revolución del 28 de Mayo*.

16. Hoover to Berle, November 18, 1943, RG 59, 822.00B/75, NARA.

17. Luna Tamayo, "Los movimientos sociales en los treinta," 213.

18. Larrea, *Estatutos, principios políticos y plan de Acción de Vanguardia Revolucionaria del Socialismo Ecuatoriano (VRSE)*, 1, 14; Paz, *Larrea Alba, nuestras izquierdas*.

19. Dawson to Secretary of State, January 29, 1931, RG 59, 822.00B/24, NARA. See Gallegos, *Rusia Soviética y la revolución mundial*; Jaramillo et al., *Manifiesto al proletariado ecuatoriano*.

20. Dawson to Secretary of State, January 29, 1931.

21. White to Dawson, 1931[?], RG 59, 822.00B/26, NARA.

22. Dawson to Secretary of State, March 10, 1933, RG 59, 822.00B/43, NARA.

23. Dawson to Secretary of State, February 7, 1931, RG 59, 822.00B/25, NARA.

24. Dawson to Secretary of State, December 9, 1930, RG 59, 822.00B/17, NARA.

25. Dawson to Thurston, December 20, 1930, RG 59, 822.00B/18, NARA.

26. Franklin, *Ecuador*, 299.

27. Henry Dearborn, "Ambursen Engineering Corporation's Activities with Regard to Revolution in Ecuador," November 16, 1945, RG 59, 822.00/11–1645, NARA.

28. Williamson to Secretary of State, March 11, 1944, RG 59, 822.00/1608, NARA.

29. Gantenbein to Secretary of State, April 18, 1944, RG 59, 822.00/1631, NARA.

30. Blasier, *The Hovering Giant*, 234.

31. Henry Dearborn, "Ecuadoran Foreign Minister's Call on Mr. Braden," January 7, 1947, RG 59, 711.22/1–747, NARA.

32. Walter C. Thurston, December 26, 1930, RG 59, 822.00B/19, NARA; White to Dawson, January 28, 1931, RG 59, 822.00B/23, NARA.

33. White to Dawson, 1931[?].

34. Dawson to Secretary of State, October 3, 1930, RG 59, 822.00B/14, NARA.

35. Dawson to Secretary of State, March 10, 1933.

36. Dawson to Thurston, December 20, 1930.

37. Gerhard Gade to Secretary of State, March 10, 1938, RG 59, 822.00B/54, NARA.

38. Hoover to Lyon, September 6, 1945, RG 59, 822.00B/9–645, NARA.

39. Scotten to Secretary of State, August 14, 1943.

40. Federal Bureau of Investigation, *Ecuador . . . Today*, 85. Many of the FBI documents cited in this section are available in an electronic appendix for this book at http://www.yachana.org/fbi.

41. Hoover to Berle, July 29, 1942, RG 59, 822.00B/62, NARA.

42. Hoover to Berle, July 29, 1942.

43. Hoover to Berle, May 18, 1942, RG 59, 822.00B/61, NARA.

44. Scotten to Secretary of State, August 14, 1943. Wade discusses drafting this report in Society of Former Special Agents of the FBI, "Interview of Former Special Agent of the FBI Wade E. Knapp (1941–1965)." Curiously, in contrast to standard practice, Ambassador Scotten, and not FBI Director Hoover, forwarded this report to the State Department. This action may either point to a warming of relations between the agencies or competition for control over the legal attaché's activities.

45. Iber, "Managing Mexico's Cold War," 13; Kofas, *The Struggle for Legitimacy*, 256; "Lombardo Toledano critica la interferencia del comunismo en entidades sindicales," *El Comercio*, December 19, 1946, 6, 9; Spenser, "El viaje de Vicente Lombardo Toledano al mundo del porvenir," 87.

46. Hoover to Berle, September 21, 1943, RG 59, 822.00B/70, NARA. The English spelling of "subsidize" may indicate that the "confidential source" was the British legation.

47. Hoover to Berle, April 7, 1944, RG 59, 822.00B/79, NARA.

48. Scotten to Secretary of State, August 14, 1943.

49. Scotten to Secretary of State, August 14, 1943.

50. Theoharis, *From the Secret Files of J. Edgar Hoover*, 86–87.

51. Barnard, "Chilean Communists, Radical Presidents and Chilean Relations with the United States," 363.

52. Dawson to Secretary of State, January 29, 1931.

53. Naval Attaché, "Intelligence Report," July 12, 1943, RG 59, 822.00B/76, NARA.

54. Hoover to Berle, September 21.

55. Hoover to Berle, November 18, 1943.

56. The FBI memos on Parades are included in an electronic appendix for this book at http://www.yachana.org/fbi.

57. Hoover to Berle, February 14, 1944, RG 59, 822.00/1626, NARA.

58. Hoover to Lyon, September 6; Hoover to Lyon, April 5, 1946, RG 59, 822.00B/4–546, NARA.

59. Hoover to Lyon, July 17, 1946, RG 59, 822.00B/7–1746, NARA.

60. Hoover to Lyon, January 17, 1946, RG 59, 822.00B/1–1746, NARA.

61. Hoover to Lyon, November 2, 1945, RG 59, 822.00B/11–245, NARA. For more on Gómez de la Torre, see Almeida, *Antología*; Rodas, *Nosotras que del amor hicimos*.

62. Hoover to Lyon, June 3, 1946, RG 59, 822.00B/6–346, NARA.

63. Hoover to Lyon, November 29, 1945, RG 59, 822.00B/11–2945, NARA.

64. Rodríguez, "Acción por el Movimiento de Mujeres," 23.

65. Hoover to Lyon, November 2, 1945; Martínez, *Yo siempre he sido Nela Martínez Espinosa*, 23. The FBI surveillance documents on Nela Martínez are available in an electronic appendix for this book at http://www.yachana.org/fbi.

66. Hoover to Lyon, November 2, 1945. On Martínez's relationship with Gallegos Lara, see Alemán and Coronel, *Vienen ganas de cambiar el tiempo*.

67. "Se reunió ayer la Asamblea de Mujeres Ecuatorianas," *El Día*, May 1, 1938, 3; "Programa de acción de la Alianza Femenina Ecuatoriana," *El Día*, May 9, 1938, 4; Alianza Femenina Ecuatoriana, *Estatutos de Alianza Femenina Ecuatoriana.*

68. Vega, *La Gloriosa*, 52, 79–80.

69. Rodríguez, "Acción por el Movimiento de Mujeres," 17, 22.

70. "Alianza Femenina Ecuatoriana eligió en reunión de ayer nuevo directorio," *El Comercio*, July 30, 1944, 16; "Llamamiento que Alianza Femenina Ecuatoriana dirige a las mujeres del país," *El Comercio*, August 8, 1944, 1, 9; Romo-Leroux, *Movimiento de mujeres en el Ecuador*, 163–65.

71. "Comités antitotalitarios del Ecuador y pro-aliados ofrecieron manifestación de simpatía a Vicente Lombardo Toledano," *El Comercio*, October 9, 1942, 2.

72. Naval Attaché, "Intelligence Report."

73. Hoover to Berle, September 11, 1943, RG 59, 822.00B/69, NARA.

74. Hoover to Berle, April 20, 1944, RG 59, 822.00/4–2045, NARA.

75. Hoover to Lyon, May 30, 1945, RG 59, 822.00B/5–3045, NARA; Hoover to Lyon, November 2, 1945.

76. Hoover to Lyon, November 2, 1945.

77. Martínez, *Yo siempre he sido Nela Martínez Espinosa*, 86.

78. Sesión Ordinaria del H. Congreso Extraordinario, Acta no. 8, December 7, 1945, APL.

79. Díaz, "Nela Martínez (Programa Número 13)"; Romo-Leroux, *Movimiento de mujeres en el Ecuador*, 63–65.

80. Hoover to Lyon, February 5, 1946, RG 59, 822.00B/2–546, NARA.

81. Hoover to Lyon, March 5, 1946, RG 59, 822.00B/3–546, NARA.

82. An agent in Argentina reported that the FBI paid "a considerable sum" to informants whose reports were taken verbatim from newspaper articles: Society of Former Special Agents of the FBI, "Interview of Former Special Agent of the FBI John J. Walsh (1938–1953)."

83. "Raymond Mériguet Cousségal," http://www.diccionariobiograficoecuador .com/tomos/tomo5/m6.htm.

84. Partido Socialista Ecuatoriano, Vanguardia Revolucionaria del Socialismo Ecuatoriano, and Partido Comunista del Ecuador, "Por la libertad, el progreso y bienestar del pueblo ecuatoriano, contra la reacción y el fascism," February 1938, private collection of Leonardo J. Muñoz. I thank Sandra Fernández Muñoz for facilitating access to this collection.

85. Partido Comunista del Ecuador, "La U.R.S.S. en guerra contra el Fascismo agresor y en defensa de los pueblos oprimidos," June 23, 1941, Hojas Volantes, BEAEP.

86. Partido Comunista del Ecuador, "Manifiesto del Partido Comunista Ecuatoriano sobre la Agresión del Perú," July 7, 1941, Hojas Volantes, BEAEP.

87. Mériguet, *Antinazismo en Ecuador*, 11.

88. "El próximo viernes se celebrará una reunión con el objeto de dejar organizado en ésta el 'Comité Antifascista,'" *El Comercio*, November 19, 1941, 1.

89. "Comité anti-fascista se formó en esta ciudad en asamblea que fue convocada con este objeto," *El Comercio*, November 22, 1941, 12.

90. Raymond Mériguet, "Por la Unión Soviética. Por España Republicana," Movimiento Popular Antitotalitario del Ecuador, November 7, 1942, Hojas Volantes, BEAEP.

91. "Perú atacó al Ecuador haciendo gala de métodos usados por totalitarios," *El Comercio*, August 8, 1941, 1.

92. "Manifiesto del Movimiento Popular Antitotalitario del Ecuador," December 11, 1941, Hojas Volantes, BEAEP.

93. Hoover to Berle, September 11, 1943. A cross-reference file note in NARA indicates that the State Department also maintained a file on Mériguet, although those documents appear to be missing from the archive: see Hoover to Berle, July 14, 1944, RG 59, 822.00B Meriguet Coussegal, Raymond Jean/7–1444, NARA.

94. Scotten to Secretary of State, August 14, 1943.

95. Federal Bureau of Investigation, *Ecuador . . . Today*, 85.

96. Naval Attaché, "Intelligence Report."

97. Hoover to Berle, September 21. See "El verdadero sentido de la doctrina monroe," *Antinazi*, August 17, 1943, 1, 7; "La disolución de la Internacional Comunista es oportuna para libertar a los pueblos de la opresión fascista, declara el mariscal José Stalin," *Antinazi*, August 17, 1943, 5.

98. Kenneth H. Vanderford, "Minutes of Meeting of Coordination Committee for Ecuador," October 26, 1942, RG 229, entry 125, box 1391, NARA; Kenneth H. Vanderford, "Minutes of Meeting of Coordination Committee for Ecuador," November 11, 1942, RG 229, entry 125, box 1391, NARA. I thank Monica Rankin for providing copies of these documents on the OIAA.

99. Office of Strategic Services, "Political Activities of French Minority Groups in Latin America since June 1940," 66.

100. "Visit of Henry A. Wallace," May 5, 1943, in "FBI Record: The Vault," http://vault.fbi.gov/Henry A Wallace /Henry A Wallace Part 1 of 2/view.

101. "Nuestro saludo de antinazistas y ecuatorianos a Henry Wallace," *Antinazi*, April 17, 1943, 1.

102. "Homenaje a Francia combatiente se realizó anoche en la Universidad," *El Comercio*, July 15, 1943, 10.

103. Hoover to Berle, September 6, 1943, RG 59, 822.00/1553, NARA.

104. Hoover to Berle, September 21, 1943; Hoover to Berle, January 26, 1944, RG 59, 822.00B/78, NARA; "La conferencia provincial antifascista se inauguró ayer en la universidad," *El Comercio*, September 21, 1943, 8.

105. "Indígenas de Cayambe forman el primer Comité Antifascista del campo en Yanahuaico," *Antinazi*, August 17, 1943, 2; "Comité indígena antifascista se organizó en Juan Montalvo," *Antinazi*, September 5, 1943, 2; Movimiento Antifasista del Ecuador, *Informe y resoluciones*, 28, 32; Nela Martínez, "Prólogo," in Mériguet, *Antinazismo en Ecuador*.

106. Scotten to Secretary of State, August 14, 1943.

107. R. Alan Reed, "Minutes of Meeting of Coordination Committee for Ecuador," July 20, 1942, RG 229, entry 125, box 1391, NARA.

108. Hoover to Berle, September 21, 1943.

109. Scotten to Secretary of State, August 14, 1943.

110. Hoover to Berle, November 27, 1944, RG 59, 822.00B/11–2744, NARA.

111. "Grupos políticos con fines subversivos," El Comercio, July 7, 1943, 1.

112. Hoover to Berle, September 21, 1943.

113. "Ciudadano francés desarrollaba actividades comunistas," El Comercio, October 31, 1943, 12.

114. "Raymond Mériguet, líder del movimiento antifascista del Ecuador," Antinazi, December 29, 1943, 1.

115. Partido Comunista del Ecuador, El Partido Comunista Ecuatoriano protesta ante la nación.

116. Rojas, Informe del c. doctor Ángel F. Rojas, 11; Aguirre, Informe del c. doctor Manuel Agustín Aguirre, 18.

117. Hoover to Berle, January 26, 1944; Hoover to Berle, April 7, 1944; Hoover to Berle, July 14, 1944; Hoover to Berle, August 18, 1944, RG 59, 822.00/8–1844, NARA.

118. Hoover to Berle, October 12, 1944, RG 59, 822.00B/10–1244, NARA. See also Hoover to Lyon, May 4, 1945, RG 59, 822.00B/5–445, NARA.

119. Federal Bureau of Investigation, History of the Special Intelligence Service Division, 489.

120. Hoover to Berle, December 7, 1944, RG 59, 822.00B/12–744, NARA; Hoover to Lyon, January 27, 1945, RG 59, 822.00B/1–2745, NARA; Hoover to Lyon, January 27, 1945, RG 59, 822.00B/1–2745, NARA.

121. Hoover to Lyon, November 14, 1945, RG 59, 822.00B/11–1445, NARA.

122. Hoover to Lyon, November 29, 1945.

123. Ayer, Yankee G-Man, 9.

124. Hoover to Berle, May 18, 1942.

125. Mexican communists similarly attempted to link Nazism and Trotskyism: see Iber, Neither Peace nor Freedom, 20, 40.

126. "Falangistas y trotzkistas: Dos enemigos de la democracia," Antinazi, November 7, 1942, 4.

127. "Los comunistas en la lucha antifascista y la disolución de la Tercera Internacional," Antinazi, June 26, 1943, 8.

128. Alexander, Trotskyism in Latin America, 245.

129. Hoover to Berle, April 7, 1944.

130. Scotten to Secretary of State, August 14, 1943.

131. Simmons to Secretary of State, July 29, 1947, RG 59, 822.00B/7–2947, NARA.

132. Hoover to Berle, September 11, 1943.

133. Hoover to Lyon, May 30, 1945.

134. Alexander and Parker, A History of Organized Labor in Peru and Ecuador, 167.

135. Isserman, Which Side Were You On? 44; Stephan and van Heurck, "Communazis," xv.

136. Robeson, *Paul Robeson Speaks*, 416–17.

137. Vernet Gresham, "Communist Activities," September 9, 1943, RG 59, 822.00B/72, NARA, and repeated in Hoover to Berle, November 18, 1943.

138. Hoover to Berle, November 18, 1943.

139. Hoover to Lyon, June 27, 1945, RG 59, 822.00B/6–2745, NARA.

140. Hoover to Berle, April 7, 1944.

141. Ellner, "Factionalism in the Venezuelan Communist Movement," 67.

142. Ibarra, "¿Qué fue la revolución de 1944?," 202.

143. Hoover to Berle, November 18, 1943.

Chapter 3. Labor

1. Pineo, *Social and Economic Reform in Ecuador*, 139.

2. Milk Ch., *Movimiento obrero ecuatoriano el desafío de la integración*.

3. FBI, *History of the Special Intelligence Service Division*, 413.

4. Hoover to Berle, December 7, 1944, RG 59, 822.00B/12–744, NARA.

5. Hoover to Berle, September 20, 1944, RG 59, 822.00B/9–2044, NARA.

6. Hoover to Lyon, September 25, 1945, RG 59, 822.00B/9–2545, NARA.

7. Rodríguez, "Ayer tomaron posesión de su cargo los profesores del Instituto Nal. 'Vicente Rocafuerte' D' Guayaquil," *El Comercio*, October 9, 1931, 1.

8. Dawson to Secretary of State, April 26, 1932, RG 59, 822.00/838, NARA; "Ecuador Exiles Teachers," *New York Times*, April 21, 1932, 7.

9. Hoover to Berle, September 20, 1944.

10. Gade to Secretary of State, March 10, 1938, RG 59, 822.00B/54, NARA.

11. Hoover to Berle, September 20, 1944.

12. Interview with Paul Reichler in Alexander, *Robert Jackson Alexander Papers, 1890 (1945)–1999, the Interview Collection*, microfilm, box 7, folder 31–32.

13. Hughes-Hallett to Bevin, October 10, 1945, AS 5659/1259/54, in *British Documents on Foreign Affairs*, series D, pt. 3, vol. 10, doc. no. 54, 403.

14. Ycaza, *Historia del movimiento obrero ecuatoriano*, 2:92; Milk Ch., *Movimiento obrero ecuatoriano el desafío de la integración*, 148.

15. Hoover to Berle, May 11, 1943, RG 59, 822.504/54, NARA.

16. Lombardo, "Informe de mi recorrido por América Latina," 19–20. The countries Lombardo Toledano visited were Cuba, Colombia, Ecuador, Peru, Chile, Bolivia, Costa Rica, Nicaragua, Honduras, El Salvador, and Guatemala, in addition to his native Mexico and the United States.

17. Lombardo, "Informe de mi recorrido por América Latina," 29–30; "En Ibarra y Cayambe se formaron comités de recepción a Lombardo Toledano," *El Comercio*, October 6, 1942, 10; "En Cayambe el Párroco Dr. Caicedo, encabeza la manifestación a Vicente Lombardo Toledano," *Antinazi*, November 7, 1942, 6.

18. "Milagro," *Antinazi*, November 7, 1942, 4, 6.

19. Among those who signed the agreement to hold a congress were Pedro Saad, Primitivo Barreto, Francisco Mora Guerrero, Ángel Fernández, José Elías Montenegro,

Segundo Naranjo, Antonio Espinosa, Alberto Torres Vera, Gilberto Pazmiño, and Víctor Hugo Briones, although eventually several of them opposed the direction that the organizing efforts took: see Rodríguez, "Informe sobre el Congreso de Unificación de los Trabajadores Ecuatorianos," 41–43; "Primer Congreso Nacional de Trabajadores se reunirá en Quito en marzo próximo," *El Comercio*, October 14, 1942, 10; Saad, *La CTE y su papel histórico*, 27.

20. "Segundo Congreso de la CTE," *La Tierra*, May 13, 1946, 1.

21. Kofas, *The Struggle for Legitimacy*, 263–64.

22. Saad, *El Ecuador y la guerra*.

23. Rodríguez, "Informe sobre el Congreso de Unificación de los Trabajadores Ecuatorianos," 44–46.

24. "El Dr. Arroyo ordena que se sitúen fondos para Congreso Nacional Obrero," *El Comercio*, February 28, 1943, 1, 4.

25. "El Congreso Nacional Obrero tiene como fundamento la estructuración de la confederación de trabajadores del Ecuador," *El Comercio*, February 28, 1943, 1, 4.

26. Rodríguez, "Informe sobre el Congreso de Unificación de los Trabajadores Ecuatorianos," 48–49, 52.

27. "No se permitirá la intervención del señor Guillermo Rodríguez en la próximo Congreso Obrero Nacional," *El Comercio*, March 11, 1943, 1, 8.

28. "Lic. Vicente Lombardo Toledano no asistirá a Congreso Obrero Nacional," *El Comercio*, March 3, 1943, 1; "El Lic. Lombardo Toledano sí asistirá al congreso obrero nacional," *El Comercio*, March 12, 1943, 10; "Lombardo Toledano no vendrá al país," *El Comercio*, March 13, 1943, 1.

29. Scotten to Secretary of State, August 14, 1943, RG 59, 822.00B/67, NARA.

30. Rodríguez, "Informe sobre el Congreso de Unificación de los Trabajadores Ecuatorianos," 57, 63–65; "El líder obrero Sr. Guillermo Rodríguez será repatriado en breve a Colombia," *El Comercio*, March 18, 1943, 1, 4.

31. Ycaza, *Historia del movimiento obrero ecuatoriano*, 2:93.

32. "El líder obrero Sr. Guillermo Rodríguez se encuentra ya en libertad en Cali," *El Comercio*, March 19, 1943, 1.

33. "El presidente de la República y su Gabinete asistirán a inauguración del Cgso. Obrero," *El Comercio*, March 15, 1943, 10.

34. "Esta tarde se inaugurará el Congreso Obrero Nacional," *El Comercio*, March 18, 1943, 1, 4.

35. "Dará una conferencia sobre el congreso de trabajadores," *El Comercio*, March 16, 1943, 4; "Sr. Pedro Saad no dió conferencia," *El Comercio*, March 17, 1943, 10.

36. "Se separaron del congreso obrero varias delegaciones," *El Comercio*, March 19, 1943, 1, 4.

37. "Nomina de delegados provinciales al Congreso Obrero Nacional," *El Comercio*, March 19, 1943, 3.

38. "Comunismo ha creído ver en Congreso Obrero una oportunidad para su labor política apasionada y anti-patriótica," *El Comercio*, March 19, 1943, 1, 4.

39. Saad, *La CTE y su papel histórico*, 28.

40. Alberto Torres Vera, Antonio Espinosa Bueno, Gilberto Pazmiño González, and José Elías Montenegro, "Pídese escolta para mantener el orden en el Congreso Obrero," *El Comercio*, March 19, 1943, 10.

41. Rodríguez, "Informe sobre el Congreso de Unificación de los Trabajadores Ecuatorianos," 54, 62.

42. "A las 4 PM se inauguró el Congreso Obrero Nacional," *El Comercio*, March 19, 1943, 10.

43. Aguirre, *Informe del c. doctor Manuel Agustín Aguirre*, 11.

44. "El Congreso Obrero Nacional se inaugurará solemnemente mañana," *El Comercio*, March 20, 1943, 1.

45. "Miembros del partido socialista fueron reducidos a prisión a medio día de ayer," *El Comercio*, March 20, 1943, 1; "El Sr. Pedro Saad, quien vino al Congreso Obrero, fue apresado en Guayaquil," *El Comercio*, March 22, 1943, 1.

46. "Hay completa calma en la República," *El Comercio*, March 23, 1943, 1.

47. "No ha cambiado la situación de los presos políticos," *El Comercio*, March 24, 1943, 1; "Juan Isaac Lovato, Ezequiel Paladines y Pedro Saad siguen presos," *Antinazi*, April 17, 1943, 6.

48. "Declaraciones del Sr. Guillermo Rodríguez," *El Comercio*, March 23, 1943, 1.

49. Aguirre, *Informe del c. doctor Manuel Agustín Aguirre*, 10.

50. Aguirre, *Informe del c. doctor Manuel Agustín Aguirre*, 12.

51. "El Congreso Obrero Nacional se inaugurará solemnemente mañana," 4.

52. "Esta tarde es inaugurará el Congreso Obrero Nacional," *El Comercio*, March 21, 1943, 1.

53. "El delegado de la Artística de Pichincha fue electo presidente de Congreso Obrero," *El Comercio*, March 22, 1943, 8.

54. "Gobierno no permitirá la reunion de otro congreso obrero," *El Comercio*, March 26, 1943, 1.

55. "Ayer a los 4 PM se inauguró el Quinto Congreso Obrero Nacional," *El Comercio*, March 22, 1943, 1, 6.

56. "Ayer a los 4 PM se inauguró el Quinto Congreso Obrero Nacional," 1, 6.

57. "Congreso Obrero Nacional recomienda que el Ecuador declare la guerra al Eje," *El Comercio*, March 24, 1943, 3.

58. "Congreso Obrero discutió en tercera la carta orgánica de la clase trabajadora," *El Comercio*, March 26, 1943, 1, 3.

59. "Congreso Obrero aprobó la carta orgánica de la clase trabajadora ecuatoriana," *El Comercio*, March 27, 1943, 8.

60. "El Ministro de Previsión Social estudia ponencias aprobadas por Cgso. Obrero," *El Comercio*, March 29, 1943, 1.

61. "La carta orgánica de la clase obrera ecuatoriana fué entregada al Ejecutivo," *El Comercio*, March 31, 1943, 10.

62. "Comisión permanente de legislación y control social," *El Comercio*, March 31, 1943, 10.

63. Aguirre, *Informe del c. doctor Manuel Agustín Aguirre*, 12.

64. Ycaza, *Historia del movimiento obrero ecuatoriano*, 2:92.

65. Albornoz, "La lucha de los trabajadores y la formación de la CTE," 80.

66. Hoover to Berle, May 12, 1943, RG 59, 822.504/57, NARA.

67. Kofas, *The Struggle for Legitimacy*, 289.

68. Saad, *La CTE y su papel histórico*, 29.

69. Milk Ch., *Movimiento obrero ecuatoriano el desafío de la integración*, 148.

70. "Visit of Vice President Henry Wallace," Quito, April 5, 1943, in "FBI Record: The Vault," http://vault.fbi.gov/Henry A Wallace /Henry A Wallace Part 1 of 2/view.

71. "Political Activity Visit of Vice President Henry Wallace," April 8, 1943, in "FBI Record: The Vault," http://vault.fbi.gov/Henry A Wallace /Henry A Wallace Part 1 of 2/view.

72. "Nuestro saludo de antinazistas y ecuatorianos a Henry Wallace," *Antinazi*, April 17, 1943, 1.

73. Hughes-Hallett to Eden, May 4, 1943, A 4786/739/54, in *British Documents on Foreign Affairs*, series D, pt. 3, vol. 6, doc. no. 85, 381–82.

74. "Visit of Henry A. Wallace," May 5, 1943, in "FBI Record: The Vault," http://vault.fbi.gov/Henry A Wallace /Henry A Wallace Part 1 of 2/view.

75. Hoover to Berle, July 14, 1943, RG 59, 822.504/59, NARA.

76. "Lic. Pedro Saad fue puesto en libertad," *El Comercio*, July 6, 1943, 1.

77. Naval Attaché, "Intelligence Report," July 12, 1943, RG 59, 822.00B/76, NARA.

78. Scotten to Secretary of State, August 14, 1943.

79. Hoover to Berle, July 14, 1943, RG 59, 822.504/60, NARA.

80. Hoover to Berle, September 11, 1943, RG 59, 822.00B/69, NARA.

81. Hoover to Berle, September 11. "Barrezeuea" was the party activist Enrique Barrezueta.

82. FBI, *Annual Report, Special Intelligence Service, Federal Bureau of Investigation, United States Department of Justice, 1943–1944*, 118.

83. Society of Former Special Agents of the FBI, http://www.nleomf.org/museum /the-collection/oral-histories.

84. Hoover to Berle, September 20, 1944.

85. Vernet Gresham, "Communist Activities," September 9, 1943, RG 59, 822.00B/72, NARA, repeated in Hoover to Berle, November 18, 1943, RG 59, 822.00B/75, NARA.

86. Hoover to Berle, September 21, 1943, RG 59, 822.00B/70, NARA.

87. Hoover to Berle, November 18, 1943.

88. Hoover to Berle, August 18, 1944, RG 59, 822.00/8–1844, NARA.

89. Hoover to Berle, April 7, 1944, RG 59, 822.00B/79, NARA.

90. Carr, *Marxism and Communism in Twentieth-Century Mexico*, 144.

Chapter 4. La Gloriosa

1. Richard P. Putrick, "Revolution in Ecuador," September 15, 1924, RG 59, 822.00/559, NARA.

2. Aguirre, *Informe del c. doctor Manuel Agustín Aguirre*, 1, 7.

3. "Un estado de barbarie," *El Comercio*, May 10, 1944, 4.

4. Parkman, *Nonviolent Insurrection in El Salvador*.

5. Bethell and Roxborough, "Introduction," 2, 5.

6. "Martínez salía de El Salvador siendo despedido con cohetes y toques de sirena," *El Comercio*, May 12, 1944, 1, 7; "Manifiesto a la nación," *El Comercio*, May 12, 1944, 1, 3.

7. Gantenbein to Secretary of State, May 12, 1944, RG 59, 822.00/1643, NARA.

8. Gantenbein to Secretary of State, May 17, 1944, RG 59, 822.00/1646, NARA.

9. FBI, *Annual Report, Special Intelligence Service, Federal Bureau of Investigation, United States Department of Justice, 1943–1944*, 55.

10. "Encendiendo la Antorcha," *La Antorcha*, vol. 1, no. 1, November 16, 1924, 1.

11. Dawson to Secretary of State, October 3, 1930, RG 59, 822.00B/14, NARA.

12. Dawson to Secretary of State, January 29, 1931, RG 59, 822.00B/24, NARA.

13. *La Vanguardia*, quoted in Aguirre, "El marxismo, la revolución y los partidos socialista y comunista del Ecuador," 91.

14. "Ricardo Paredes, Candidato del Partido Comunista," 1933, Private collection of Leonardo J. Muñoz, Quito.

15. Naval Attaché, July 12, 1943, RG 59, 822.00B/76, NARA.

16. Interview with Hugo Larrea Benalcazar, in Alexander, *Robert Jackson Alexander papers, 1890 (1945)–1999, the Interview Collection*, microfilm, box 7, folder 31–32.

17. Aguilar Vazquez, *Informe a la nación*, 21.

18. Hoover to Berle, September 11, 1943, RG 59, 822.00B/69, NARA.

19. Hoover to Berle, September 11, 1943.

20. Naval Attaché, July 12, 1943.

21. Hoover to Berle, September 11, 1943.

22. Hoover to Berle, August 18, 1944, RG 59, 822.00/8–1844, NARA.

23. Torre, *Populist Seduction in Latin America*.

24. Alianza Democrática Ecuatoriana, *Los postulados de la Revolución de Mayo*, 7–12.

25. Pólit Ortiz, "A los 40 años de la 'Gloriosa Revolución' del 28 de mayo de 1944," 46.

26. Gustavo Becerra, "Es indispensable la unidad de todos los ecuatorianos sobre la base de un programa democrático," *El Día*, July 29, 1943, 1, 6.

27. Hoover to Berle, September 11, 1943.

28. Manuel Agustín Aguirre, Juan I. Lovato, Alfonso Calderón, Pablo Duque Arias, Hugo Carrera Andrade, Gonzalo Oleas, and Gonzalo Maldonado Jarrín, "El Partido Socialista Ecuatoriano a la nación," *El Día*, August 6, 1943, 1, 2.

29. Hoover to Berle, September 11, 1943.

30. Hoover to Berle, November 18, 1943, RG 59, 822.00B/75, NARA.

31. Hoover to Berle, June 13, 1944, RG 59, 822.00/6–1344, NARA.

32. Hoover to Berle, February 29, 1944, RG 59, 822.00/1616, NARA.

33. For detailed examinations of the May 1944 revolution, see Araujo Hidalgo, *El 28 de mayo, balance de una revolución popular*; Cabrera, *La Gloriosa*; Girón, *La*

revolución de mayo; Torre, *Populist Seduction in Latin America*; Universidad de Guayaquil, *El 28 de mayo de 1944*; Vega, *La Gloriosa*.

34. Aguirre, *El Partido Socialista en la Revolución del 28 de Mayo*, 11.

35. Rodas, *Nosotras que del amor hicimos*, 60. On the role of women in the May revolution, see León Galarza, "Las mujeres y la 'Gloriosa'"; Romo-Leroux, *Movimiento de mujeres en el Ecuador*, 162–63. On the role of Indigenous activists, see Vega, *La Gloriosa*, 96.

36. Guarnición Militar de Guayaquil, "Proclama de la Guarnición Militar de Guayaquil," 171.

37. Blanksten, *Ecuador*, 46; Muñoz Vicuña, "Prólogo," 10; Oña Villarreal, *Presidentes del Ecuador*, 53. In Guayaquil, the Junta Provisional de Gobierno (Provisional Governing Board) included Francisco Arízaga Luque (liberal), Pedro Saad (communist), Ángel Felicísimo Rojas (socialist), Alfonso Larrea Alba (VRSE), and Efraín Camacho Santos (conservative). In Quito, the ADE's political bureau that claimed control included Julio Teodoro Salem (independent liberal), Gustavo Becerra (communist), Manuel Agustín Aguirre (socialist), Camilo Ponce Enríquez (Ecuadorian Democratic Front/conservative), Mariano Suárez Veintimilla (conservative), and General Luis Larrea Alba (VRSE).

38. Girón, *La revolución de mayo*, 122.

39. Girón, *La revolución de mayo*, 355; Vega, *La Gloriosa*, 96.

40. Sosa-Buchholz, "The Strange Career of Populism in Ecuador," 144.

41. Ayala Mora, "La represión arroísta," 35–38.

42. "Immense muchedumbre participó en el impotent desfile fúnebre efectuado ayer," *El Comercio*, May 24, 1944, 12.

43. Aguirre, *El Partido Socialista en la Revolución del 28 de Mayo*, 10, 13.

44. Williamson to Secretary of State, May 29, 1944, RG 59, 822.00/1651, NARA.

45. Scotten to Secretary of State, May 29, 1944, RG 59, 822.00/1652, NARA. At the start of the insurrection, militants attacked the telegraph office in Guayaquil and cut off communication with the rest of the country.

46. Williamson to Secretary of State, May 29, 1944, RG 59, 822.00/1658.

47. Hoover to Berle, May 27, 1944, RG 59, 822.00/1730, NARA. Hoover's sequence of letters on La Gloriosa are available in an electronic appendix for this book at http://www.yachana.org/FBI.

48. Gantenbein to Secretary of State, May 22, 1944, RG 59, 822.00/1650, NARA.

49. Memo from Hanley to Keith and Berle, May 24, 1944, RG 59, 822.00/1669, NARA.

50. Gantenbein to Secretary of State, March 8, 1944, RG 59, 822.00/1601, NARA.

51. Gantenbein to Secretary of State, May 22, 1944.

52. Scotten to Secretary of State, May 23, 1944, RG 59, 822.00/1670, NARA.

53. Hoover to Berle, June 2, 1944, RG 59, 822.00/6–244, NARA.

54. Hoover to Berle, May 29, 1944, RG 59, 822.00/5–2944, NARA. U.S. officials in Ecuador consistently referred to ARNE mistakenly as the Asociación (rather than the correct Acción) Revolucionaria Nacionalista Ecuatoriana.

55. http://es.metapedia.org/wiki/Acción_Revolucionaria_Nacionalista_Ecuatoriana

56. Hoover to Berle, February 14, 1944, RG 59, 822.00/1626.

57. Bueno, "Sinopsis de acciones y secuencias constituyentes de la actuación de José María Plaza," 136, 140.

58. Hoover to Berle, February 14, 1944.

59. Hoover to Berle, March 3, 1944, RG 59, 822.00/1618, NARA.

60. Gantenbein to Secretary of State, May 17, 1944.

61. "Los hermanos Plaza," *Newsweek* (June 19, 1944): 62.

62. Williamson to Secretary of State, May 29, 1944, RG 59, 822.00/1654.

63. Williamson to Secretary of State, May 29, 1944, RG 59, 822.00/1663.

64. Scotten to Secretary of State, May 29, 1944, RG 59, 822.00/1662, NARA; Scotten to Secretary of State, June 1, 1944, RG 59, 822.01/99, telegram, in *FRUS* 7 (1944): 1041.

65. Pineo, *Ecuador and the United States*, 116–17.

66. Hoover to Berle, April 20, 1944, RG 59, 822.00/4–2045, NARA.

67. Scotten to Secretary of State, May 30, 1944, RG 59, 822.00/1672, NARA.

68. Scotten to Secretary of State, June 1, 1944, RG 59, 822.01/100, telegram, in *FRUS* 7 (1944): 1040.

69. Scotten to Secretary of State, June 1, 1944, RG 59, 822.01/99.

70. Stettinius to the Diplomatic Representatives in the American Republics except Argentina, Bolivia, and Ecuador, June 5, 1944, in *FRUS* 7 (1944): 1045–46.

71. Scotten to Secretary of State, May 29, 1944, RG 59, 822.00/1664.

72. Scotten to Secretary of State, June 3, 1944, RG 59, 822.00/1708.

73. Hoover to Berle, June 2, 1944. The FBI was concerned with the threat of Ecuadorian support for the "Gran Colombian ideal," but politicians rarely mentioned this concept. One of the few examples was President Carlos Julio Arosemena Tola's statement on the anniversary of Ecuadorian independence that was won with Venezuelan support: see "Mensaje del Excmo. Presidente Constitucional de la República señor don Carlos Julio Arosemena en homenaje a la Gran Colombia," *La Tierra*, May 24, 1948, 3.

74. Williamson to Secretary of State, May 31, 1944, RG 59, 822.00/1685, NARA.

75. Scotten to Secretary of State, May 31, 1944, RG 59, 822.00/1684, NARA.

76. Hoover to Berle, June 2, 1944. The leaders mentioned in the memo included José María Velasco Ibarra (political chameleon), Francisco Arízaga Luque (liberal), General Luis Larrea Alba (VRSE), Julio Teodoro Salem (independent), Mariano Suárez Veintimilla (conservative), Manuel Agustín Aguirre (socialist), Gustavo Becerra (communist), Camilo Ponce Enríquez (Frente Democrático/conservative), Major Leonardo Chiriboga Ordóñez (army), Pedro Saad (communist), Ángel Felicísimo Rojas (ADE/socialist), Enrique Gil Gilbert (communist), Efrain Camacho Santos (conservative), and Colonel Pablo Larrea Borja (army).

77. FBI, *Annual Report, Special Intelligence Service, Federal Bureau of Investigation, United States Department of Justice, 1943-1944*, 55.

78. FBI, *Annual Report, Special Intelligence Service, Federal Bureau of Investigation, United States Department of Justice, 1943-1944*, 58–59.

79. FBI, *Annual Report, Special Intelligence Service, Federal Bureau of Investigation, United States Department of Justice, 1943–1944*, 55.

80. FBI, *History of the Special Intelligence Service Division*, 408.

81. FBI, *Annual Report, Special Intelligence Service, Federal Bureau of Investigation, United States Department of Justice, 1943–1944*, 117.

82. FBI, *History of the Special Intelligence Service Division*, 415–16.

83. Scotten to Secretary of State, May 29, 1944, RG 59, 822.00/1664.

84. Scotten to Secretary of State, May 29, 1944, RG 59, 822.00/1659.

85. Scotten to Secretary of State, May 29, 1944, RG 59, 822.00/1661.

86. Scotten to Secretary of State, May 29, 1944, RG 59, 822.00/1655.

87. Williamson to Secretary of State, May 31, 1944, RG 59, 822.00/1690.

88. Edward A. Tamm, "Memorandum from the Director's Assistant (Tamm) to the Director of the Federal Bureau of Investigation (Hoover)," in U.S. Department of State, *Emergence of the Intelligence Establishment*, 30. An FBI agent in Paraguay confirms that embassy's reliance on the bureau's infrastructure during similar disturbances in that country: see Society of Former Special Agents of the FBI, "Former Special Employee of the FBI William Horan," http://www.nleomf.org/museum/the -collection/oral-histories/william-horan.html, July 23, 2003.

89. Harold Williamson, "Interview between the Legal Attaché and the de facto A.D.E. Authorities Concerning the Origin of the Revolutionary Movement in Guayaquil," May 31, 1944, included in Williamson to Secretary of State, June 1, 1944, RG 59, 822.00/1700, NARA; Scotten to Secretary of State, June 3, 1944, RG 59, 822.00/1708, NARA. See "Movimiento subversivo estallo en Guayaquil," *El Comercio*, May 29, 1944, 1.

90. Hoover to Lyon, June 16, 1944, RG 59, 822.00/6–1645, NARA.

91. Scotten to Secretary of State, August 14, 1943, RG 59, 822.00B/67, NARA.

92. Williamson to Secretary of State, May 30, 1944, RG 59, 822.00/1678, NARA.

93. Hoover to Berle, June 13, 1944.

94. Hoover to Berle, June 6, 1944, RG 59, 822.00/1721, NARA.

95. Hoover to Berle, June 19, 1944, RG 59, 822.00/6–1944, NARA.

96. Hoover to Berle, September 20, 1944, RG 59, 822.00B/9–2044, NARA.

97. Scotten to Secretary of State, June 3, 1944, RG 59, 822.00/1707; Scotten to Secretary of State, June 14, 1944, RG 59, 822.00/1723, NARA.

98. Scotten to Secretary of State, June 14, 1944.

99. Williamson to Secretary of State, May 2, 1944, RG 59, 822.00/1637, NARA.

100. José María Velasco Ibarra, "Transfórmase el cuerpo de carabineros en un organismo de policía civil," decree 11, *Registro Oficial* 1, no. 10 (June 13, 1944): 37.

101. Williamson to Secretary of State, July 26, 1944, RG 59, 822.00/7–2644, NARA.

102. Federal Bureau of Investigation, *History of the Special Intelligence Service Division*, 200–2.

103. Hoover to Lyon, June 16, 1944.

104. Hoover to Berle, August 18, 1944.

105. Federal Bureau of Investigation, *Annual Report, Special Intelligence Service, Federal Bureau of Investigation, United States Department of Justice, 1944–1945*, 86–87.

106. Williamson to Secretary of State, June 1, 1944.

107. Long to Secretary of State, June 2, 1944, RG 59, 822.00/1698, NARA.

108. Scotten to Secretary of State, June 3, 1944, RG 59, 822.00/1708.

109. Memorandum from Otis Bosworth, June 7, 1944, in Gantenbein to Secretary of State, June 10, 1944, RG 59, 822.00/1718, NARA.

110. Scotten to Secretary of State, June 3, 1944, RG 59, 822.00/1708.

111. Scotten to Secretary of State, July 18, 1944, RG 59, 822.00/7–1844, NARA.

Chapter 5. Constitution

1. Williamson to Secretary of State, June 1, 1944, RG 59, 822.00/1700, NARA.

2. Gustavo Becerra, "Manifiesto a la nación del Partido Comunista del Ecuador," 1943, Hojas Volantes, BEAEP.

3. Aguirre, "Breves memorias sobre la Revolución del 28 de Mayo de 1944," 218–21. The communist Alfredo Vera presents a similar view of these events in "Una insurrección triunfante que no pudo ser Revolución," 104.

4. Confederación de Trabajadores del Ecuador, "Estatutos de la Confederación de Trabajadores del Ecuador," 194.

5. Aguirre, *El Partido Socialista en la Revolución del 28 de Mayo*, 19.

6. Scotten to Secretary of State, June 14, 1944, RG 59, 822.00/1723, NARA.

7. Memo from Dearborn to Woodward, Lyon, and McGurk, September 11, 1944, RG 59, 822.00/9–1144, NARA; Scotten to Secretary of State, September 14, 1944, RG 59, 822.00/9–1444, NARA.

8. Aguirre, "Breves memorias sobre la Revolución del 28 de Mayo de 1944," 230.

9. Williamson to Secretary of State, July 26, 1944, RG 59, 822.00/7–2644, NARA.

10. Memo from Keith to McGurk, July 27, 1944, RG 59, 822.00/7–2744, NARA.

11. "Congreso de Trabajadores eligió representantes a la Asamblea Constituyente," *El Comercio*, July 10, 1944, 1.

12. "El Dr. Francisco Arízaga Luque fue nombrado Presidente por 52 votos," *El Comercio*, August 11, 1944, 3.

13. "Alizana Femenina Ecuatoriana eligió en reunión de ayer nuevo directorio," *El Comercio*, July 30, 1944, 16; "Llamamiento que Alianza Femenina Ecuatoriana dirige a las mujeres del país," *El Comercio*, August 8, 1944, 1, 9; Romo-Leroux, *Movimiento de mujeres en el Ecuador*, 163–65.

14. Hoover to Berle, July 23, 1944, RG 59, 822.00/7–2344, NARA.

15. Hoover to Berle, July 30, 1944, RG 59, 822.00/7–3044, NARA.

16. Hoover to Berle, September 1, 1944, RG 59, 822.00/9–144, NARA.

17. "Actas de la Asamblea Constituyente de 1944," vol. 1, August 10, 1944, 32, Archivo Palacio Legislativo (APL), Quito; "Miembros de la Constituyente juraron trabajar por la grandeza de la Patria," *El Comercio*, August 11, 1944, 1; "Opinan que el período de sesiones de la Asamblea no debe pasar de dos meses," *El Comercio*, August 11, 1944, 2.

18. "Actas de la Asamblea Constituyente de 1944," vol. 1 (August 19, 1944), 564, APL; "Sectores capitalistas no deben temer que la legislativa de emergencia haga la revolución," *El Comercio*, August 20, 1944, 12.

19. "Actas de la Asamblea Constituyente de 1944," vol. 1, August 24, 1944, 804, APL; "Descentralización administrativa y centralización política propunga la Asamblea," *El Comercio*, August 25, 1944, 3.

20. "La Asamblea Constituyente inició la discusión de la Carta Política," *El Comercio*, August 22, 1944, 1; "Actas de la Asamblea Constituyente de 1944," vol. 1, August 21, 1944, 618, APL.

21. Hoover to Lyon, January 27, 1945, RG 59, 822.00B/1–2745, NARA.

22. Hoover to Lyon, September 6, 1945, RG 59, 822.00B/9–645, NARA.

23. Scotten to Secretary of State, March 5, 1945, RG 59, 711.22/3–545, NARA.

24. Hoover to Berle, November 27, 1944, RG 59, 822.00B/11–2744, NARA.

25. Hoover to Berle, December 7, 1944, RG 59, 822.00B/12–744, NARA.

26. Hoover to Berle, September 20, 1944, RG 59, 822.00B/9–2044, NARA.

27. Hoover to Lyon, June 27, 1945, RG 59, 822.00B/6–2745, NARA.

28. Scotten to Secretary of State, November 3, 1944, RG 59, 822.00/11–344, NARA.

29. Hoover to Berle, November 27, 1944.

30. Scotten to Secretary of State, December 5, 1944, RG 59, 822.00/12–544, NARA.

31. Blanksten, *Ecuador*, 51–52. See also Linke, *Ecuador*, 47–49.

32. Bossano, *Evolución del derecho constitucional ecuatoriano*, 164.

33. Federal Bureau of Investigation, *History of the Special Intelligence Service Division*, 414.

34. Aguirre, *El Partido Socialista en la Revolución del 28 de Mayo*, 21–22, 26, 28.

35. Vega, *La Gloriosa*, 118–19.

36. Scotten to Secretary of State, July 29, 1944, RG 59, 822.00/7–2944, NARA.

37. Hoover to Lyon, March 14, 1945, RG 59, 822.00B/3–1445, NARA; Hoover to Lyon, April 20, 1945, RG 59, 822.00B/4–2045, NARA.

38. "Contramanifestaciones rechazaron a los agitadores extremistas," *El Comercio*, January 17, 1945, 10; "Ecuador Groups Clash at Quito," *New York Times*, January 18, 1945, 4; Hoover to Lyon, March 14, 1945, NARA; Hoover to Lyon, April 4, 1945, RG 59, 822 .00B/4–445, NARA.

39. "Versión oficial de levantamiento de los indígenas en el anejo Sanguicel," *El Comercio*, January 13, 1945, 1; "Contramanifestaciones rechazaron a los agitadores extremistas"; "Prodújose lavantamiento de indígenas de cantón Cayambe contra la autoridad," *El Comercio*, January 30, 1945, 1–2; Vega, *La Gloriosa*, 117; Cueva, *The Process of Political Domination*, 37; Muñoz, *Testimonio de lucha*, 86–88.

40. Hoover to Lyon, August 2, 1945, RG 59, 822.00B/8–245, NARA.

41. For a parallel in Chile, see Barnard, "Chilean Communists, Radical Presidents and Chilean Relations with the United States," 359. Barnard argues that "revolution was far from the party's intentions."

42. L. C. Hughes-Hallett, "Ecuador: Political Review for the Year 1943," January 4, 1944, AS 526/192/54, in *British Documents on Foreign Affairs*, series D, pt. 3, vol. 8, doc. no. 101, 188.

43. Burt to Dearborn, July 14, 1945, RG 59, 822.00/7–1445, NARA.

44. "Luego de analizar actual situación del país, CTE hace presente su rechazo a todo intento de dictadura," *El Universo*, July 13, 1945, 1, 3.

45. Lichtenstein, *Labor's War at Home*.

46. Dearborn to Monro, July 26, 1945, RG 59, 822.00B/7–2645, NARA.

47. Leonard, "The New Pan Americanism in U.S.-Central American Relations," 106.

48. Shaw's response indicated that the instructions came in "File No. 810.00B/9–2145." A handwritten annotation on Shaw's letter at NARA attached to this file number cryptically notes "rap ba ara sea ma al ar our neve": see Shaw to Secretary of State, Quito, November 9, 1945, RG 59, 822.00B/11–945, NARA.

49. Shaw to Secretary of State, November 9, 1945.

50. Hughes-Hallett to Bevin, December 17, 1945, N 137/137/38, in *British Documents on Foreign Affairs*, series D, Part IV, vol. 1, doc. no. 54, 139.

51. Kofas, *The Struggle for Legitimacy*, 304.

52. Browder, *Teheran*.

53. Carr, *Marxism and Communism in Twentieth-Century Mexico*, 106.

54. Healey, *California Red*, 92, 236.

55. Duclos, "On the Dissolution of the American Communist Party," originally published as "A propos de la dissolution du P.C.A.," *Cahiers du communism* 6, new series (April 1945): 21–38.

56. Using documents from the Comintern archives, Harvey Klehr, John Earl Haynes, and K. M. Anderson argue for "the wholly Soviet origins of the Duclos article": see Klehr et al., *The Soviet World of American Communism*, 100.

57. Isserman, *Which Side Were You On?* 221; Ryan, *Earl Browder*, 246–61; Starobin, *American Communism in Crisis*, 78–83.

58. Carr, *Marxism and Communism in Twentieth-Century Mexico*, 140–41.

59. Barnard, "Chilean Communists, Radical Presidents and Chilean Relations with the United States," 356.

60. Caballero, *Latin America and the Comintern*, 134–37.

61. Ellner, "Factionalism in the Venezuelan Communist Movement," 60, 68.

62. Kinoshita, *Mário Schenberg*, 35.

63. Nuñez, "Los partidos politicos en el Ecuador," 54.

64. Ibarra, "Los idearios de la izquierda comunista ecuatoriana," 49–51.

65. Herrería and Moreno de Safadi, "El 28 de Mayo de 1944," 251–52. Some Venezuelans also complained about Roca's advocacy for Browder's positions: see Ellner, "Factionalism in the Venezuelan Communist Movement," 62.

66. Quoted in Scotten to Secretary of State, August 14, 1943, RG 59, 822.00B/67, NARA.

67. Juan L. Gorrell, "Reaction in Quito to the Announced Dissolution of the Communist International," June 3, 1943, RG 59, 800.00B/Communist International/295, NARA, cited in Caballero, *Latin America and the Comintern*, 147.

68. PCE, *Unidad Progresista para derrotar a los reaccionarios en las elecciones*, 4, 6.

69. Asamblea Constituyente, Acta no. 26, September 7, 1944, APL.

70. Carr, "From Caribbean Backwater to Revolutionary Opportunity," 248.

71. Aguirre, *Informe del c. doctor Manuel Agustín Aguirre*, 21.

72. Hoover to Berle, August 18, 1944, RG 59, 822.00/8–1844, NARA.

73. Office of Strategic Services, "The First Half Year of the Velasco Ibarra Administration in Ecuador," 8, 12.

74. Hoover to Berle, December 7, 1944.

75. Hoover to Lyon, March 14, 1945; Hoover to Lyon, June 27, 1945.

76. Churchill and Vander Wall, *The Cointelpro Papers*.

77. Hoover to Lyon, June 27, 1945.

78. Carr, *Marxism and Communism in Twentieth-Century Mexico*, 127.

79. Hoover to Lyon, June 27, 1945.

80. Hoover to Lyon, September 6, 1945.

81. Hoover to Lyon, April 4, 1945.

82. PCE, *Unidos para la democracia y el progreso*, 6–7.

83. PCE, *Unidos para la democracia y el progreso*, 8–9.

84. PCE, *Unidos para la democracia y el progreso*, 10–11.

85. PCE, *Unidos para la democracia y el progreso*, 12–15.

86. Hoover to Lyon, September 6, 1945; Hoover to Lyon, August 2, 1945.

87. Hoover to Lyon, September 6, 1945.

88. Hoover to Lyon, November 14, 1945, RG 59, 822.00B/11–1445, NARA.

89. Hoover to Lyon, October 11, 1945, RG 59, 822.00B/10–1145, NARA.

90. Ellner, "Factionalism in the Venezuelan Communist Movement," 69.

91. Martínez, "Pedro Saad y el browderismo," 15–16.

92. Martínez, *Yo siempre he sido Nela Martínez Espinosa*, 58.

93. Ellner, "Factionalism in the Venezuelan Communist Movement," 59.

94. Shaw to Secretary of State, November 9, 1945.

95. Hoover to Lyon, November 29, 1945, RG 59, 822.00B/11–2945, NARA.

96. "El Comité Central Electoral de Trabajadores, Estudiantes y Partidos de Izquierda, a la ciudadanía del Cantón Quito," October 20, 1945, Hojas Volantes, BEAEP; El Comité Central Electoral, "Lista no. 3," 1945, Hojas Volantes, BEAEP.

97. "Ampliamente triunfaron ayer los conservadores en las elecciones," *El Comercio*, November 25, 1945, 1.

98. Burt to Secretary of State, March 12, 1946, RG 59, 822.00/3–1246, NARA.

99. Hoover to Berle, November 27, 1944.

100. Hoover to Berle, November 18, 1943, RG 59, 822.00B/75, NARA.

101. Hoover to Berle, June 13, 1944, RG 59, 822.00/6–1344, NARA.

102. Hoover to Lyon, November 29, 1945.

103. Hoover to Berle, November 27, 1944.

104. Herrería and Moreno de Safadi, "El 28 de Mayo de 1944," 251–52.

105. Wright to Bevin, July 5, 1946, AS 11648/5/54, in *British Documents on Foreign Affairs*, series D, pt. 4, vol. 2, doc. no. 97, 201.

106. Aguirre, *Una etapa política del socialismo ecuatoriano*, 19–20, 48–49.

107. PCE, *Fundamentos ideológicos y programa mínimo.*

108. Hughes-Hallett to Bevin, December 17, 1945, 140.

109. PCE, "Terminemos con la dictadura de Velasco!" May 8, 1946, Hojas Volantes, BEAEP.

Chapter 6. Coup

1. Hoover to Berle, November 27, 1944, RG 59, 822.00B/11–2744, NARA.

2. Hoover to Lyon, November 15, 1945, RG 59, 822.00B/11–1545, NARA.

3. Barnard, "Chilean Communists, Radical Presidents and Chilean Relations with the United States," 363–74.

4. Bethell and Roxborough, "Introduction," 16.

5. Ellner, "Venezuela," 166.

6. Barnard, "Chile," 91.

7. "No soy hombre de derecha. Mi alma es netamente izquierdista," *El Comercio*, June 12, 1944, 1, 8.

8. Williamson to Secretary of State, June 7, 1944, RG 59, 822.00/1715, NARA.

9. Williamson to Secretary of State, June 23, 1944, RG 59, 822.00/6–2344, NARA.

10. Hoover to Berle, November 27, 1944.

11. Hoover to Berle, December 7, 1944, RG 59, 822.00B/12–744, NARA.

12. Hoover to Berle, November 27, 1944.

13. Hoover to Lyon, June 27, 1945, RG 59, 822.00B/6–2745, NARA.

14. Hoover to Berle, December 7, 1944.

15. Hoover to Lyon, April 4, 1945, RG 59, 822.00B/4–445, NARA.

16. Hoover to Lyon, November 14, 1945, RG 59, 822.00B/11–1445, NARA.

17. Vera, "Una insurrección triunfante que no pudo ser Revolución," 105–6.

18. Cueva, "El Ecuador de 1925 a 1960," 110.

19. Ospina Peralta, "Matrimonio de compromiso," 130.

20. Garaycoa, "La estructura económica del Ecuador en los años 40," 46–47; Cueva, *The Process of Political Domination in Ecuador*, 40.

21. Jirón, "La transformación política del 28 de Mayo de 1944," 30.

22. Egas, *28 de mayo de 1944*, 128; Ordeñana, "Una revolución traicionada," 55.

23. Vera, "Una insurrección triunfante que no pudo ser Revolución," 105.

24. Aguirre, "Breves memorias sobre la Revolución del 28 de Mayo de 1944," 223.

25. Aguirre, *Una etapa política del socialismo ecuatoriano*, 46.

26. "Actas de la Asamblea Nacional Constituyente de 1944," vol. 3, 511 (September 23, 1944), APL.

27. Linke, *Ecuador*, 49.

28. Quoted in Gerassi, *The Great Fear in Latin America*, 143.

29. FBI, *Annual Report, Special Intelligence Service, Federal Bureau of Investigation, United States Department of Justice, 1944–1945*, 87.

30. Hoover to Lyon, October 11, 1945, RG 59, 822.00B/10–1145, NARA.

31. Shaw to Secretary of State, June 24, 1947, RG 59, 822.00B/6–2447, NARA; Shaw to Secretary of State, June 30, 1947, RG 59, 822.00B/6–3047, NARA.

32. Scotten to Secretary of State, December 5, 1944, RG 59, 822.00/12–544, NARA.

33. Hoover to Lyon, September 6, 1945, RG 59, 822.00B/9–645, NARA.

34. Hoover to Lyon, June 27, 1945.

35. Hoover to Lyon, October 11, 1945.

36. Scotten to Secretary of State, March 5, 1946, RG 59, 822.00/3–546, NARA.

37. Becker, "Ecuador's Early No-Foreign Military Bases Movements."

38. Hoover to Lyon, Washington, DC, May 17, 1946, RG 59, 822.00B/5–1746, NARA.

39. Hoover to Lyon, Washington, DC, July 17, 1946, RG 59, 822.00B/7–1746, NARA.

40. Hoover to Lyon, Washington, DC, September 12, 1946, RG 59, 822.00B/9–1246, NARA.

41. Hoover to Lyon, Washington, DC, September 17, 1946, RG 59, 822.00B/9–1746, NARA.

42. Simmons to Secretary of State, August 19, 1947, RG 59, 822.00B/8–1947, NARA.

43. Hoover to Lyon, May 17, 1946.

44. José María Velasco Ibarra, "Expúlsase del territorio nacional a varios ciudadanos por alterar la paz y Constitución de la República," decree 425-A, *Registro Oficial*, vol. 2, no. 547, March 30, 1946, 4548–49. See also "Esta madrugada fue apresado el General Alberto Enríquez Gallo," *La Tierra*, March 30, 1946, 1, 4; "El gobierno declara que tiene en su poder documentos sobre un complot," *El Comercio*, March 31, 1946, 1, 5.

45. Bethell and Roxborough, "Introduction," 2.

46. "Varias manifestaciones fueron impedidas ayer," *El Comercio*, April 2, 1946, 1.

47. "Autoridades impidieron en Guayaquil la realización de un miting izquierdista," *El Comercio*, April 4, 1946, 1; "Varios ciudadanos fueron apresados ayer por la policía de Guayaquil," *El Comercio*, April 4, 1946, 1.

48. "Embajador Plaza niegase a comentar los sucesos," *El Comercio*, April 6, 1946, 1.

49. Edmond to Bevin, May 7, 1947, AS 3090/1151/54, in *British Documents on Foreign Affairs*, series D, pt. 4, vol. 4, doc. no. 78, 352.

50. M. Agustín Aguirre, Gustavo Becerra, and Sergio Lasso Meneses, "Velasco Ibarra asumió dictadura por segunda vez," *La Tierra*, April 1, 1946, 1, 4.

51. "Dr. Manuel Agustín Aguirre fue reducido a prisión," *El Comercio*, April 2, 1946, 1.

52. See, e.g., Emilio Gangotena, "Manifiesto del partido socialista a la nación," *El Comercio*, April 4, 1946, 1, 3.

53. See, e.g., Manuel Agustín Aguirre, "Mensaje del secretario general del P.S.E. a los partidos democráticos de América y en especial a los partidos socialistas," *La Tierra*, April 21, 1946, 4.

54. PCE, "Dictadura y democracia," 1946, Hojas Volantes, BEAEP.

55. "La verdad ante todo," *La Tierra*, April 1, 1946, 1; "El tribunal de garantías hubiera concedido al ejecutivo las facultades extraordinarias," *El Comercio*, April 1, 1946, 1.

56. "Diario 'La Tierra' fue asaltado esta madrugada," *El Comercio*, April 2, 1946, 1; "Como fué asaltado el diario La Tierra por guardias civiles y agentes de pesquisa," *El Comercio*, April 3, 1946, 10.

57. "Federación de Universitarios suscribió un manifiesto dirigido a la nación," *El Comercio*, April 4, 1946, 1.

58. Confederación de Trabajadores del Ecuador, "Manifiesto de la Confederación de Trabajadores del Ecuador," *La Tierra*, May 1, 1946, 1; "Acuerdos y resoluciones tomadas en la asamblea organizada por la C.T.E. y la C.T.P. en conmemoración del 10 de mayo," *La Tierra*, May 5, 1946, 2.

59. "Se inauguró ayer el Tercer Congreso Federación de Trabajadores de Pichincha," *El Comercio*, May 19, 1946, 3.

60. "Federación de Trabajadores de Pichincha tuvo una sesión ampliada conmemorativa," *El Comercio*, May 29, 1946, 10.

61. "El señor Gustavo Buendía, fue reducido a prisión el día de ayer," *La Tierra*, May 9, 1946, 1, 4; "El señor Raimond Meriguet debió salir ayer de mañana con dirección a Colombia," *La Tierra*, May 11, 1946, 4.

62. "Ciudadano fue apresado por orden del gobierno," *El Comercio*, May 19, 1946, 3.

63. "El Sr. Luis F. Alvaro está preso por no ser 'terrorista,'" *La Tierra*, May 18, 1946, 4.

64. See, e.g., "¿Quién es el terrorista?," *La Tierra*, May 16, 1946, 4.

65. Scotten to Secretary of State, February 28, 1946, RG 59, 822.00/2-2846, NARA.

66. Edmond to Bevin, May 7, 1947, 353.

67. Wright to Bevin, April 6, 1946, AS 2223/5/54, in *British Documents on Foreign Affairs*, series D, pt. 4, vol. 1, doc. no. 92, 444–45.

68. Hoover to Lyon, June 3, 1946, RG 59, 822.00B/6-346, NARA.

69. Hoover to Lyon, June 3, 1946; Nela Martínez E., Ester Núñez de Castrejón, Luisa Gómez de la Torre, Judith Cevallos, Isabel A. Saad, Clemencia Salazar, and Laura Rodríguez, "Carta abierta al señor doctor José María Velasco Ibarra," *La Tierra*, April 17, 1946, 3–4.

70. Hoover to Lyon, July 26, 1946, RG 59, 822.00B/7-2646, NARA. See "Ayer se rindió un homenaje en el Hotel Savoy a la maestra Sta. María L. Gómez," *El Día*, May 5, 1946, 2; "En reunión de mujeres se acordó formar comité de defensa de derechos humanos," *El Comercio*, May 5, 1946, 16. The gendered usage (e.g., "Mrs. Saad" instead of Isabel Herrería) is from the press coverage. It is not clear whether the women employed traditional language as a ploy to advance their political agenda or the reporter used the terms in a demeaning manner.

71. "Mujeres ecuatorianas lucharán abnegadamente por la conquista de los derechos humanos," *La Tierra*, May 5, 1946, 1, 4.

72. "El Partido Comunista tiene una sola línea de conducta en el país," *El Comercio*, May 6, 1946, 8.

73. "El día d hoy debe hacerse la convocatoria a elecciones," *El Comercio*, April 5, 1946, 1.

74. José María Velasco Ibarra, "Se convoca a elecciones para diputados provinciales y funcionales al congreso nacional que deberá reunirse el diez de agosto del presente año," decree 459, *Registro Oficial*, vol. 2, no. 555, April 9, 1946, 4605–6; "Sólo el Tribunal Superior Electoral y el Tribunal de Garantías pueden convocar a elecciones al próximo congress," *El Comercio*, April 6, 1946, 1, 5.

75. "Parece que sólo dos partidos de derecha intervendrán en las próximas elecciones," *El Comercio*, May 13, 1946, 1.

76. Emilio Gangotena, "El Partido Socialista al Pueblo Ecuatoriano," May 1946, in Hojas Volantes, BEAEP; "Protesta contra orden de prision del Dr. Emilio Gangotena," *El Comercio*, May 17, 1946, 10.

77. PCE, "Terminemos con la dictadura de Velasco!" May 8, 1946, Hojas Volantes, BEAEP.

78. "La directiva conservadora ha seguido eligiendo candidatos a diputados por provincias," *El Comercio*, May 10, 1946, 1; Hoover to Lyon, August 30, 1946, RG 59, 822.00B/8–3046, NARA.

79. Hoover to Lyon, August 30, 1946; "Apresan a otro ciudadano," *La Tierra*, May 14, 1946, 4; "Pusieron en libertad a dos detenidos políticos," *El Comercio*, May 19, 1946, 1.

80. Ricardo Paredes, "El Comité Ejecutivo del Partido Comunista del Ecuador," June 20, 1946, Hojas Volantes, BEAEP.

81. "Grave situación del Sr. R. Meriguet," *La Tierra*, June 22, 1946, 4; "Doctor Héctor Vásconez Valencia y señor Raymond Meriguet libertados," *La Tierra*, June 25, 1946, 1.

82. "Bienvenido compañero Dr. Manuel A. Aguirre," *La Tierra*, August 31, 1946, 1.

83. Hoover to Lyon, September 12, 1946.

84. Hoover to Lyon, September 17, 1946.

85. Hoover to Lyon, July 26, 1946.

86. Edmond to Bevin, May 7, 1947, 354.

87. Aguirre, *Una etapa política del socialismo ecuatoriano*, 55.

88. Ricardo Paredes, "Abajo la farsa electoral," *La Tierra*, June 30, 1946, 4.

89. "P. Comunista hace un llamamiento pueblo y al ejército de la patria," *La Tierra*, July 17, 1946, 1.

90. Hoover to Lyon, June 3, 1946.

91. Hoover to Neal, October 10, 1946, RG 59, 822.00B/10–1046, NARA.

92. Hoover to Lyon, November 15, 1945.

93. "Secretario Gral. del PSE fue apresado anoche," *La Tierra*, July 31, 1946, 1.

94. "Asamblea concede amnistía a presos y expatriados políticos," *El Comercio*, August 13, 1946, 1.

95. "Continúa persecución a socialistas," *La Tierra*, August 15, 1946, 1.

96. Ricardo Paredes, "Partido Comunista Ecuatoriano contesta a Mtro. d' Gobierno," *La Tierra*, August 23, 1946, 1, 4.

97. "Partido Socialista ha mirado con complacencia circular del Ministro de Gobierno," *El Comercio*, August 27, 1946, 1, 7.

98. Bossano, *Evolución del derecho constitucional ecuatoriano*, 181.

99. PCE, *Unidad Progresista para derrotar a los reaccionarios en las elecciones*, 1.

100. Aguirre, *Una etapa política del socialismo ecuatoriano*, 56.

101. Ricardo Paredes, "El partido comunista defiende la enseñanza laica," *La Tierra*, October 18, 1946, 1.

102. General Aurelio Baquero, "Manifiesto de Vanguardia Revolucionaria Socialista Ecuatoriana a la Nación," *La Tierra*, October 27, 1946, 1, 4.

103. Edmond to Bevin, March 4, 1947, AS 1649/1151/54, in *British Documents on Foreign Affairs*, series D, pt. 4, vol. 4, doc. no. 76, 349.

104. Hoover to Lyon, March 18, 1946, RG 59, 822.00B/3-1846, NARA.

105. Hoover to Lyon, July 17, 1946; Hoover to Lyon, July 26, 1946.

106. Hoover to Lyon, June 3, 1946.

107. Hoover to Neal, December 16, 1946, RG 59, 822.00B/12-1646.

108. Kofas, *The Struggle for Legitimacy*, 299; Welch, "Labor Internationalism," 62–65.

109. Barnard, "Chile," 68.

110. Romualdi, "Labor and Democracy in Latin America," 477–89.

111. Dearborn to Hall, Wells, and Trueblood, September 19, 1946, RG 59, 822.5043/9-1946, NARA.

112. Romualdi, *Presidents and Peons*, 41.

113. Romualdi, "Labor and Democracy in Latin America," 488.

114. Fishburn, "Memorandum," August 6, 1947, RG 59, 822.5043/8-647, NARA.

115. Dearborn to Schnee, Wells, and Trueblood, December 10, 1946, RG 59, 822.504/12-1046, NARA.

116. Romualdi, *Presidents and Peons*, 41, 69.

117. Scipes, *AFL-CIO's Secret War against Developing Country Workers*.

118. Hoover to Neal, October 10, 1946.

119. "Mañana debe inaugurarse el congreso p. comunista," *La Tierra*, September 30, 1946, 1.

120. "Congreso Nacional de Vanguardia se realizará en Diciembre," *El Comercio*, November 16, 1946, 10.

121. "Ayer inauguró sus sesiones el III congreso ncnal. del partido comunista," *La Tierra*, November 17, 1946, 1.

122. "Reclamos por las aguas de caciques en Urcuquí," *El Día*, August 13, 1931, 8.

123. Asamblea Nacional Constituyente, Acta no. 125, December 23, 1944, APL; "La Asamblea aprobó la expropiación de aguas de Acequías Grande y Caciques," *El Comercio*, December 24, 1944, 1, 3.

124. Jorge Gallegos and Segundo Peñafiel, "Urcuquí a la nación ecuatoriano," *El Comercio*, November 15, 1946, 3.

125. "Defensa de los derechos del pueblo de Urcuquí," *La Tierra*, November 22, 1946, 1.

126. Jorge Gallegos and Héctor Romero, "Protesta del pueblo de Urcuquí," *El Comercio*, November 30, 1946, 3; Benjamín Montaquiza and Norberto Valverde, "Adhesión y respaldo al pueblo de Urcuquí," *El Comercio*, December 13, 1946, 3; Armando Cruz Cobos, "La confederación campesina de Cuba con el pueblo campesino de Urcuquí," *La Tierra*, January 17, 1947, 1, 2.

127. Asamblea Nacional Constituyente, Acta no. 121, December 23, 1946, APL; "Asamblea Nacional reformó el decreto sobre problema de aquas de Urcuquí," *El Comercio*, December 24, 1946, 5, 12.

128. "Dr. Ricardo Paredes fue reelecto secretario general del comunismo," *La Tierra*, November 24, 1946, 1.

129. Dearborn to Hall and Wells, January 16, 1947, RG 59, 822.00B/1–1647, NARA.

130. Shaw to Secretary of State, June 16, 1947, RG 59, 822.00B/6–1647, NARA.

131. Asamblea Nacional Constituyente, Acta no. 100, December 2, 1946, APL.

132. "Comunistas y autores de asalto a varios comercios de Guayaquil fueron apresados," *El Comercio*, December 4, 1946, 1, 5.

133. Ricardo Paredes, "Acuerdo del Partido Comunista Ecuatoriano," *La Tierra*, December 3, 1946, 4.

134. "Comunistas empeñarán sus fuerzas para libertad de sus copartidarios," *La Tierra*, December 6, 1946, 1.

135. Ricardo Paredes, "Una nueva ola de terror contra las fuerzas democráticas se ha iniciado detengámosla," December 8, 1946, Hojas Volantes, BEAEP.

136. Luis F. Alvaro, "La Federación Ecuatoriana de Indios," December 4, 1946, Hojas Volantes, BEAEP.

137. "Piden poner en libertad a los detenidos políticos," *El Comercio*, December 15, 1946, 16; "Un comité se encargada de la defensa de los detenidos políticos," *El Comercio*, December 8, 1946, 5.

138. "Los señores Pedro Saad y Enrique Gil Gilbert fueron puestos en libertad," *El Comercio*, December 22, 1946, 16.

Chapter 7. Departures

1. Partido Comunista del Ecuador, *Unidad Progresista para derrotar a los reaccionarios en las elecciones*, 4, 6.

2. Partido Comunista del Ecuador, *Unidad Progresista para derrotar a los reaccionarios en las elecciones*, 6–8.

3. "Manifiesto de los candidatos del Frente Popular de Izquierda," May 28, 1947, in Hojas Volantes, BEAEP.

4. "Cinco listas de candidatos se han presentado al Tribunal Electoral de Pichincha," *El Comercio*, May 18, 1947, 1, 5.

5. Shaw to Secretary of State, June 6, 1947, RG 59, 822.00B/6–647, NARA.

6. Shaw to Secretary of State, May 26, 1947, RG 59, 822.00/5–2647, NARA.

7. Shaw to Secretary of State, June 6, 1947.

8. "Dos listas de candidatos por Pichichincha fueron anuladas," *El Comercio*, May 25, 1947, 1.

9. Rafael Quevedo Coronel and Telmo Aguinaga, "A los patrocinantes de las Listas A y B, de Candidatos a Senadores y Diputados por Pichincha y al pública en general," *La Tierra*, May 27, 1947, 1, 2.

10. Shaw to Secretary of State, June 12, 1947, RG 59, 822.00B/6–1247, NARA.

11. "Hay entusiasmo entre los ciudadanos para terciar en próximas elecciónes," *El Comercio*, May 23, 1947, 5.

12. "Ecuador Will Vote Today," *New York Times*, June 1, 1947, 5.

13. "Manifiesto de los candidatos del Frente Popular de Izquierda."

14. "Los partidos políticos prosiguen con entusiasmo sus actividades electorales," *El Comercio*, May 29, 1947, 1.

15. "Frente Popular de Guayaquil lanza lista de candidatos," *El Comercio*, May 23, 1947, 5.

16. Shaw to Secretary of State, June 12, 1947.

17. "En Guayaquil se trató de convertir un conflicto obrero en actividad subversiva," *El Comercio*, May 27, 1947, 1, 3.

18. "Ecuador Foils Coup; Red Leader Seized," *New York Times*, May 27, 1947, 3.

19. "Versión del intento subversivo enviado a la prensa extranjera," *El Comercio*, May 27, 1947, 12.

20. "Hay tranquilidad en Guayaquil y no se han hecho nuevas detenciones," *El Comercio*, May 28, 1947, 1.

21. "Parece que se quiere justificar por anticipado la alteración del orden público en el país," *El Comercio*, May 30, 1947, 6; "Sobre la prisión de dos candidatos comunistas del Guayas," *El Comercio*, June 1, 1947, 13.

22. Shaw to Secretary of State, June 23, 1947, RG 59, 822.00B/6–2347, NARA; "Revocó la orden de detención contra sindicado de rebelión," *El Comercio*, June 12, 1947, 14.

23. "Ecuador Voting Is Orderly," *New York Times*, June 2, 1947, 11. See also Julian Sorel, "La mujer," *La Tierra*, June 6, 1947, 3.

24. "Oficialmente se informó que las elecciones se realizaron en todo el país," *La Tierra*, June 2, 1947, 1.

25. "La lista de M.C.D.N. triunfó ampliamente en las elecciones de ayer," *El Comercio*, June 2, 1947, 1, 4; "En Tungurahua y Loja los socialistas triunfaron ayer en las elecciones," *El Comercio*, June 2, 1947, 4.

26. Shaw to Secretary of State, June 12, 1947.

27. Shaw to Secretary of State, June 12, 1947.

28. Shaw to Secretary of State, July 9, 1947, RG 59, 822.00B/7–947, NARA.

29. Simmons to Secretary of State, September 18, 1947, RG 59, 822.00B/9–1847, NARA.

30. Simmons to Secretary of State, July 31, 1947, RG 59, 822.00B/7–3147, NARA.

31. Shaw to Secretary of State, June 12, 1947.

32. Simmons to Secretary of State, August 12, 1947, RG 59, 822.00B/8–1247, NARA.

33. Simmons to Secretary of State, September 18, 1947.

34. Ellner, "Factionalism in the Venezuelan Communist Movement."

35. Partido Comunista del Ecuador, "Declaración del Partido Comunista del Ecuador sobre proyecto de establecimiento de pacto de asistencia mutua de carácter internacional," August 15, 1947, Hojas Volantes, BEAEP.

36. OIR, "Political Developments and Trends in the Other American Republics in the Twentieth Century," 49, 51.

37. Schwartzberg, "Rómulo Betancourt," 614–15, 661.

38. "Dr. Velasco Ibarra renuncia y entrega el mando al Ministro de Defensa," *El Comercio*, August 24, 1947, 1.

39. George H. Owen, "Memorandum of Conversation," August 27, 1947, RG 59, 822.00/8–2747, in *FRUS* 1947, vol. 8, 667–68.

40. Ospina Peralta, "Matrimonio de compromiso," 148.

41. Wright to Bevin, September 8, 1947, AS 5445/1151/54, in *British Documents on Foreign Affairs*, series D, pt. 4, vol. 4, doc. no. 82, 365.

42. Simmons to Secretary of State, August 23, 1947, RG 59, 822.00/8–2347, telegram, in *FRUS*, vol. 8, 1947, 664–65.

43. Ricardo Paredes, "El Partido Comunista y el Pueblo frente al momento político," August 24, 1947, Hojas Volantes, BEAEP.

44. Lovett to Petropolis (Brazil) U.S. Delegation, August 28, 1947, RG 59, 822.01/8–2847, NARA.

45. Hughes-Hallett to Eden, September 7, 1943, A 8685/683/54, in *British Documents on Foreign Affairs*, series D, pt. 3, vol. 7, doc. no. 60, 482.

46. Edmond to Bevin, March 4, 1947, AS 1649/1151/54, in *British Documents on Foreign Affairs*, series D, pt. 4, vol. 4, doc. no. 76, 349.

47. "Revolt that Wasn't," *Newsweek* 34 (August 8, 1949): 32.

48. Simmons to Secretary of State, August 25, 1947, RG 59, 822.00/8–2547, telegram, in *FRUS*, vol. 8, 1947, 665–66.

49. Simmons to Secretary of State, September 2, 1947, RG 59, 822.00/9–247, telegram, in *FRUS*, vol. 8, 1947, 669–70.

50. Partido Comunista del Ecuador, "Luchemos contra los conservadores," September 2, 1947, Hojas Volantes, BEAEP.

51. "Triunfó en el país el movimiento constitucionalista," *El Comercio*, September 3, 1947, 1.

52. Carvell to Bevin, May 24, 1949, AS 3046/1011/54, in *British Documents on Foreign Affairs*, series D, pt. 4, vol. 7, doc. no. 17, 423.

53. FBI, *History of the Special Intelligence Service Division*, 656–57.

54. FBI, *History of the Special Intelligence Service Division*, 415. See FBI, *Annual Report, Special Intelligence Service, Federal Bureau of Investigation, United States Department of Justice, 1946–1947*, 33.

55. Shaw to Secretary of State, July 15, 1947, RG 59, 822.00B/7–1547, NARA.

56. Simmons to Secretary of State, August 19, 1947, RG 59, 822.00B/8–1947, NARA.

57. Shaw to Secretary of State, July 7, 1947, RG 59, 822.00B/7–747, NARA; Simmons to Secretary of State, July 23, 1947, RG 59, 822.00B/7–2347, NARA.

58. Shaw to Secretary of State, June 23, 1947.

59. Simmons to Secretary of State, July 29, 1947, RG 59, 822.00B/7–2947, NARA.

60. Shaw to Secretary of State, June 30, 1947, RG 59, 822.00B/6–3047, NARA. See "Comunicación de los 'Comandos' a Junta Consultiva del Ministerio de Relaciones Exteriores causó gran inquietud en toda la ciudadanía," *La Tierra*, March 2, 1946, 1–2.

61. Simmons to Secretary of State, July 29, 1947.

62. Simmons to Secretary of State, January 20, 1948, RG 59, 822.00B/1–2048, NARA.

63. Marshall to Amembassy, February 10, 1948, RG 59, 822.00B/1–848, NARA.

64. Simmons to Secretary of State, March 3, 1948, RG 59, 822.00B/3–348, NARA.

65. Simmons to Secretary of State, July 31, 1947.

66. Simmons to Secretary of State, July 29, 1947.

67. Simmons to Secretary of State, December 31, 1947, RG 59, 822.00B/12–3147, NARA.

68. Shaw to Secretary of State, July 9, 1947.

69. Simmons to Secretary of State, April 13, 1948, RG 59, 822.00B/4–1348, NARA.

70. Simmons to Secretary of State, April 21, 1948, RG 59, 822.00B/4–2148, NARA.

71. Drew Pearson, "U.S. Agents in Latin America," Bell Syndicate, December 11, 1947, http://hdl.handle.net/2041/21966, published as Drew Pearson, "Carrousel de Washington," *El Comercio*, December 14, 1947, 4.

72. Simmons to Secretary of State, March 4, 1948, RG 59, 811.20200(D)/3–448, in *FRUS*, vol. 9, 1948, 581–85.

73. Simmons to Secretary of State, April 15, 1948, RG 59, 822.00B/4–1548, NARA.

Conclusion

1. Valeria Coronel, "La revolución Gloriosa," 94.

2. Agee, *Inside the Company*.

3. See, e.g., Marchetti and Marks, *The CIA and the Cult of Intelligence*; Stockwell, *In Search of Enemies*; Donner, *The Age of Surveillance*; McGehee, *Deadly Deceits*.

4. Main, Johnston, and Beeton, "Latin America and the Caribbean," 484.

5. See http://rt.com/news/ecuado-correa-cia-attack-429.

6. Democracy Now! "Ecuadoran President Rafael Correa on WikiLeaks, the September Coup, U.S. Denial of Climate Funding, and Controversial Forest Scheme REDD," December 9, 2010, http://www.democracynow.org/2010/12/9/ecuadoran_president_rafael_correa_on_the.

7. Petrich, "En el país todos los cuadros de inteligencia trabajaban para la CIA," 2.

8. Hillary Rodham Clinton, "Events in Ecuador," September 30, 2010, http://www.state.gov/secretary/rm/2010/09/148481.htm.

9. Proaño, "Ni anticapitalista, ni antiimperialist," 5.

10. "En Ecuador sí somos antiimperialistas," *Opción*, vol. 9, no. 195, June 16–30, 2010, 4.

11. Clinton, *Hard Choices*, 246–68.

12. Paz Salinas, *Strategy, Security, and Spies*, 208.

13. Stephan and van Heurck, *"Communazis,"* 232.

BIBLIOGRAPHY

Archives

Archivo del Ministerio de Previsión Social, Archivo Intermedio, Quito
Archivo Nacional de Ecuador (ANE), Quito
Archivo Palacio Legislativo (APL), Quito
Biblioteca Ecuatoriana Aurelio Espinosa Pólit (BEAEP), Cotocollao
National Archives Records Administration (NARA), College Park, MD
Private collection of Leonardo J. Muñoz, Quito

Periodicals

British Documents on Foreign Affairs: Reports and Papers from the Foreign Office Confidential Print (Bethesda, MD: University Publications of America).
Foreign Relations of the United States (FRUS) (Washington, DC: U.S. Government Printing Office)
Registro Oficial (Quito)

Newspapers

Antinazi (Quito)
La Antorcha (Quito)
El Comercio (Quito)
El Día (Quito)
New York Times
El Telégrafo (Guayaquil)
La Tierra (Quito)
El Universo (Guayaquil)

Books and Articles

"Los hermanos Plaza." *Newsweek* 23 (June 19, 1944): 62.
"Pan-American Labor Urged to Fight U.S. Trusts." *Daily Worker* 22, no. 279 (November 21, 1945): 8.
"Revolt that Wasn't." *Newsweek* 34 (August 8, 1949): 32.

Agee, Philip. *Inside the Company: CIA Diary.* New York: Bantam, 1975.

Aguilar Vazquez, A. *Informe a la nación, 1943.* Quito: Imprenta del Ministerio de Gobierno, 1943.

Aguirre, Manuel Agustín. "Breves memorias sobre la Revolución del 28 de Mayo de 1944." In *El 28 de mayo de 1944: Testimonio,* ed. Universidad de Guayaquil, 213–35. Guayaquil: Universidad de Guayaquil, 1984.

———. "El marxismo, la revolución y los partidos socialista y comunista del Ecuador: Notas para discusión." In *Marx ante América Latina: Homenaje a Carlos Marx por el centenario de su muerte,* ed. Manuel Agustín Aguirre, 69–131. Quito: Universidad Central, 1985.

———. *El Partido Socialista en la Revolución del 28 de Mayo.* Quito: Departamento de Publicaciones, 1945.

———. *Informe del c. doctor Manuel Agustín Aguirre, Secretario General del Partido Socialista Ecuatoriano al X Congreso.* Quito: Partido Socialista Ecuatoriano, 1943.

———. *Una etapa política del socialismo ecuatoriano.* Quito: Editora Ecuador, 1946.

Albornoz, Osvaldo. "La lucha de los trabajadores y la formación de la CTE." In *28 de mayo y fundación de la C.T.E.,* ed. Instituto de Investigaciones y Estudios Socio-económicos del Ecuador (INIESEC), 77–110. Quito: Editora Nacional, 1984.

Alemán, Gabriela, and Valeria Coronel, ed. *Vienen ganas de cambiar el tiempo: Epistolario entre Nela Martínez Espinosa y Joaquín Gallegos Lara—1930 a 1938.* Quito: Instituto Metropolitano de Patrimonio; and Archivo Martínez-Meriguet, 2012.

Alexander, Robert Jackson. *Trotskyism in Latin America.* Stanford, CA: Hoover Institution Press, 1973.

Alexander, Robert Jackson, and John D. French. *Robert Jackson Alexander Papers, 1890 (1945)–1999, the Interview Collection.* Microfilm. Leiden: Inter Documentation Company (IDC), 2002.

Alexander, Robert Jackson, and Eldon M. Parker. *A History of Organized Labor in Peru and Ecuador.* Westport, CT: Praeger, 2007.

Alianza Democrática Ecuatoriana. *Los postulados de la Revolución de Mayo: Programa de Alianza Democrática Ecuatoriana.* Quito: Talleres Gráficos Nacionales, 1944.

Alianza Femenina Ecuatoriana. *Estatutos de Alianza Femenina Ecuatoriana.* Quito: Talleres Gráficos de Educación, 1938.

Almeida Cabrera, Laura. *Antología.* Quito: Ediciones La Tierra, 2007.

Ameringer, Charles D. *U.S. Foreign Intelligence: The Secret Side of American History.* Lexington, MA: Lexington Books, 1990.

Araujo Hidalgo, Manuel. *El 28 de mayo, balance de una revolución popular. Documentos para la historia.* Quito: Talleres Gráfico Nacionales, 1946.

Ayala Mora, Enrique. "La represión arroísta: caldo de cultivo de la 'Gloriosa.'" In *La Gloriosa ¿Revolución que no fue?,* ed. Santiago Cabrera Hanna, 19–38. Quito: Editora Nacional, Universidad Andina Simón Bolívar, 2016.

Ayer, Frederick. *Yankee G-Man*. Chicago: H. Regnery, 1957.

Barnard, Andrew. "Chile." In *Latin America between the Second World War and the Cold War, 1944–1948*, ed. Leslie Bethell and Ian Roxborough, 66–91. Cambridge: Cambridge University Press, 1992.

———. "Chilean Communists, Radical Presidents and Chilean Relations with the United States, 1940–1947." *Journal of Latin American Studies* 13, no. 2 (November 1981): 347–74.

Batvinis, Raymond. *The Origins of FBI Counterintelligence*. Lawrence: University Press of Kansas, 2007.

Becker, Marc. "Ecuador's Early No-Foreign Military Bases Movement." *Diplomatic History* 41, no. 3 (June 2017): 518–42.

———. "La historia del movimiento indígena escrita a través de las páginas de Ñucanchic Allpa." In *Estudios ecuatorianos: Un aporte a la discusión*, ed. Ximena Sosa-Buchholz and William F. Waters, 133–53. Quito: Facultad Latinoamericana de Ciencias Sociales Sede Ecuador (FLACSO) and Editorial Universitaria Abya-Yala, 2006.

———. *Indians and Leftists in the Making of Ecuador's Modern Indigenous Movements*. Durham, NC: Duke University Press, 2008.

Berle, Adolf. *Navigating the Rapids, 1918–1971: From the Papers of Adolf A. Berle*. New York: Harcourt Brace Jovanovich, 1973.

Bethell, Leslie, and Ian Roxborough. "Conclusion: The Post-War Conjuncture in Latin America and Its Consequences." In *Latin America between the Second World War and the Cold War, 1944–1948*, ed. Leslie Bethell and Ian Roxborough, 317–34. Cambridge: Cambridge University Press, 1992.

———. "Introduction: The Post-War Conjuncture in Latin America: Democracy, Labor and the Left." In *Latin America between the Second World War and the Cold War, 1944–1948*, ed. Leslie Bethell and Ian Roxborough, 1–32. Cambridge: Cambridge University Press, 1992.

Blanksten, George. *Ecuador: Constitutions and Caudillos*. Berkeley: University of California Press, 1951.

Blasier, Cole. *The Hovering Giant: U.S. Responses to Revolutionary Change in Latin America, 1910–1985*. Rev. ed. Pittsburgh, Pa.: University of Pittsburgh Press, 1985.

Blum, William. *Killing Hope: U.S. Military and CIA Interventions since World War II*, 2nd ed. Monroe, ME: Common Courage, 2004.

Bonilla, Adrián. *En busca del pueblo perdido: Diferenciación y discurso de la izquierda marxista en los sesenta*. Quito: FLACSO and Editorial Universitaria Abya-Yala, 1991.

Bossano, Guillermo. *Evolución del derecho constitucional ecuatoriano*, 2nd ed. Quito: Editorial Casa de la Cultura Ecuatoriana, 1975.

Bratzel, John. "Introduction." In *Latin America during World War II*, ed. Thomas Leonard and John Bratzel, 1–13. Lanham, MD: Rowman and Littlefield, 2007.

Browder, Earl. *Teheran: Our Path in War and Peace*. New York: International, 1944.

Bueno, J. E. "Sinopsis de acciones y secuencias constituyentes de la actuación de José María Plaza, en el proceso culminante en el '28 de Mayo de 1944.'" In *El 28 de mayo de 1944: Testimonio*, ed. Universidad de Guayaquil, 123–40. Guayaquil: Universidad de Guayaquil, 1984.

Caballero, Manuel. *Latin America and the Comintern, 1919–1943*. Cambridge: Cambridge University Press, 1986.

Cabrera, Santiago, ed. *La Gloriosa ¿Revolución que no fue?* Quito: Editora Nacional, Universidad Andina Simón Bolívar, 2016.

Carr, Barry. "From Caribbean Backwater to Revolutionary Opportunity: Cuba's Evolving Relationship with the Comintern, 1925–34." In *International Communism and the Communist International, 1919–43*, ed. Tim Rees and Andrew Thorpe, 234–53. New York: St. Martin's Press, 1998.

———. *Marxism and Communism in Twentieth-Century Mexico*. Lincoln: University of Nebraska Press, 1992.

Churchill, Ward, and Jim Vander Wall. *The Cointelpro Papers: Documents from the FBI's Secret Wars against Domestic Dissent*. Boston: South End, 1990.

Clinton, Hillary Rodham. *Hard Choices*. New York: Simon and Schuster, 2014.

Confederación de Trabajadores del Ecuador. "Estatutos de la Confederación de Trabajadores del Ecuador." In *28 de mayo y fundación de la CTE*, ed. Osvaldo Albornoz et al., 194–211. Quito: Editora Nacional, 1984.

Coordinator of Information. "Preliminary Analysis of Elements of Insecurity in Ecuador," November 4, 1941. In *OSS/State Department Intelligence and Research Reports, Part XIV, Latin America, 1941–1961*. Microfilm. Washington, DC: University Publications of America, 1979.

Coronel, Valeria. "La revolución Gloriosa: una relectura desde la estrategia de la hegemonía de la izquierda de entreguerras." In *La Gloriosa ¿Revolución que no fue?*, ed. Santiago Cabrera Hanna, 75–94. Quito: Editora Nacional, Universidad Andina Simón Bolívar, 2016.

———. "A Revolution in Stages: Subaltern Politics, Nation-State Formation, and the Origins of Social Rights in Ecuador, 1834–1943." Ph.D. diss., New York University, 2011.

Cramer, Gisela, and Ursula Prutsch. *¡Américas unidas! Nelson A. Rockefeller's Office of Inter-American Affairs (1940–46)*. Madrid: Iberoamericana Vervuert, 2012.

———. "Nelson A. Rockefeller's Office of Inter-American Affairs (1940–1946) and Record Group 229." *Hispanic American Historical Review* 86, no. 4 (November 2006): 785–806.

Cueva, Agustín. "El Ecuador de 1925 a 1960." In *Nueva Historia del Ecuador, Volumen 10: Epoca republicana III: El Ecuador entre los años veinte y los sesenta*, ed. Enrique Ayala Mora, 87–121. Quito: Editora Nacional, 1990.

———. *The Process of Political Domination in Ecuador*. New Brunswick, NJ: Transaction, 1982.

Díaz, Ruth. "Nela Martínez (Programa Número 13)." In *Mujeres de Nuestra América*, tape recording. Quito: Ciespal, 1994.

Donner, Frank. *The Age of Surveillance: The Aims and Methods of America's Political Intelligence System*. New York: Vintage, 1981.

Duclos, Jacques. "On the Dissolution of the American Communist Party." *Political Affairs*, no. 24 (July 1945): 656–72.

Egas Egas, Edison. *28 de mayo de 1944: La gloriosa o la revolución traicionada y la constitución de 1945*. Quito: Facultad de Filosofía, Letras y Ciencias de la Educación, 1992.

Ellner, Steve. "Factionalism in the Venezuelan Communist Movement, 1937–1948." *Science and Society* 45, no. 1 (Spring 1981): 52–70.

———. "Venezuela." In *Latin America between the Second World War and the Cold War, 1944–1948*, ed. Leslie Bethell and Ian Roxborough, 147–69. Cambridge; New York, NY, USA: Cambridge University Press, 1992.

Federal Bureau of Investigation. *Annual Report, Special Intelligence Service, Federal Bureau of Investigation, United States Department of Justice, 1941–1942*. Washington, DC: FBI, 1942.

———. *Annual Report, Special Intelligence Service, Federal Bureau of Investigation, United States Department of Justice, 1942–1943*. Washington, DC: FBI, 1943.

———. *Annual Report, Special Intelligence Service, Federal Bureau of Investigation, United States Department of Justice, 1943–1944*. Washington, DC: FBI, 1944.

———. *Annual Report, Special Intelligence Service, Federal Bureau of Investigation, United States Department of Justice, 1944–1945*. Washington, DC: FBI, 1945.

———. *Annual Report, Special Intelligence Service, Federal Bureau of Investigation, United States Department of Justice, 1945–1946*. Washington, DC: FBI, 1946.

———. *Annual Report, Special Intelligence Service, Federal Bureau of Investigation, United States Department of Justice, 1946–1947*. Washington, DC: FBI, 1947.

———. *Ecuador . . . Today*. United States Department of Justice: FBI, 1942.

———. *History of the Special Intelligence Service Division*. Washington, DC: FBI, 1947.

———. *Report of the Director of the Federal Bureau of Investigation John Edgar Hoover for the Fiscal Year 1942*. Washington, DC: FBI, 1942.

———. *Report of the Director of the Federal Bureau of Investigation John Edgar Hoover for the Fiscal Year 1947*. Washington, DC: FBI, 1947.

Franklin, Albert B. *Ecuador: Portrait of a People*. New York: Doubleday, Doran and Company, Inc., 1943.

Friedman, Max Paul. *Nazis and Good Neighbors: The United States Campaign against the Germans of Latin America in World War II*. Cambridge: Cambridge University Press, 2003.

Gallegos, Luis Gerardo. *Rusia Soviética y la revolución mundial*. Quito: Universidad Central, 1931.

Galvis, Silvia, and Alberto Donadío. *Colombia Nazi, 1939–1945: espionaje alemán: la cacería del FBI: Santos, López y los pactos secretos*. Bogotá: Planeta, 1986.

Garaycoa, Xavier. "La estructura económica del Ecuador en los años 40." In *28 de mayo y fundación de la CTE*, ed. Instituto de Investigaciones y Estudios Socioeconómicos del Ecuador (INIESEC), 39–53. Quito: Editora Nacional, 1984.

Gerassi, John. *The Great Fear in Latin America*. New York: Collier, 1965.

Girón, Sergio Enrique. *La revolución de mayo*. Quito: Editorial Atahualpa, 1945.

Goldstein, Robert Justin. *Political Repression in Modern America from 1870 to the Present*. Cambridge, MA: Schenkman, 1978.

Grandin, Greg. *Empire's Workshop: Latin America and the Roots of U.S. Imperialism*. New York: Metropolitan, 2006.

Guarnición Militar de Guayaquil. "Proclama de la Guarnición Militar de Guayaquil." In *28 de mayo de 1944: Documentos*, ed. Universidad de Guayaquil, 171. Guayaquil: Universidad de Guayaquil, 1983.

Healey, Dorothy. *California Red: A Life in the American Communist Party*. Urbana: University of Illinois Press, 1993.

Herrería, Isabel, and Ana Moreno de Safadi. "El 28 de Mayo de 1944: Alianza Democrática Ecuatoriana." In *El 28 de mayo de 1944: Testimonio*, ed. Universidad de Guayaquil, 237–59. Guayaquil: Universidad de Guayaquil, 1984.

Huggins, Martha Knisely. *Political Policing: The United States and Latin America*. Durham, NC: Duke University Press, 1998.

Ibarra, Hernán. "Los idearios de la izquierda comunista ecuatoriana (1928–1961)." In *El pensamiento de la izquierda comunista (1928–1961)*, ed. Hernán Ibarra, 11–64. Quito: Ministerio de Coordinación de la Política y Gobiernos Autónomos Descentralizados, 2013.

———. "¿Qué fue la revolución de 1944?" In *La Gloriosa ¿Revolución que no fue?*, ed. Santiago Cabrera Hanna, 191–204. Quito: Editora Nacional, Universidad Andina Simón Bolívar, 2016.

Iber, Patrick. "Managing Mexico's Cold War: Vicente Lombardo Toledano and the Uses of Political Intelligence." *Journal of Iberian and Latin American Research* 19, no. 1 (2013): 11–19.

———. *Neither Peace nor Freedom: The Cultural Cold War in Latin America*. Cambridge, MA: Harvard University Press, 2015.

Isserman, Maurice. *Which Side Were You On? The American Communist Party during the Second World War*. Middletown, CT: Wesleyan University Press, 1982.

Jaramillo, Juan G., Enrique A. Terán, and Juan F. Karolys et al. *Manifiesto al proletariado ecuatoriano*. Quito: Imprenta y Fotograbado Kaleda, 1931.

Jirón, Sergio Enrique. "La transformación política del 28 de Mayo de 1944." In *El 28 de mayo de 1944: Testimonio*, ed. Universidad de Guayaquil, 13–30. Guayaquil: Universidad de Guayaquil, 1984.

Johnson, Chalmers. *The Sorrows of Empire: Militarism, Secrecy, and the End of the Republic*. New York: Metropolitan, 2004.

Kessler, Ronald. *The Bureau: The Secret History of the FBI*. New York: St. Martin's Press, 2002.

Kinoshita, Dina Lida. *Mário Schenberg: O cientista e o político*. Brasília: Fundação Astrojildo Pereira, 2014.

Klehr, Harvey, John Earl Haynes, and Fridrikh Igorevich Firsov. *The Secret World of American Communism*. New Haven, CT: Yale University Press, 1995.

Kofas, Jon V. *The Struggle for Legitimacy: Latin American Labor and the United States, 1930–1960.* Tempe: Arizona State University, 1992.

Langguth, A. J. *Hidden Terrors.* New York: Pantheon, 1978.

Larrea Alba, Luis. *Estatutos, principios políticos y plan de Acción de Vanguardia Revolucionaria del Socialismo Ecuatoriano (VRSE).* Quito: Imprenta Fernández, 1936.

Lauderbaugh, George M. "Estados Unidos y Ecuador durante la Segunda Guerra Mundial: conflicto y convergencia." In *Ecuador: Relaciones exteriores a la luz del bicentenario,* ed. Beatriz Zepeda, 265–96. Quito: FLACSO, Sede Ecuador, 2009.

Leonard, Thomas. "The New Pan Americanism in U.S.-Central American Relations, 1933–1954." In *Beyond the Ideal: Pan Americanism in Inter-American Affairs,* ed. David Sheinin, 95–114. Westport, CT: Greenwood, 2000.

León Borja, Daniel. *Hombres de Mayo, album deccaricaturas Poder Ejecutivo, Asamblea Constituyente.* Quito, 1945.

León Galarza, Catalina. "Las mujeres y la 'Gloriosa': mayo de 1944." In *La Gloriosa ¿Revolución que no fue?,* ed. Santiago Cabrera Hanna, 39–56. Quito: Editora Nacional, Universidad Andina Simón Bolívar, 2016.

Lichtenstein, Nelson. *Labor's War at Home: The CIO in World War II.* Philadelphia, PA: Temple University Press, 2003.

Linke, Lilo. *Ecuador: Country of Contrasts,* 2d ed. London: Oxford University Press, 1955.

Lombardo Toledano, Vicente. "Informe de mi recorrido por América Latina: Ecuador." In *Formación y pensamiento de la CTE,* ed. Jorge León, Hernán Ibarra, and Patrico Icaza, 17–36. Quito: Centro de Documentación e Información de los Movimientos Sociales del Ecuador (CEDIME), 1983.

Luna Tamayo, Milton. "Los movimientos sociales en los treinta. El rol protagónico de la multitud." *Revista Ecuatoriana de Historia Económica* 3, no. 6 (1989): 199–235.

Main, Alexander, Jake Johnston, and Dan Beeton. "Latin America and the Caribbean." In *The WikiLeaks Files: The World According to US Empire,* ed. Julian Assange, 483–514. New York: Verso, 2015.

Marchetti, Victor, and John D. Marks. *The CIA and the Cult of Intelligence.* New York: Dell, 1974.

Martínez, Nela. "Pedro Saad y el browderismo. A propósito de sus discursos en Moscú." *Mañana,* no. 225 (January 1968): 15–16.

———. *Yo siempre he sido Nela Martínez Espinosa: Una autobiografía hablada.* Quito: Consejo Nacional de las Mujeres (CONAMU); Fondo de Desarrollo de las Naciones Unidas para la Mujer (UNIFEM), 2006.

McGehee, Ralph W. *Deadly Deceits: My Twenty-Five Years in the CIA.* New York: Sheridan Square, 1983.

McIntosh, Elizabeth. *Sisterhood of Spies: The Women of the OSS.* Annapolis, MD: Naval Institute Press, 1998.

———. *Undercover Girl.* New York: Macmillan Co., 1947.

McPherson, Alan L. *The Invaded: How Latin Americans and Their Allies Fought and Ended U.S. Occupations*. Oxford: Oxford University Press, 2014.

Medsger, Betty. *The Burglary: The Discovery of J. Edgar Hoover's Secret FBI*. New York: Alfred A. Knopf, 2014.

Mériguet, Raymond. *Antinazismo en Ecuador, años 1941–1944: Autobiografía del Movimiento Antinazi de Ecuador (MPAE-MAE)*. Quito: R. Mériguet Coussegal, 1988.

Milk Ch., Richard L. *Movimiento obrero ecuatoriano el desafío de la integración*. Quito: Ediciones Abya-Yala, 1997.

Movimiento Antifascista del Ecuador (MAE). *Informe y resoluciones, Conferencia Provincial de Pichincha*. Quito: Movimiento Antifascista del Ecuador (MAE), 1943.

Muñoz, Leonardo. *Testimonio de lucha: Memorias sobre la historia del socialismo en el Ecuador*. Quito: Editora Nacional, 1988.

Muñoz Vicuña, Elías. "Prólogo." In *28 de mayo de 1944: Documentos*, ed. Universidad de Guayaquil, 9–11. Guayaquil: Universidad de Guayaquil, 1983.

Navarro, Aaron. *Political Intelligence and the Creation of Modern Mexico, 1938–1954*. University Park: Pennsylvania State University Press, 2010.

Newton, Ronald C. *The "Nazi Menace" in Argentina, 1931–1947*. Stanford, CA: Stanford University Press, 1992.

Núñez del Arco Proaño, Francisco. *El Ecuador y la Alemania nazi: Los secretos de una relación ocultada*. Quito: Editorial JB, 2013.

Nuñez, Jorge. "Los partidos politicos en el Ecuador. 3. El Partido Comunista." *Nueva* 69 (September 1980): 52–56.

Office of the Coordinator of Inter-American Affairs. *History of the Office of the Coordinator of Inter-American Affairs: Historical Reports on War Administration*. Washington, DC: U.S. Government Printing Office, 1947.

Office of Intelligence Research. "A Survey of the Principal Newspapers of the Other American Republics," February 9, 1948. In *OSS/State Department Intelligence and Research Reports, Part XIV, Latin America, 1941–1961*. Microfilm. Washington, DC: University Publications of America, 1979.

———. "Political Developments and Trends in the Other American Republics in the Twentieth Century," October 1, 1949. In *OSS/State Department Intelligence and Research Reports, Part XIV, Latin America, 1941–1961*. Microfilm. Washington, DC: University Publications of America, 1979.

Office of Strategic Services. "The First Half Year of the Velasco Ibarra Administration in Ecuador," November 28, 1944. In *OSS/State Department Intelligence and Research Reports, Part XIV, Latin America, 1941–1961*. Microfilm. Washington, DC: University Publications of America, 1979.

———. "Political Activities of French Minority Groups in Latin America since June 1940," December 28, 1943. In *OSS/State Department Intelligence and Research Reports, Part XIV, Latin America, 1941–1961*. Microfilm. Washington, DC: University Publications of America, 1979.

Oña Villarreal, Humberto. *Presidentes del Ecuador*, 3d ed. Quito: Multigráficas Sur, 1994.

Ordeñana Trujillo, José Vicente. "Una revolución traicionada." In *El 28 de mayo de 1944: Testimonio*, ed. Universidad de Guayaquil, 55–66. Guayaquil: Universidad de Guayaquil, 1984.

Ospina Peralta, Pablo. "La aleación inestable. Origen y consolidación de un Estado transformista: Ecuador, 1920–1960." Ph.D. diss., University of Amsterdam, Amsterdam, 2016.

———. "Matrimonio de compromiso. El ejército liberal y el Partido Conservador (1941–1948)." In *La Gloriosa ¿Revolución que no fue?*, ed. Santiago Cabrera Hanna, 129–52. Quito: Editora Nacional, Universidad Andina Simón Bolívar, 2016.

Padilla, Tanalís, and Louise Walker. "In the Archives: History and Politics." *Journal of Iberian and Latin American Research* 19, no. 1 (2013): 1–10.

Páez, Alexei. *Los orígenes de la izquierda ecuatoriana*. Quito: Fundación de Investigaciones Andino Amazónica and Ediciones Abya-Yala, 2001.

———, ed. *El anarquismo en el Ecuador*. Quito: Editora Nacional and Instituto Nacional de Formación Obrero y Campesina (INFOC), 1986.

Parkman, Patricia. *Nonviolent Insurrection in El Salvador: The Fall of Maximiliano Hernández Martínez*. Tucson: University of Arizona Press, 1988.

Partido Comunista del Ecuador. *Fundamentos ideológicos y programa mínimo*. Quito: Partido Comunista del Ecuador, 1945.

———. *El Partido Comunista Ecuatoriano protesta ante la nación*. Quito: Imprenta Editorial Pichincha, 1943.

———. *Unidad Progresista para derrotar a los reaccionarios en las elecciones*. Quito: Editorial Quito, 1947.

———. *Unidos para la democracia y el progreso: Posición del Partido Comunista del Ecuador en el momento actual*. Quito: Partido Comunista del Ecuador, 1945.

Paz, Clotario. *Larrea Alba, nuestras izquierdas*. Guayquil: Tribuna Libre, 1938.

Paz Salinas, María Emilia. *Strategy, Security, and Spies: Mexico and the U.S. as Allies in World War II*. University Park: Pennsylvania State University Press, 1997.

Pearson, Drew. "U.S. Agents in Latin America." December 11, 1947, The Bell Syndicate, Inc., http://hdl.handle.net/2041/21966.

Petrich, Blanche. "En el país todos los cuadros de inteligencia trabajaban para la CIA." *La Jornada* (Mexico City), October 25, 2010, 2.

Pineo, Ronn. *Ecuador and the United States: Useful Strangers*. Athens: University of Georgia Press, 2007.

———. *Social and Economic Reform in Ecuador: Life and Work in Guayaquil*. Gainesville: University Press of Florida, 1996.

Pólit Ortiz, Francisco. "A los 40 años de la 'Gloriosa Revolución' del 28 de mayo de 1944." In *El 28 de mayo de 1944: Testimonio*, ed. Universidad de Guayaquil, 41–54. Guayaquil: Universidad de Guayaquil, 1984.

Proaño A., Guido. "Ni anticapitalista, ni antiimperialist." *Opción* 9, no. 195 (June 16–30, 2010): 5.

Raat, W. Dirk. "U.S. Intelligence Operations and Covert Action in Mexico, 1900–47." *Journal of Contemporary History* 22, no. 4 (October 1987): 615–38.

Randall, Stephen James. "Colombia, the United States and Inter-American Aviation Rivalry, 1927–1940." *Journal of Inter-American Studies and World Affairs* 14, no. 3 (August 1972): 297–324.

Rankin, Monica A. *¡México, la patria! Propaganda and Production during World War II*. Lincoln: University of Nebraska Press, 2009.

Ratner, Michael, and Michael Steven Smith. *Che Guevara and the FBI: The U.S. Political Police Dossier on the Latin American Revolutionary*. Brooklyn, NY: Ocean, 1997.

Robeson, Paul. *Paul Robeson Speaks: Writings, Speeches, Interviews, 1918–1974*. New York: Brunner/Mazel, 1978.

Rodas Chaves, Germán. *La izquierda ecuatoriana en el siglo XX (Aproximación histórica)*. Quito: Ediciones Abya-Yala, 2000.

Rodas, Raquel. *Nosotras que del amor hicimos . . .* Quito: Raquel Rodas, 1992.

Rodríguez, Guillermo. "Informe sobre el Congreso de Unificación de los Trabajadores Ecuatorianos. Marzo de 1943." In *Formación y pensamiento de la C.T.E.*, ed. Jorge León, Hernán Ibarra, and Patrico Icaza, 41–88. Quito: Centro de Documentación e Información de los Movimientos Sociales del Ecuador (CEDIME), 1983.

Rodríguez, Lilya. "Acción por el Movimiento de Mujeres." In *Homenaje a Nela Martínez Espinosa*, ed. Acción por el Movimiento de Mujeres, 16. Quito: Acción por el Movimiento de Mujeres, 1990.

Rojas, Ángel F. *Informe del c. doctor Ángel F. Rojas, Secretario General del X Congreso del Partido Socialista Ecuatoriano*. Quito: Partido Socialista Ecuatoriano, 1943.

Romo-Leroux, Ketty. *Movimiento de mujeres en el Ecuador*. Guayaquil: Universidad de Guayaquil, 1997.

Romualdi, Serafino. "Labor and Democracy in Latin America." *Foreign Affairs* 25, no. 3 (April 1947): 477–89.

———. *Presidents and Peons: Recollections of a Labor Ambassador in Latin America*. New York: Funk and Wagnalls, 1967.

Rosenfeld, Seth. *Subversives: The FBI's War on Student Radicals, and Reagan's Rise to Power*. New York: Farrar, Straus and Giroux, 2012.

Rout, Leslie, and John Bratzel. *The Shadow War: German espionage and United States counterespionage in Latin America during World War II*. Frederick, Md.: University Publications of America, 1986.

Ryan, James. *Earl Browder: The Failure of American Communism*. Tuscaloosa, Ala: University of Alabama Press, 1997.

Saad, Pedro. *La CTE y su papel histórico*. Guayaquil: Ed. Claridad, 1968.

———. *El Ecuador y la guerra*. Guayaquil: Emperio Gráfico, 1943.

Sadlier, Darlene. *Americans All: Good Neighbor Cultural Diplomacy in World War II*. Austin: University of Texas Press, 2012.

Schwartzberg, Steven. "Rómulo Betancourt: From a Communist Anti-Imperialist to a Social Democrat with US Support." *Journal of Latin American Studies* 29, no. 3 (October 1997): 613–65.

Scipes, Kim. AFL-CIO's *Secret War against Developing Country Workers: Solidarity or Sabotage?* Lanham, MD: Lexington Books, 2010.

Society of Former Special Agents of the FBI Inc. *Society of Former Special Agents of the FBI*, 2d ed. Paducah, KY: Turner, 1999.

Sosa-Buchholz, Ximena. "The Strange Career of Populism in Ecuador." In *Populism in Latin America*, ed. Michael L. Conniff, 138–56. Tuscaloosa: University of Alabama Press, 1999.

Spenser, Daniela. "El viaje de Vicente Lombardo Toledano al mundo del porvenir." *Desacatos* 34 (September–December 2010): 77–96.

Starobin, Joseph. *American Communism in Crisis, 1943–1957*. Cambridge: Harvard University Press, 1972.

Stephan, Alexander and Jan van Heurck. *"Communazis": FBI Surveillance of German Emigré Writers*. New Haven: Yale University Press, 2000.

Stockwell, John. *In Search of Enemies: A CIA Story*. New York: W. W. Norton and Company, 1978.

Stuart, Graham. *The Department of State: A History of Its Organization, Procedure, and Personnel*. New York: Macmillan, 1949.

Theoharis, Athan G. *From the Secret Files of J. Edgar Hoover*. Chicago: I. R. Dee, 1991.

Torre, Carlos de la. *Populist Seduction in Latin America*. 2d ed. Athens: Ohio University Press, 2010.

Tota, Antônio Pedro. *The Seduction of Brazil: The Americanization of Brazil during World War II*. Austin: University of Texas Press, 2009.

Troy, Thomas F. *Donovan and the CIA: A History of the Establishment of the Central Intelligence Agency*. Frederick, MD: Aletheia Books, 1981.

Ungar, Sanford. *FBI*. Boston: Little, Brown, 1976.

United States Department of State. *Emergence of the Intelligence Establishment*. Washington, DC: U.S. Government Printing Office, 1996.

Universidad de Guayaquil, ed. *El 28 de mayo de 1944: Testimonio*. Guayaquil: Universidad de Guayaquil, 1984.

Vega, Silvia. *La Gloriosa: De la revolución del 28 de mayo de 1944 a la contrarrevolución velasquista*. Quito: Editorial El Conejo, 1987.

Vera, Alfredo. "Una insurrección triunfante que no pudo ser Revolución." In *El 28 de mayo de 1944: testimonio*, ed. Universidad de Guayaquil. Guayaquil: Litografía e Imprenta de la Universidad de Guayaquil, 1984.

Vera, Pedro Jorge. "La Insurrección del 28 de Mayo: Un vistazo." In *El 28 de mayo de 1944: testimonio*, ed. Universidad de Guayaquil, 31–39. Guayaquil: Universidad de Guayaquil, 1984.

Webb, G. Gregg. "Intelligence Liaison between the FBI and State, 1940–44: Effective Interagency Collaboration." *Studies in Intelligence* 49, no. 3 (2005): 25–38.

Weiner, Tim. *Enemies: A History of the FBI*. New York: Random House, 2012.

Welch, Cliff. "Labor Internationalism: U.S. Involvement in Brazilian Unions, 1945–1965." *Latin American Research Review* 30, no. 2 (1995): 61–89.

Weld, Kirsten. *Paper Cadavers: The Archives of Dictatorship in Guatemala*. Durham: Duke University Press, 2014.

Whitehead, Don. *The FBI Story: A Report to the People*. New York: Random House, 1956.

Ycaza, Patricio. *Historia del movimiento obrero ecuatoriano: De la influencia de la táctica del frente popular a las luchas del FUT*, vol. 2. Quito: Centro de Documentación e Información de los Movimientos Sociales del Ecuador (CEDIME), 1991.

INDEX

Italicized page numbers refer to photos and illustrations

Catholic church: and labor organizing, 67, 96, 99–100, 103, 161; and May 1944 revolution, 145, 155; and National Labor Congress (Quito, 1943), 108; political attitudes of, 129–30, 174; strength of, 44, 64, 67

Catucuamba, Luis, 82

Cayambe, *vi*, 65, 69, 82, 101

Cedeño (teachers' representative), 70

CEDOC (Confederación Ecuatoriana de Obreros Católicos, Ecuadorian Confederation of Catholic Workers), 67, 96

Chacaguaza, Toribio, 170

chauffeurs' union, 143

Chávez: Hugo, 130, 254; Leopoldo N., 109–11

Checa Murillo, David, 110

Chile: Communist Party, 14–15, 172, 176–77, 194–95, 243; populist government in, 194–95; surveillance in, 3, 18, 38–40, 50, 55, 67, 221, 260n16

Chilean Communist Party, 15, 176, 243

Churchill, Winston, 171

CIA (Central Intelligence Agency), vii, 2, 47–51, 233–34, 252

CIG (Central Intelligence Group), 49–51, 246

CIO (Congress of Industrial Organizations, U.S.), 171, 214

citizenship and political participation, 163–64, 198–99, 228

civil attachés, 39. *See also* Legal Attaché's Offices

Clinton: Bill, 254–55; Hillary, 253–54

COE (Confederación de Obreros del Ecuador, Confederation of Ecuadorian Laborers), 112

coffee, 46

COI (Coordinator of Information), 12, 27

Cointelpro (Counterintelligence Program, U.S.), 181

Cold War, 195, 202–3, 214, 224, 232, 251, 254

Colegio Vicente Rocafuerte, 97

Colombia, 3, 21, 23–24, 29–30, 37, 41, 176, 194

Columbe, 65

Columbus, Christopher, 251

Combate (PCE), 6, 72, 211

Comintern (Communist International): and communist parties, 56, 61–62, 67; dissolution of, 81, 87, 170; and popular front strategy, 66, 176; seventh congress, 58, 66, 171, 175, 177–78

"Communism and Trade Unions in Guayaquil" (FBI), 62

Communist International. See Comintern (Communist International)

Communist League of America, 88

Communist Political Association, 175

Confederación del Guayas (Guayas Confederation), 99

Congreso Nacional de Trabajadores (National Workers' Congress), 101

Consejo Administrativo Revolucionario (Revolutionary Administrative Council), 150

Conservative Party, 26, 67, 112, 172, 190, 209, 225–26

Constituent Assembly (1944–45), 17, 53, 158, 161–70, 202

constitution (Ecuador): of 1869, 213; of 1906, 202; of 1929, 212; of 1945, 158–91, 199, 201–5, 207–10, 212, 235; of 1946, 5, 211–14, 224, 227, 235

constitution: Mexico (1917), 63; U.S., 36

Constitutional Court, 202, 204

cooperatives, 69–70, 95, 153, 173, 187, 196, 213

Córdova Malo, Joaquín, 108

Cordovez, Aurelio, 239

Coronel, Valeria, 250

Corporación Ecuatoriana de Fomento, 74–76

corporatism, 27, 197–98

Correa, Rafael, 252–53

Cosse, Charles, 89

Costa Rica, 37, 97, 117, 127, 172, 277n16127

Council of National Defense, 262n46

CPUSA (Communist Party of the USA), 173, 175–76

Seventh International Conference of American States (Uruguay, 1933), 6
sexism, 77, 210, 291n70. *See also* women
Shadow War, The (Rout and Bratzel), 19
Shaw, George P., 172, 218, 230
shoemakers' union, 188
Silva, Eduardo, 228
Simmons, John, 231, 233–36, 239–47, 250–51
SIS (Special Intelligence Service), 2–3, 6–7, 12, 18–23, 37–38, 55–56
Sittenfeld, Kurt, 88
SOAW (School of the Americas Watch), 8
Sociedad de Carpinteros de Guayaquil (Society of Guayaquil Carpenters), 105
Solano, Celso Nicolas, 85
Somoza García, Anastasio, 127
Soria, Raúl, 228
Sosa-Buchholz, Ximena, 138
Soviet Union: and fight against fascism, 170; and PCE, 68; recognition of, 165–66, 181, 183–84; and United States, 161
Spanish Civil War (1930s), 78, 85, 100
Spanish inquisition, 55
Speakes, John, 10, 49
Special Activities Branch (Office of Naval Intelligence), 19
Special Intelligence Section (Office of Naval Intelligence), 19
Stalin, Joseph, 81, 86–87, 170–71
State Department: and AFL (U.S.), 214; alliances with liberals and leftists, 3, 130–31, 153–54, 171–73, 233–34, 257; and departure of FBI from Ecuador, 238–47; Division of Foreign Activity Correlation, 9–10; and foreign intelligence, 9–14; interagency competition and rivalry, 9–14, 24, 49–51, 273n44; OIR (Office of Intelligence Research), 26, 233; and police training, 33; and political intervention, 59–61, 195; and Rafael Correa, 252–53; and SIS, 21; surveillance reports as source for history of left, vii
Stephan, Alexander, 259–60n10
Stern, Heinz Alfred (Bobby Astor), 85

Suárez Veintimilla, Mariano, 26, 150, 154, 237, 282n37
Sundberg, Ronald, 18–19, 22, 54
surveillance reports as source for history of left, vii–viii, 4–6, 15, 78, 92–93, 99, 128, 155, 255–57

Tamm, Edward, 148
Teheran Conference, 171, 175–76, 182
Terán Varea, Benjamín, 212
Theoharis, Athan, 67
third-way movement, 142
Thompson, Edgar K., 23–28
Tigua, *vi*, 65, 105, 187
Tinajero, Ciro Luis, 28
Tinker Salas, Miguel, ix, 260nn11–12
Tomlinson, Edward, 29–30, 32
Torres Vera, Alberto, 106, 110
Transocean news service, 26, 29, 79, 154
Tribunal of Constitutional Guarantees (Tribunal de Garantías Constitucionales), 173, 190, 204–5, 208, 212, 214
Trotsky, Leon, 20, 86
Trotskyism, 86–92
Trujillo, José Vicente, 235
Truman, Harry, 12, 48–50, 232
Truman Doctrine, 232
Tucker McClure Company, 116–17
Tulio Oramas, Marco, 239

Ubico, Jorge, 154
UDE (Unión Democrática Universitaria, University Democratic Union), 134
Unión Sindical de Pichincha (Trade Union of Pichincha), 108
Unión Sindical de Trabajadores (Workers' Trade Union), 102
"United for Democracy and Progress—Position of the Communist Party of Ecuador at the Present Time" (PCE), 182
united front strategy. *See* popular front strategy
United Nations charter, 77
United Press, 26